The Moynihan Report
and the Politics of Controversy

The Moynihan Report and the Politics of Controversy

Lee Rainwater

William L. Yancey

A *Trans-action* Social Science and Public Policy Report

Including the full text of
The Negro Family: The Case for National Action
by Daniel Patrick Moynihan

THE M.I.T. PRESS
Massachusetts Institute of Technology
Cambridge, Massachusetts, and London, England

The distinctive character of social science discourse is to be sought in the fact that every assertion, no matter how objective it may be, has ramifications extending beyond the limits of science itself. Since every assertion of a "fact" about the social world touches the interests of some individual or group, one cannot even call attention to the existence of certain "facts" without courting the objections of those whose very *raison d'être* in society rests upon a divergent interpretation of the "factual" situation.

Louis Wirth, Preface to Karl Mannheim,
Ideology and Utopia (New York: Harcourt, Brace & World, 1936).

Preface

The events with which this book deals provide a particularly
sensitive vantage point for examining the relationship of social
science endeavors to public policy formation and for studying the
complex interactions between the federal government and the civil
rights organizations. As social scientists, we have a general interest in the former; and as sociologists engaged in research on the
situation of Negro Americans, we have a particular interest in the
latter subject.

When the events of the Moynihan Report controversy reached
their apotheosis in November 1965, we decided to undertake a
study of the controversy to be published as an article in *Trans-
action* magazine, as one of a series of articles dealing with issues
of social science and public policy. By the time we had completed
the study, our appreciation of the complexity and importance of
the subject was such that we also decided to publish this more
detailed examination.

It was apparent from the public events connected with the
controversy that four groups were importantly involved — the
White House staff, Permanent Government civil servants, civil
rights organizations, and social scientists. Therefore, we compiled
a list of persons in each of these sectors who had been publicly

involved in the controversy in one way or another. In order not to miss others whose involvement had been less public we asked several knowledgeable informants in each sector for the names of others whose views could shed light on the relevant events. In this way, we developed a sample of sixty-odd individuals who seem to be the main participants in the controversy.

During January, we interviewed these persons, most of them in face-to-face interviews in New York and Washington, D.C., some of them by telephone when schedules did not permit our getting together in person. With each person, we sought three things: his version of the events that had transpired and his role in them, his evaluation of the Moynihan Report and the controversy it precipitated, and his views of how these events were related to other, larger issues of civil rights. Because the men and women involved were experienced and sophisticated participants in the political process, we found them highly verbal and incisive informants, although in the manner of busy people not always too clear on details. While most of the informants were gratifyingly frank and open, a few were considerably less so.

The interviews provided us with two kinds of data. First, the informants gave us information that could be used in a straightforward way (usually quite readily cross-checked against information from other informants or from documents). Second, the interview interaction itself provided information — informants would talk about some subjects quite freely and dry up on others; they would try to persuade us of the accuracy of particular interpretations of the significance of events; and occasionally they would try to co-opt us to one side of the many-sided controversy. In some cases, the manner of the interview told us more than the content.

The interviews were distributed as follows:

Academic social science	18
Civil rights organizations	18
Federal government	
Presidential government	4
Welfare establishment	7
Civil rights agencies	3
Women's organizations	3
Church organizations	4
News media	3
Other	1
	61

The second main source of data came from documents, although the documentation of events in the controversy is perhaps slight compared to many political events and many of the documents are still considered internal to the government. However, on certain crucial issues those documents that were available to us served to clarify hitherto fuzzy issues and to provide a check against assertions made in interviews.

Because the press coverage of the Moynihan Report and controversy played a critical role in the event, we have collected an extensive file of press clippings and magazine articles. We have sought to take the press coverage as problematic rather than definitive and to show how what was written as factual description itself played a key role in the development of the controversy.

Finally, some of our data came from participation rather than interview. Although less systematic than the interviewing, such participation provided us with a chance to observe some of the events of the controversy as they unfolded. Rainwater was a participant in the fall White House planning conference, as a member of the panel on the family; Yancey attended the spring White House conference as a *Trans-action* correspondent.

The analysis of the data from these various sources presented typical problems of trying to reconstruct events and their significance. It should be remembered that the Moynihan controversy was still ongoing during the time our study was being done and that the participants in the events it touched on had to be concerned with what effects our work might have — this was not a dead issue. Therefore, we have sought to piece together a reconstruction of events and meanings that is not dependent in any crucial way on information gained in only one interview, and we have sought to separate our interpretation of events from the description of events themselves.

It will be apparent to the reader that we have our own views about the issues raised in the controversy and that our interpretations from time to time are influenced by those views. We make no apology for this as we have sought to describe the events as accurately as we could determine them and to communicate the views of participants in the controversy as clearly as possible whether or not we disagree with those views.

Perhaps a note of personal history will clarify our own position and inform the reader about the perspective from which we view the events described in the book. We have been involved for several years in conducting a research on the experience of one par-

ticular Negro population — families living in a large public housing project in St. Louis. For longer than that, we have been students of Negro and white lower-class life and of efforts to change
the way society imposes disadvantage on these groups. Therefore, in July 1965, we read the first news article about the Moynihan report with great interest. Our concern after reading that
article, which discussed budding federal attempts to "better the
structure of the Negro family," was much the same as that of
Herbert J. Gans (see pages 445-457). The tone of the article suggested some kind of direct intervention into family life. Because of
these concerns, Rainwater noted in an article he was writing on the
Negro family that such intervention might distract "the country
from the pressing needs for socio-economic reform, and provide
an alibi for failure to embark on the basic institutional changes
that are needed to do anything about abolishing both white and
Negro poverty."

Early in the fall of 1965, when we were able to read Moynihan's
report, *The Negro Family: The Case for National Action,* however,
we did not find in it any such suggestion of distraction from the
basic institutional sources of Negro disadvantage. Instead, we
were impressed with the "fit" between Moynihan's summary of
previous research and current statistics on the situation of lower-
class Negro families and our own intensive participant observation and interview data from our St. Louis research, as well as
Rainwater's earlier studies of both white and Negro lower-class
life-style. To us, Moynihan's report seemed very much in line with
studies of lower-class life that were initiated in the 1930's by such
scholars as Allison Davis, Burleigh Gardner, John Dollard, Horace
Cayton, St. Clair Drake, and others. While we recognized that currently there is much re-examination and re-evaluation of these
pioneering works as social scientists turn their attention again to
questions of poverty and of Negro disadvantage, our current research and that of other contemporary scholars suggest that future
reformulations will not refute the essential accuracy of the earlier
scholars' descriptions of the dynamics of lower-class life. Therefore, Moynihan's formulation seemed to us a useful starting point
for the kind of policy-planning approach Moynihan called for at
the end of his report.

When, later in the fall, we learned that the Moynihan Report
had precipitated a major controversy among persons interested in
civil rights, we were both puzzled and concerned. The controversy
seemed to reflect two kinds of dangers in the application of social
science to policy issues which had already impressed us in connec-

tion with our research. The first had to do with the misuse of social science findings in public conflicts (for example, the use of data on Negro family instability by school board lawyers to defend school boards against charges of inferior education through de facto segregated schools), and the second had to do with the threats posed to the autonomy of social science by direct or indirect pressures on social scientists to conceal findings that policy makers and activitists thought made their work more difficult.*

In the first case, we wanted to better understand how social scientists can do honest research on "sensitive" subjects and at the same time guard against misuse and intentionally destructive applications. In the second case, we wanted to discover how social scientists can resist the pressures of action groups, with which they themselves are sympathetic, to avoid or conceal data that seem damaging to the particular strategies of those groups. We felt that it would be impossible for social scientists to develop more adequate comprehension of such complex issues as the situations of Negro Americans if they felt constant pressure (either from within themselves or from others) to tailor their findings to preferred civil rights strategies; from our point of view, the strategies should be tailored to the reality uncovered by social science investigations and not the reverse. And there must be sufficient tolerance of ambiguity for social science research to develop at its necessarily slow pace while civil rights action proceeds at its own, hopefully faster, pace.

Should social scientists allow themselves to be pressured into restrictive rationalization of their research in terms of the interests of any of the participants in a complex policy issue such as civil rights — the civil rights organizations, or the agencies that deal with the disadvantaged, or the political representatives of broader white power groups — they would be engaged in apologetics and not social science. Yet, if they simply retreated from the policy area altogether, refusing to discuss the policy implications of their work, they would be avoiding responsibility for the way their work was applied and be morally implicated should their work be used to bolster injustice or to slow progress toward justice.

It was with these concerns that we began the study, and they

*We had dealt with these issues in two papers prepared earlier in 1965: Lee Rainwater and David J. Pittman, "Ethical Problems in Studying Politically Sensitive & Deviant Communities," *Social Problems* (forthcoming); presented at the Society for the Study of Social Problems meetings, Chicago, August 1965; William Yancey, "Political Implications of Poverty Research," presented at Missouri Society for Sociology and Anthropology meetings, October 1965.

have shaped the manner in which we approached our study. We have relied heavily on two other social scientists, Herbert J. Gans and Hylan Lewis, with considerable experience in research and private and government consultation in the areas touched on in this report. Many of the insights and interpretations presented here were developed in discussion with them. This does not mean that they agree with all that we say — indeed, they do not — but even the areas of disagreement have helped us in sharpening our views. Needless to say, neither they nor any of the other persons whose contributions we acknowledge below are responsible for the shortcomings of our analysis.

Our approach to this study has been much influenced by conversations with two of our colleagues at Washington University, Alvin W. Gouldner and Irving L. Horowitz, and by the example of their own work in the sociology of knowledge, of sociology, and of politics. Another colleague, Charles A. Valentine, was kind enough to discuss with us some of the general civil rights issues raised by the controversy and to serve informally as an additional pair of eyes and ears at the spring White House conference. Norman E. Whitten brought a clarifying anthropological perspective to help us work through some of the issues connected with matrifocal families among New World Negroes.

Ira L. Reiss and John Gagnon were kind enough to give us technical advice concerning the determinants of Negro and white illegitimacy, and William F. Pratt went to considerable trouble to make available to us his unpublished study of illegitimate conceptions and births in the Detroit area.

We owe a special debt to Daniel P. Moynihan, without whose cooperation our study would have been far less complete. He was kind enough to make all his files dealing with the report and related events available to us and to speak with us at whatever length we desired and with considerable forthrightness and candor.

We are grateful to *Trans-action* magazine, its Editorial Board and its editor, Leonard Zweig, for their encouragement and for their financial support of the study. In small part, the study can be considered a part of an ongoing research project supported by the National Institutes of Mental Health (MH09189).

Some of the persons we interviewed prefer to remain unnamed; therefore, we acknowledge with gratitude the assistance of all of those whom we interviewed, who often also took the time to find and make available to us documents that were relevant. Many of these same persons also took the time to give us their reactions to the draft of this document, thus allowing us to make corrections of factual errors and interpretations and often providing us with valuable additional data. For such assistance we wish to thank the following persons: Paul Barton, Wiley Branton, Robert Carter, Kenneth Clark, Robert Coles, Fred Davis, Robert Dentler, Leonard Duhl, Frank E. Erwin, Alan Gartner, Elizabeth Herzog, Adelaide Hill, Herbert Hill, Norman Hill, Carl Holman, Frederick Jaffe, Mary Keyserling, Myron Lefcowitz, Bernard Mackler, S. M. Miller, Thomas Pettigrew, Richard Rovere, William Ryan, Alvin Schorr, Harold Sheppard, Charles Silberman, Robert Spike, and W. Willard Wirtz.

We acknowledge our indebtedness to Patricia Rutherford and Margaret Wedel for the demanding work of tracking down and keeping track of documents, interviews, and sundry details, and to them and Betty Higgins, Irma Morose, and Dianne Sattley for typing and proofreading the several drafts of this study.

Finally, we thank our wives for their encouragement and their toleration of the after-hours work and preoccupation that accompany a research carried out over the condensed time period that this study necessitated.

Lee Rainwater
William L. Yancey

St. Louis, Missouri
June 1966

Contents

1

Introduction

On June 4, 1965, President Johnson spoke at a Howard University commencement. His remarks were unique among presidential utterances on the situation of Negro Americans in that the emphasis was not upon federal efforts to do away with traditional Jim Crow practices but rather on the social and economic situation of Negroes. The focus of his concern was similarly a break with tradition; he dealt not so much with the plight of Negroes in the South but of those in the great northern ghettos.

The President said, "Negroes have been another nation: deprived of freedom, crippled by hatred, the doors of opportunity closed to hope." After brief mention of the civil rights legislative accomplishments of the past eight years, which he characterized as only "the end of the beginning," he announced the "next and more profound stage of the battle for civil rights," in which the goal would be that "all our citizens must have the ability to walk through [the gates of opportunity]." He emphasized that although some Negroes, including the graduating class before him, were steadily narrowing the gap between themselves and their white counterparts, for the great majority of Negro Americans "the walls are rising and the gulf is widening."

Detailing the facts of "this American failure" he noted increasing disparity between Negroes and whites in unemployment rates, in income, in poverty, in infant mortality. He asked why this should be and then answered the question: "Negroes are trapped in inherited, gateless poverty."

While the increasing and accelerating attack of his administration on poverty would help, Negro poverty was of a special, more desperate kind. It was the product of ancient brutality, past injustice, and present prejudice which had produced a twisted and battered cultural heritage, a community excluded from the rest of society and buried under a blanket of circumstance. To lift just a corner of that blanket would provide no lasting solution, the entire cover must be raised "if we are to liberate our fellow citizens."

The injustice that Negroes suffer was now an urban injustice. Negroes lived separate lives in a world of decay which shaped them, crippled the youth, and desolated the men who knew not the saving pressures of a more hopeful society. Unemployment strikes most swiftly at the Negro and this burden erodes hope and breeds despair, which in turn brings indifference to the learning that offers a way out; together these burdens and responses were "often the source of destructive rebellion against the fabric of society." Success and achievement could wipe away the lacerating hurt of prejudice, distaste, and condescension. "It can be overcome. But for many the wounds are always open."

As a final element in his diagnosis, the President emphasized the importance of the breakdown of the Negro family structure, "its influence radiating to every part of life." White America must accept responsibility for this breakdown that flows from oppression and persecution of the Negro man, from long years of degradation and discrimination which have attacked his dignity and assaulted his ability to provide for his family. Again the facts: Only a minority of Negro children reach the age of eighteen having lived all their lives with both parents; a majority of all Negro children receive public assistance at some time during their childhood. And the consequences: "When the family collapses, it is the children that are usually damaged. When it happens on a massive scale, the community itself is crippled." Unless the family is strengthened, conditions created under which most parents will stay together, all other public activity "will never be enough to cut completely the circle of despair and deprivation."

The President announced that we knew part of the answer to the problem — jobs, a decent family income, decent homes and decent surroundings, an equal chance to learn, better designed welfare and social programs, medical care, an understanding heart by all Americans — but that there were other answers still to be found. Therefore, he intended to call a White House Conference "To Fulfill These Rights," inviting scholars, experts, outstanding Negro leaders and officials of the government at every level. Its goal would be to "shatter forever not only the barriers of law and public practice but the walls which bound the condition of man by the color of his skin." He pledged that it would be a chief goal of his administration and his program in the years to come to end this "one huge wrong of the American nation."

For anyone who still maintained some belief in the sincerity and credibility of federal civil rights policy, the President's speech was remarkable for its eloquence and for its insights into the basic plight of Negro Americans. Beyond eloquence and insights, however, it seemed to signal an important shift in the stance of the federal government toward civil rights issues. The "next and more profound stage" of the civil rights struggle would not have to do with the legal protection of rights, but with the provision of resources that would enable Negro Americans to turn freedom into an equal life. The emphasis seemed to be not so much on law- and court-guaranteed justice, but on the social and economic factors of jobs, housing, education, community and family life.

The social scientist could see in this speech a distillation of over three decades of economic, sociological, and psychological research on the "Negro problem." Despite the voracious appetite of the federal government for social science findings and consultation, it was still unique to find a social science perspective so clearly central to a major presidential address.

How could such a thing come about?

The Howard University speech gave a public face to a then confidential ("for official use only") report, *The Negro Family: The Case for National Action,* from the Office of Policy Planning and Research of the Department of Labor. The report had been completed in March 1965 by Daniel Patrick Moynihan,

Assistant Secretary of Labor, in collaboration with two members of his staff, Paul Barton and Ellen Broderick. It gave voice to views that Moynihan had been formulating for over a year and reflected his belief that policy making in the government should make greater use of the social sciences for problem diagnosis and description.

In the report and several related memorandums, Moynihan had sought to inform the President and his staff of what he felt should be some of the central issues in formulating a more effective national effort for carrying out the complex task of bringing Negro Americans into full participation in the society. With the speech and the announcement of a fall conference to develop a program in line with the goals it enunciated, it seemed that Moynihan's report had borne its first fruit.

At the direction of the President, presidential assistant Richard N. Goodwin and Moynihan had drafted the speech, using drafts that Moynihan had already prepared, on the night of June 3rd and into the early hours of June 4th. Part of the speech's crispness and assertive tone was perhaps due to the fact that it was not exhaustively reviewed and criticized nor negotiated with the various departments affected by its content — it was closer to a pure "Presidential Act" than most presidents' speeches. (The President's "We Shall Overcome" speech was another example.) Before the speech was given, however, approval was sought and obtained from three civil rights leaders — Martin Luther King, Jr., Roy Wilkins, and Whitney Young.

Yet, by the following October it also seemed that this might perhaps be all that the report would accomplish except to precipitate one of the angriest and most bitter controversies yet among government and private individuals all presumably dedicated to realizing Negro rights. From anonymous layers of the federal government, in the inner councils of some civil rights groups, in unpublished memoranda and private denunciations, in the professional conversations of some social scientists, and finally, in public meetings and in the press the report (but not the President's speech) increasingly came under attack during the late summer and fall of the year.

Finally, early in November, a week before the White House Conference (now scaled down to a planning conference for a larger one to be held the following spring), sixty representatives of New York churches and civil rights organizations, under the leadership of the Commission on Religion and Race of the National Council of Churches and the Office of Church and Race of the Protestant Council of New York City, met to adopt a resolution urging the President to strike the questions of "family stability" from the agenda of the conference.

When the White House Conference met, its director announced to the amusement of the audience that he had been reliably informed that no such person as Daniel Patrick Moynihan existed, the report on the Negro family became one of several subjects about which the civil rights leaders expressed indignation, the press searched out these rumblings and characterized them as one of the main events at the conference, and the controversy was used to support the apparent view of some high administration figures that the conference was a "total disaster."

From the report in March, then, to the conference in November, a great deal had transpired. These events shed considerable light on complexities of formulating national policy concerning our most sensitive domestic problem and on what can happen to social science information as it makes its way through the political mill.

The skeletal features of Moynihan's Report are simple indeed. As the government removes barriers to Negro liberty through various kinds of antidiscrimination action, the problem of equality will become dominant. Here the question is not so much the freedom of Negroes to live their lives as whites do if they wish but the question of having equal resources to enable them to live in the way that whites do. Moynihan argued that this was not now the case and that equality (in the sense of the Negro's equal ability to produce equal results for himself) will not result simply from lifting legal barriers to full participation. He argued that the effect of the way Negroes have been and are treated in American society has been to create conditions in the Negro community that make it all but impossible for the great majority of Negroes to take advantage of the new opportunities the laws provide. He felt that "at the heart of the deterioration of the fabric of Negro society is the deterioration of the Negro family." His report built the following argument:

1. The deterioration of the Negro family is demonstrated by these facts (a) nearly a quarter of urban Negro marriages are dissolved; (b) nearly one quarter of Negro births are now illegitimate; (c) as a consequence, almost one fourth of Negro families are headed by females, and (d) this breakdown of the Negro family has led to a startling increase in welfare dependency. Why should this be so?

2. Moynihan found "the roots of the problem" in slavery, in the effects of reconstruction on the family and, particularly, on the position of the Negro man, in urbanization, in unemployment and poverty, in the wage system that often does not provide a family wage. He noted that the dimensions of all of these problems are growing because of the high fertility of Negroes (for example, the Negro population and labor force will be increasing twice as fast as that of whites between now and 1970).

3. Having demonstrated that the socioeconomic system, past and present, produces an unstable family system for Negroes, he went on to discuss "the tangle of pathology" in the Negro community (a phrase borrowed from social-psychologist Kenneth Clark's description of Harlem ghetto life). This tangle of pathology involves the matriarchy of the Negro family (by which he meant the tendency for women to fare better interpersonally and economically than men and thereby to dominate family life), the failure of youth (by which he referred to the fact that Negro children do not learn as much in school as white children and that they leave school earlier), higher rates of delinquency and crime among Negroes, the fact that Negroes disproportionately fail the Armed Forces qualification test (and that this suggests their poor competitive position in the job market as well), and the alienation of Negro men which results in their withdrawal from stable family-oriented society, in higher rates of drug addiction, in despair of achieving a stable life.

Moynihan, then, saw a vicious cycle operating. Negro men have no stable place in the economic system; as a result, they cannot be strong husbands and fathers. Therefore Negro families break up, and women must assume the task of rearing children without male assistance; often the women must assume the task of bringing in income also. Since the children do not grow up in a stable home and so learn that they cannot look forward to a stable life, they are not able to accomplish in school, leave school early, and therefore are in a very poor position to qualify for jobs that will produce a decent family income; and the cycle starts again.

With this, Moynihan had achieved his main goal of defining a problem rather than proposing a solution. He concluded his report with what he felt was its most immediate policy implications:

The policy of the United States is to bring the Negro American to full and equal sharing in the responsibilities and rewards of citizenship. To this end the programs of the federal government bearing on this objective shall be designed to have the effect, directly or indirectly, of enhancing the stability and resources of the Negro American family.

One of the most frequent criticisms of the Report was that its author spoke of "the Negro family" and thus did an injustice to those Negroes whose lives are not characterized by the kind of instability and pathology with which he dealt. Yet at two points in the report, he indicated that the Negro community contained two broad groupings — an increasingly successful middle class, and an increasingly disorganized lower class. Even so, those who wished to emphasize the sources of strength within the Negro community or who wished to preserve the "good name" of Negro families were highly displeased with Moynihan's characterizations.

To sociologists and psychologists with a professional interest in the situation of Negro Americans, the report presented little that was new or startling. Rather, it presented in a dramatic and policy-oriented way a well-established, though not universally supported, view of the afflictions of Negro Americans. Indeed, the basic paradigm of Negro life that Moynihan's report reflected had been laid down by the great Negro sociologist, E. Franklin Frazier, over thirty years before. The most direct contemporary source for the thinking in the report probably lay in the work of Kenneth Clark whose book, *Dark Ghetto,* was published at about the time the report was sent to the White House. Moynihan's work took the form of testing the accuracy of and then restating Frazier's predictions about the intertwining effects of socioeconomic deprivation and family disorganization on the situation of Negro Americans as they migrated to the cities. Further, he sought to show that Clark's work in Harlem, initially published as a report of the HARYOU project (*Youth in The Ghetto,* 1964), described a process that could be said to apply generally in the Negro ghettos of American cities. The report provided data indicating the situation of Negroes over the past fifteen years, particularly in relation to government labor and welfare programs.

Yet, if there was "nothing really new" in the report, why should it have elicited such a positive response from the White House; why the uneasy and critical response within certain segments of the government; why the strong negative response from some in the civil rights movement and in academic social science circles? How, in short, does "nothing new" become both new national policy and a controversy?

We seek in the balance of this book to elucidate the sources of both acceptance and rejection of the report. In the chapters that follow, we will consider the political situation of the government and the civil rights movement during the time when the report was first made and later surfaced; and we will examine in detail Moynihan's strategy and the report which he wrote in the service of that strategy, reactions to the report within the government, reactions to the report in those outside agencies involved, the press treatment of the report and the intellectual debate that followed, and finally the apotheosis of the controversy in the White House conferences and publicity about them.

2

The Political Context of the Report: The Government and Civil Rights Movement

One can view the Moynihan report as an experimental stimulus, a natural intervention, which provides an opportunity to understand not only the dynamics of the controversy it precipitated but also the political context in which it took place. Necessary to an understanding of the Moynihan controversy is some knowledge of the status of the civil rights movement and of the administration at the time the Moynihan report was issued.

The Movement in the Spring of 1965

Bayard Rustin wrote in February 1965, "The decade spanned by the 1954 Supreme Court decision on school desegregation and the Civil Rights Act of 1964 will undoubtedly be recorded as the period in which the legal foundations of racism in America were destroyed. To be sure, pockets of resistance remain; but it would be hard to quarrel with the assertion that the elaborate legal structure of segregation and discrimination, particularly

in relation to public accommodation, has virtually collapsed." *
In the spring of 1965, the civil rights movement was entering a
new and undefined phase, but it did not know what this new phase
would be. As a social movement, like social movements have in
the past, it has faced the threat of destruction because of its
victories. Charles Silberman has suggested that the leaders were
estranged from their rank and file, were divided and uncertain
where to turn.†

Not only was there growing uncertainty and conflict at the
intellectual level but the civil rights organizations were experiencing a marked decline in public support in the form of contributions. From the NAACP to the newer, more radical organizations, the high-water mark of contributions had been a year or
two earlier, and the concrete expression of concern and support
that contributions represent had fallen off. There was good
reason to fear that legislative successes were lowering motivations to dig into the pocketbook.

Without belittling the importance of the direct-action tactics
that have proved successful within the last ten years, it should
be pointed out that the institution of Jim Crow in the South is
much different from the institutions of discrimination and segregation in urban centers, both North and South. In many ways
one could view the South as an underdeveloped country which,
perhaps beginning with the boll weevil, has been moving away
from single-crop farming to an industrial economy. The need
for labor in industrial centers in the South as well as the North
encouraged migration from rural to urban centers. It is more
efficient to hire people in an industrial economy according to
their skill; to arbitrarily hire or not hire someone because of
his skin color is not congruent with the requirements of an
industrial society. The removal of Jim Crow can be seen as
required for the South's industrial development. Similarly, segregation of public accommodations only impedes the flow of commerce. By the 1960's, segregated lunch counters were to a large
degree symbolic manifestations of the previous society. Segregation in these forms is like the barnacles on a boat; once the
boat begins moving, they produce friction that must be eliminated before full speed can be attained.

---

* Bayard Rustin, "From Protest to Politics: The Future of the Civil Rights Movement." *Commentary*, Vol. 39, No. 2 (February 1965).

† Charles Silberman, "Beware the Day They Change Their Minds." *Fortune*,
November 1965.

The movement attacked these forms of racism at their weakest point. Because they were only symbolic and furthermore were barriers to industrial progress, small numbers of civil rights workers could, by "placing their bodies on the line," attack segregation in the South with success.

Also, supporters of white supremacy in the South had proved themselves to be considerably less skillful than the northern functionaries and power figures who support de facto segregation and discrimination. The southern racists strengthened the civil rights movement by accommodatingly playing their roles in open, often brutal, public confrontations; the northerners avoided or minimized open confrontations.

But while legal racism was destroyed in the United States, the decade of 1954 to 1964 can also be seen as the period of the development of de facto segregation. The year 1965 may be known in history as the time when the civil rights movement discovered, in the sense of becoming explicitly aware, that abolishing legal racism would not produce Negro equality. As Robert Carter, general counsel of the NAACP, said, "The 1954 Supreme Court decision did not produce integration of schools, marching on Washington did not produce equality, and demonstrating in lunch counters did not give people money to buy a dinner."

It was at this time that it became especially clear that de facto segregation and subtle racism were tied to our most fundamental socioeconomic institutions. More Negroes were unemployed in 1964 than in 1954. The unemployment gap between the races was wider. The relative income of Negroes had risen in the decade of the 50's, but not in the 1960's. A large percentage of Negro workers remained in jobs of the unskilled category — those most vulnerable to automation.

Now the problems of racism became very subtle. Again from Robert Carter: "This is an urban problem, not as crystal clear as other civil rights problems. The new problem is in urban centers in the North. Of course this problem is mixed up with problems of class, culture, subculture and so forth. It is not easy to tackle but we must do it."

In summary, then, we can say that in the spring of 1965 the Negro faced obstacles far more diffuse than the legal barriers he had been attacking. As Bayard Rustin wrote:

... automation, urban decay, de facto school segregation. These are problems which, while conditioned by Jim Crow, do not vanish upon its demise. They are more deeply rooted in our social-economic order; they are the result of the total society's failure to meet not only the Negro's needs, but human needs generally.

While the problem became more subtle, Negro leaders faced the additional problem of having generated the aspirations of Negro masses. That is, the decade of 1954 to 1964 can also be seen as the decade of the development of the "new Negro." The public image of the Negro American changed from the passive, downtrodden, Uncle Tom who hoped for integration to an active mass seeking to join American society. And more recently there are those few who question whether or not they really want to join the society; they found after they had integrated the lunch counter they didn't like the menu.

While a new activism has begun to develop in the Negro masses, the civil rights leaders were estranged from, even afraid of, the urban masses. James Farmer wrote of the necessity for a mass movement, but sensed the potential violence of the urban Negro. The strategy of nonviolence that was effective against the lunch counters in the South may not be so effective with these new activists. Violence on the part of white tormentors in the South had not hurt the movement because the trained and disciplined small cadre of civil rights workers did not return the violence. This may not be so in the case of the urban northern Negro; he may well reciprocate.

Perhaps the best indication of the estrangement of the urban Negro is the experience of Bayard Rustin, who after the Harlem riots of 1964 found jobs for 120 teenagers in Harlem. A few weeks later, only twelve of them were still working. One boy told Rustin he could make more playing pool than the $50 a week he had been earning; another could make more than his $60 salary by selling "pot"; another turned down a four-year basketball scholarship to a major university because he preferred to be a "pimp."

While it is clear that the "movement" was unsure of what to do in the spring of 1965 it is also clear that it is difficult to speak about the "movement" as a single force in American society. There is a considerable amount of variation within it. Rustin, its "strategist," was appealing to the Negro leaders for the development of a mass political movement in coalition with labor. On the other hand, James Farmer and CORE, feeling the malaise of 1965, were looking for something else. Farmer's decision to resign from CORE and develop a new organization to fight illiteracy was made in the spring of 1965, seven or eight months before it was announced. The NAACP continued to fight the subtle legal battle of de facto segregation and announced a program of "citizenship clinics" in the Negro community. The National Urban League with its program of self-help within the urban slum seemed in tune with the new phase of the movement. Only the young radicals of SNCC were not faced with the dilemma of 1965 because they continued to fight segregation in the South, where more than half the Negro Americans remained.

Rustin has written the best summary of the status of the movement in 1965: "The civil rights movement is evolving from a protest movement into a full-fledged *social movement* — an evolution calling its very name into question. It is now concerned not merely with removing the barriers to full *opportunity* but with achieving the fact of *equality*." James Farmer, writing in 1966 after the Moynihan controversy, said,

There have been great gains in job opportunities and educational opportunities for Negroes over the last few years and with organizations like CORE demanding justice, these opportunities will continue to expand. But we can no longer evade the knowledge that *most* Negroes will not be helped by equal opportunity. These are staggering problems for which the traditional CORE program of anti-discrimination is ill-equipped. We are now seeking new techniques and emphasis that will serve not only today's Negro masses but also tomorrow's teeming millions.

The Government and Civil Rights, Spring 1965

"To move a nation, a president has first to have the nation's ear. . . ." * Arthur Schlesinger, Jr. suggests that a major problem for any administration is to generate popular support for any program that it wishes to initiate. Schlesinger's discussion of the early Kennedy administration leaves one with a feeling of a country with an ambiguous malady and no national economic collapse or war to move it into action: "Kennedy's was an invisible and intangible crisis and the nation had elected him president by the slimmest of margins."

An analogous situation in connection with civil rights existed in Washington in 1965 when it became clear that the voting rights bill would be passed. With legal equality now on the

* Arthur Schlesinger, Jr., *One Thousand Days* (Boston: Houghton Mifflin, 1965).

law books there was a fear that popular support of the civil rights movement would diminish.

The difference between the Johnson and the Kennedy administration can be seen in the different strategies each used in developing a public issue and generating popular support. Unlike Johnson, Kennedy "communicated a deeply critical attitude toward the ideas and institutions which American society had come in the 50's to regard with enormous self-satisfaction." Kennedy had a pervasive effect on the national mood which had left for Johnson a "radical critique of American society."

In contrast, Johnson with the wide margin of votes that he received in 1964 had used the strategy of developing a "consensus image" in order to push his administrative programs. He wanted to be President of "all the people"; yet it was clear that the coalition that elected him in 1964, an important part of which was the Negro vote, had within it major conflicts. The Mississippi Freedom Democratic Party not only gained recognition at Atlantic City but in its rejection of compromise gave the Johnson Administration a stinging indication of how real and overt was the conflict with the civil rights movement. Unlike the War on Poverty, the civil rights movement began outside of the government and had since its inception been beyond governmental control.

There is little question that Bayard Rustin and Tom Kahn are correct in suggesting that much of Johnson's "place in history" will be determined by the demands made upon his administration by the civil rights movement.* Because of this pressure, he has been able to move in areas that otherwise would have been impossible even if they had been desired by the administration.

But, having reacted to the movement's demands for a decade, the government had learned that it was impossible to satiate the new Negro American. For each demand that was met another was made. Something had to be done by the Administration, not only to insure equality of the Negro American, but also so the government would not continue to be merely a "reacting" force. To quote one government source, "We could never catch those guys — the only thing to do is to get ahead of them." Another government source said that much of the Howard speech was designed to "leap frog the movement." And another, a man

---

* Bayard Rustin and Tom Kahn, "Civil Rights." *Commentary*, Vol. 39, No. 6 (June 1965).

primarily identified with the civil rights group in the government, said of the Howard speech, "Johnson had, more than any President, come out very strong, probably as strong as a President could be expected to, in the civil rights area. But the Howard speech went beyond this and surprised everyone."

One can imagine that men in the Administration, after seeing the Voting Rights Bill of 1965 passed through Congress, would begin to sit back and believe that the job had been done. But, if nothing else the 1964 Civil Rights Bill taught the Administration (1) that the passing of the civil rights bills did not solve the problem of discrimination in American society, and (2) that as strong as the 1964 bill might have been, it did little to reduce the amount of conflict between the government and the "movement." Thus it was clear in the spring of 1965 that the passing of the voting rights bill would not solve the problem of discrimination nor would it achieve consensus. That spring marked the time when the government began to seriously look around for an answer to the question of what to do next. High officials realized that laws would not solve the problem; and they were feeling around for some way to move toward a next step that would make it possible for the Negro Americans to realize the gains that the laws made possible.

In addition to the realization of limitations to the legal apparatus as an effective force in the final solution of the civil rights problem, there was also realization of the weakness, if not the lack, of a bureaucracy to deal effectively with civil rights matters. This was particularly true for those aspects of civil rights that involve social and economic aspects of the Negro's position in American society. As within the movement, the government was beginning to realize that the civil rights laws and the Supreme Court would not produce equality or consensus. A new administration policy had to be developed if the task was to be accomplished, but there was little or no bureaucratic or administrative apparatus designed to tackle social and economic problems in their racial manifestations. Perhaps the best indications of these difficulties are the number of civil rights agencies that have been developed within the government and the shifting of responsibilities among them.

It was in this atmosphere that Moynihan first introduced the White House staff to the ideas that were later to be written down in the "Moynihan Report." Long before the report was in its final form, Moynihan discussed his views with people in

the Administration and found his listeners anxious for new
ideas. The report itself fitted an existing need within the Administration. It gave the Administration a specific target and a
specific means to measure the effectiveness of existing or new
programs aimed at the pathologies of the urban slums. It is little
wonder that after distributing the paper, Moynihan received
very positive feedback from high administrative officials — "Pat,
I think you've got it."

The liaison between the government and the civil rights groups
had come a long way since Franklin Roosevelt's White House
cook provided the main link between the two, but the easy and
frequent interaction at high levels that exists between business,
or labor, or other pressure groups and the White House was still
not in existence. For their part, recent administrations had been
reluctant to develop close relations for fear of stimulating demands that could not be met. The rights groups had a comparable
reluctance; too much camaraderie might be taken for "Uncle
Tomism" particularly since it was not likely to lead to significant changes in law or more vigorous government enforcement of existing law. The Johnson Administration had settled
on a kind of symbolic liaison — from time to time, the President
would talk with the top civil rights leaders or call them on the
telephone and tell them how much he hoped to accomplish with
them and how much he needed their help. But beneath this,
the eleborate staff linkages between pressure groups and White
House that exist in other areas simply did not exist.

In such a context, the rights groups were distinctly nervous
about the President's vigorous utterances on civil rights ("We
Shall Overcome"). If the President succeeded in persuading the
public, including the Negro public, that he was now in charge
of the civil rights movement it could only weaken their already
small influence, particularly because they had no compensatory
power base in the Congress. This was the civil rights manifestation of the "benign Machiavellianism" of the Johnson Administration. By embracing the movement figuratively (and its leaders
physically), the President maximized his own options in action
and minimized theirs. The Moynihan Report and the controversy
it created were eventually pressed into the service of this
strategy.

3

Moynihan's Strategy

The Moynihan Report is clearly not an article prepared for a learned journal nor an ordinary position paper prepared by a political executive. Rather, it is a hybrid that seeks to present certain social science facts and at the same time to argue a particular and rather unusual policy position. As such, it reflects some of the intellectual difficulties of each one of the elements that go into making the hybrid and some additional ones that come from the combination of the two approaches. In order to fully understand the document we need to know something of the man who wrote it, the office he held, the problem he sought to deal with, and the strategy he developed.

The Man

Daniel Patrick Moynihan joined the New Frontier in 1961 as special assistant to Secretary of Labor Goldberg and by 1963 was appointed Assistant Secretary of Labor in charge of the Office of Policy Planning and Research. He was one of a new

17

breed of public servants, the social scientist-politicos, who combine in their background both social science training and experience and full-time involvement in political activity. He had attended the City College of New York and Tufts University and received a Ph.D. in political science from the Fletcher School of Law and Diplomacy in 1961. He had attended the London School of Economics on a Fulbright fellowship. From 1955 to 1959 he had worked as an assistant to Governor Harriman of New York. From 1959 to 1961 he had been the director of the New York State Government Research Project at Syracuse University. His particular interests in political science, coupled with his experience in New York politics, had moved him in the direction of an increasing emphasis on the sociological study of urban life; his work in the Department of Labor was to sharpen further his sociological bent.

The Office

An Assistant Secretary of Labor and Director of the Office of Policy Planning and Research, with an additional over-all responsibility for the work of the Bureau of Labor Statistics, Moynihan was concerned with the development of information from which the effectiveness of the Department's activities could be assessed and with the development of programmatic ideas and policy goals in line with the Department's responsibilities. As an assistant secretary his constituency involved most naturally the higher level members of the Department of Labor and the White House staff. Cabinet officers and their assistants stand between the Presidential Government of each administration and the Permanent Government of civil servants and appointed officials who serve for longer periods of time than the elected administration. Moynihan's political experience and personal conception of public service pointed him very strongly in the direction of the Presidential Government. He clearly defined himself over the years of his service in Washington as a member of the "Presidential party." In addition to the normal privileges of his office, Moynihan had close personal relationships with the White House staff, relations that grew out of the Kennedy period and antedated his appointment as Assistant Secretary.

He had conceived President Kennedy's study of selective service rejectees (the Task Force on Manpower Conservation), that had been part of the groundwork for planning the War on

Poverty. The Task Force had produced a report, "One-Third of a Nation," which provided Moynihan a model as he began to work on his Negro family report. Moynihan had been a member of the four-man team that developed the War on Poverty legislative proposals (the others were Sargent Shriver, Adam Yarmolinsky, and James Sundquist). In his effort, he had been particularly concerned to strengthen the employment aspects of the poverty program.

The office that Moynihan held is of crucial importance in understanding the report and the controversy. The report itself was written from the standpoint of a member of the Presidential Government who has the right to suggest policy of the sweeping nature that Moynihan had in mind. Only a person in this position would have been able to write a report relatively free of the long review process typical of government reports or to ensure that it received high-level distribution. Only a person in this position would have been able to speak directly and on a relatively equal footing with the White House staff. Finally, only a person who was defined as solidly part of the Presidential Government would have a chance of resisting the counter-pressures that would come from other departments who might feel the report had policy implications inimicable to their programs.

Once the existence of the report became public knowledge, the fact that its author occupied such a high position meant that it must be taken seriously. The government produces thousands of reports every year, many of which have implications that considered on their merits alone deserve consideration by the public and by representatives of organizations and interest groups likely to be affected. However, very seldom are such reports given the kind of public notoriety and serious attention that was given the Moynihan Report. The attention reflected the seriousness implicit in its authorship as much or more than it derived from the content of the report itself. This is, of course, one of the reasons why "nothing new" caused a controversy.

The Problem

Moynihan's experience in Washington, then, had been such as to acquaint him with the problems of formulating programs that would deal effectively with unemployment, underemployment, poverty, and the like. Although he had a strong belief that modern government is capable of formulating policies and programs to deal with problems before there is a surge of popular demand or well-formulated political pressure, he had strong misgivings about the extent to which the vast range of federal activity designed to cope with problems of poverty was likely to be effective.

His own views on social welfare were strongly influenced by Catholic welfare philosophy, which has emphasized the idea that family interests are the central objective of social welfare and of social policy in general. He had observed that most European nations and Canada had adopted family-allowance programs to cope with difficulties of income maintenance at low-income levels. Early in his career in Washington he had tried to work up some interest in such a policy, but with no success. As the Kennedy Administration managed to stimulate the national economy, Moynihan felt he saw interest in unemployment problems declining; he came to the conclusion that the "unemployment rate was simply a shorthand for the gross national product." As the War on Poverty was put together, he felt that its main emphasis on community action programs contributed little in terms of support of families. Increasingly, he had come to feel that the idea of family welfare could provide both a focus for working out social and economic programs to deal with the problems of those cut off from the great society and a standard by which to evaluate the success of the programs. Thus, he told a conference on poverty in America held at the University of California, Berkeley, in February of 1965:

. . . it is very clear that after only a year of general discussion the question of poverty is leading us to a major reassessment of the effect upon family structure of the way we do things in this country.

Several things emerge. First it becomes more obvious that the primary function of community welfare programs is to provide surrogate family services. The logic of this relationship has taken us well beyond the original provision of food and clothing and money to far more complex matters of providing proper attitudes toward work, reasonable expectations of success and so forth. Obviously these are matters which for most persons are handled within the family system, and most of us would risk the speculation that the traditional family arrangement is probably the more efficient one.

It also emerges, however, that in general our arrangements do not pay much heed to this fact . . . .

We are beginning to see something of the relation of unemployment to family structure . . . . It may be that this line of inquiry will enable us to redefine the problem of unemployment — so easily viewed as a matter of economic waste, and therefore of relatively marginal importance in an age of economic abundance — *and cast it in terms of the problem of delinquency and crime and welfare dependence and such, which by and large are problems the nation knows it has and would like to see dealt with* [emphasis ours].

In any event, I would think it is becoming clear that the discussion of poverty is leading us steadily towards a much more realistic view of the importance of maintaining a stable family structure at all levels of society — and more importantly, of the ease with which well-meaning or unthinking social policies can work against that objective . . . .

The next great social issue raised in America ought to be the question of how to insure a decent family income and a decent family setting for the working people of America, as we have already done — and as a result of no inconsiderable intervention of the Federal Government — for middle class Americans.

Thus Moynihan saw the War on Poverty as a logical outgrowth of the success of the early Kennedy years in getting the economy moving again. But he was concerned that the policies worked out to achieve these goals might actually be "counterproductive" or at least inadequate to the problem. For his part, he wished to use the notion of family welfare as a reference point by which to evaluate the desirability and the success of particular poverty programs. Using that standard, he had considerable doubt about two of the main lines of attack, community action programs and welfare services. Instead, he felt there should be greater emphasis on employment, income maintenance, and education. (It is not clear to us the extent to which Moynihan's general views on poverty were widely known within the government; if they were, this would help to account for some of the negative reactions to the report by those in the Permanent Government.)

Therefore when Moynihan turned his attention to the situation of Negro Americans, it seemed clear to him that the question of Negro family welfare should be central. Early in the 1960's he had collaborated with Nathan Glazer on a book, *Beyond The Melting Pot,** which dealt with the role of ethnicity in New York City. In 1964, the book won a *Saturday Review of Literature* Anisfield-Wolf Award as a significant contribution toward im-

---

* Nathan Glazer, and Daniel P. Moynihan, *Beyond the Melting Pot: The Negroes, Puerto Rican, Jews, Italians, and Irish of New York City* (Cambridge, Mass.: The M.I.T. Press, 1963).

proving race relations. One section of the book, written by Glazer, dealt with Negroes. The concern with family stability and pathology that was later to loom so large in the report had been foreshadowed in the short discussion of the Negro family in this book.

In addition, Moynihan remembered his own childhood. He had grown up in a broken family in Hell's Kitchen in New York City and had become a shoeshine boy when he was thirteen. On the corners that he worked, his companions were Negro shoeshine boys. He got to know something of their world and they something of his; and he was impressed by the fact that these seemed to be much the same worlds. This led him much later to work out systematically some of the parallels between the "wild Irish slums" of the late nineteenth century and the Negro ghettos of today. His work with Glazer reinterested him in these issues; and the interest deepened during his time at the Department of Labor as he observed that the various programs designed to increase the employment level of Negroes seemed to have very uneven success.

All of these issues were brought into sharp focus in April 1964 when Moynihan attended a planning conference for a study on the Negro in America to be sponsored by *Daedalus* and the American Academy of Arts and Sciences. Seventeen persons were assembled to discuss the current state of knowledge in this area and to develop a plan for a major work that would be at once scholarly and relevant to policy.* Moynihan listened to the early discussion, making a few comments about labor-force projections; and then, as the discussion centered on the transmission of social science ideas into public policy, he pointed out that one of the most important issues of race relations policy at that time was the question of preferential or compensatory treatment for Negroes. He said that there was resistance to the idea from such organs of the Establishment as *The New York Times,*

"And I was thinking that the Academy might do a great service if it were to look into the question . . . were to come to a conclusion that if you were ever going to have anything like an equal Negro community, you are for the next thirty years going to have to give them

---

* The other participants, in addition to *Daedalus* editor, Stephen Graubard, were Daniel Bell, Eric H. Erikson, Rashi Fein, Paul A. Freund, Clifford Geertz, Oscar Handlin, Everett C. Hughes, Carl Kaysen, Edward H. Levi, Jean Mayer, Robert Merton, Thomas F. Pettigrew, Talcott Parsons, Arthur Singer, and William M. Schmidt.

unequal treatment. I think the possibilities of thus legitimizing such treatment might have some relevance to public policy right now.

The introduction of this specific programmatic idea stimulated a great deal of discussion pro and con, which focussed, among other things, on the whole question of the extent to which there were various kinds of restraints on policy that sought to improve the position of Negro Americans. This led one distinguished sociologist, with a record of contributions in both theoretical and applied areas, to make a prophetic comment:

If we summarize a part of the discussion of the past fifteen minutes or so, we have shifted our attention to the restraints on some current activities that have been initiated to deal with the problem. I think we ought to perhaps consider the implication of such an emphasis. . . . If this volume . . . were inadvertently to have an emphasis on the value constraints, the moral constraints, the social constraints, the sources of resistance, so that the volume could be read in effect by those who read it selectively [to say] that "the Negro must be contained and that the Negro movement is getting out of hand, and if you really stop to think about it, the alternatives are severely restricted and limited." . . . If we in an effort to diagnose [the] realities, emphasize the obstacles and the restraints and so on, there could be an imbalance in the resulting volume which might be very easily misunderstood. It could be interpreted as an effort to sap the energies, almost a plot to sap the energies, of the grass roots movement. Thus we could be presented as the white liberals of the American Academy who are engaged in rationalizing not the status quo, but the future status [quo].

Much of what was said by the conference participants seemed to reinforce for Moynihan his twin concern with employment and the family. Thus, toward the end of the conference he said, "The biggest question is, will the Negro community itself get pulled apart by the problems of employment? It would seem to us to be absolutely devastating, and they are not Negro problems, they are American problems generally, but their differential effect on the Negro is potentially disastrous." He then quickly summarized what were actually to become the main points of the first part of his Negro family report, the differentials having to do with wages, with unemployment, with illegitimacy, with family breakup.

At the end of the conference, he was asked what kind of information the government needed from the scholarly community.

He emphasized the problem of the family, saying:

I think that the problem of the Negro family is practically the property of the American government. I mean we spend most of our money on this, in one form or another, in health, in welfare, and on employment, and yet we know nothing about it, or not much about it, and one of the reasons is that we are not supposed to know anything about it. It's none of your business that 40 per cent of the kids are illegitimate (a reference to the figures from Harlem) and don't, for heaven's sake, try to get it published, you can't. And if it is getting worse, that's even less of your business. All you're supposed to do is keep on supplying welfare, and if we knew something about the dynamics of that and if we could, for heaven's sake, find something besides the inheritance from slavery, which sort of leaves you there — that's it, that's it — but if there is something that is new, if it's getting worse because of reasons that are new, then there is a possibility of public policy reacting to it.

The idea of preferential treatment, which the participants discussed in considerable detail, highlighted the ambiguities of that idea in relation to traditional American political thought. The participants all agreed that the situation of Negro Americans required special treatment, but they were very unclear as to how this could be rationalized in traditional political rhetoric. It would seem that in the course of the following year Moynihan worked out what he believed to be one solution. This solution involved an emphasis on equality and particularly the introduction of the standard of "equal results," which Moynihan incorporated into his report and which was subsequently incorporated into the President's Howard University speech:

We seek not just freedom but opportunity — not just legal equity but human ability — not just equality as a right and a theory but equality as a fact and a result. For the task is to give twenty million Negroes the same chance as every other American to learn and grow, to work and share in society, to develop their abilities — physical, mental and spiritual — and to pursue their individual happiness.

If this were the national goal, then, and if it were to follow that this goal could be achieved only by special efforts on the behalf of Negroes, the logic of the argument of "equal results" would justify them.

Even so, Moynihan came to recognize that as a political slogan or program direct preferential treatment was not feasible. At a subsequent *Daedalus* conference in May 1965, he said:

> . . . in order to do anything about the Negro Americans on the scale that our data would indicate, we have to declare that we are doing it for *everybody*. I think, however, that the problem of the Negro American is now a special one and is not just an intense case of the problem of all poor people . . . Congressmen vote for everyone more readily than they vote for anyone . . . . In terms of the working of the system we are trying to influence by our thinking here, it will be done for "everybody," whatever may be in the back of the minds of the people who do it.

As the *Daedalus* volume was planned, Moynihan himself was selected to write the article that dealt with problems of employment, income, and the Negro family, and so, beginning in the fall of 1964, he started to think more seriously about the issue.

The Strategy

Over the fall, Moynihan mulled the question of Negro poverty and the family and began to examine some of the data already in his office on unemployment rates and rates of marital disruption over a fifteen year period. At the same time, he thought he sensed in Washington a tendency on the part of some administration officials to think that the Civil Rights Act of 1964 had solved a good part of the civil rights problem. He was concerned with the credence given public opinion polls that showed that a majority of Negroes in Harlem felt that the Civil Rights Act would make a "very great difference" in their lives. The sharp contrast between this optimistic mood and the depressing figures on social and economic status disturbed him. Late in November of 1964, he decided to write a report on the Negro family for internal use in the government:

> I woke up a couple of nights later (that is, after one such conversation with a highly placed optimist) at four o'clock in the morning and felt I had to write a paper about the Negro family to explain to the fellows how there was a problem more difficult than they knew and also to explain some of the issues of unemployment and housing in terms that would be new enough and shocking enough that they would say, "Well, we can't let this sort of thing go on. We've got to do something about it."

He organized a small working staff and through them began to collect government statistics that in one way or another had bearing on the problem. He had available to him not only the vast range of published and indexed government statistics but also the services of Labor Department economists and of the Bureau of Labor Statistics to pull together information that was not already in published form. The basic paradigm he worked with was that of the social and economic analysis that had laid the ground work for the poverty program, except that he was doing this on his own and on a much smaller scale. From December through March, then, Moynihan and his staff put together the document and in the process worked out a strategy of placement and presentation. At the same time, he laid the groundwork for the reception of the report by speaking from time to time to those he wished in the end to persuade. In March, the document was formally cleared by Secretary of Labor Wirtz and one hundred nicely printed and bound copies run off in the basement of the Department of Labor. Despite its small audience he wanted a handsome, finished-looking document. No more than eighty of the numbered copies of the report were distributed by July, when it was decided to make the document public and turn it over to the Government Printing Office.

Moynihan was writing for a very small audience. His concern was to have adopted at the highest levels of the administration the view that family welfare provided a central point of reference in evaluating the effectiveness of programs to deal with disadvantaged groups. He sought to achieve a basic redefinition of the civil rights problem at the highest level of the administration as a preliminary to a broader redefinition by the government as a whole. In order to do this, he wanted to formulate a clear diagnosis of the problem, to acquaint officials with facts that he felt they either did not know or of which they did not see the full implications.

While the document was to be an unusual one for government policy papers, it must at least have some kinship with them. Therefore, there was heavy emphasis on government statistics, since these are the "authoritative data" with which high level officials are accustomed to working. Though it sought to present a complex argument, the document must be short and sharply focused. Although early in his planning Moynihan had thought of suggesting solutions as well as defining a problem, he finally determined not to include any reference to solutions in the report itself in order to force his readers to focus their attention on understanding the problem qua problem.

Thus, the report was distributed to only a few persons within the Department of Labor and the White House. As time went on, particularly as the reputation of the report spread within the Administration and demands for it increased, the circle of distribution grew wider. But at least from April through most of June only a handful of persons outside the White House and the Department of Labor had seen copies. During April and May, with the report as the formal basis for his views, Moynihan pursued his goal in personal conversations and with briefer memoranda. The events of the first week of June provided the first indication that his report had found its target.

In the meantime, Moynihan had completed a slightly different version of the same ideas for publication in *Daedalus*; the draft of this paper was discussed at a *Daedalus* conference on May 14th and 15th. Though the essential points contained in the report are also found in the article prepared for publication, some of the issues that were to prove sensitive when the report made its way into the press are much subdued in the paper — there are a scant two sentences dealing with illegitimacy and no discussion of slavery and other historical factors.

On May 4th, Secretary Wirtz forwarded to the White House a memorandum for the President that summarized the report and added several recommendations. Secretary Wirtz indicated that the memorandum had been prepared by Moynihan but that he agreed with the analysis and concurred in the recommendations. The memorandum was sent to Presidential Assistant Bill Moyers; it is not clear whether the President in fact ever read it (apparently he did not read the report), but the effect of the memorandum was to place the report and several recommendations on the White House agenda.

Moynihan sought to present a sharply focused argument leading to the conclusion that the government's economic and social welfare programs, existing and prospective ones, should be systematically designed to encourage the stability of the Negro family. He sought to show, first, that the Negro family was highly unstable (female-headed households produced by marital breakup and illegitimacy). This instability resulted from the systematic weakening of the position of the Negro male. Slavery, reconstruction, urbanization, and unemployment had produced a problem as old as America and as new as the April unemployment rate. This problem of unstable families in turn was a central feature of the tangle of pathology of the urban ghetto, involving problems of delinquency, crime, school dropouts, unemployment, and poverty. Finally, Moynihan wanted the Administration to understand that some evidence supported the conclusion that these problems fed on themselves and that matters were rapidly getting worse.

In the report, in conversations, and in memorandums, Assistant Secretary of Labor Moynihan sought to persuade his peers and his superiors in the Presidential Government that they were confronted with a crisis situation no less dangerous than that of Birmingham, Selma, or Mississippi for all that it might be somewhat drawn out. Though he did not deal with the summer riots of 1964 in the report, he was quite willing to point out to anyone who was interested that these riots had at their core Negro youth who knew how bad off they were and that there would be more such riots.

In the May 4th memorandum to the President, he sought to emphasize the necessity for planning. The first step in the solution of these problems was simply that the government must acknowledge the problem and its urgency — agencies and key individuals must be brought together, focus on the problem, and agree that the basic strategy must be to strengthen the family. There must be a stop to decision-making processes in which policy makers rush off after solutions before really agreeing on what the problem is. Once the focus was on the stability of the family, the government would have an absolute measure of whether or not its efforts were producing any results. The government would not be able to tell itself that it had changed anything until it really had; that is, until the proportion of Negro marriages that break up begins to decline and the proportion of Negro families with male heads begins to increase. Moynihan believed that should the government be able to create the conditions in which this would happen, other indices of disorganization would also show improvement — more children would complete school and they would do better in school, there would be less crime and delinquency, less dope addiction, and so forth. In short, the mutually reinforcing tangle of pathology would begin to unravel.

Though he had decided not to include recommendations in his report — for fear that all of the attention would go to the recommended programs rather than to the definition of the problem and also that there would be premature budget estimates of the cost of the recommended programs — in the memorandum he suggested several steps as a start. These reflected two kinds of concerns, one administrative and the other programmatic.

The first had to do with institutionalizing the kind of policy-assessment approach he had sought to essay in his report. He felt a group should be appointed to review all the programs of the federal government with a view to determining whether they were helping to strengthen the Negro family or simply perpetuating its weaknesses. In line with this, the government should establish a place at which relevant data on the changing situation of Negroes could be brought together, organized, and made available to other agencies. Such an information center would provide a better means of measuring the success or failure of programs than the present widely dispersed source of information allowed.

In the area of concrete programs, Moynihan felt that jobs had primacy and that the government should not rest until every able-bodied Negro man was working even if this meant that some women's jobs had to be redesigned to enable men to fulfill them. He felt that housing programs should be initiated that provide decent family housing and, in particular, that the housing in suburbs must be planned so that families could escape the ghetto.

In addition, birth control programs were sorely needed so that Negroes could limit their families in line with their needs and desires and the illegitimacy rate could be reduced. Then, finally, Negro youths should be given a greater opportunity to serve in the Armed Forces. It would be possible to set up training programs to allow more Negroes who volunteer for the services but are rejected to qualify on the standard tests and thus be accepted.

In short, though he felt that the general direction of solutions to the problems he had posed — employment, income maintenance (in the form of family allowances perhaps), better housing and family planning — were clear, he did not formulate specific program proposals. Rather, he hoped that if he were successful in persuading the Administration to adopt his view of the nature and urgency of the situation, working groups would be set up to develop such specific programs.

Moynihan's principal immediate goal was to stimulate a commitment by the Administration to engage in long-range policy planning. At the time he formulated his strategy there were many senior career men in the government (and others outside) who were desperately trying to elicit from the Administration this kind of commitment and who were trying to put together social science materials of various kinds to demonstrate the value of such policy planning. Moynihan's position as Assistant Secretary and his personal relations with the White House staff allowed him a kind of access that the career men did not have (some had had such access under Kennedy). He had the ear of the White House and the political status and skill to make use of it. One career planner credited him with "making the one main inroad into the White House" to get action, though he noted that Moynihan's goal and ability to use social science data in its services were not unique to him.

That Moynihan was not very successful in his efforts to win White House aides over to the philosophy of careful policy planning before program development and something of the nature of the resistance to such an approach are suggested by the following experience related by one of the nation's best informed experts on ghetto problems. This man had been called to the White House in the summer of 1965 to meet with the President's top aides to discuss what should be accomplished in the fall conference. He found the senior man at the meeting "terribly impatient";

He kept demanding specific proposals for specific programs and specific legislation: "Our job is to legislate." I tangled with him because I saw my function as trying to suggest the complexity of the problem and the need for co-ordination between programs and community organization or social action from within the Negro community. I was terribly conscious of the enormous obstacles in the way of any attempt by government to stimulate authentic social action within a community. I was also terribly aware of what seemed to me then — and still seems — the serious failures of many of the governmental programs that had already been established. I was trying to suggest that we might come closer to a solution of the problem if the government tried to do a few things well instead of doing a great many things badly. He was extremely impatient with any discussion of complexity and disinterested in any critique of weakness of the existing programs. His orientation — stemming, I assume, from the fact that he had to report directly to the President — was "what do we do next?" He just was not interested in anything that did not lead directly to a specific proposal which he could place before the President — and before the Congress.

Other experts have made similar observations about White House aides in the meetings of that summer.

There is an interesting contrast between the internal policy statement that the report represents and the political statement which the Howard University speech represents. The report is addressed to the concerns of those who manage the nation. That is, it presents a problem rather than an argument about rights and justice. It says that things are going badly in one segment of the society and will continue to go badly until the government sets them right. The argument rests less on moral considerations than it does on a certain kind of high-level administrative rationality. If the nation is to be *governed* properly, or indeed be governable, national social and economic policy must operate in such a way that Negroes have different life experiences than they now have. The Howard University speech, on the other hand, places the same views in the context of justice and morality and thereby lacks the highly impersonal and detached tone that the report brings to bear. While this latter tone is appropriate and desirable for an internal document, it can seem almost heartless if considered outside of that context.

One other aspect of the tone of the report deserves mention. Moynihan was concerned to demonstrate the extent of family disorganization among poor Negroes and the relation of family disorganization to various social problems in the ghetto. In line with this goal, he emphasized very strongly the destructive potential of disorganized family life much as Frazier, Clark and others before him had done. However, there is another way of looking at Negro lower-class family forms — one concerns oneself with how particular family patterns function to enable individuals to adapt to their depriving lower-class existence and to maintain themselves biologically, psychically, and socially in the one world in which they must live. From this perspective some of the same behaviors that appear pathological (in terms of ability to function in line with the demands of stable working or middle-class norms and institutions) are functional in terms of the ability to make as gratifying a life as possible in a ghetto milieu. Had Moynihan dealt with this aspect of the situation he might have avoided some of the criticism of the report — but probably would have earned other kinds of criticism. As many sociologists have noted, functional analysis tends to appear as rather conservative; bowdlerizer versions of the adaptive quality of "pathological" lower-class patterns could undoubtedly be made to appear to support the view that lower-class Negroes are really not so dissatisfied with their situation. In any case, this line of argument would hardly be persuasive with high officials for the federal initiatives Moynihan hoped to stimulate. For that purpose, he needed to point to what poor Negroes were deprived of, not to how they managed to make out despite their deprivations.

The Results

The report had sought to establish in the Presidential Government a new view of the situation of Negro Americans and to set in motion program planning in line with that new view. (This, despite the fact that there was nothing at all new to a wide group of social scientists and citizens well-informed in the civil rights area about the views Moynihan advanced.) The strategy seemed to have paid off handsomely. Moynihan's White House constituency was already concerned as to the direction the government should move after the 1965 Civil Rights Bill, and they seemed to understand his contention that purely antidiscrimination programs would not alone solve the problems of the northern ghettos. They were sympathetic to the notion that the family provided a worthwhile focus for evaluating the effectiveness of programs and some of them developed a fairly thorough intellectual sophistication in what all of this implied. Finally, the President decided to use Moynihan's work as the basis for his speech at Howard University. (The facts are unclear to us, but there is some reason to believe that the President decided to accept the invitation from Howard *because* he wanted a forum at which to test out these ideas concerning "the next more profound stage of the battle for civil rights.") In line with this thinking, the White House decided to call a conference to discuss the problems that would now be confronted in this next stage.

While those in the government who were privy to Moynihan's views saw in them a powerful tool for understanding and planning, they also recognized considerable danger should the report's ideas be communicated to the public in the wrong way. Interestingly enough, some persons in the Administration saw the dangers not so much in a negative reaction from persons concerned with civil rights but rather in the unpleasant prospect of Southern newsmen and public figures seeking to twist the argument to substantiate their views of the inferiority of Negroes. As knowledge of the main ideas in the report became more widespread within the government, however, some individuals began to warn of the backlash from Negro leaders who would be concerned about the discussion of such sensitive issues as family instability, illegitimacy, and the like.

In any case, when Moynihan left the country on June 4th to attend a conference in Yugoslavia on multiethnic societies, he had every reason to believe that the initial goals of his strategy had been achieved and that the road was open to the ultimate goal of a revised national strategy for Negro equality. Though he was to be involved in the conference planning that followed the speech, his central role was ended. The staff job of "preplanning" was turned over to an ad hoc group, which used the staff facilities of the President's Council on Equal Opportunity headed by Vice-President Humphrey and staffed by men primarily identified with him. Moynihan returned to Washington late in June and left on July 18th to run in the New York Democratic Primary for the office of President of the City Council.

The Follow-Up

A series of preparatory meetings for the conference were held in a White House conference room during the month of July. At these meetings, social experts presented their views to a group of about ten White House assistants and staff members of the "preplanning" group. The experts came in one at a time so that each man gave his own views but without an opportunity for exchange of views with any of the other experts. Several of the experts found this arrangement a rather uncomfortable one since they felt very much on the spot vis-à-vis the government people; they found it difficult to present their arguments as vigorously or as broadly as they would have liked or as would have been possible working in concert with other experts. From the point of view of the government, of course, this arrangement was desirable since it did not want to be lobbied or instructed but simply informed and left free to decide what to do with the knowledge. It was, of course, also in a very good position to see the extent of spontaneous consensus among the experts since no expert knew what the others were saying.

Those called to the White House for these meetings included a distinguished list of social scientists — Professors Talcott Parsons, Eric Erikson, Kenneth Clark, Robert Coles, Thomas Pettigrew, Urie Bronfenbrenner, and James Wilson. During this period no civil rights leaders attended the preparatory meetings; the staff had wished to invite John Turner, Professor of Social Work at Western Reserve University and consultant to the National Urban League, and Bayard Rustin, but they were out of the country at the time the schedule was arranged.

The experts scheduled for these meetings could be expected to deepen considerably the officials' understanding of the problems of the Negro family and of ghetto pathology. With the exception of Erikson and Parsons, all of them were men who had devoted a considerable part of their professional careers to studying the impact on individuals and group of living in a lower-class environment. Almost all of the academicians had also participated in the *Daedalus* conferences and reflected its "Eastern Establishment" cast: five were Harvard professors.

It is important to note that these preparatory meetings and the staff work connected with them did not involve an officially appointed planning group for the conference but a preplanning group which was beginning to work out tentative ideas as to what the conference might be like. For a number of reasons the planning staff was not appointed until early October. Nevertheless this preplanning group worked out an over-all design that was to persist through the actual planning conference held in November.

Much of the later controversy about the conference and the Moynihan Report had to do with whether or not the conference was going to be "about the family." As best we can determine the answer to this question can be yes or no depending on what "about the family" is taken to mean. It is clear that at no time and in no way was the conference planned as a conference on the Negro family (that is, as a conference that would deal solely with the subject of the Negro family even in the relatively broad way it had been treated in Moynihan's work of Spring 1965). On the other hand, it seems quite reasonable to believe that the White House had in mind that the main overarching theme of the conference would be the welfare of Negro families in the sense in which Moynihan used the idea: as the basis from which to evaluate the effectiveness of programs designed to cope with the next stage of the civil rights struggle. From this point of view, then, the discussions in the prospective conference dealing with employment, education, health and welfare programs, and the like would have been subjected to the standard of whether or not they seemed to be likely to pay off in greater family stability and well-being. However, some of the other areas of persisting concern in civil rights — voting, the administration of justice, protection of civil rights workers — could not be so directly related to this concern.

In any case, quite early in the July discussions, government officials in the preplanning group pointed out that the family emphasis would prove a very sensitive and touchy issue with people involved in civil rights activity and argued against heavy emphasis on the subject, even in the form of an overarching standard of program effectiveness. In late July, therefore, an outline of panels for the conference was developed, using a traditional subgrouping around topics that had long been dealt with by the U.S. Civil Rights Commission in its hearings — jobs, education, voting, protection of persons, and so on. In addition, it was obvious that some new areas needed to be introduced to cope with northern and urban problems. At one point, it was thought that there should be a panel on "the dynamics of the ghetto" that would consider both the family and the community, but in the end this was broken up into two sessions — one on family and one on community. From this time, late July, until the planning conference there were frequent expressions of concern both within the government and from outside about the existence of even one session dealing specifically with the family — for reasons that we trust will become apparent in the sections that follow.

One final point can be raised concerning the connection between the conference and Moynihan's thesis. This has to do with why there should have been a conference at all. The White House decision to call a conference was apparently not subjected to a great deal of discussion and consideration; it just seemed a good idea in the context of the President's speech, the new issues that he raised, and the Administration's continuing concern about where to go next in civil rights. (Apparently while drafting the speech, Richard Goodwin conceived the idea of the conference and included it in the draft sent to the President, who adopted the idea.) Since the new theme was clearly aimed at a significant departure from previous ways of dealing with the problem (although in line with the War on Poverty philosophy), it seemed a good idea to call together experts, civil rights leaders, and government officials to map out the new territory.

However, White House conferences do not generally serve this function. In the past most, but not all, conferences had served primarily to ratify programs already on the drawing board and to build public support for them. Most of the questions and an-

swers are known in rough outline and the conference provides
a stage on which they can be made public in a context that sym-
bolizes their importance. Yet here a conference was going to
take on the task of solving the most sensitive domestic issue
confronting the country and do so in the full light of publicity.
It was this disparity between the goal of the conference and
the administrative and political realities of a sensitive issue that
caused the fall meeting to be scaled down to a planning conference; nor was the spring meeting able to overcome these obstacles. In a very real sense, it seems that the White House did
not understand what it was getting into.

To highlight this point, let us note briefly that there was another frequently used alternative open to the President if he
wished to get moving on the next stage and make some kind of
dramatic public acknowledgment of his desire in the Howard
speech.

This would have involved a President's Commission that could
have taken Moynihan's work as an initial proposal and developed
its implications, subjecting the thesis to thorough correction and
elaboration. Perhaps this route was awkward because there were
already three commissions operating in this area — the United
States Civil Rights Commission, the President's Commission on
Equal Opportunity, and a Commission on Fair Housing. A fourth
commission, even a temporary one, would seem to indicate a
preference for studying the problem to death rather than doing
something about it.

Yet such a commission would also have highlighted some of
the inadequacies of the government bureaucracy currently dealing with civil rights problems. The approach of the Civil Rights
Commission and other agencies had been heavily dominated by
the thinking of the "first stage" of the civil rights struggle: that
concerned centrally and single-mindedly with questions of discrimination and segregation. Their staffs tended to be uncomfortable about approaches that departed from this simple, primarily legal, model. On the other hand, the welfare bureaucracy
that did exist to deal with the social and economic issues that
Moynihan raised was deeply implicated in his implicit critique
of the government's approach to the welfare of the disadvantaged.
Since one of the main goals of the re-examination that Moynihan
was proposing would be to point out the inadequacies and destructive effects of many government programs, one could hardly
turn the job over to any of the already existing poverty and

welfare agencies no matter how much their technical skills and experience might be necessary to the success of such a re-examination.

Thus, none of the alternatives to a conference would seem very attractive from the point of view of the Administration, although subsequent events do suggest that a somewhat less public and longer term inquiry would have been desirable.

4

The Moynihan Report
and the Howard University Address

THE

THE CASE FOR NATIONAL ACTION

NEGRO
FAMILY

OFFICE OF POLICY PLANNING AND RESEARCH
UNITED STATES DEPARTMENT OF LABOR

MARCH, 1965

The United States is approaching a new crisis in race relations.

In the decade that began with the school desegregation decision of the Supreme Court, and ended with the passage of the Civil Rights Act of 1964, the demand of Negro Americans for full recognition of their civil rights was finally met.

The effort, no matter how savage and brutal, of some State and local governments to thwart the exercise of those rights is doomed. The nation will not put up with it—least of all the Negroes. The present moment will pass. In the meantime, a new period is beginning.

In this new period the expectations of the Negro Americans will go beyond civil rights. Being Americans, they will now expect that in the near future equal opportunities for them as a group will produce roughly equal results, as compared with other groups. This is not going to happen. Nor will it happen for generations to come unless a new and special effort is made.

There are two reasons. First, the racist virus in the American blood stream still afflicts us: Negroes will encounter serious personal prejudice for at least another generation. Second, three centuries of sometimes unimaginable mistreatment have taken their toll on the Negro people. The harsh fact is that as a group, at the present time, in terms of ability to win out in the competitions of American life, they are not equal to most of those groups with which they will be competing. Individually, Negro Americans reach the highest peaks of achievement. But collectively, in the spectrum of American ethnic and religious and regional groups, where some get plenty and some get none, where some send eighty percent of their children to college and others pull them out of school at the 8th grade, Negroes are among the weakest.

The most difficult fact for white Americans to understand is that in these terms the circumstances of the Negro American community in recent years has probably been getting *worse, not better.*

Indices of dollars of income, standards of living, and years of education deceive. The gap between the Negro and most other groups in American society is widening.

The fundamental problem, in which this is most clearly the case, is that of family structure. The evidence—not final, but powerfully persuasive—is that the Negro family in the urban ghettos is crumbling. A middle-class group has managed to save itself, but for vast numbers of the unskilled, poorly educated city working class the fabric of conventional social relationships has all but disintegrated. There are indications that the situation may have been arrested in the past few years, but the general post-war trend is unmistakable. So long as this situation persists, the cycle of poverty and disadvantage will continue to repeat itself.

The thesis of this paper is that these events, in combination, confront the nation with a new kind of problem. Measures that have worked in the past, or would work for most groups in the present, will not work here. A national effort is required that will give a unity of purpose to the many activities of the Federal government in this area, directed to a new kind of national goal: the establishment of a stable Negro family structure.

This would be a new departure for Federal policy. And a difficult one. But it almost certainly offers the only possibility of resolving in our time what is, after all, the nation's oldest, and most intransigent, and now its most dangerous social problem. What Gunnar Myrdal said in *An American Dilemma* remains true today: *"America is free to choose whether the Negro shall remain her liability or become her opportunity."*

TABLE OF CONTENTS

Chapter I

The Negro American Revolution

The Negro American revolution is rightly regarded as the most important domestic event of the postwar period in the United States.

Nothing like it has occurred since the upheavals of the 1930's which led to the organization of the great industrial trade unions, and which in turn profoundly altered both the economy and the political scene. There have been few other events in our history—the American Revolution itself, the surge of Jacksonian Democracy in the 1830's, the Abolitionist movement, and the Populist movement of the late 19th century—comparable to the current Negro movement.

There has been none more important. The Negro American revolution holds forth the prospect that the American Republic, which at birth was flawed by the institution of Negro slavery, and which throughout its history has been marred by the unequal treatment of Negro citizens, will at last redeem the full promise of the Declaration of Independence.

Although the Negro leadership has conducted itself with the strictest propriety, acting always and only as American citizens asserting their rights within the framework of the American political system, it is no less clear that the movement has profound international implications.

It was in no way a matter of chance that the nonviolent tactics and philosophy of the movement, as it began in the South, were consciously adapted from the techniques by which the Congress Party undertook to free the Indian nation from British colonial rule. It was not a matter of chance that the Negro movement caught fire in America at just that

moment when the nations of Africa were gaining their freedom. Nor is it merely incidental that the world should have fastened its attention on events in the United States at a time when the possibility that the nations of the world will divide along color lines seems suddenly not only possible, but even imminent.

(Such racist views have made progress within the Negro American community itself—which can hardly be expected to be immune to a virus that is endemic in the white community. The Black Muslim doctrines, based on total alienation from the white world, exert a powerful influence. On the far left, the attraction of Chinese Communism can no longer be ignored.)

It is clear that what happens in America is being taken as a sign of what can, or must, happen in the world at large. The course of world events will be profoundly affected by the success or failure of the Negro American revolution in seeking the peaceful assimilation of the races in the United States. The award of the Nobel Peace Prize to Dr. Martin Luther King was as much an expression of the hope for the future, as it was recognition for past achievement.

It is no less clear that carrying this revolution forward to a successful conclusion is a first priority confronting the Great Society.

The End of the Beginning

The major events of the onset of the Negro revolution are now behind us.

The *political events* were three: First, the Negroes themselves organized as a mass movement. Their organizations have been in some ways better disciplined and better led than any in our history. They have established an unprecedented alliance with religious groups throughout the nation and have maintained close ties with both political parties and with most segments of the trade union movement. Second, the Kennedy-Johnson Administration committed the Federal government to the cause of Negro equality. This had never happened before. Third, the 1964 Presidential election was practically a referendum on this commitment: if these were terms made by the opposition, they were in effect accepted by the President.

The overwhelming victory of President Johnson must be taken as emphatic popular endorsement of the unmistakable, and openly avowed course which the Federal government has pursued under his leadership.

The *administrative events* were threefold as well: First, beginning with the establishment of the President's Committee on Equal Employment Opportunity and on to the enactment of the Manpower Development and Training Act of 1962, the Federal government has launched a major national effort to redress the profound imbalance between the economic position of the Negro citizens and the rest of the nation that derives primarily from their unequal position in the labor market. Second, the Economic Opportunity Act of 1964 began a major national effort to abolish poverty, a condition in which almost half of Negro families are living. Third, the Civil Rights Act of 1964 marked the end of the era of legal and formal discrimination against Negroes and created important new machinery for combating covert discrimination and unequal treatment. (The Act does not guarantee an end to harassment in matters such as voter registration, but does make it more or less incumbent upon government to take further steps to thwart such efforts when they do occur.)

The *legal events* were no less specific. Beginning with *Brown* v. *Board of Education* in 1954, through the decade that culminated in the recent decisions upholding Title II of the Civil Rights Act, the Federal judiciary, led by the Supreme Court, has used every opportunity to combat unequal treatment of Negro citizens. It may be put as a general proposition that the laws of the United States now look upon any such treatment as obnoxious, and that the courts will strike it down wherever it appears.

The Demand for Equality

With these events behind us, the nation now faces a different set of challenges, which may prove more difficult to meet, if only because they cannot be cast as concrete propositions of right and wrong.

The fundamental problem here is that the Negro revolution, like the industrial upheaval of the 1930's, is a movement for equality as well as for liberty.

Liberty and Equality are the twin ideals of American democracy. But they are not the same thing. Nor, most importantly, are they equally attractive to all groups at any given time; nor yet are they always compatible, one with the other.

Many persons who would gladly die for liberty are appalled by equality. Many who are devoted to equality are puzzled and even troubled by liberty. Much of the political history of the American nation can be seen as a competition between these two ideals, as for example, the unending troubles between capital and labor.

By and large, liberty has been the ideal with the higher social prestige in America. It has been the middle class aspiration, par excellence. (Note the assertions of the conservative right that ours is a republic, not a democracy.) Equality, on the other hand, has enjoyed tolerance more than acceptance. Yet it has roots deep in Western civilization and "is at least coeval with, if not prior to, liberty in the history of Western political thought."[1]

American democracy has not always been successful in maintaining a balance between these two ideals, and notably so where the Negro American is concerned. "Lincoln freed the slaves," but they were given liberty, not equality. It was therefore possible in the century that followed to deprive their descendants of much of their liberty as well.

The ideal of equality does not ordain that all persons end up, as well as start out equal. In traditional terms, as put by Faulkner, "there is no such thing as equality *per se,* but only equality *to*: equal right and opportunity to make the best one can of one's life within one's capability, without fear of injustice or oppression or threat of violence."[2] But the evolution of American politics, with the distinct persistence of ethnic and religious groups, has added a profoundly significant new dimension to that egalitarian ideal. It is increasingly demanded that the distribution of success and failure within one group be roughly comparable to that within other groups. It is not enough that all individuals start out on even terms, if the members of one group almost invariably end up well to the fore, and those of another far to the rear. This is what ethnic politics are all about in America, and in the main the Negro American demands are being put forth in this now traditional and established framework.[3]

Here a point of semantics must be grasped. The demand for Equality of Opportunity has been generally perceived by white Americans as a demand for liberty, a demand not to be excluded from the competitions of life—at the polling place, in the scholarship examinations, at the personnel office, on the housing market. Liberty does, of course, demand that everyone be free to try his luck, or test his skill in such matters. But these opportunities do not necessarily produce equality: on the contrary, to the extent that winners imply losers, equality of opportunity almost insures inequality of results.

The point of semantics is that equality of opportunity now has a different meaning for Negroes than it has for whites. It is not (or at least no longer) a demand for liberty alone, but also for equality—in terms of group results. In Bayard Rustin's terms, "It is now concerned not merely with removing the barriers to full *opportunity* but with achieving the fact of *equality.*"[4] By equality Rustin means a distribution of achievements among Negroes roughly comparable to that among whites.

As Nathan Glazer has put it, "The demand for economic equality is now not the demand for equal opportunities for the equally qualified: it is now the demand for equality of economic results . . . The demand for equality in education . . . has also become a demand for equality of results, of outcomes."[5]

Some aspects of the new laws do guarantee results, in the sense that upon enactment and enforcement they bring about an objective that is an end in itself, e.g., the public accommodations title of the Civil Rights Act.

Other provisions are at once terminal and intermediary. The portions of the Civil Rights Act dealing with voting rights will achieve an objective that is an end in itself, but the exercise of those rights will no doubt lead to further enlargements of the freedom of the Negro American.

But by and large, the programs that have been enacted in the first phase of the Negro revolution—Manpower Retraining, the Job Corps, Community Action, et al.—only make opportunities available. They cannot insure the outcome.

The principal challenge of the next phase of the Negro revolution is to make certain that equality of results will now follow. If we do not, there will be no social peace in the United States for generations.

787-326 O-65—2

The Prospect for Equality

The time, therefore, is at hand for an unflinching look at the present potential of Negro Americans to move from where they now are to where they want, and ought to be.

There is no very satisfactory way, at present, to measure social health or social pathology within an ethnic, or religious, or geographical community. Data are few and uncertain, and conclusions drawn from them, including the conclusions that follow, are subject to the grossest error.* Nonetheless, the opportunities, no less than the dangers, of the present moment. demand that an assessment be made.

That being the case, it has to be said that there is a considerable body of evidence to support the conclusion that Negro social structure, in particular the Negro family, battered and harassed by discrimination, injustice, and uprooting, is in the deepest trouble. While many young Negroes are moving ahead to unprecedented levels of achievement, many more are falling further and further behind.

After an intensive study of the life of central Harlem, the board of directors of Harlem Youth Opportunities Unlimited, Inc. summed up their findings in one statement: "Massive deterioration of the fabric of society and its institutions..."[6]

It is the conclusion of this survey of the available national data, that what is true of central Harlem, can be said to be true of the Negro American world in general.

If this is so, it is the single most important social fact of the United States today.

---

*As much as possible, the statistics used in this paper refer to Negroes. However, certain data series are available only in terms of the white and nonwhite population. Where this is the case, the nonwhite data have been used as if they referred only to Negroes. This necessarily introduces some inaccuracies, but it does not appear to produce any significant distortions. In 1960, Negroes were 92.1 percent of all nonwhites. The remaining 7.9 percent is made up largely of Indians, Japanese, and Chinese. The combined male unemployment rates of these groups is lower than that of Negroes. In matters relating to family stability, the smaller groups are probably more stable. Thus 21 percent of Negro women who have ever married are separated, divorced, or their husbands are absent for other reasons. The comparable figure for Indians is 14 percent; Japanese, 7 percent; Chinese 6 percent. Therefore, the statistics on nonwhites generally **understate** the degree of disorganization of the Negro family and underemployment of Negro men.

Chapter II

The Negro American Family

At the heart of the deterioration of the fabric of Negro society is the deterioration of the Negro family.

It is the fundamental source of the weakness of the Negro community at the present time.

There is probably no single fact of Negro American life so little understood by whites. The Negro situation is commonly perceived by whites in terms of the visible manifestations of discrimination and poverty, in part because Negro protest is directed against such obstacles, and in part, no doubt, because these are facts which involve the actions and attitudes of the white community as well. It is more difficult, however, for whites to perceive the effect that three centuries of exploitation have had on the fabric of Negro society itself. Here the consequences of the historic injustices done to Negro Americans are silent and hidden from view. But here is where the true injury has occurred: unless this damage is repaired, all the effort to end discrimination and poverty and injustice will come to little.

The role of the family in shaping character and ability is so pervasive as to be easily overlooked. The family is the basic social unit of American life; it is the basic socializing unit. By and large, adult conduct in society is learned as a child.

A fundamental insight of psychoanalytic theory, for example, is that the child learns a way of looking at life in his early years through which all later experience is viewed and which profoundly shapes his adult conduct.

It may be hazarded that the reason family structure does not loom larger in public discussion of social issues is that people tend to assume that the nature of family life is about the same throughout American society. The mass media and the development of suburbia have created an image of the American family as a highly standardized phenomenon. It is therefore easy to assume that whatever it is that makes for differences among individuals or groups of individuals, it is not a different family structure.

There is much truth to this; as with any other nation, Americans are producing a recognizable family system. But that process is not completed by any means. There are still, for example, important differences in family patterns surviving from the age of the great European migration to the United States, and these variations account for notable differences in the progress and assimilation of various ethnic and religious groups.[7] A number of immigrant groups were characterized by unusually strong family bonds; these groups have characteristically progressed more rapidly than others.

But there is one truly great discontinuity in family structure in the United States at the present time: that between the white world in general and that of the Negro American.

The white family has achieved a high degree of stability and is maintaining that stability.

By contrast, the family structure of lower class Negroes is highly unstable, and in many urban centers is approaching complete breakdown.

N.b. There is considerable evidence that the Negro community is in fact dividing between a stable middle-class group that is steadily growing stronger and more successful, and an increasingly disorganized and disadvantaged lower-class group. There are indications, for example, that the middle-class Negro family puts a higher premium on family stability and the conserving of family resources than does the white middle-class family.[8] The discussion of this paper is not, obviously, directed to the first group excepting as it is affected by the experiences of the second—an important exception. (See Chapter IV, The Tangle of Pathology.)

There are two points to be noted in this context.

First, the emergence and increasing visibility of a Negro middle-class may beguile the nation into supposing that the circumstances of the remainder of the Negro community are equally prosperous, whereas just the opposite is true at present, and is likely to continue so.

Second, the lumping of all Negroes together in one statistical measurement very probably conceals the extent of the disorganization among the lower-class group. If conditions are improving for one and deteriorating for the other, the resultant statistical averages might show no change. Further, the statistics on the Negro family and most other subjects treated in this paper refer only to a specific point in time. They are a vertical measure of the situation at a given moment. They do not measure the experience of individuals over time. Thus the average monthly unemployment rate for Negro males for 1964 is recorded as 9 percent. But *during* 1964, some 29 percent of Negro males were unemployed at one time or another. Similarly, for example, if 36 percent of Negro children are living in broken homes *at any specific moment,* it is likely that a far higher proportion of Negro children find themselves in that situation *at one time or another* in their lives.

Nearly a Quarter of Urban Negro Marriages are Dissolved.

Nearly a quarter of Negro women living in cities who have ever married are divorced, separated, or are living apart from their husbands.

Percent Distribution of Ever-Married Females with Husbands Absent or Divorced, Rural-Urban, 1960

	Urban		Rural nonfarm		Rural farm	
	Nonwhite	white	Nonwhite	White	Nonwhite	White
Total, husbands absent or divorced...............	22.9	7.9	14.7	5.7	9.6	3.0
Total, husbands absent..	17.3	3.9	12.6	3.6	8.6	2.0
Separated............	12.7	1.8	7.8	1.2	5.6	0.5
Husbands absent for other reasons.......	4.6	2.1	4.8	2.4	3.0	1.5
Total, divorced........	5.6	4.0	2.1	2.1	1.0	1.0

Source: *U.S. Census of Population, 1960, Nonwhite Population by Race,* PC (2) 1c, table 9, pp. 9-10.

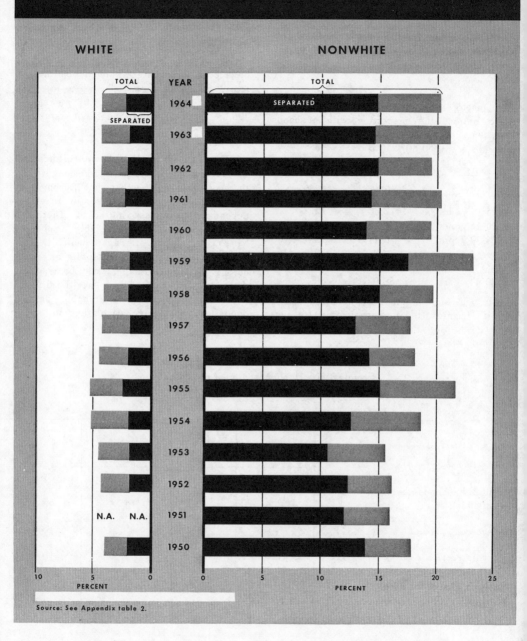

PERCENT OF WOMEN WITH HUSBANDS ABSENT

WHITE

NONWHITE

Source: See Appendix table 2.

- 7 -

The rates are highest in the urban Northeast where 26 percent of Negro women ever married are either divorced, separated, or have their husbands absent.

On the urban frontier, the proportion of husbands absent is even higher. In New York City in 1960, it was 30.2 percent, *not* including divorces.

Among ever-married nonwhite women in the nation, the proportion with husbands present *declined* in *every* age group over the decade 1950-60, as follows:

Age	Percent with Husbands Present	
	1950	1960
15-19 years	77.8	72.5
20-24 years	76.7	74.2
25-29 years	76.1	73.4
30-34 years	74.9	72.0
35-39 years	73.1	70.7
40-44 years	68.9	68.2

Although similar declines occurred among white females, the proportion of white husbands present never dropped below 90 percent except for the first and last age group.[9]

Nearly One-Quarter of Negro Births are now Illegitimate.

Both white and Negro illegitimacy rates have been increasing, although from dramatically different bases. The white rate was 2 percent in 1940; it was 3.07 percent in 1963. In that period, the Negro rate went from 16.8 percent to 23.6 percent.

The number of illegitimate children per 1,000 live births increased by 11 among whites in the period 1940-63, but by 68 among nonwhites. There are, of course, limits to the dependability of these statistics. There are almost certainly a considerable number of Negro children who, although technically illegitimate, are in fact the offspring of stable unions. On the other hand, it may be assumed that many births that are in fact illegitimate are recorded otherwise. Probably the two opposite effects cancel each other out.

Percent Distribution of Ever-Married Negro Females with Husbands Absent or Divorced, in Urban Areas, by Region, 1960

	Northeast	North Central	South	West
Total, husbands absent or divorced	25.6	22.6	21.5	24.7
Divorced......................	3.9	7.3	4.8	9.9
Separated	16.0	11.7	11.9	10.7
Husbands absent for other reasons.....................	5.7	3.6	4.8	4.1

Source: *U.S. Census of Population, 1960, Nonwhite Population by Race,* PC (2) 1c, table 9, pp. 9-10.

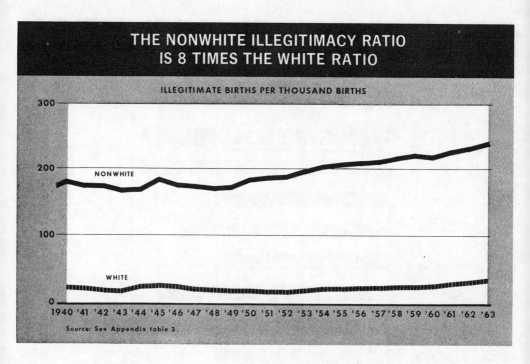

THE NONWHITE ILLEGITIMACY RATIO IS 8 TIMES THE WHITE RATIO

ILLEGITIMATE BIRTHS PER THOUSAND BIRTHS

NONWHITE

WHITE

1940 '41 '42 '43 '44 '45 '46 '47 '48 '49 '50 '51 '52 '53 '54 '55 '56 '57 '58 '59 '60 '61 '62 '63

Source: See Appendix table 3.

On the urban frontier, the nonwhite illegitimacy rates are usually higher than the national average, and the increase of late has been drastic.

In the District of Columbia, the illegitimacy rate for nonwhites grew from 21.8 percent in 1950, to 29.5 percent in 1964.

A similar picture of disintegrating Negro marriages emerges from the divorce statistics. Divorces have increased of late for both whites and nonwhites, but at a much greater rate for the latter. In 1940 both groups had a divorce rate of 2.2 percent. By 1964 the white rate had risen to 3.6 percent, but the nonwhite rate had reached 5.1 percent—40 percent greater than the formerly equal white rate.

Almost One-Fourth of Negro Families are Headed by Females.

As a direct result of this high rate of divorce, separation, and desertion, a very large percent of Negro families are headed by females. While the percentage of such families among whites has been dropping since 1940, it has been rising among Negroes.

The percent of nonwhite families headed by a female is more than double the percent for whites. Fatherless nonwhite families increased by a sixth between 1950 and 1960, but held constant for white families.

It has been estimated that only a minority of Negro children reach the age of 18 having lived all their lives with both their parents.

ILLEGITIMACY RATIOS PER 1,000 NONWHITE BIRTHS, BY CITY, 1950 AND 1962

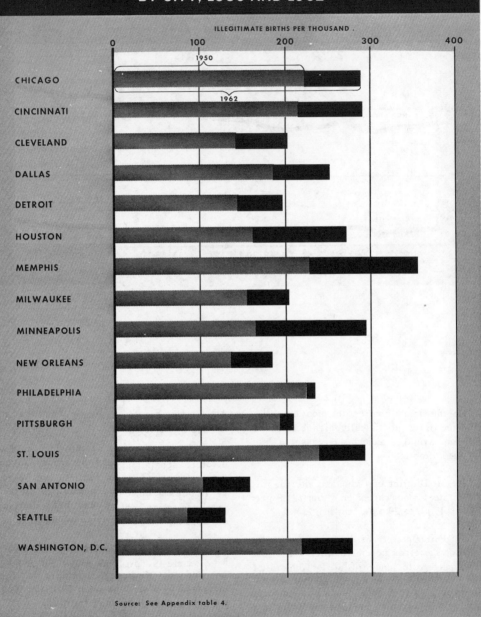

ILLEGITIMATE BIRTHS PER THOUSAND .

Source: See Appendix table 4.

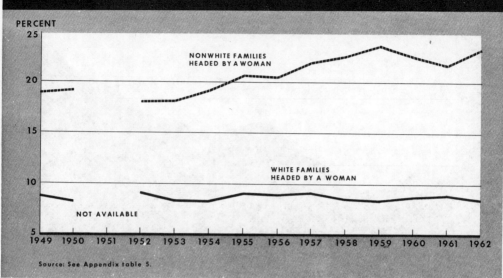

ALMOST ONE FOURTH OF NONWHITE FAMILIES
ARE HEADED BY A WOMAN

PERCENT

NONWHITE FAMILIES
HEADED BY A WOMAN

WHITE FAMILIES
HEADED BY A WOMAN

NOT AVAILABLE

Source: See Appendix table 5.

Percent Distribution of White and Nonwhite Families
in the United States, by Type of Family
1950 and 1960

Type of family	1960			1950		
	White	Non-white	Difference	White	Non-white	Difference
All families	100	100		100	100	
Husband-wife......	88	74	14	87	78	9
Other male head....	3	5	−2	4	4	0
Female head.......	9	21	−12	9	18	−9

Source: *U.S. Census of Population, 1960, U.S. Summary (Detailed Characteristics)*,
table 186, p. 464.

- 11-

787-326 O-65—3

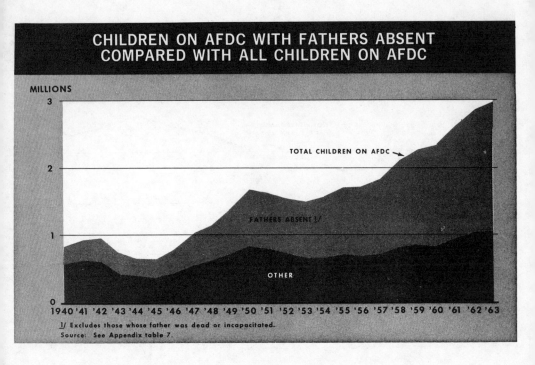

CHILDREN ON AFDC WITH FATHERS ABSENT COMPARED WITH ALL CHILDREN ON AFDC

MILLIONS

TOTAL CHILDREN ON AFDC →

FATHERS ABSENT 1/

OTHER

1940 '41 '42 '43 '44 '45 '46 '47 '48 '49 '50 '51 '52 '53 '54 '55 '56 '57 '58 '59 '60 '61 '62 '63

1/ Excludes those whose father was dead or incapacitated.
Source: See Appendix table 7.

Once again, this measure of family disorganization is found to be diminishing among white families and increasing among Negro families.

The Breakdown of the Negro Family Has Led to a Startling Increase in Welfare Dependency.

The majority of Negro children receive public assistance under the AFDC program at one point or another in their childhood.

At present, 14 percent of Negro children are receiving AFDC assistance, as against 2 percent of white children. Eight percent of white children receive such assistance at some time, as against 56 percent of non-whites, according to an extrapolation based on HEW data. (Let it be noted, however, that out of a total of 1.8 million nonwhite illegitimate children in the nation in 1961, 1.3 million were *not* receiving aid under the AFDC program, although a substantial number have, or will, receive aid at some time in their lives.)

Again, the situation may be said to be worsening. The AFDC program, deriving from the long established Mothers' Aid programs, was established in 1935 principally to care for widows and orphans, although the legislation covered all children in homes deprived of parental support because one or both of their parents are absent or incapacitated.

In the beginning, the number of AFDC families in which the father was absent because of desertion was less than a third of the total. Today it is two-thirds. HEW estimates "that between two-thirds and three-fourths of the 50 percent increase from 1948 to 1955 in the number of absent-father families receiving ADC may be explained by an increase in broken homes in the population."[10]

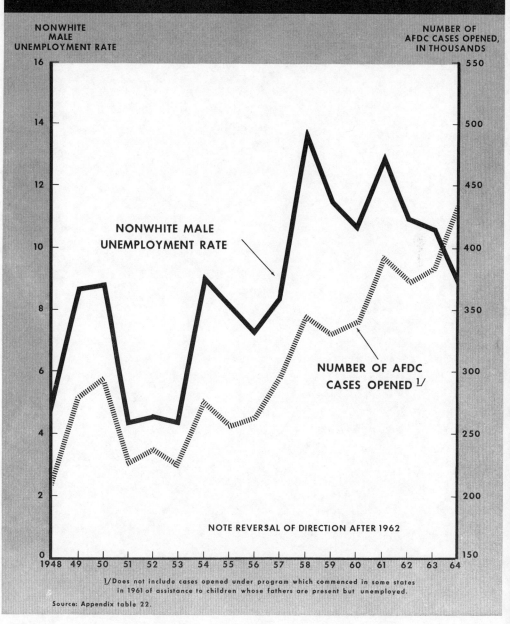

CASES OPENED UNDER AFDC COMPARED WITH UNEMPLOYMENT RATE FOR NONWHITE MALES

NONWHITE
MALE
UNEMPLOYMENT RATE

NUMBER OF
AFDC CASES OPENED,
IN THOUSANDS

NONWHITE MALE
UNEMPLOYMENT RATE

NUMBER OF AFDC
CASES OPENED [1]

NOTE REVERSAL OF DIRECTION AFTER 1962

[1] Does not include cases opened under program which commenced in some states in 1961 of assistance to children whose fathers are present but unemployed.

Source: Appendix table 22.

A 1960 study of Aid to Dependent Children in Cook County, Ill.[11] stated:

The 'typical' ADC mother in Cook County was married and had children by her husband, who deserted; his whereabouts are unknown, and he does not contribute to the support of his children. She is not free to remarry and has had an illegitimate child since her husband left. (Almost 90 percent of the ADC families are Negro.)[11]

The steady expansion of this welfare program, as of public assistance programs in general, can be taken as a measure of the steady disintegration of the Negro family structure over the past generation in the United States.

Chapter III

The Roots of the Problem

Slavery

The most perplexing question about American slavery, which has never been altogether explained, and which indeed most Americans hardly know exists, has been stated by Nathan Glazer as follows: "Why was American slavery the most awful the world has ever known?"[12] The only thing that can be said with certainty is that this is true: it was.

American slavery was profoundly different from, and in its lasting effects on individuals and their children, indescribably worse than, any recorded servitude, ancient or modern. The peculiar nature of American slavery was noted by Alexis de Tocqueville and others, but it was not until 1948 that Frank Tannenbaum, a South American specialist, pointed to the striking differences between Brazilian and American slavery. The feudal, Catholic society of Brazil had a legal and religious tradition which accorded the slave a place as a human being in the hierarchy of society—a luckless, miserable place, to be sure, but a place withal. In contrast, there was nothing in the tradition of English law or Protestant theology which could accommodate to the fact of human bondage—the slaves were therefore reduced to the status of chattels—often, no doubt, well cared for, even privileged chattels, but chattels nevertheless.

Glazer, also focusing on the Brazil-United States comparison, continues.

In Brazil, the slave had many more rights than in the United States: he could legally marry, he could, indeed had to, be baptized and become a member of the Catholic Church, his family could not be broken up for sale, and he had many days on which he could either rest or earn money to buy his freedom. The Government encouraged manumission,

and the freedom of infants could often be purchased for a small sum at the baptismal font. In short: the Brazilian slave knew he was a man, and that he differed in degree, not in kind, from his master.[13]

[In the United States,] the slave was totally removed from the protection of organized society (compare the elaborate provisions for the protection of slaves in the Bible), his existence as a human being was given no recognition by any religious or secular agency, he was totally ignorant of and completely cut off from his past, and he was offered absolutely no hope for the future. His children could be sold, his marriage was not recognized, his wife could be violated or sold (there was something comic about calling the woman with whom the master permitted him to live a "wife"), and he could also be subject, without redress, to frightful barbarities—there were presumably as many sadists among slaveowners, men and women, as there are in other groups. The slave could not, by law, be taught to read or write; he could not practice any religion without the permission of his master, and could never meet with his fellows, for religious or any other purposes, except in the presence of a white; and finally, if a master wished to free him, every legal obstacle was used to thwart such action. This was not what slavery meant in the ancient world, in medieval and early modern Europe, or in Brazil and the West Indies.

More important, American slavery was also awful in its effects. If we compared the present situation of the American Negro with that of, let us say, Brazilian Negroes (who were slaves 20 years longer), we begin to suspect that the differences are the result of very different patterns of slavery. Today the Brazilian Negroes are Brazilians; though most are poor and do the hard and dirty work of the country, as Negroes do in the United States, they are not cut off from society. They reach into its highest strata, merging there—in smaller and smaller numbers, it is true, but with complete acceptance—with other Brazilians of all kinds. The relations between Negroes and whites in Brazil show nothing of the mass irrationality that prevails in this country.[14]

Stanley M. Elkins, drawing on the aberrant behavior of the prisoners in Nazi concentration camps, drew an elaborate parallel between the two institutions. This thesis has been summarized as follows by Thomas F. Pettigrew:

Both were closed systems, with little chance of manumission, emphasis on survival, and a single, omnipresent authority. The profound personality change created by Nazi internment, as independently reported by a number of psychologists and psychiatrists who survived, was toward childishness and total acceptance of the SS guards as father-figures—a syndrome strikingly similar to the "Sambo" caricature of the Southern slave. Nineteenth-century racists readily believed that the "Sambo" personality was simply an inborn racial type. Yet no African anthropological data have ever shown any personality type resembling Sambo; and the concentration camps molded the equivalent personality pattern in a wide variety of Caucasian prisoners. Nor was Sambo merely a product of "slavery" in the abstract, for the less devastating Latin American system never developed such a type.

Extending this line of reasoning, psychologists point out that slavery in all its forms sharply lowered the need for achievement in slaves...Negroes in bondage, stripped of their African heritage, were placed in a completely dependent role. All of their rewards came, not from individual initiative and enterprise, but from absolute obedience—a situation that severely depresses the need for achievement among all peoples. Most important of all, slavery vitiated family life... Since many slaveowners neither fostered Christian marriage among their slave couples nor hesitated to separate them on the auction block, the slave household often developed a fatherless matrifocal (mother-centered) pattern.[15]

The Reconstruction

With the emancipation of the slaves, the Negro American family began to form in the United States on a widespread scale. But it did so in an atmosphere markedly different from that which has produced the white American family.

The Negro was given liberty, but not equality. Life remained hazardous and marginal. Of the greatest importance, the Negro male, particularly in the South, became an object of intense hostility, an attitude unquestionably based in some measure on fear.

When Jim Crow made its appearance towards the end of the 19th century, it may be speculated that it was the Negro male who was most humiliated thereby; the male was more likely to use public facilities, which rapidly became segregated once the process began, and just as important, segregation, and the submissiveness it exacts, is surely more destructive to the male than to the female personality. Keeping the Negro "in his place" can be translated as keeping the Negro male in his place: the female was not a threat to anyone.

Unquestionably, these events worked against the emergence of a strong father figure. The very essence of the male animal, from the bantam rooster to the four-star general, is to strut. Indeed, in 19th century America, a particular type of exaggerated male boastfulness became almost a national style. Not for the Negro male. The "sassy nigger" was lynched.

In this situation, the Negro family made but little progress toward the middle-class pattern of the present time. Margaret Mead has pointed out that while "In every known human society, everywhere in the world, the young male learns that when he grows up one of the things which he must do in order to be a full member of society is to provide food for some female and her young."[16] This pattern is not immutable, however: it can be broken, even though it has always eventually reasserted itself.

Within the family, each new generation of young males learn the appropriate nurturing behavior and superimpose upon their biologically given maleness this learned parental role. When the family breaks down—as it does under slavery, under certain forms of indentured labor and serfdom, in periods of extreme social unrest during wars, revolutions, famines, and epidemics, or in periods of abrupt transition from one type of economy to another—this delicate line of transmission is broken. Men may flounder badly in these periods, during which the primary unit may again become mother and child, the biologically given, and the special conditions under which man has held his social traditions in trust are violated and distorted.[17]

E. Franklin Frazier makes clear that at the time of emancipation Negro women were already "accustomed to playing the dominant role in family and marriage relations" and that this role persisted in the decades of rural life that followed.

Urbanization

Country life and city life are profoundly different. The gradual shift of American society from a rural to an urban basis over the past century and a half has caused abundant strains, many of which are still much in evidence. When this shift occurs suddenly, drastically, in one or two generations, the effect is immensely disruptive of traditional social patterns.

It was this abrupt transition that produced the wild Irish slums of the 19th Century Northeast. Drunkenness, crime, corruption, discrimination, family disorganization, juvenile delinquency were the routine of that era. In our own time, the same sudden transition has produced the Negro slum—different from, but hardly better than its predecessors, and fundamentally the result of the same process.

Negroes are now more urbanized than whites.

Urban Population as Percent of Total, by Color, by Region, 1960

Region	White	Negro
United States	69.5	73.2
Northeast	79.1	95.7
North Central	66.8	95.7
South	58.6	58.4
West	77.6	92.6

Source: *U.S. Census of Population,* PC(1)-1D, 1960, *U.S. Summary,* table 155 and 233; PC (2)-1C, *Nonwhite Population by Race,* table 1.

Negro families in the cities are more frequently headed by a woman than those in the country. The difference between the white and Negro proportions of families headed by a woman is greater in the city than in the country.

Percent of Negro Families with Female Head, by Region and Area, 1960

Region	Urban	Rural Nonfarm	Rural Farm
United States	23.1	19.5	11.1
Northeast	24.2	14.1	4.3
North Central	20.8	14.7	8.4
South	24.2	20.0	11.2
West	20.7	9.4	5.5

Source: *U.S. Census of Population, 1960, Nonwhite Population by Race,* PC (2) 1C, table 9, pp. 9-10.

The promise of the city has so far been denied the majority of the Negro migrants, and most particularly the Negro family.

In 1939, E. Franklin Frazier described its plight movingly in that part of *The Negro Family* entitled "In the City of Destruction:"

> The impact of hundreds of thousands of rural southern Negroes upon northern metropolitan communities presents a bewildering spectacle. Striking contrasts in levels of civilization and economic well-being among these newcomers to modern civilization seem to baffle any attempt to discover order and direction in their mode of life.[18]
>
> In many cases, of course, the dissolution of the simple family organization has begun before the family reaches the northern city. But, if these families have managed to preserve their integrity until they reach the northern city, poverty, ignorance, and color force them to seek homes in deteriorated slum areas from which practically all institutional life has disappeared. Hence, at the same time that these simple rural families are losing their internal cohesion, they are being freed from the controlling force of public opinion and communal institutions. Family desertion among Negroes in cities appears, then, to be one of the inevitable consequences of the impact of urban life on the simple family organization and folk culture which the Negro has evolved in the rural South. The distribution of desertions in relation to the general economic and cultural organization of Negro communities that have grown up in our American cities shows in a striking manner the influence of selective factors in the process of adjustment to the urban environment.[19]

Frazier concluded his classic study, *The Negro Family*, with the prophesy that the "travail of civilization is not yet ended."

> First, it appears that the family which evolved within the isolated world of the Negro folk will become increasingly disorganized. Modern means of communication will break down the isolation of the world of the black folk, and, as long as the bankrupt system of southern agriculture exists, Negro families will continue to seek a living in the towns and cities of the country. They will crowd the slum areas of southern cities or make their way to northern cities where their family life will become disrupted and their poverty will force them to depend upon charity.[20]

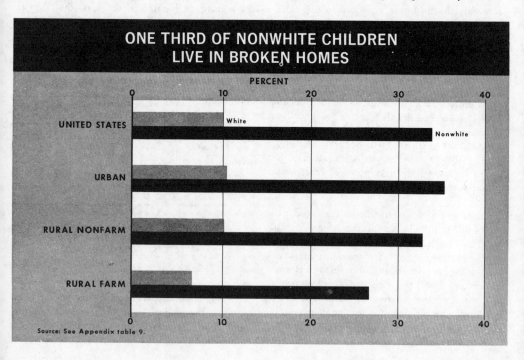

ONE THIRD OF NONWHITE CHILDREN
LIVE IN BROKEN HOMES

Source: See Appendix table 9.

In every index of family pathology—divorce, separation, and desertion, female family head, children in broken homes, and illegitimacy—the contrast between the urban and rural environment for Negro families is unmistakable.

Harlem, into which Negroes began to move early in this century, is the center and symbol of the urban life of the Negro American. Conditions in Harlem are not worse, they are probably better than in most Negro ghettos. The social disorganization of central Harlem, comprising ten health areas, was thoroughly documented by the HARYOU report, save for the illegitimacy rates. These have now been made available to the Labor Department by the New York City Department of Health. There could hardly be a more dramatic demonstration of the crumbling—the breaking—of the family structure on the urban frontier.

Estimated Illegitimacy Ratios Per 1,000 Livebirths For Nonwhites In Central Harlem by Health Area, 1963

Health area [1]	Nonwhite
Total	434.1
No. 8	367.6
No. 10	488.9
No. 12	410.1
No. 13	422.5
No. 15	455.1
No. 16	449.4
No. 19	465.2
No. 24	424.8
No. 85.10	412.3
No. 85.20	430.8

[1]Statistics are reported by geographical areas designated "Health Areas."

Source: Department of Health, New York City.

Unemployment and Poverty

The impact of unemployment on the Negro family, and particularly on the Negro male, is the least understood of all the developments that have contributed to the present crisis. There is little analysis because there has been almost no inquiry. Unemployment, for whites and nonwhites alike, has on the whole been treated as an economic phenomenon, with almost no attention paid for at least a quarter-century to social and personal consequences.

In 1940, Edward Wight Bakke described the effects of unemployment on family structure in terms of six stages of adjustment.[21] Although the families studied were white, the pattern would clearly seem to be a general one, and apply to Negro families as well.

The first two stages end with the exhaustion of credit and the entry of the wife into the labor force. The father is no longer the provider and the elder children become resentful.

The third stage is the critical one of commencing a new day-to-day existence. At this point two women are in charge:

Consider the fact that relief investigators or case workers are normally women and deal with the housewife. Already suffering a loss in prestige and authority in the family because of his failure to be the chief bread winner, the male head of the family feels deeply this obvious transfer of planning for the family's well-being to two women, one of them an outsider. His role is reduced to that of errand boy to and from the relief office.[22]

If the family makes it through this stage Bakke finds that it is likely to survive, and the rest of the process is one of adjustment. *The critical element of adjustment was not welfare payments, but work.*

Having observed our families under conditions of unemployment with no public help, or with that help coming from direct [sic] and from work relief, we are convinced that after the exhaustion of self-produced resources, work relief is the only type of assistance which can restore the strained bonds of family relationship

787-326 O-65—4

in a way which promises the continued functioning of that family in meeting the responsibilities imposed upon it by our culture.[23]

Work is precisely the one thing the Negro family head in such circumstances has not received over the past generation.*

The fundamental, overwhelming fact is that *Negro unemployment*, with the exception of a few years during World War II and the Korean War, *has continued at disaster levels for 35 years.*

Once again, this is particularly the case in the northern urban areas to which the Negro population has been moving.

The 1930 Census (taken in the spring, before the depression was in full swing) showed Negro unemployment at 6.1 percent, as against 6.6 percent for whites. But taking out the South reversed the relationship: white 7.4 percent, nonwhite 11.5 percent.

By 1940, the 2 to 1 white-Negro unemployment relationship that persists to this day had clearly emerged. Taking out the South again, whites were 14.8 percent, nonwhites 29.7 percent.

*An exception is the rather small impact of the ADC-U program since 1961, now expanded by Title V of the Economic Opportunity Act.

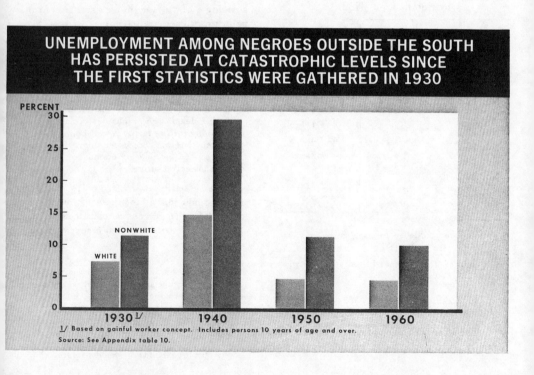

UNEMPLOYMENT AMONG NEGROES OUTSIDE THE SOUTH HAS PERSISTED AT CATASTROPHIC LEVELS SINCE THE FIRST STATISTICS WERE GATHERED IN 1930

PERCENT

NONWHITE

WHITE

1930 [1]/   1940   1950   1960

1/ Based on gainful worker concept. Includes persons 10 years of age and over.

Source: See Appendix table 10.

Since 1929, the Negro worker has been tremendously affected by the movements of the business cycle and of employment. He has been hit worse by declines than whites, and proportionately helped more by recoveries.

From 1951 to 1963, the level of Negro male unemployment was on a long-run rising trend, while at the same time following the short-run ups and downs of the business cycle. During the same period, the number of broken families in the Negro world was also on a long-run rise, with intermediate ups and downs.

A glance at the chart on page 22 reveals that the series move in the same directions— up and down together, with a long-run rising trend—but that the peaks and troughs are 1 year out of phase. Thus unemployment peaks 1 year before broken families, and so on. By plotting these series in terms of deviation from trend, and moving the unemployment curve *1 year ahead,* we see the clear relation of the two otherwise seemingly unrelated series of events; the cyclical swings in unemployment have their counterpart in increases and decreases in separations.

The effect of recession unemployment on divorces further illustrates the economic roots of the problem. The nonwhite divorce rates dipped slightly in high unemployment years like 1954-55, 1958, and 1961-62. (See table 21 on page 77 .)

Divorce is expensive: those without money resort to separation or desertion. While divorce is not a desirable goal for a society, it recognizes the importance of marriage and family, and for children some family continuity and support is more likely when the institution of the family has been so recognized.

The conclusion from these and similar data is difficult to avoid: During times when jobs were reasonably plentiful (although at no time during this period, save perhaps the first 2 years, did the unemployment rate for Negro males drop to anything like a reasonable level) the Negro family became stronger and more stable. As jobs became more and more difficult to find, the stability of the family became more and more difficult to maintain.

This relation is clearly seen in terms of the illegitimacy rates of census tracts in the District of Columbia compared with male unemployment rates in the same neighborhoods.

In 1963, a prosperous year, 29.2 percent of all Negro men in the labor force were unemployed at some time during the year. Almost half of these men were out of work 15 weeks or more.

The impact of poverty on Negro family structure is no less obvious, although again it may not be widely acknowledged. There would seem to be an American tradition, agrarian in its origins but reinforced by attitudes of urban immigrant groups, to the effect that family morality and stability decline as income and social position rise. Over the years this may have provided some consolation to the poor, but there is little evidence that it is true. On the contrary, higher family incomes are unmistakably associated with greater family stability— which comes first may be a matter for conjecture, but the conjunction of the two characteristics is unmistakable.

The Negro family is no exception. In the District of Columbia, for example, census tracts with median incomes over $8,000 had an illegitimacy rate one-third that of tracts in the category under $4,000.

The Wage System

The American wage system is conspicuous in the degree to which it provides high incomes for individuals, but is rarely adjusted to insure that family, as well as individual needs are met. Almost without exception, the social welfare and social insurance systems of other industrial democracies provide for some adjustment or supplement of a

UNEMPLOYMENT RATE OF NONWHITE MEN COMPARED WITH PERCENT OF NONWHITE WOMEN SEPARATED FROM HUSBANDS

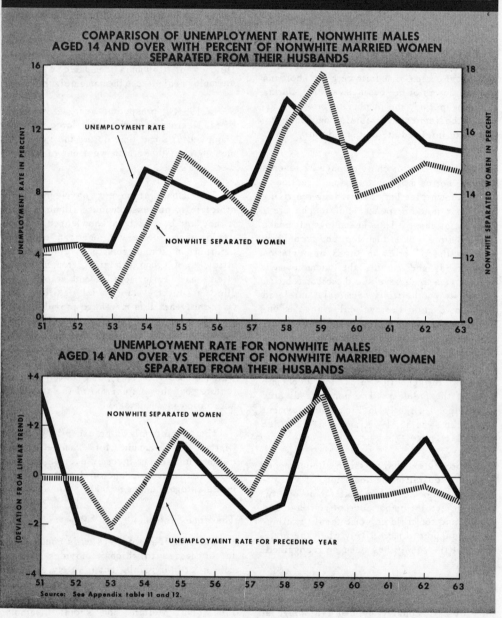

COMPARISON OF UNEMPLOYMENT RATE, NONWHITE MALES AGED 14 AND OVER WITH PERCENT OF NONWHITE MARRIED WOMEN SEPARATED FROM THEIR HUSBANDS

UNEMPLOYMENT RATE

NONWHITE SEPARATED WOMEN

UNEMPLOYMENT RATE FOR NONWHITE MALES AGED 14 AND OVER VS PERCENT OF NONWHITE MARRIED WOMEN SEPARATED FROM THEIR HUSBANDS

NONWHITE SEPARATED WOMEN

UNEMPLOYMENT RATE FOR PRECEDING YEAR

Source: See Appendix table 11 and 12.

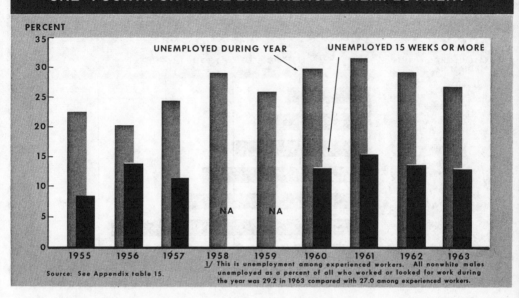

AMONG NONWHITE MEN WORKING DURING THE YEAR, ONE-FOURTH OR MORE EXPERIENCE UNEMPLOYMENT [1]

PERCENT

UNEMPLOYED DURING YEAR   UNEMPLOYED 15 WEEKS OR MORE

1955 1956 1957 1958 1959 1960 1961 1962 1963

Source: See Appendix table 15.

[1] This is unemployment among experienced workers. All nonwhite males unemployed as a percent of all who worked or looked for work during the year was 29.2 in 1963 compared with 27.0 among experienced workers.

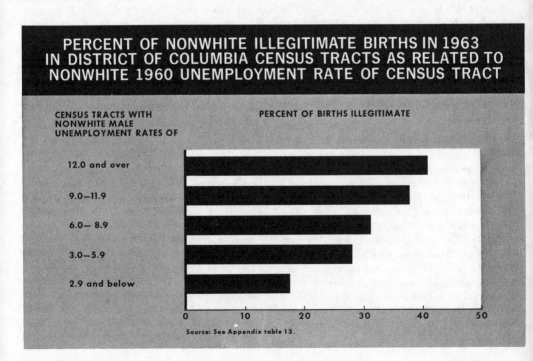

PERCENT OF NONWHITE ILLEGITIMATE BIRTHS IN 1963 IN DISTRICT OF COLUMBIA CENSUS TRACTS AS RELATED TO NONWHITE 1960 UNEMPLOYMENT RATE OF CENSUS TRACT

CENSUS TRACTS WITH NONWHITE MALE UNEMPLOYMENT RATES OF

PERCENT OF BIRTHS ILLEGITIMATE

12.0 and over

9.0—11.9

6.0— 8.9

3.0—5.9

2.9 and below

0   10   20   30   40   50

Source: See Appendix table 13.

PERCENT OF NONWHITE ILLEGITIMATE BIRTHS IN 1963 IN D.C. CENSUS TRACTS AS RELATED TO MEDIAN NONWHITE FAMILY INCOME IN 1959 OF CENSUS TRACT 1/

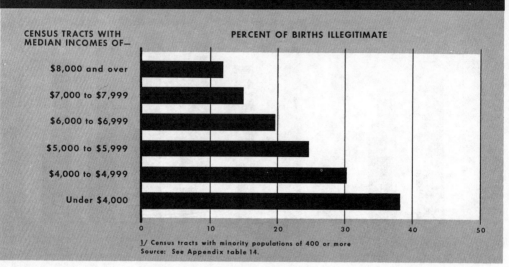

CENSUS TRACTS WITH MEDIAN INCOMES OF—

PERCENT OF BIRTHS ILLEGITIMATE

1/ Census tracts with minority populations of 400 or more
Source: See Appendix table 14.

worker's income to provide for the extra expenses of those with families. American arrangements do not, save for income tax deductions.

The Federal minimum wage of $1.25 per hour provides a basic income for an individual, but an income well below the poverty line for a couple, much less a family with children.

The 1965 Economic Report of the President revised the data on the number of persons living in poverty in the United States to take account of the varying needs of families of different sizes, rather than using a flat cut off at the $3,000 income level. The resulting revision illustrates the significance of family size. Using these criteria, the number of poor families is smaller, but the number of large families who are poor increases, and the number of children in poverty rises by more than one-third—from 11 million to 15 million. This means that one-fourth of the Nation's children live in families that are poor.[24]

A third of these children belong to families in which the father was not only present, but was employed the year round. In overall terms, median family income is lower for large families than for small families. Families of six or more children have median incomes 24 percent below families with three. (It may be added that 47 percent of young men who fail the Selective Service education test come from families of six or more.)

During the 1950-60 decade of heavy Negro migration to the cities of the North and West, the ratio of nonwhite to white family income in cities increased from 57 to 63 percent. Corresponding declines in the ratio in the rural nonfarm and farm areas kept the national ratio virtually unchanged. But between 1960 and 1963, median nonwhite family income slipped from 55 percent to 53 percent of white income. The drop occurred in three regions, with only the South, where a larger proportion of Negro families have more than one earner, showing a slight improvement.

Ratio of Nonwhite to White Family Median Income, United States and Regions, 1960-63

Region	1960	1961	1962	1963
United States..	55	53	53	53
Northeast ...	68	67	66	65
North Central.	74	72	68	73
South	43	43	47	45
West	81	87	73	76

Source: U. S. Department of Commerce. Bureau of the Census, Current Population Reports, Series P-60, *Income of Families and Persons in the United States,* No. 37 (1960), No. 39 (1961), No. 41 (1962), No. 43 (1963). Data by region, table 11 in P-60, No. 41, for 1962, table 13 in P-60, No. 43, for 1963 and, for 1960 and 1961, unpublished tabulations from the Current Population Survey.

Because in general terms Negro families have the largest number of children and the lowest incomes, many Negro fathers literally cannot support their families. Because the father is either not present, is unemployed, or makes such a low wage, the Negro woman goes to work. Fifty-six percent of Negro women, age 25 to 64, are in the work force, against 42 percent of white women. This dependence on the mother's income undermines the position of the father and deprives the children of the kind of attention, particularly in school matters, which is now a standard feature of middle-class upbringing.

The Dimensions Grow

The dimensions of the problems of Negro Americans are compounded by the present extraordinary growth in Negro population. At the founding of the nation, and into the first decade of the 19th century, 1 American in 5 was a Negro. The proportion declined steadily until it was only 1 in 10 by 1920, where it held until the 1950's, when it began to rise. Since 1950, the Negro population

has grown at a rate of 2.4 percent per year compared with 1.7 percent for the total population. If this rate continues, in seven years 1 American in 8 will be nonwhite.

These changes are the result of a declining Negro death rate, now approaching that of the nation generally, and a fertility rate that grew steadily during the postwar period. By 1959, the ratio of white to nonwhite fertility rates reached 1:1.42. Both the white and nonwhite fertility rates have declined since 1959, but the differential has not narrowed.

Family size increased among nonwhite families between 1950 and 1960—as much for those without fathers as for those with fathers. Average family size changed little among white families, with a slight increase in the size of husband-wife families balanced by a decline in the size of families without fathers.

Average Number of Family Members by Type of Family and Color, Conterminous United States, 1960 and 1950

Type of family	1950 White	1950 Nonwhite	1960 White	1960 Nonwhite
All families...	3.54	4.07	3.58	4.30
Husband-wife..	3.61	4.16	3.66	4.41
Other male head	3.05	3.63	2.82	3.56
Female head ..	3.06	3.82	2.93	4.04

Source: *U.S. Census of Population, 1960, U.S. Summary (Detailed Characteristics),* table 187, p. 469.

Negro women not only have more children, but have them earlier. Thus in 1960, there were 1,247 children ever born per thousand ever-married nonwhite women 15 to 19 years of age, as against only 725 among white women, a ratio of 1.7:1. The Negro fertility rate overall is now 1.4 times the white, but what might be called the generation rate is 1.7 times the white.

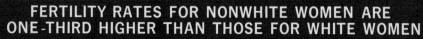

FERTILITY RATES FOR NONWHITE WOMEN ARE ONE-THIRD HIGHER THAN THOSE FOR WHITE WOMEN

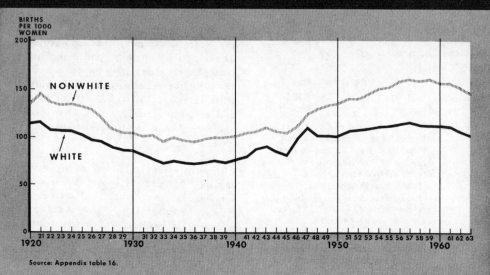

Source: Appendix table 16.

This population growth must inevitably lead to an unconcealable crisis in Negro unemployment. The most conspicuous failure of the American social system in the past 10 years has been its inadequacy in providing jobs for Negro youth. Thus, in January 1965 the unemployment rate for Negro teenagers stood at 29 percent. This problem will now become steadily more serious.

Population and Labor Force Projections, by Color

	Percent increase	
	Actual 1954-64	Projected* 1964-70
Civilian population age 14 and over		
White	15.6	9.7
Nonwhite	23.9	19.9
Civilian labor force		
White	14.6	10.8
Nonwhite	19.3	20.0

*Population and labor force projections by color were made by the Bureau of Labor Statistics. They have not been revised since the total population and labor force were re-estimated, but are considered accurate measures of the relative magnitudes of increase.

Source: Bureau of Labor Statistics.

During the rest of the 1960's the nonwhite civilian population 14 years of age and over will increase by 20 percent—more than double the white rate. The nonwhite labor force will correspondingly increase 20 percent in the next 6 years, double the rate of increase in the nonwhite labor force of the past decade.

Family income in 1959	Number of Children per Nonwhite Mother Age 35-39, 1960
Under $2,000	5.3
$2,000 to $3,999	4.3
$4,000 to $4,999	4.0
$5,000 to $5,999	3.8
$6,000 to $6,999	3.5
$7,000 to $9,999	3.2
$10,000 to $14,999	2.9
$15,000 and over	2.9

Source: 1960 Census, *Women by Number of Children Ever Born,* PC (2) 3A, table 38, p. 188.

As with the population as a whole, there is much evidence that c h i l d r e n are being born most rapidly in those Negro families with the least financial resources. This is an ancient pattern, but because the needs of children are greater today it is very possible that the education and opportunity gap between the offspring of these families and those of stable middle-class unions is not closing, but is growing wider.

A cycle is at work; too many children too early make it most difficult for the parents to finish school. (In February, 1963, 38 percent of the white girls who dropped out of school did so because of marriage or pregnancy, as against 49 percent of nonwhite girls.)[25] An Urban League study in New York reported that 44 percent of girl dropouts left school because of pregnancy.[26]

Low education levels in turn produce low income levels, which deprive children of many opportunities, and so the cycle repeats itself.

787-326 O-65—5

Chapter IV

The Tangle of Pathology

That the Negro American has survived at all is extraordinary—a lesser people might simply have died out, as indeed others have. That the Negro community has not only survived, but in this political generation has entered national affairs as a moderate, humane, and constructive national force is the highest testament to the healing powers of the democratic ideal and the creative vitality of the Negro people.

But it may not be supposed that the Negro American community has not paid a fearful price for the incredible mistreatment to which it has been subjected over the past three centuries.

In essence, the Negro community has been forced into a matriarchal structure which, because it is so out of line with the rest of the American society, seriously retards the progress of the group as a whole, and imposes a crushing burden on the Negro male and, in consequence, on a great many Negro women as well.

There is, presumably, no special reason why a society in which males are dominant in family relationships is to be preferred to a matriarchal arrangement. However, it is clearly a disadvantage for a minority group to be operating on one principle, while the great majority of the population, and the one with the most advantages to begin with, is operating on another. This is the present situation of the Negro. Ours is a society which presumes male leadership in private and public affairs. The arrangements of society facilitate such leadership and reward it. A subculture, such as that of the Negro American, in which this is not the pattern, is placed at a distinct disadvantage.

Here an earlier word of caution should be repeated. There is much evidence that a considerable number of Negro families have managed to break out of the tangle of pathology and to establish themselves as stable, effective units, living according to patterns. of American society in general. E. Franklin Frazier has suggested that the middle-class Negro American family is, if anything, more patriarchal and protective of its children than the general run of such families.[27] Given equal opportunities, the children of these families will perform as well or better than their white peers. They need no help from anyone, and ask none.

While this phenomenon is not easily measured, one index is that middle-class Negroes have even fewer children than middle-class whites, indicating a desire to conserve the advances they have made and to insure that their children do as well or better. Negro women who marry early to uneducated laborers have more children than white women in the same situation; Negro women who marry at the common age for the middle class to educated men doing technical or professional work have only four-fifths as many children as their white counterparts.

It might be estimated that as much as half of the Negro community falls into the middle class. However, the remaining half is in desperate and deteriorating circumstances. Moreover, because of housing segregation it is immensely difficult for the stable half to escape from the cultural influences of the unstable one. The children of middle-class Negroes often as not must grow up in, or next to the slums, an experience almost unknown to white middle-class children. They are therefore constantly exposed to the pathology of the disturbed group and constantly

Children Born per Woman Age 35 to 44: Wives of Uneducated Laborers
who Married Young, Compared with Wives of Educated Professional
Workers who Married After Age 21, White and Nonwhite, 1960[1]

	Children per Woman	
	White	Nonwhite
Wives married at age 14 to 21 to husbands who are laborers and did not go to high school	3.8	4.7
Wives married at age 22 or over to husbands who are professional or technical workers and have completed 1 year or more of college	2.4	1.9

[1]Wives married only once, with husbands present.

Source: 1960 Census, *Women by Number of Children ever Born,* PC (2) 3A, table 39 and 40, pp. 199-238.

in danger of being drawn into it. It is for this reason that the propositions put forth in this study may be thought of as having a more or less general application.

In a word, most Negro youth are in *danger* of being caught up in the tangle of pathology that affects their world, and probably a majority are so entrapped. Many of those who escape do so for one generation only: as things now are, their children may have to run the gauntlet all over again. That is not the least vicious aspect of the world that white America has made for the Negro.

Obviously, not every instance of social pathology afflicting the Negro community can be traced to the weakness of family structure. If, for example, organized crime in the Negro community were not largely controlled by whites, there would be more capital accumulation among Negroes, and therefore probably more Negro business enterprises. If it were not for the hostility and fear many whites exhibit towards Negroes, they in turn would be less afflicted by hostility and fear and so on. There is no one Negro community. There is no one Negro problem. There is no one solution. Nonetheless, at the center of the

tangle of pathology is the weakness of the family structure. Once or twice removed, it will be found to be the principal source of most of the aberrant, inadequate, or anti-social behavior that did not establish, but now serves to perpetuate the cycle of poverty and deprivation.

It was by destroying the Negro family under slavery that white America broke the will of the Negro people. Although that will has re-asserted itself in our time, it is a resurgence doomed to frustration unless the viability of the Negro family is restored.

Matriarchy

A fundamental fact of Negro American family life is the often reversed roles of husband and wife.

Robert O. Blood, Jr. and Donald M. Wolfe, in a study of Detroit families, note that "Negro husbands have unusually low power,"[28] and while this is characteristic of all low income families, the pattern pervades the Negro social structure: "the cumulative re-sult of discrimination in jobs..., the segre-gated housing, and the poor schooling of Negro men."[29] In 44 percent of the Negro families studied, the wife was dominant, as against 20 percent of white wives. "Whereas the majority of white families are equalitarian, the largest percentage of Negro families are dominated by the wife."[30]

The matriarchal pattern of so many Negro families reinforces itself over the generations. This process begins with education. Although the gap appears to be closing at the moment, for a long while, Negro females were better educated than Negro males, and this remains true today for the Negro population as a whole.

Educational Attainment of the Civilian Noninstitutional Population 18 Years of Age and Over, March 1964

Color and sex	Median school years completed
White:	
Male	12.1
Female . . .	12.1
Nonwhite:	
Male	9.2
Female . . .	10.0

Source: Bureau of Labor Statistics, unpublished data.

The difference in educational attainment between nonwhite men and women in the labor force is even greater; men lag 1.1 years behind women.

The disparity in educational attainment of male and female youth age 16 to 21 who were out of school in February 1963, is striking. Among the nonwhite males, 66.3 percent were not high school graduates, compared with 55.0 percent of the females. A similar difference existed at the college level, with 4.5 percent of the males having completed 1 to 3 years of college compared with 7.3 percent of the females.

The poorer performance of the male in school exists from the very beginning, and the magnitude of the difference was documented by the 1960 Census in statistics on the number of children who have fallen one

or more grades below the typical grade for children of the same age. The boys have more frequently fallen behind at every age level. (White boys also lag behind white girls, but at a differential of 1 to 6 percentage points.)

Percent of Nonwhite Youth Enrolled in School Who are 1 or More Grades Below Mode for Age, by Sex, 1960

Age	Male	Female
7 to 9 years old	7.8	5.8
10 to 13 years old	25.0	17.1
14 and 15 years old	35.5	24.8
16 and 17 years old	39.4	27.2
18 and 19 years old	57.3	46.0

Source: 1960 Census, *School Enrollment*, PC(2) 5A, table 3, p. 24.

In 1960, 39 percent of all white persons 25 years of age and over who had completed 4 or more years of college were women. Fifty-three percent of the nonwhites who had attained this level were women.

However, the gap is closing. By October 1963, there were slightly more Negro men in college than women. Among whites there were almost twice as many men as women enrolled.

There is much evidence that Negro females are better students than their male counterparts.

Daniel Thompson of Dillard University, in a private communication on January 9, 1965, writes:

As low as is the aspirational level among lower class Negro girls, it is considerably higher than among the boys. For example, I have examined the honor rolls in Negro high schools for about 10 years. As a rule, from 75 to 90 percent of all Negro honor students are girls.

**Fall Enrollment of Civilian Noninstitutional Population in College,
by Color and Sex - October 1963**

(in thousands)

Color and Sex	Population, age 14-34, Oct. 1, 1963	Number enrolled	Percent of youth, age 14-34
Nonwhite			
Male	2,884	149	5.2
Female.	3,372	137	4.1
White			
Male	21,700	2,599	12.0
Female	20,613	1,451	7.0

Source: U.S. Bureau of the Census, *Current Population Reports,* Series P-20, No. 129
July 24, 1964, tables 1, 5.

Dr. Thompson reports that 70 percent of all applications for the National Achievement Scholarship Program financed by the Ford Foundation for outstanding Negro high school graduates are girls, despite special efforts by high school principals to submit the names of boys.

The finalists for this new program for outstanding Negro students were recently announced. Based on an inspection of the names, only about 43 percent of all the 639 finalists were male. (However, in the regular National Merit Scholarship program, males received 67 percent of the 1964 scholarship awards.)

Inevitably, these disparities have carried over to the area of employment and income.

In 1 out of 4 Negro families where the husband is present, is an earner, and someone else in the family works, the husband is not the principal earner. The comparable figure for whites is 18 percent.

More important, it is clear that Negro females have established a strong position for themselves in white collar and professional employment, precisely the areas of the economy which are growing most rapidly, and to which the highest prestige is accorded.

The President's Committee on Equal Employment Opportunity, making a preliminary report on employment in 1964 of over 16,000 companies with nearly 5 million employees, revealed this pattern with dramatic emphasis.

In this work force, Negro males outnumber Negro females by a ratio of 4 to 1. Yet Negro males represent only 1.2 percent of all males in white collar occupations, while Negro females represent 3.1 percent of the total female white collar work force. Negro males represent 1.1 percent of all male professionals, whereas Negro females represent roughly 6 percent of all female professionals. Again, in technician occupations, Negro males represent 2.1 percent of all male technicians while Negro females represent roughly 10 percent of all female technicians. It would appear therefore that there are proportionately 4 times as many Negro females in significant white collar jobs than Negro males.

Although it is evident that office and clerical jobs account for approximately 50 percent of all Negro female white collar

DEPARTMENT OF LABOR EMPLOYMENT
AS OF DECEMBER 31, 1964

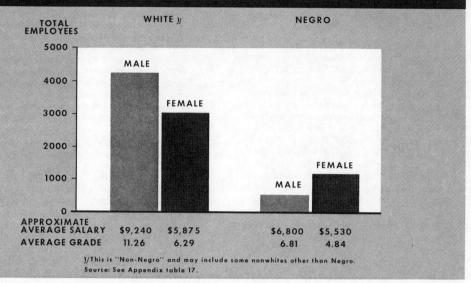

	WHITE 1/		NEGRO	
APPROXIMATE AVERAGE SALARY	$9,240	$5,875	$6,800	$5,530
AVERAGE GRADE	11.26	6.29	6.81	4.84

1/This is "Non-Negro" and may include some nonwhites other than Negro.
Source: See Appendix table 17.

workers, it is significant that 6 out of every 100 Negro females are in professional jobs. This is substantially similar to the rate of all females in such jobs. Approximately 7 out of every 100 Negro females are in technician jobs. This exceeds the proportion of all females in technician jobs—approximately 5 out of every 100.

Negro females in skilled jobs are almost the same as that of all females in such jobs. Nine out of every 100 Negro males are in skilled occupations while 21 out of 100 of all males are in such jobs.[31]

This pattern is to be seen in the Federal government, where special efforts have been made recently to insure equal employment opportunity for Negroes. These efforts have been notably successful in Departments such as Labor, where some 19 percent of employees are now Negro. (A not disproportionate per-

centage, given the composition of the work force in the areas where the main Department offices are located.) However, it may well be that these efforts have redounded mostly to the benefit of Negro women, and may even have accentuated the comparative disadvantage of Negro men. Seventy percent of the Negro employees of the Department of Labor are women, as contrasted with only 42 percent of the white employees.

Among nonprofessional Labor Department employees—where the most employment opportunities exist for all groups—Negro women outnumber Negro men 4 to 1, and average almost one grade higher in classification.

The testimony to the effects of these patterns in Negro family structure is widespread, and hardly to be doubted.

Whitney Young:

Historically, in the matriarchal Negro society, mothers made sure that if one of
their children had a chance for higher education the daughter was the one to pursue
it.[32]

The effect on family functioning and role
performance of this historical experience
[economic deprivation] is what you might
predict. Both as a husband and as a father
the Negro male is made to feel inadequate,
not because he is unlovable or unaffectionate, lacks intelligence or even a gray
flannel suit. But in a society that measures a man by the size of his pay check,
he doesn't stand very tall in a comparison with his white counterpart. To this
situation he may react with withdrawal,
bitterness toward society, aggression
both within the family and racial group,
self-hatred, or crime. Or he may escape
through a number of avenues that help
him to lose himself in fantasy or to compensate for his low status through a variety of exploits.[33]

Thomas Pettigrew:

The Negro wife in this situation can easily become disgusted with her financially
dependent husband, and her rejection of
him further alienates the male from family
life. Embittered by their experiences with
men, many Negro mothers often act to perpetuate the mother-centered pattern by
taking a greater interest in their daughters
than their sons.[34]

Deton Brooks:

In a matriarchal structure, the women are
transmitting the culture.[35]

Dorothy Height:

If the Negro woman has a major underlying concern, it is the status of the Negro
man and his position in the community and
his need for feeling himself an important
person, free and able to make his contribution in the whole society in order that
he may strengthen his home.[36]

Duncan M. MacIntyre:

The Negro illegitimacy rate always has
been high—about eight times the white
rate in 1940 and somewhat higher today
even though the white illegitimacy rate
also is climbing. The Negro statistics
are symtomatic of some old socioeconomic
problems, not the least of which are underemployment among Negro men and compensating higher labor force propensity among
Negro women. Both operate to enlarge
the mother's role, undercutting the status
of the male and making many Negro families essentially matriarchal. The Negro
man's uncertain employment prospects,
matriarchy, and the high cost of divorces
combine to encourage desertion (the poor
man's divorce), increases the number of
couples not married, and thereby also increases the Negro illegitimacy rate. In
the meantime, higher Negro birth rates
are increasing the nonwhite population,
while migration into cities like Detroit,
New York, Philadelphia, and Washington,
D.C. is making the public assistance rolls
in such cities heavily, even predominantly,
Negro.[37]

**Robin M. Williams, Jr. in a study of
Elmira, New York:**

Only 57 percent of Negro adults reported
themselves as married—spouse present,
as compared with 78 percent of native
white American gentiles, 91 percent of
Italian-American, and 96 percent of Jewish
informants. Of the 93 unmarried Negro
youths interviewed, 22 percent did not
have their mother living in the home with
them, and 42 percent reported that their
father was not living in their home. One-
third of the youths did not know their
father's present occupation, and two-
thirds of a sample of 150 Negro adults did
not know what the occupation of their
father's father had been. Forty percent of
the youths said that they had brothers and
sisters living in other communities:
another 40 percent reported relatives living in their home who were not parents,
siblings, or grandparent.[38]

The Failure of Youth

Williams' account of Negro youth growing
up with little knowledge of their fathers,
less of their fathers' occupations, still less
of family occupational traditions, is in sharp
contrast to the experience of the white child.

The white family, despite many variants, remains a powerful agency not only for transmitting property from one generation to the next, but also for transmitting no less valuable contracts with the world of education and work. In an earlier age, the Carpenters, Wainwrights, Weavers, Mercers, Farmers, Smiths acquired their names as well as their trades from their fathers and grandfathers. Children today still learn the patterns of work from their fathers even though they may no longer go into the same jobs.

White children without fathers at least perceive all about them the pattern of men working.

Negro children without fathers flounder—and fail.

Not always, to be sure. The Negro community produces its share, very possibly more than its share, of young people who have the something extra that carries them over the worst obstacles. But such persons are always a minority. The common run of young people in a group facing serious obstacles to success do not succeed.

A prime index of the disadvantage of Negro youth in the United States is their consistently poor performance on the mental tests that are a standard means of measuring ability and performance in the present generation.

There is absolutely no question of any genetic differential: Intelligence potential is distributed among Negro infants in the same proportion and pattern as among Icelanders or Chinese or any other group. American society, however, impairs the Negro potential. The statement of the HARYOU report that "there is no basic disagreement over the fact that central Harlem students are performing poorly in school"[39] may be taken as true of Negro slum children throughout the United States.

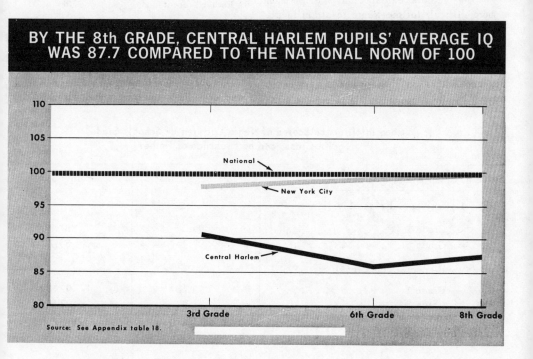

BY THE 8th GRADE, CENTRAL HARLEM PUPILS' AVERAGE IQ WAS 87.7 COMPARED TO THE NATIONAL NORM OF 100

National

New York City

Central Harlem

3rd Grade
6th Grade
8th Grade

Source: See Appendix table 18.

787-326 O-65—6

Eighth grade children in central Harlem have a median IQ of 87.7, which means that perhaps a third of the children are scoring at levels perilously near to those of retardation. IQ *declines* in the first decade of life, rising only slightly thereafter.

The effect of broken families on the performance of Negro youth has not been extensively measured, but studies that have been made show an unmistakable influence.

Martin Deutch and Bert Brown, investigating intelligence test differences between Negro and white 1st and 5th graders of different social classes, found that there is a direct relationship between social class and IQ. As the one rises so does the other: but more for whites than Negroes. This is surely a result of housing segregation, referred to earlier, which makes it difficult for middle-class Negro families to escape the slums.

The authors explain that "it is much more difficult for the Negro to attain identical middle- or upper-middle-class status with whites, and the social class gradations are less marked for Negroes because Negro life in a caste society is considerably more homogeneous than is life for the majority group."[40]

Therefore, the authors look for background variables other than social class which might explain the difference: "One of the most striking differences between the Negro and white groups is the consistently higher frequency of broken homes and resulting family disorganization in the Negro group."[41]

Father Absent From the Home

Lowest social class level		Middle social class level		Highest social class level	
Percent of		Percent of		Percent of	
White	Negro	White	Negro	White	Negro
15.4	43.9	10.3	27.9	0.0	13.7

(Adapted from authors' table)

Further, they found that children from homes where fathers are present have significantly higher scores than children in homes without fathers.

	Mean Intelligence Scores
Father Present	97.83
Father Absent	90.79

The influence of the father's presence was then tested *within* the social classes and school grades for Negroes alone. They found that "a consistent trend within both

Mean Intelligence Scores of Negro Children by School, Grade, Social Class, and by Presence of Father

Social Class and School Grade	Father present	Father absent
Lowest social class level:		
Grade 1	95.2	87.8
Grade 5	92.7	85.7
Middle social class level:		
Grade 1	98.7	92.8
Grade 5	92.9	92.0

(Adapted from authors' table)

Percent of Nonwhite Males Enrolled in School, by Age and Presence of Parents, 1960

Age	Both parents present	One parent present	Neither parent present
5 years	41.7	44.2	34.3
6 years	79.3	78.7	73.8
7 to 9 years	96.1	95.3	93.9
10 to 13 years	96.2	95.5	93.0
14 and 15 years	91.8	89.9	85.0
16 and 17 years.	78.0	72.7	63.2
18 and 19 years.	46.5	40.0	32.3

Source: 1960 Census, *School Enrollment,* PC (2) 5A, table 3, p. 24.

grades at the lower SES [social class] level appears, and in no case is there a reversal of this trend: for males, females, and the combined group, the IQ's of children with fathers in the home are always higher than those who have no father in the home." [42]

The authors say that broken homes "may also account for some of the differences between Negro and white intelligence scores." [43]

The scores of fifth graders with fathers absent were lower than the scores of first graders with fathers absent, and while the authors point out that it is cross sectional data and does not reveal the duration of the fathers' absence, "What we might be tapping is the cumulative effect of fatherless years." [44]

This difference in ability to perform has its counterpart in statistics on actual school performance. Nonwhite boys from families with both parents present are more likely to be going to school than boys with only one parent present, and enrollment rates are even lower when neither parent is present.

When the boys from broken homes are in school, they do not do as well as the boys from whole families. Grade retardation is higher when only one parent is present, and highest when neither parent is present.

The loneliness of the Negro youth in making fundamental decisions about education is shown in a 1959 study of Negro and white dropouts in Connecticut high schools.

Only 29 percent of the Negro male dropouts discussed their decision to drop out of school with their fathers, compared with 65 percent of the white males (38 percent of the Negro males were from broken homes). In fact, 26 percent of the Negro males did not discuss this major decision in their lives with anyone at all, compared with only 8 percent of white males.

A study of Negro apprenticeship by the New York State Commission Against Discrimination in 1960 concluded:

Negro youth are seldom exposed to influences which can lead to apprenticeship. Negroes are not apt to have relatives, friends, or neighbors in skilled occupations. Nor are they likely to be in secondary schools where they receive encouragement and direction from alternate role models. Within the minority community, skilled Negro 'models' after whom the Negro youth might pattern himself are rare, while substitute sources which could provide the direction, encouragement, resources, and information needed to achieve skilled craft standing are nonexistent. [45]

Percent of Nonwhite Males Enrolled in School Who are 1 or More Grades Below Mode for Age, by Age Group and Presence of Parents, 1960

Age group	Both parents present	One parent present	Neither parent present
7-9 years	7.5	7.7	9.6
10-13 years	23.8	25.8	30.6
14-15 years	34.0	36.3	40.9
16-17 years.	37.6	40.9	44.1
18-19 years.	60.6	65.9	46.1

Source: 1960 Census, *School Enrollment,* PC(2) 5A, table 3, p. 24.

Delinquency and Crime

The combined impact of poverty, failure, and isolation among Negro youth has had the predictable outcome in a disastrous delinquency and crime rate.

In a typical pattern of discrimination, Negro children in all public and private orphanages are a smaller proportion of all children than their proportion of the population although their needs are clearly greater.

On the other hand Negroes represent a third of all youth in training schools for juvenile delinquents.

Children in Homes for Dependent and Neglected Children, 1960

	Number	Percent
White	64,807	88.4
Negro.	6,140	8.4
Other races	2,359	3.2
All races	73,306	100.0

Source: 1960 Census, *Inmates of Institutions,* PC (2) 3A, table 31, p. 44.

It is probable that at present, a majority of the crimes against the person, such as rape, murder, and aggravated assault are committed by Negroes. There is, of course, no absolute evidence; inference can only be made from arrest and prison population statistics. The data that follow unquestionably are biased against Negroes, who are arraigned much more casually than are whites, but it may be doubted that the bias is great enough to affect the general proportions.

Number of arrests in 1963

	White	Negro
Offences charged total . .	31,988	38,549
Murder and nonnegligent manslaughter	2,288	2,948
Forcible rape	4,402	3,935
Aggravated assault.	25,298	31,666

Source: *Crime in the United States* (Federal Bureau of Investigation, 1963) table 25, p. 111.

Again on the urban frontier the ratio is worse: 3 out of every 5 arrests for these crimes were of Negroes.

In Chicago in 1963, three-quarters of the persons arrested for such crimes were Negro; in Detroit, the same proportions held.

In 1960, 37 percent of all persons in Federal and State prisons were Negro. In that year, 56 percent of the homicide and 57 percent of the assault offenders committed to State institutions were Negro.

	Number of city arrests in 1963[1]	
	White	Negro
Offenses charged total . .	24,805	35,520
Murder and nonnegligent manslaughter	1,662	2,593
Forcible rape	3,199	3,570
Aggravated assault	19,944	29,357

[1]In 2,892 cities with population over 2,500

Source: *Crime in the United States* (Federal Bureau of Investigation, 1963) table 31, p. 117.

The overwhelming number of offenses committed by Negroes are directed toward other Negroes: the cost of crime to the Negro community is a combination of that to the criminal and to the victim.

Some of the research on the effects of broken homes on delinquent behavior recently surveyed by Thomas F. Pettigrew in *A Profile of the Negro American* is summarized below, along with several other studies of the question.

Mary Diggs found that three-fourths—twice the expected ratio—of Philadelphia's Negro delinquents who came before the law during 1948 did not live with both their natural parents.[46]

In predicting juvenile crime, Eleanor and Sheldon Glueck also found that a higher proportion of delinquent than nondelinquent boys came from broken homes. They identified five critical factors in the home environment that made a difference in whether boys would become delinquents: discipline of boy by father, supervision of boy by mother, affection of father for boy, affection of mother for boy, and cohesiveness of family.

In 1952, when the New York City Youth Board set out to test the validity of these five factors as predictors of delinquency, a problem quickly emerged. The Glueck sample consisted of white boys of mainly Irish, Italian, Lithuanian, and English descent.

However, the Youth Board group was 44 percent Negro and 14 percent Puerto Rican, and the frequency of broken homes within these groups was out of proportion to the total number of delinquents in the population.[47]

In the majority of these cases, the father was usually never in the home at all, absent for the major proportion of the boy's life, or was present only on occasion.

(The final prediction table was reduced to three factors: supervision of boy by mother, discipline of boy by mother, and family cohesiveness within what family, in fact, existed, but was, nonetheless, 85 percent accurate in predicting delinquents and 96 percent accurate in predicting nondelinquents.)

Researchers who have focussed upon the "good" boy in high delinquency neighborhoods noted that they typically come from exceptionally stable, intact families.[48]

Recent psychological research demonstrates the personality effects of being reared in a disorganized home without a father. One study showed that children from fatherless homes seek immediate gratification of their desires far more than children with fathers present.[49] Others revealed that children who hunger for immediate gratification are more prone to delinquency, along with other less social behavior.[50] Two psychologists, Pettigrew says, maintain that inability to delay gratification is a critical factor in immature, criminal, and neurotic behavior.[51]

Finally, Pettigrew discussed the evidence that a stable home is a crucial factor in counteracting the effects of racism upon Negro personality.

A warm, supportive home can effectively compensate for many of the restrictions the Negro child faces outside of the ghetto; consequently, the type of home life a Negro enjoys as a child may be far more crucial for governing the influence of segregation upon his personality than the form the segregation takes—legal or informal, Southern or Northern. [52]

A Yale University study of youth in the lowest socioeconomic class in New Haven in 1950 whose behavior was followed through their 18th year revealed that among the delinquents in the group, 38 percent came from broken homes, compared with 24 percent of nondelinquents. [53]

The President's Task Force on Manpower Conservation in 1963 found that of young men rejected for the draft for failure to pass the mental tests, 42 percent of those with a court record came from broken homes, compared with 30 percent of those without a court record. Half of all the nonwhite rejectees in the study with a court record came from broken homes.

An examination of the family background of 44,448 delinquency cases in Philadelphia between 1949 and 1954 documents the frequency of broken homes among delinquents. Sixty-two percent of the Negro delinquents and 36 percent of white delinquents were not living with both parents. In 1950, 33 percent of nonwhite children and 7 percent of white children in Philadelphia were living in homes without both parents. Repeaters were even more likely to be from broken homes than first offenders. [54]

The Armed Forces

The ultimate mark of inadequate preparation for life is the failure rate on the Armed Forces mental test. The Armed Forces Qualification Test is not quite a mental test, nor yet an education test. It is a test of ability to perform at an acceptable level of competence. It roughly measures ability that ought to be found in an average 7th or 8th grade student. A grown young man who cannot pass this test is in trouble.

Fifty-six percent of Negroes fail it.

This is a rate almost four times that of the whites.

The Army, Navy, Air Force, and Marines conduct by far the largest and most important education and training activities of the Federal Government, as well as provide the largest single source of employment in the nation.

Juvenile Delinquents—Philadelphia by presence of parents, 1949-54

	White			Negro		
	All Court cases	First Offenders	Recidivists	All court cases	First Offenders	Recidivists
Number of Cases	20,691	13,220	4,612	22,695	11,442	6,641
Number not living with both parents	7,422	4,125	2,047	13,980	6,586	4,298
Percent not living with both parents	35.9	31.2	44.4	61.6	57.6	64.7

Source: Adapted from table 1, p. 255, "Family Status and the Delinquent Child," Thomas P. Monahan, *Social Forces,* March 1957.

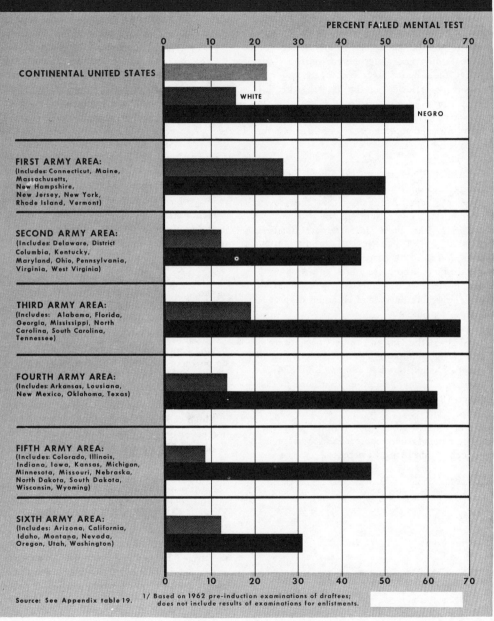

ALMOST FOUR TIMES AS MANY NEGROES AS WHITES
FAIL THE ARMED FORCES MENTAL TEST 1/

PERCENT FAILED MENTAL TEST

CONTINENTAL UNITED STATES

WHITE

NEGRO

FIRST ARMY AREA:
(Includes: Connecticut, Maine,
Massachusetts,
New Hampshire,
New Jersey, New York,
Rhode Island, Vermont)

SECOND ARMY AREA:
(Includes: Delaware, District
Columbia, Kentucky,
Maryland, Ohio, Pennsylvania,
Virginia, West Virginia)

THIRD ARMY AREA:
(Includes: Alabama, Florida,
Georgia, Mississippi, North
Carolina, South Carolina,
Tennessee)

FOURTH ARMY AREA:
(Includes: Arkansas, Lousiana,
New Mexico, Oklahoma, Texas)

FIFTH ARMY AREA:
(Includes: Colorado, Illinois,
Indiana, Iowa, Kansas, Michigan,
Minnesota, Missouri, Nebraska,
North Dakota, South Dakota,
Wisconsin, Wyoming)

SIXTH ARMY AREA:
(Includes: Arizona, California,
Idaho, Montana, Nevada,
Oregon, Utah, Washington)

Source: See Appendix table 19.

1/ Based on 1962 pre-induction examinations of draftees;
does not include results of examinations for enlistments.

Military service is disruptive in some respects. For those comparatively few who are killed or wounded in combat, or otherwise, the personal sacrifice is inestimable. But on balance service in the Armed Forces over the past quarter-century has worked greatly to the advantage of those involved. The training and experience of military duty itself is unique; the advantages that have generally followed in the form of the G.I. Bill, mortgage guarantees, Federal life insurance, Civil Service preference, veterans hospitals, and veterans pensions are singular, to say the least.

Although service in the Armed Forces is at least nominally a duty of all male citizens coming of age, it is clear that the present system does not enable Negroes to serve in anything like their proportionate numbers. This is not a question of discrimination. Induction into the Armed Forces is based on a variety of objective tests and standards, but these tests nonetheless have the effect of keeping the number of Negroes disproportionately small.

In 1963 the United States Commission on Civil Rights reported that "A decade ago, Negroes constituted 8 percent of the Armed Forces. Today . . . they continue to constitute 8 percent of the Armed Forces."[55]

In 1964 Negroes constituted 11.8 percent of the population, but probably remain at 8 percent of the Armed Forces.

Enlisted Men:	Percent Negro
Army	12.2
Navy	5.2
Air Force	9.1
Marine Corps	7.6
Officers:	
Army	3.2
Navy	.2
Air Force	1.2
Marine Corps	.2

The significance of Negro under-representation in the Armed Forces is greater than might at first be supposed. If Negroes were represented in the same proportions in the military as they are in the population, they would number 300,000 plus. This would be over 100,000 more than at present (using 1964 strength figures). If the more than 100,000 unemployed Negro men were to have gone into the military the Negro male unemployment rate would have been 7.0 percent in 1964 instead of 9.1 percent.

In 1963 the Civil Rights Commission commented on the occupational aspect of military service for Negroes. "Negro enlisted men enjoy relatively better opportunities in the Armed Forces than in the civilian economy in every clerical, technical, and skilled field for which the data permit comparison."[56]

There is, however, an even more important issue involved in military service for Negroes. Service in the United States Armed Forces is the *only* experience open to the Negro American in which he is truly treated as an equal: not as a Negro equal to a white, but as one man equal to any other man in a world where the category "Negro" and "white" do not exist. If this is a statement of the ideal rather than reality, it is an ideal that is close to realization. In food, dress, housing, pay, work—the Negro in the Armed Forces *is* equal and is treated that way.

There is another special quality about military service for Negro men: it is an utterly masculine world. Given the strains of the disorganized and matrifocal family life in which so many Negro youth come of age, the Armed Forces are a dramatic and desperately needed change: a world away from women, a world run by strong men of unquestioned authority, where discipline, if harsh, is nonetheless orderly and predictable, and where rewards, if limited, are granted on the basis of performance.

The theme of a current Army recruiting message states it as clearly as can be: "In the U.S. Army you get to know what it means to feel like a man."

At the recent Civil Rights Commission hearings in Mississippi a witness testified that his Army service was in fact "the only time I ever felt like a man."

Yet a majority of Negro youth (and probably three-quarters of Mississippi Negroes) fail the Selective Service education test and are rejected. Negro participation in the Armed Forces would be less than it is, were it not for a proportionally larger share of voluntary enlistments and reenlistments. (Thus 16.3 percent of Army sergeants are Negro.)

Alienation

The term alienation may by now have been used in too many ways to retain a clear meaning, but it will serve to sum up the equally numerous ways in which large numbers of Negro youth appear to be withdrawing from American society.

One startling way in which this occurs is that the men are just not there when the Census enumerator comes around.

According to Bureau of Census population estimates for 1963, there are only 87 nonwhite males for every 100 females in the 30-to-34-year age group. The ratio does not exceed 90 to 100 throughout the 25-to-44-year age bracket. In the urban Northeast, there are only 76 males per 100 females 20-to-24-years of age, and males as a percent of females are below 90 percent throughout all ages after 14.

There are not really fewer men than women in the 20-to-40 age bracket. What obviously is involved is an error in counting: the surveyors simply do not find the Negro

Ratio of Males per 100 Females in the Population, by Color, July 1, 1963

Age	Males per 100 Females	
	White	Nonwhite
Under 5	104.4	100.4
5-9 years	103.9	100.0
10-14 years	104.0	100.0
15-19 years.	103.2	99.5
20-24 years	101.2	95.1
25-29 years.	100.1	89.1
30-34 years	99.2	86.6
35-39 years.	97.5	86.8
40-44 years.	96.2	89.9
45-49 years.	96.5	90.6

Source: *Current Population Reports*, Series P-25, No. 276, table 1, (Total Population Including Armed Forces Abroad)

man. Donald J. Bogue and his associates, who have studied the Federal count of the Negro man, place the error as high as 19.8 percent at age 28; a typical error of around 15 percent is estimated from age 19 through 43.[57] Preliminary research in the Bureau of the Census on the 1960 enumeration has resulted in similar conclusions, although not necessarily the same estimates of the extent of the error. The Negro male *can* be found at age 17 and 18. On the basis of birth records and mortality records, the conclusion must be that he is there at age 19 as well.

When the enumerators do find him, his answers to the standard questions asked in the monthly unemployment survey often result in counting him as "not in the labor force." In other words, Negro male unemployment may in truth be somewhat greater than reported.

The labor force participation rates of nonwhite men have been falling since the beginning of the century and for the past decade have been lower than the rates for white men. In 1964, the participation rates were 78.0 percent for white men and 75.8 percent for nonwhite men. Almost one percentage point of this difference was due to a higher proportion of nonwhite men unable to work because of long-term physical or mental illness; it seems reasonable to assume that the rest of the difference is due to discouragement about finding a job.

If nonwhite male labor force participation rates were as high as the white rates, there would have been 140,000 more nonwhite males in the labor force in 1964. If we further assume that the 140,000 would have been unemployed, the unemployment rate for nonwhite men would have been 11.5 percent instead of the recorded rate of 9 percent, and the ratio between the nonwhite rate and the white rate would have jumped from 2:1 to 2.4:1.

Understated or not, the official unemployment rates for Negroes are almost unbelievable.

The unemployment statistics for Negro teenagers—29 percent in January 1965—reflect lack of training and opportunity in the greatest measure, but it may not be doubted that they also reflect a certain failure of nerve.

"Are you looking for a job?" Secretary of Labor Wirtz asked a young man on a Harlem street corner. "Why?" was the reply.

Richard A. Cloward and Robert Ontell have commented on this withdrawal in a discussion of the Mobilization for Youth project on the lower East Side of New York.

> What contemporary slum and minority youth probably lack that similar children in earlier periods possessed is not motivation but some minimal sense of competence.

> We are plagued, in work with these youth, by what appears to be a low tolerance for frustration. They are not able to absorb setbacks. Minor irritants and rebuffs are magnified out of all proportion to reality. Perhaps they react as they do because they are not equal to the world that confronts them, and they know it. And it is

the knowing that is devastating. Had the occupational structure remained intact, or had the education provided to them kept pace with occupational changes, the situation would be a different one. But it is not, and that is what we and they have to contend with.[58]

Narcotic addiction is a characteristic form of withdrawal. In 1963, Negroes made up 54 percent of the addict population of the United States. Although the Federal Bureau of Narcotics reports a decline in the Negro proportion of new addicts, HARYOU reports the addiction rate in central Harlem rose from 22.1 per 10,000 in 1955 to 40.4 in 1961.[59]

There is a larger fact about the alienation of Negro youth than the tangle of pathology described by these statistics. It is a fact particularly difficult to grasp by white persons who have in recent years shown increasing awareness of Negro problems.

The present generation of Negro youth growing up in the urban ghettos has probably less personal contact with the white world than any generation in the history of the Negro American.[60]

Until World War II it could be said that in general the Negro and white worlds lived, if not together, at least side by side. Certainly they did, and do, in the South.

Since World War II, however, the two worlds have drawn physically apart. The symbol of this development was the construction in the 1940's and 1950's of the vast white, middle- and lower-middle class suburbs around all of the Nation's cities. Increasingly the inner cities have been left to Negroes—who now share almost no community life with whites.

In turn, because of this new housing pattern—most of which has been financially assisted by the Federal government—it is probable that the American school system has become *more*, rather than less segregated in the past two decades.

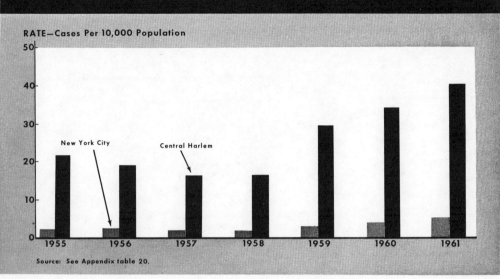

THE RATE OF NARCOTIC USERS IN CENTRAL HARLEM WAS 8 TIMES AS HIGH AS THAT FOR NEW YORK CITY IN 1961

RATE—Cases Per 10,000 Population

New York City

Central Harlem

1955   1956   1957   1958   1959   1960   1961

Source: See Appendix table 20.

School integration has not occurred in the South, where a decade after *Brown v. Board of Education* only 1 Negro in 9 is attending school with white children.

And in the North, despite strenuous official efforts, neighborhoods and therefore schools are becoming more and more of one class and one color.

In New York City, in the school year 1957-58 there were 64 schools that were 90 percent of more Negro or Puerto Rican. Six years later there were 134 such schools.

Along with the diminution of white middle-class contacts for a large percentage of Negroes, observers report that the Negro churches have all but lost contact with men in the Northern cities as well. This may be a normal condition of urban life, but it is probably a changed condition for the Negro American and cannot be a socially desirable development.

The only religious movement that appears to have enlisted a considerable number of lower class Negro males in Northern cities of late is that of the Black Muslims: a movement based on total rejection of white society, even though it emulates whites more.

In a word: the tangle of pathology is tightening.

Chapter V

The Case For National Action

The object of this study has been to define a problem, rather than propose solutions to it. We have kept within these confines for three reasons.

First, there are many persons, within and without the Government, who do not feel the problem exists, at least in any serious degree. These persons feel that, with the legal obstacles to assimilation out of the way, matters will take care of themselves in the normal course of events. This is a fundamental issue, and requires a decision within the Government.

Second, it is our view that the problem is so inter-related, one thing with another, that any list of program proposals would necessarily be incomplete, and would distract attention from the main point of inter-relatedness. We have shown a clear relation between male employment, for example, and the number of welfare dependent children. Employment in turn reflects educational achievement, which depends in large part on family stability, which reflects employment. Where we should break into this cycle, and how, are the most difficult domestic questions facing the United States. We must first reach agreement on what the problem is, then we will know what questions must be answered.

Third, it is necessary to acknowledge the view, held by a number of responsible persons, that this problem may in fact be out of control. This is a view with which we emphatically and totally disagree, but the view must be acknowledged. The persistent rise in Negro educational achievement is probably the main trend that belies this thesis. On the other hand our study has produced some clear indications that

the situation may indeed have begun to feed on itself. It may be noted, for example, that for most of the post-war period male Negro unemployment and the number of new AFDC cases rose and fell together as if connected by a chain from 1948 to 1962. The correlation between the two series of data was an astonishing .91. (This would mean that 83 percent of the rise and fall in AFDC cases can be statistically ascribed to the rise and fall in the unemployment rate.) In 1960, however, for the first time, unemployment declined, but the number of new AFDC cases rose. In 1963 this happened a second time. In 1964 a third. The possible implications of these and other data are serious enough that they, too, should be understood before program proposals are made.

However, the argument of this paper does lead to one central conclusion: Whatever the specific elements of a national effort designed to resolve this problem, those elements must be coordinated in terms of one general strategy.

What then is that problem? We feel the answer is clear enough. Three centuries of injustice have brought about deep-seated structural distortions in the life of the Negro American. At this point, the present tangle of pathology is capable of perpetuating itself without assistance from the white world. The cycle can be broken only if these distortions are set right.

In a word, a national effort towards the problems of Negro Americans must be directed towards the question of family structure. The object should be to strengthen the Negro family so as to enable it to raise and support its members as do other families. After that, how this group of Americans chooses to run its affairs, take advantage of its opportunities, or fail to do so, is none of the nation's business.

The fundamental importance and urgency of restoring the Negro American Family structure has been evident for some time. E. Franklin Frazier put it most succinctly in 1950:

> As the result of family disorganization a large proportion of Negro children and youth have not undergone the socialization which only the family can provide. The disorganized families have failed to provide for their emotional needs and have not provided the discipline and habits which are necessary for personality development. Because the disorganized family has failed in its function as a socializing agency, it has handicapped the children in their relations to the institutions in the community. Moreover, family disorganization has been partially responsible for a large amount of juvenile delinquency and adult crime among Negroes. Since the widespread family disorganization among Negroes has resulted from the failure of the father to play the role in family life required by American society, the mitigation of this problem must await those changes in the Negro and American society which will enable the Negro father to play the role required of him.[61]

Nothing was done in response to Frazier's argument. Matters were left to take care of themselves, and as matters will, grew worse not better. The problem is now more serious, the obstacles greater. There is, however, a profound change for the better in one respect. The President has committed the nation to an all out effort to eliminate poverty wherever it exists, among whites or Negroes, and a militant, organized, and responsible Negro movement exists to join in that effort.

Such a national effort could be stated thus:

The policy of the United States is to bring the Negro American to full and equal sharing in the responsibilities and rewards of citizenship. To this end, the programs of the Federal government bearing on this objective shall be designed to have the effect, directly or indirectly, of enhancing the stability and resources of the Negro American family.

FOOTNOTE REFERENCES
AND
APPENDIX TABLES

FOOTNOTE REFERENCES

1. Robert Harris, *The Quest for Equality*, (Baton Rouge, Louisiana State University Press, 1960), p. 4.

2. William Faulkner, in a speech before the Southern Historical Society in November 1955, quoted in *Mississippi: The Closed Society*, by James W. Silver, (New York, Harcourt, Brace and World, Inc., 1964), p. xiii.

3. For a view that present Negro demands go beyond this traditional position see Nathan Glazer, "Negroes and Jews: The Challenge to Pluralism," *Commentary*, December 1964, pp. 29-34.

4. Bayard Rustin, "From Protest to Politics: The Future of the Civil Rights Movement," *Commentary*, February 1965, p. 27.

5. Nathan Glazer, op. cit., p. 34.

6. *Youth in the Ghetto*, Harlem Youth Opportunities Unlimited, Inc., New York, 1964, p. xi.

7. Nathan Glazer and Daniel Patrick Moynihan, *Beyond the Melting Pot*, (MIT Press and Harvard University Press, Cambridge, 1963), pp. 290-291.

8. E. Franklin Frazier, *Black Bourgeoisie*, (New York, Collier Books, 1962).

9. Furnished by Dr. Margaret Bright, in a communication on January 20, 1965.

10. Maurine McKeany, *The Absent Father and Public Policy in the Program of Aid to Dependent Children*, (Berkeley, University of California Press, 1960), p. 3.

11. "Facts, Fallacies and Future: A Study of the Aid to Dependent Children of Cook County, Illinois," (New York, Greenleigh Associates, Inc., 1960), p. 5.

12. Nathan Glazer, "Introduction," *Slavery*, Stanley M. Elkins, (New York, Grosset and Dunlap, 1963), p. ix.

13. Ibid., pp. xi-xii.

14. Ibid., pp. ix-x.

15. Thomas F. Pettigrew, *A Profile of the Negro American*, (Princeton, New Jersey, D. Van Nostrand Company, Inc., 1964), pp. 13-14.

16. Margaret Mead, *Male and Female*, (New York, New American Library, 1962), p. 146.

17. Ibid., p. 148.

18. E. Franklin Frazier, *The Negro Family in the United States*, (Chicago, The University of Chicago Press, 1939), p. 298.

19. Ibid., pp. 340-341.

20. Ibid., p. 487.

21. Edward Wight Bakke, *Citizens Without Work*, (New Haven, Yale University Press, 1940.)

22. Ibid., p. 212.

23. Ibid., p. 224.

24. Economic Report of the President, January 1965, p. 163.

25. Vera C. Perrella and Forrest A. Bogan, "Out of School Youth, February 1963," *Special Labor Force Report*, No. 46, Bureau of Labor Statistics, U. S. Department of Labor.

26. *Youth in the Ghetto*, op. cit., p. 185.

27. E. Franklin Frazier, *Black Bourgeoisie*, (New York, Collier Books, 1962.)

28. Robert O. Blood, Jr. and Donald M. Wolfe, *Husbands and Wives: The Dynamics of Married Living*, (Illinois, The Free Press of Glencoe, 1960), p. 34.

29. Ibid., p. 35.

30. Ibid.

31. Based on preliminary draft of a report by the President's Committee on Equal Employment Opportunity.

32. Whitney Young, *To Be Equal*, (New York, McGraw Hill Book Company, 1964), p. 25.

33. Ibid., p. 175.

34. Thomas F. Pettigrew, op. cit., p. 16.

35. Deton Brooks, quoted in *The New Improved American* by Bernard Asbell, (New York, McGraw Hill Book Company, 1965), p. 76.

36. Dorothy Height, in the Report of Consultation of Problems of Negro Women, President's Commission on the Status of Women, April 19, 1963, p. 35.

37. Duncan M. MacIntyre, *Public Assistance: Too Much or Too Little?* (New York, New York State School of Industrial Relations, Cornell University, Bulletin 53-1, December 1964), pp. 73-74.

38. Robin M. Williams, Jr., *Strangers Next Door*, (Englewood Cliffs, New Jersey, Prentice-Hall, Inc., 1964), p. 240.

39. *Youth in the Ghetto*, op. cit., p. 195.

40. Martin Deutch and Bert Brown, "Social Influences in Negro-White Intelligence Differences," *Social Issues*, April 1964, p. 27.

41. Ibid., p. 29.

42. Ibid.

43. Ibid., p. 31.

44. Ibid.

45. "Negroes in Apprenticeship, New York State," *Monthly Labor Review*, September 1960, p. 955.

46. Mary H. Diggs, "Some Problems and Needs of Negro Children as Revealed by Comparative Delinquency and Crime Statistics," *Journal of Negro Education*, 1950, 19, pp. 290-297.

47. Maude M. Craig and Thelma J. Glick, "Ten Years Experience with the Glueck Social Prediction Table," *Journal of Crime and Delinquency*, July 1963, p. 256.

48. F. R. Scarpitti, Ellen Murray, S. Dinitz and W. C. Reckless, "The 'Good' Boy in a High Delinquency Area: Four Years Later," *American Sociological Review*, 1960, 25, pp. 555-558.

49. W. Mischel, "Father-Absence and Delay of Gratification: Cross-Cultural Comparisons," *Journal of Abnormal and Social Psychology*, 1961, 63, pp. 116-124.

50. W. Mischel, "Preference for Delayed Reinforcement and Social Responsibility," *Journal of Social and Abnormal Psychology,* 1961, 62, pp. 1-7.
"Delay of Gratification, Need for Achievement, and Acquiescence in Another Culture," *Journal of Abnormal and Social Psychology,* 1961, 62, pp. 543-552.

51. O. H. Mowrer and A. D. Ullman, "Time as a Determinant in Integrative Learning," *Psychological Review*, 1945, 52, pp. 61-90.

52. Thomas F. Pettigrew, op. cit., p. 22.

53. Erdman Palmore, "Factors Associated with School Dropouts on Juvenile Delinquency Among Lower Class Children," *Social Security Bulletin,* October 1963, p. 6.

54. Thomas P. Monahan, "Family Status and the Delinquent Child," *Social Forces*, March 1957, p. 254.

55. Report of the U. S. Commission on Civil Rights, September 1963. p. 173.

56. Ibid., p. 174.

57. Donald J. Bogue, Bhaskar D. Misra, and D. P. Dandekar, "A New Estimate of the Negro Population and Negro Vital Rates in the United States, 1930-1960," *Demography*, Vol. 1, No. 1, 1964, p. 350.

58. Richard A. Cloward and Robert Ontell, "Our Illusions about Training," *American Child,* January 1965, p. 7.

59. *Youth in the Ghetto,* op. cit., p. 144.

60. Nathan Glazer and Daniel Patrick Moynihan, op. cit.

61. E. Franklin Frazier, "Problems and Needs of Negro Children and Youth Resulting from Family Disorganization," *Journal of Negro Education,* Summer 1950, pp. 276-277.

APPENDIX TABLES

Table 1

PERCENT OF NONWHITE MARRIED WOMEN WITH HUSBANDS ABSENT DUE TO SEPARATION AND OTHER REASONS, 1960

City	Percent with Husband Absent due to Separation and Other Reasons	Percent Separated
Akron	16.1	11.9
Birmingham	18.5	13.8
Mobile	23.5	16.4
Denver	14.2	9.5
Hartford	25.7	19.9
Wilmington	23.9	17.3
Washington	23.5	16.1
Chicago	23.5	18.7
Detroit	19.2	14.9
St. Louis	23.1	18.5
New York City	30.2	21.5
Buffalo	22.3	17.7
Philadelphia	25.3	19.5
Pittsburgh	19.7	15.1
Baltimore	23.0	16.6
Houston	15.3	11.4
Dallas	17.2	11.8
San Antonio	16.1	9.0
Cleveland	18.5	14.1
Cincinnati	20.6	15.7
Milwaukee	18.2	13.5
Boston	23.5	15.9
New Orleans	22.2	15.7
Seattle	13.8	8.7
Memphis	22.6	17.7
Atlanta	22.6	16.8

Source: *U.S. Census of Population*, Vol. 1 —Selected States, table 105.

Table 2

PERCENT OF MARRIED WOMEN WITH HUSBANDS ABSENT DUE TO SEPARATION AND OTHER REASONS, BY COLOR, 1950-64

Year	White		Nonwhite	
	Total[1]	Separated	Total[1]	Separated
1964	4.4	2.2	20.4	14.8
1963	4.4	1.9	21.2	14.6
1962	4.4	2.0	20.5	14.9
1961	4.3	2.2	19.6	14.3
1960	4.1	1.9	19.4	13.8
1959	4.4	1.8	23.3	17.6
1958	4.0	1.9	19.8	16.0
1957	4.2	1.7	17.9	13.1
1956	4.5	1.9	18.2	14.2
1955	5.3	2.3	21.9	15.1
1954	5.1	1.9	18.8	12.7
1953	4.7	1.8	15.7	10.6
1952	4.5	1.8	16.2	12.4
1951	n.a.	n.a.	16.1	12.1
1950	4.0	2.0	18.0	13.9

[1]Includes figures not shown separately.

Source: U.S. Bureau of the Census, *Current Population Series*, P-20.

Data for 1950 from 1950 Decennial Census because color break for 1950 is not available from *Current Population Survey*.

Table 3

ESTIMATED NUMBER OF ILLEGITIMATE LIVE BIRTHS
AND RATIO OF ILLEGITIMATE BIRTHS TO ALL LIVE BIRTHS
BY COLOR, 1940-63

Year	Number of Illegitimate Births (in thousands)			Illegitimacy Ratio [2]		
	Total	White	Nonwhite	Total	White	Nonwhite
1963[1]	259.4	102.2	150.7	63.3	30.7	235.9
1962	245.1	93.5	147.5	58.8	27.5	229.9
1961	240.2	91.1	149.1	56.3	25.3	223.4
1960	224.3	82.5	141.8	52.7	22.9	215.8
1959	220.6	79.6	141.1	52.0	22.1	218.0
1958	208.7	74.6	134.1	49.6	20.9	212.3
1957	201.7	70.8	130.9	47.4	19.6	206.7
1956	193.5	67.5	126.0	46.5	19.0	204.0
1955	183.3	64.2	119.2	45.3	18.6	202.4
1954	176.6	62.7	113.9	44.0	18.2	198.5
1953	160.8	56.6	104.2	41.2	16.9	191.1
1952	150.3	54.1	96.2	39.1	16.3	183.4
1951	146.5	52.6	93.9	39.1	16.3	182.8
1950	141.6	53.5	88.1	39.8	17.5	179.6
1949	133.2	53.5	79.7	37.4	17.3	167.5
1948	129.7	54.8	74.9	36.7	17.8	164.7
1947	131.9	60.5	71.5	35.7	18.5	168.0
1946	125.2	61.4	63.8	38.1	21.1	170.1
1945	117.4	56.4	60.9	42.9	23.6	179.3
1944	105.2	49.6	55.6	37.6	20.2	163.4
1943	98.1	42.8	55.4	33.4	16.5	162.8
1942	96.5	42.0	54.5	34.3	16.9	169.2
1941	95.7	41.9	53.8	38.1	19.0	174.5
1940	89.5	40.3	49.2	37.9	19.5	168.3

[1] Preliminary figures

[2] Per 1,000 total live births.

Source: U.S. Department of Health, Education, and Welfare; Public Health Service, National Vital Statistics Division; annual *Vital Statistics of the United States*.

Table 4

RATIO OF ILLEGITIMATE BIRTHS TO ALL LIVE BIRTHS, NONWHITE, BY CITY, 1950 AND 1962[1]

City	1950 Ratio	1962 Ratio	Percent Increase
Chicago.	222.9	289.9	30
Cincinnati	214.6	290.6	35
Cleveland	141.0	202.2	43
Dallas.	187.2	252.4	35
Detroit	143.8	197.8	38
Houston.	160.8	272.9	70
Memphis	228.6	356.8	56
Milwaukee	153.5	203.2	32
Minneapolis	165.4	294.5	78
New Orleans	134.8	183.8	36
Philadelphia	223.9	233.3	4
Pittsburgh	191.5	208.1	9
St. Louis	237.8	292.3	23
San Antonio	100.5	157.8	57
Seattle	81.9	128.9	57
Washington, D. C. . . .	218.2	278.4	28

[1]Per 1,000 total live births.

Source: 1950 Rates: "Illegitimate Births: United States, 1938-57", U.S. Department of Health, Education and Welfare, 1963
1962 Rates: Computed from live birth and illegitimate birth statistics, *Vital Statistics of the U.S.* Volume I.

Table 5

FAMILIES HEADED BY A WOMAN AS PERCENT OF ALL FAMILIES
BY COLOR, SELECTED PERIODS, 1949-62

Year	Families Headed by a Woman as Percent of Total	
	White	Nonwhite
1962.	8.6	23.2
1961.	8.9	21.6
1960.	8.7	22.4
1959.	8.4	23.6
1958.	8.6	22.4
1957.	8.9	21.9
1956.	8.8	20.5
1955.	9.0	20.7
1954.	8.3	19.2
1953.	8.4	18.1
1952.	9.2	17.9
1950.	8.4	19.1
1949.	8.8	18.8

Source: U.S. Department of Commerce, Bureau of the Census:
Current Population Reports, P-20, No. 125, 116, 106,
100, 88, 83, 75, 67, 53, 44, 33, and 26. Figures are
for March or April of each year.

Table 6

PERCENT DISTRIBUTION OF ALL FAMILIES BY TYPE OF FAMILY, BY COLOR, SELECTED PERIODS, 1949-62

Year	White				Nonwhite			
	All Families	Husband-Wife Families	Other Families With Male Head	Families With Female Head	All Families	Husband-Wife Families	Other Families With Male Head	Families With Female Head
1962	100.0	88.8	2.6	8.6	100.0	72.3	4.4	23.2
1961	100.0	88.6	2.5	9.0	100.0	74.4	3.9	21.6
1960	100.0	88.7	2.6	8.7	100.0	73.6	4.0	22.4
1959	100.0	88.8	2.8	8.4	100.0	72.0	4.4	23.6
1958	100.0	88.6	2.8	8.6	100.0	73.4	4.2	22.4
1957	100.0	88.4	2.8	8.9	100.0	74.7	3.4	21.9
1956	100.0	87.9	3.3	8.8	100.0	76.1	3.4	20.5
1955	100.0	87.9	3.0	9.0	100.0	75.3	4.0	20.7
1954	100.0	88.5	3.2	8.3	100.0	77.0	3.8	19.2
1953	100.0	88.2	3.4	8.4	100.0	78.6	3.4	18.1
1952	100.0	87.8	3.0	9.2	100.0	78.8	3.6	17.9
1950	100.0	88.4	3.1	8.4	100.0	76.8	4.3	19.1
1949	100.0	88.0	3.3	8.8	100.0	76.8	4.1	18.8

NOTE: Because of rounding, sums of individual items may not equal 100.

Source: U.S. Department of Commerce, Bureau of the Census: *Current Population Reports,* P-20, Nos. 125, 116, 106, 100, 88, 83, 75, 67, 53, 44, 33, and 26. Figures are for March or April of each year.

Table 7

CHILDREN ON AFDC WITH FATHERS ABSENT
COMPARED WITH ALL CHILDREN ON AFDC

Year	Total Children on AFDC	Children on AFDC Father Absent [1]	Percent
1963	2,952,000	1,889,000	64.0
1962	2,849,000	1,803,000	63.3
1961	2,613,000	1,666,000	63.8
1960	2,330,000	1,498,000	64.3
1959	2,247,000	1,404,000	62.5
1958	2,092,000	1,280,000	61.2
1957	1,832,000	1,104,000	60.3
1956	1,708,000	1,016,000	59.5
1955	1,692,000	983,000	58.1
1954	1,567,000	885,000	56.5
1953	1,494,000	820,000	54.9
1952	1,528,000	809,000	52.9
1951	1,618,000	827,000	51.1
1950	1,660,000	818,000	49.3
1949	1,366,000	648,000	47.4
1948	1,146,000	522,000	45.5
1947	1,009,000	441,000	43.7
1946	799,000	334,000	41.8
1945	647,000	257,000	39.7
1944	651,000	247,000	37.9
1943	746,000	269,000	36.1
1942	952,000	325,000	34.1
1941	946,000	304,000	32.1
1940	835,000	253,000	30.3

[1] Excludes those whose father was dead or incapacitated.

Source: *Trend Report,* "Graphic Presentation of Public Assistance and Related Data", HEW, 1963.

Table 8

PERCENT OF NEGRO FAMILIES WITH FEMALE HEAD, BY REGION AND AREA, 1960

Region	Urban	Rural Nonfarm	Rural Farm
United States.	23.1	19.5	11.1
Northeast	24.2	14.1	4.3
North Central	20.8	14.7	8.4
South	24.2	20.0	11.2
West.	20.7	9.4	5.5

Source: *U.S. Census of Population, 1960, Nonwhite Population by Race,* PC (2) 1C, table 9, pp 9-10.

Table 9

PERCENT OF WHITE AND NONWHITE CHILDREN UNDER 18 NOT LIVING WITH BOTH PARENTS, UNITED STATES, URBAN AND RURAL, 1960

Area	Children Under 18 Without Both Parents	
	White	Nonwhite
United States	10.0	33.7
Urban...............................	10.3	35.1
Rural Nonfarm	10.1	32.7
Rural Farm	6.6	26.5

Source: *U.S. Census of Population, 1960, Social and Economic Characteristics* PC (1)-1(C), table 79, p. 210.

Table 10

UNEMPLOYMENT RATES, BY COLOR, U.S. AND U.S. EXCLUDING SOUTH, 1930-1960

Color and Area	1960	1950	1940	1930[1]
United States				
White	4.7	4.5	14.2	6.6
Nonwhite	8.7	7.8	16.8	6.1
United States Excluding South				
White	4.8	4.9	14.8	7.4
Nonwhite	10.1	11.4	29.7	11.5

[1] Based in gainful worker concept. Includes persons 10 years of age and over.

Source: Bureau of Labor Statistics, computed from decennial censuses of population.

Table 11

PERCENT OF NONWHITE MARRIED WOMEN WITH HUSBANDS ABSENT AND UNEMPLOYMENT RATES OF NONWHITE MALES AGED 14 AND OVER.

Year	Percent of Nonwhite Married Women Separated from Their Husbands	Unemployment Rate for Nonwhite Males Aged 14 and Over
1963	14.6	10.6
1962	14.9	11.0
1961	14.3	12.9
1960	13.8	10.7
1959	17.6	11.5
1958	16.0	13.7
1957	13.1	8.4
1956	14.2	7.3
1955	15.1	8.2
1954	12.7	9.2
1953	10.6	4.4
1952	12.4	4.5
1951	12.1	4.4
1950		8.9
1949		8.8
1948		5.1

Source: Bureau of Labor Statistics, Department of Labor.

Table 12

PERCENT OF NONWHITE MARRIED WOMEN WITH HUSBANDS ABSENT COMPARED WITH UNEMPLOYMENT OF NONWHITE MALES AGED 14 AND OVER–DEVIATIONS FROM LINEAR TREND

Year	Percent of Nonwhite Married Women Separated from Their Husbands, Deviation from 1951-63 Linear Trend	Unemployment Rate for Nonwhite Males Aged 14 and Over, Deviation from 1948-62 Linear Trend
1963	−1.1	
1962	−0.5	−1.0
1961	−0.8	+1.4
1960	−1.0	−0.3
1959	+3.1	+0.9
1958	+1.8	+3.6
1957	−0.9	−1.2
1956	+0.5	−1.8
1955	+1.7	−0.4
1954	−0.4	+1.1
1953	−2.2	−3.2
1952	−0.1	−2.6
1951	−0.1	−2.2
1950		+2.7
1949		+3.1
1948		−0.1

Source: Bureau of Labor Statistics, Department of Labor.

Table 13

PERCENT OF NONWHITE ILLEGITIMATE BIRTHS IN 1963 IN DISTRICT OF COLUMBIA CENSUS TRACTS AS RELATED TO NONWHITE 1960 UNEMPLOYMENT RATE OF CENSUS TRACTS[1]

Census Tracts With Nonwhite Male Unemployment Rates of:–	Percent of Births Illegitimate
12.0 and over	40.8
9.0 -- 11.9	37.9
6.0 -- 8.9	31.1
3.0 -- 5.9	28.1
2.9 and below	17.6

[1]Census tracts with minority populations of 400 or more.

Source: Illegitimate Birth Statistics from D. C. Department of Public Health; nonwhite male unemployment rates from *Income, Education, and Unemployment in Neighborhoods, Washington, D. C.* Bureau of Labor Statistics, Department of Labor.

Table 14

PERCENT OF NONWHITE ILLEGITIMATE BIRTHS IN 1963 IN DISTRICT OF COLUMBIA CENSUS TRACTS AS RELATED TO MEDIAN NONWHITE FAMILY INCOME IN 1959 OF CENSUS TRACTS[1]

Census Tracts With Median Incomes of:—	Percent of Births Illegitimate
$8,000 and over.	12.0
$7,000 to $7,999	15.0
$6,000 to $6,999.	19.8
$5,000 to $5,999	24.8
$4,000 to $4,999	30.2
under $4,000.	38.2

[1]Census tracts with minority populations of 400 or more.

Source: Illegitimate Birth Statistics from D. C. Department of Public Health; nonwhite family income from *Income, Education, and Unemployment in Neighborhoods, Washington, D. C.,* Bureau of Labor Statistics, Department of Labor.

Table 15

EXTENT OF UNEMPLOYMENT AMONG NONWHITE MEN, 1955-63

Year	All Unemployed as a Percent of Total Working or Looking for work	Unemployed who Worked During the Year as a Percent of Total Working	Percent of Unemployed who Worked During the Year Having Unemployment of 15 weeks or More
1963.....	29.2	27.0	48.5
1962.....	31.9	29.3	47.9
1961.....	34.1	31.6	48.2
1960.....	31.8	29.7	43.3
1959.....	27.8	26.0	NA
1958.....	31.6	29.1	NA
1957.....	NA	24.3	46.3
1956.....	NA	20.0	38.2
1955.....	NA	22.3	38.0

Source: Bureau of Labor Statistics, Department of Labor.

118

Table 16

FERTILITY RATES, BY COLOR, 1920-63
(Births per 1,000 Women, Age 15-44[1])

Year	White	Nonwhite	Year	White	Nonwhite
1963[2]	104.3	149.3	1941	80.7	105.4
1962	108.3	153.9	1940	77.1	102.4
1961	113.0	158.9	1939	74.8	100.1
1960	114.0	159.3	1938	76.5	100.5
1959	114.6	162.3	1937	74.4	99.4
1958	114.8	160.5	1936	73.3	95.9
1957	117.5	162.8	1935	74.5	98.4
1956	115.6	160.5	1934	75.8	100.4
1955	113.3	154.8	1933	73.7	97.3
1954	113.1	152.5	1932	79.0	103.0
1953	110.7	146.8	1931	82.4	102.1
1952	109.8	143.0	1930	87.1	105.9
1951	107.5	141.9	1929	87.3	106.1
1950	102.3	137.3	1928	91.7	111.0
1949	103.6	135.1	1927	97.1	121.7
1948	104.3	131.6	1926	99.2	130.3
1947	111.8	125.9	1925	103.3	134.0
1946	100.4	113.9	1924	107.8	135.6
1945	83.4	106.0	1923	108.0	130.5
1944	86.3	108.5	1922	108.8	130.8
1943	92.3	111.0	1921	117.2	140.8
1942	89.5	107.6	1920	115.4	137.5

[1] Adjusted for underregistration of births.
[2] Preliminary

Source: *Vital Statistics of the United States, 1962*, Volume I—Natality, table 1-2, pp. 1-4. The National Vital Statistics Division discontinued making adjustments for underregistration in 1959. Adjusted rates for 1960-1963 are based on estimates of underregistration supplied by the National Vital Statistics Division.

Table 17

DEPARTMENT OF LABOR EMPLOYMENT
AS OF DECEMBER 31, 1964

Grade	White[1]		Negro	
	Male	Female	Male	Female
Total	4,245	3,027	511	1,190
Average grade	11.26	6.29	6.81	4.84
Approximate Average salary	$9,240	$5,875	$6,800	$5,530
GS-18	7		1	
GS-17	23	2	1	
GS-16	38	3	3	
GS-15	261	21	3	
GS-14	408	53	9	1
GS-13	640	114	26	5
GS-12	877	147	36	13
GS-11	1,043	136	47	17
GS-10		9		
GS-9	448	210	59	40
GS-8	6	27	3	5
GS-7	221	282	55	82
GS-6	13	270	13	109
GS-5	104	757	70	350
GS-4	57	632	69	296
GS-3	84	313	78	238
GS-2	12	51	22	33
GS-1	3		16	1

[1]This is "Non-Negro" and may include some nonwhites other than Negro.

Source: Department of Labor.

Table 18

MEDIAN IQ SCORES FOR CENTRAL HARLEM AND NEW YORK CITY PUPILS COMPARED TO NATIONAL NORMS

Grade in School	Central Harlem	New York City	National
Third	90.6	98.6	100.0
Sixth	86.3	99.8	100.0
Eighth	87.7	100.0	100.0

Source: Harlem Youth Opportunities Unlimited, Inc., *Youth in the Ghetto,* Adapted from chart 4, p. 193.

Table 19

REJECTION RATES FOR FAILURE TO PASS
THE ARMED FORCES MENTAL TEST, BY COLOR

	Number Examined, 1962	Failed Mental Test	
		Number	Percent
Continental United States	**286,152**	**64,536**	**22.6**
White	235,678	36,204	15.4
Negro	50,474	28,332	56.1
First Army Area:			
(Connecticut, Maine, Massachusetts, New Hampshire, New Jersey, New York, Rhode Island, Vermont)			
White	49,171	12,989	26.4
Negro	7,937	3,976	50.1
Second Army Area:			
(Delaware, District of Columbia, Kentucky, Maryland, Ohio, Pennsylvania, Virginia, West Virginia)			
White	48,641	5,888	12.1
Negro	9,563	4,255	44.5
Third Army Area:			
(Alabama, Florida, Georgia, Mississippi, North Carolina, South Carolina, Tennessee)			
White	30,242	5,786	19.1
Negro	20,343	13,772	67.7
Fourth Army Area:			
(Arkansas, Louisiana, New Mexico, Oklahoma, Texas)			
White	15,048	2,039	13.5
Negro	4,796	2,988	62.3
Fifth Army Area:			
(Colorado, Illinois, Indiana, Iowa, Kansas, Michigan, Minnesota, Missouri, Nebraska, North Dakota, South Dakota, Wisconsin, Wyoming)			
White	51,117	4,495	8.9
Negro	5,723	2,684	46.9
Sixth Army Area:			
(Arizona, California, Idaho, Montana, Nevada, Oregon, Utah, Washington)			
White	41,459	5,007	12.1
Negro	2,112	657	31.1

Source: Department of Defense, 1962. Examinations for the draft; does not include examination of applicants for enlistment.

Table 20

HABITUAL NARCOTICS USE – CASES AND RATE PER 10,000
POPULATION FOR CENTRAL HARLEM AND NEW YORK CITY,
1955-61

Year	Central Harlem		New York City	
	Cases	Rate[1]	Cases	Rate[1]
1961.........	934	40.4	4,006	5.2
1960.........	798	34.3	3,054	3.9
1959.........	693	29.5	2,413	3.1
1958.........	396	16.7	1,637	2.1
1957.........	395	16.5	1,654	2.1
1956.........	449	18.6	1,835	2.4
1955.........	542	22.1	1,828	2.3

[1] Per 10,000 population.

Source: Harlem Youth Opportunities Unlimited, Inc., *Youth in the Ghetto,* p. 144
(Based on data from New York City Department of Health, Bureau of
Preventable Diseases).

Table 21

DIVORCES, AS PERCENT OF WOMEN EVER MARRIED, UNITED STATES, BY COLOR, 1940 AND 1947-64

Year	Total	White	Nonwhite
1940	2.2	2.2	2.2
1947	2.7	2.6	3.1
1948	2.8	n.a.	n.a.
1949	2.8	n.a.	n.a.
1950	3.0[1]	3.0[1]	3.5[1]
1950	2.7	n.a.	n.a.
1951	2.6	n.a.	3.1
1952	2.8	2.7	3.5
1953	2.8	2.7	3.8
1954	2.8	2.7	3.9
1955	2.8	2.7	3.2
1956	3.0	2.9	4.0
1957	2.8	2.7	3.8
1958	2.9	2.8	3.5
1959	3.0	2.9	4.0
1960	3.3	3.0	5.4
1961	3.5	3.3	4.8
1962	3.3	3.1	5.0
1963	3.5	3.3	5.5
1964	3.8	3.6	5.1

[1]Data for 1950 from 1950 Decennial Census because color break for 1950 is not available from *Current Population Survey*; CPS total figure is 2.7 percent for 1950, so the same approximate difference can be assumed for white and nonwhite percents.

Source: U.S. Bureau of the Census, *Current Population Series*, P-20.

Table 22

CASES OPENED UNDER AFDC (EXCLUDING UNEMPLOYED PARENT SEGMENT) COMPARED WITH UNEMPLOYMENT RATE OF NONWHITE MALES

Year	AFDC Cases Opened [1]	Nonwhite Male Unemployment Rate
1964	429,048	9.1
1963	380,985	10.6
1962	370,008	11.0
1961	391,238	12.9
1960	338,730	10.7
1959	329,815	11.5
1958	345,950	13.7
1957	294,032	8.4
1956	261,663	7.3
1955	256,881	8.2
1954	275,054	9.2
1953	222,498	4.4
1952	234,074	4.5
1951	225,957	4.4
1950	291,273	8.9
1949	278,252	8.8
1948	210,193	5.1

[1]Does not include cases opened under program which commenced in some States in 1961 of assistance to children whose fathers are present but unemployed. There were 70,846 such cases opened in 1961, 81,192 in 1962, 80,728 in 1963, and 105,094 in 1964.

Source: AFDC cases opened from HEW; nonwhite male unemployment rates from Department of Labor.

☆U. S. GOVERNMENT PRINTING OFFICE : 1965 O - 794-628

For sale by the Superintendent of Documents, U.S. Government Printing Office
Washington, D.C., 20402 – Price 45 cents

B. REMARKS OF THE PRESIDENT AT
HOWARD UNIVERSITY, JUNE 4, 1965

[Editors' note: The speech was drafted by Richard N. Goodwin and Daniel P. Moynihan.]

TO FULFILL THESE RIGHTS
June 4, 1965

Our earth is the home of revolution.

In every corner of every continent men charged with hope contend with ancient ways in the pursuit of justice. They reach for the newest of weapons to realize the oldest of dreams; that each may walk in freedom and pride, stretching his talents, enjoying the fruits of the earth.

Our enemies may occasionally seize the day of change. But it is the banner of our revolution they take. And our own future is linked to this process of swift and turbulent change in many lands in the world. But nothing in any country touches us more profoundly, nothing is more freighted with meaning for our own destiny, than the revolution of the Negro American.

In far too many ways American Negroes have been another nation: deprived of freedom, crippled by hatred, the doors of opportunity closed to hope.

In our time change has come to this Nation too. The American Negro, acting with impressive restraint, has peacefully protested and marched, entered the courtrooms and the seats of government, demanding a justice that has long been denied. The voice of the Negro was the call to action. But it is a tribute to America that, once aroused, the courts and the Congress, the President and most of the people, have been the allies of progress.

Legal Protection for Human Rights

Thus we have seen the high court of the country declare that discrimination based on race was repugnant to the Constitution, and therefore void. We have seen in 1957, 1960, and again in 1964, the first civil rights legislation in this Nation in almost an entire century.

As majority leader of the United States Senate, I helped to guide two of these bills through the Senate. As your President,

I was proud to sign the third. And now very soon we will have the fourth — a new law guaranteeing every American the right to vote.

No act of my entire administration will give me greater satisfaction than the day when my signature makes this bill too the law of this land.

The voting rights bill will be the latest, and among the most important, in a long series of victories. But this victory — as Winston Churchill said of another triumph for freedom — "is not the end. It is not even the beginning of the end. But it is, perhaps, the end of the beginning."

That beginning is freedom. And the barriers to that freedom are tumbling down. Freedom is the right to share fully and equally in American society — to vote, to hold a job, to enter a public place, to go to school. It is the right to be treated in every part of our national life as a person equal in dignity and promise to all others.

Freedom Is Not Enough

But freedom is not enough. You do not wipe away the scars of centuries by saying: Now you are free to go where you want, do as you desire, and choose the leaders you please.

You do not take a person who, for years, has been hobbled by chains and liberate him, bring him up to the starting line of a race and then say, "you are free to compete with all the others," and still justly believe that you have been completely fair.

Thus it is not enough just to open the gates of opportunity. All our citizens must have the ability to walk through those gates.

This is the next and more profound stage of the battle for civil rights. We seek not just freedom but opportunity — not just legal equity but human ability — not just equality as a right and a theory but equality as a fact and as a result.

For the task is to give 20 million Negroes the same chance as every other American to learn and grow, to work and share in society, to develop their abilities — physical, mental and spiritual, and to pursue their individual happiness.

To this end equal opportunity is essential, but not enough. Men and women of all races are born with the same range of abilities. But ability is not just the product of birth. Ability is stretched or stunted by the family you live with, and the neighborhood you live in, by the school you go to and the poverty or the richness of your surroundings. It is the product of a hundred unseen forces playing upon the infant, the child, and the man.

Progress for Some

This graduating class at Howard University is witness to the indomitable determination of the Negro American to win his way in American life.

The number of Negroes in schools of higher learning has almost doubled in 15 years. The number of nonwhite professional workers has more than doubled in 10 years. The median income of Negro college women exceeds that of white college women. And there are also the enormous accomplishments of distinguished individual Negroes — many of them graduates of this institution, and one of them the first lady ambassador in the history of the United States.

These are proud and impressive achievements. But they tell only the story of a growing middle class minority, steadily narrowing the gap between them and their white counterparts.

A Widening Gulf

But for the great majority of Negro Americans — the poor, the unemployed, the uprooted and the dispossessed — there is a much grimmer story. They still are another nation. Despite the court orders and the laws, despite the legislative victories and the speeches, for them the walls are rising and the gulf is widening.

Here are some of the facts of this American failure.

Thirty-five years ago the rate of unemployment for Negroes and whites was about the same. Today the Negro rate is twice as high.

In 1948 the 8 percent unemployment rate for Negro teenage boys was actually less than that of whites. By last year that rate had grown to 23 percent, as against 13 percent for whites.

Between 1949 and 1959, the income of Negro men relative to white men declined in every section of this country. From 1952 to 1963 the median income of Negro families compared to white actually dropped from 57 percent to 53 percent.

In the years 1955 through 1957, 22 percent of experienced Negro workers were out of work at some time during the year. In 1961 through 1963 that proportion had soared to 29 percent.

Since 1947 the number of white families living in poverty has decreased 27 percent, while the number of poor nonwhite families decreased only 3 percent.

The infant mortality of nonwhites in 1940 was 70 percent greater than whites. Twenty-two years later it was 90 percent greater.

Moreover, the isolation of Negro from white communities is increasing, rather than decreasing, as Negroes crowd into the central cities and become a city within a city.

Of course Negro Americans as well as white Americans have shared in our rising national abundance. But the harsh fact of the matter is that in the battle for true equality too many are losing ground every day.

The Causes of Inequality

We are not completely sure why this is. The causes are complex and subtle. But we do know the two broad basic reasons. And we do know that we have to act.

First, Negroes are trapped — as many whites are trapped — in inherited, gateless poverty. They lack training and skills. They are shut in slums, without decent medical care. Private and public poverty combine to cripple their capacities.

We are trying to attack these evils through our poverty program, through our education program, through our medical care and our other health programs and a dozen more of the Great Society programs that are aimed at the root causes of this poverty.

We will increase, and accelerate, and broaden this attack in years to come until this most enduring of foes finally yields to our unyielding will. But there is a second cause — much more difficult to explain, more deeply grounded, more desperate in its force. It is the devasting heritage of long years of slavery; and a century of oppression, hatred and injustice.

Special Nature of Negro Poverty

For Negro poverty is not white poverty. Many of its causes and many of its cures are the same. But there are differences — deep, corrosive, obstinate differences — radiating painful roots into the community, the family, and the nature of the individual.

These differences are not racial differences. They are solely and simply the consequence of ancient brutality, past injustice, and present prejudice. They are anguishing to observe. For the Negro they are a constant reminder of oppression. For the white they are a constant reminder of guilt. But they must be faced and dealt with and overcome, if we are ever to reach the time when the only difference between Negroes and whites is the color of their skin.

Nor can we find a complete answer in the experience of other American minorities. They made a valiant and a largely successful effort to emerge from poverty and prejudice. The Negro, like these others, will have to rely mostly on his own efforts. But he just cannot do it alone. For they did not have the heritage of centuries to overcome. They did not have a cultural tradition which had been twisted and battered by endless years of hatred and hopelessness. Nor were they excluded because of race or color — a feeling whose dark intensity is matched by no other prejudice in our society.

Nor can these differences be understood as isolated infirmities. They are a seamless web. They cause each other. They result from each other. They reinforce each other. Much of the Negro community is buried under a blanket of history and circumstance. It is not a lasting solution to lift just one corner of that blanket. We must stand on all sides and raise the entire cover if we are to liberate our fellow citizens.

The Roots of Injustice

One of the differences is the increased concentration of Negroes in our cities. More than 73 percent of all Negroes live in urban areas compared with less than 70 percent of the whites. Most of these Negroes live in slums. Most of them live together — a separated people. Men are shaped by their world. When it is a world of decay, ringed by an invisible wall — when escape is arduous and uncertain, and the saving pressures of a more hopeful society are unknown — it can cripple the youth and desolate the man.

There is also the burden that a dark skin can add to the search for a productive place in society. Unemployment strikes most swiftly and broadly at the Negro. This burden erodes hope. Blighted hope breeds despair. Despair brings indifference to the learning which offers a way out. And despair, coupled with indifference, is often the source of destructive rebellion against the fabric of society.

There is also the lacerating hurt of early collision with white hatred or prejudice, distaste, or condescension. Other groups have felt similar intolerance. But success and achievement could wipe it away. They do not change the color of a man's skin. I have seen this uncomprehending pain in the eyes of the little Mexican-American schoolchildren that I taught many years ago. It can be overcome. But for many, the wounds are always open.

Family Breakdown

Perhaps most important — its influence rediating to every part of life — is the breakdown of the Negro family structure. For this, most of all, white America must accept responsibility. It flows from centuries of oppression and persecution of the Negro man. It flows from long years of degradation and discrimination, which have attacked his dignity and assaulted his ability to provide for his family.

This, too, is not pleasant to look upon. But it must be faced by those whose serious intent is to improve the life of all Americans.

Only a minority — less than half — of all Negro children reach the age of 18 having lived all their lives with both of their parents. At this moment little less than two-thirds are living with both of their parents. Probably a majority of all Negro children receive federally aided public assistance sometime during their childhood.

The family is the cornerstone of our society. More than any other force it shapes the attitudes, the hopes, the ambitions, and the values of the child. When the family collapses it is the children that are usually damaged. When it happens on a massive scale the community itself is crippled.

So, unless we work to strengthen the family, to create conditions under which most parents will stay together — all the rest: schools and playgrounds, public assistance and private concern, will never be enough to cut completely the circle of despair and deprivation.

To Fulfill These Rights

There is no single easy answer to all of these problems.

Jobs are part of the answer. They bring the income which permits a man to provide for his family.

Decent homes in decent surroundings, and a chance to learn — an equal chance to learn — are part of the answer.

Welfare and social programs better designed to hold families together are part of the answer.

Care of the sick is part of the answer.

An understanding heart by all Americans is also a large part of the answer.

To all these fronts — and a dozen more — I will dedicate the expanding efforts of the Johnson Administration.

But there are other answers still to be found. Nor do we fully understand all of the problems. Therefore, I want to announce tonight that this fall I intend to call a White House conference of scholars, and experts, and outstanding Negro leaders — men of both races — and officials of government at every level.

This White House conference's theme and title will be "To Fulfill These Rights."

Its object will be to help the American Negro fulfill the rights which, after the long time of injustice, he is finally about to secure.

To move beyond opportunity to achievement.

To shatter forever not only the barriers of law and public practice but the walls which bound the condition of man by the color of his skin.

To dissolve, as best we can, the antique enmities of the heart which diminish the holder, divide the great democracy, and do wrong — great wrong — to the children of God.

I pledge you tonight this will be a chief goal of my administration, and of my program next year, and in years to come. And I hope, and I pray, and I believe, it will be a part of the program of all America.

What Is Justice?

For what is justice?

It is to fulfill the fair expectations of man.

Thus, American justice is a very special thing. For, from the first, this has been a land of towering expectations. It was to be a nation where each man could be ruled by the common consent of all — enshrined in law, given life by institutions, guided by men themselves subject to its rule. And all — all of every station and origin — would be touched equally in obligation and in liberty.

Beyond the law lay the land. It was a rich land, glowing with more abundant promise than man had ever seen. Here, unlike any place yet known, all were to share the harvest.

And beyond this was the dignity of man. Each could become whatever his qualities of mind and spirit would permit — to strive, to seek, and, if he could, to find his happiness.

This is American justice. We have pursued it faithfully to the edge of our imperfections. And we have failed to find it for the American Negro.

It is the glorious opportunity of this generation to end the one huge wrong of the American Nation and, in so doing, to find America for ourselves, with the same immense thrill of discovery which gripped those who first began to realize that here, at last, was a home for freedom.

All it will take is for all of us to understand what this country is and what this country must become.

The Scripture promises: "I shall light a candle of understanding in thine heart, which shall not be put out."

Together, and with millions more, we can light that candle of understanding in the heart of all America.

And, once lit, it will never again go out.

The Report Becomes Public

The fact that the report existed, and was being considered in high places, as well as the nature of its contents slowly became public over the summer and the early fall. The process of becoming public can be conveniently considered in three phases. First there was the discussion of the report's ideas as these were reflected in the President's Howard University speech and in background briefing about it. Later, in mid-July and early August, came the first fairly full summaries of the report. Finally, after the Watts riot came background articles that drew in one way or another on the report's contents.

Press Coverage of the Howard University Speech

From the beginning, in the background stories on the President's speech, two somewhat contradictory themes that were to plague the Moynihan thesis in the coming months were apparent. *The New York Times* coverage picked up one of these themes; a column by *The Washington Star's* Mary McGrory picked up the second.

In a *New York Times* story of June 5th, "White House sources" are quoted to the effect that the Howard speech was the first major Presidential civil rights speech conceived independently of the direct pressure of racial crisis. Mr. Johnson's target was not the South but "the whole nation and the total social and economic plight of its Negro citizens." Further, the speech was said to have been under study for about two months: "Much consultation with civil rights leaders and experts in the social sciences went into its preparation."

The White House sources said that there would be two specific steps following up the speech. One involved the conference that was "to produce specific ideas and to chart programs for implementing them." Also, "each government agency will be asked to review its programs in the light of the speech and to see what can be done by the government to carry the Negro beyond 'legal equity.' " The speech's emphasis on Negro family breakdown "could ultimately affect federal, state, and local administration of a number of existing welfare programs, particularly as they relate to unwed or abandoned mothers and their dependent children." Thus the White House sources were playing back to the press one of Moynihan's main concerns, that the effect of federal programs on Negro family stability be systematically evaluated. Finally, the White House sources were quoted as telling a favorite Johnson story which illustrated his feelings on the matter — a little boy tells his mother that he has received a new toy from a friend in return for a favor; the favor was that he stop hitting the other little boy over the head. "Mr. Johnson's view is said to be that it isn't enough for white people to 'stop hitting the Negro over the head.' Their problem now, he believes, is to help the Negro reach the point where the only thing different about him is the color of his skin." The following day a *New York Times* editorial, taking as its point of departure the President's speech and some recent remarks by Bayard Rustin, made the following programmatic suggestions:

The cures for the social afflictions that hold the Negro in thrall lie in public and private programs that make the present War on Poverty and all its related undertakings for expanded education, urban renewal and improved welfare services seem incredibly puny. In the absence of much more massive action to engender full employment, clear the slums and make more schooling available to more people, the chief effect of these programs may be to confront the United States with problems not unlike those of the "revolutions of rising expectations" in Africa and Asia.

The conference . . . will have as its mission the development of an action program as crucial for the country as it is for the Negro.

On the other hand, Mary McGrory of The Washington Star, also drawing on "White House aides," told quite a different story. Her views could not be taken lightly by Washingtonians since she was regarded as one of the most influential Washington columnists, with good access to the President and his staff. McGrory's story said that in the speech "President Johnson suggested that the time had come for them [Negroes] to come to grips with their own worst problem, "the breakdown of Negro family life.' " Self-improvement was said to be the key to the announced next stage in civil rights; Miss McGrory noted that the NAACP and James Farmer of CORE had both been concerned "about the necessity for efforts within the Negro community to make life better." This was a delicate subject because of the risk of being called an "Uncle Tom." But, with the President's encouragement and approval, more Negroes were expected to speak out on this hitherto most delicate subject. His aides are quoted as saying that the President was determined "that the unprecedented White House Conference he has called for next fall will not turn into a seminar for reliving old woes and grievances or generate only new demands for help from the federal government." Rather he hoped that Negroes would find solutions of their own. Mc-Grory's emphasis, sometimes referred to as the "they-should-pull-up-their-own-socks" school, counterposed "self-improvement" to "new demands for help from the federal government."

Thus the speech that The New York Times saw as legitimating massive federal programs which would make present ones seem incredibly puny was put in a very different light by Miss McGrory. The Washington Post, in its editorial of June 6th, reported a very subdued version of the latter line:

Implicit in his discussion is the fact that the government cannot reach all of these sources of maladjustment, except in a remote way. In addition to all the government can do there is need for human understanding, individual and group efforts and a general improvement of the social, moral and intellectual environment in which people live.

You could pay your money and take your choice. The President sought to encourage Negroes to pull up their socks and stop asking the government for so much money or he was building toward massive federal programs to bring about equal results by dealing with the social and economic plight of Negro citizens.

An interesting and perhaps prophetic treatment of the President's speech appeared in James Reston's column of June 6th. He juxtaposed the problems of peace in Vietnam and racial equality at home and suggested that there was an anxiety in the country about many of the Administration's policies and much of its evangelic rhetoric. People had begun to doubt

that the Administration is willing or able to provide the means to achieve the exalted aims it proclaims . . . It is well and good for the President to say that the inequality of the American Negro is intolerable . . . How this is to be done, however, without a massive public works and public housing policy is not clear. Again the objectives are expressed in eloquent words, but not carried out in public policy. . . . On this question, as on Vietnam, the disparity between ends and means is startling and disturbing. . . . [The means proposed are clearly inadequate and] "this is what creates the uneasiness over what is said in Washington and what is done."

The events of the following six months could hardly have shaken Mr. Reston's confidence in the correctness of his views.

Press Coverage of the Early Conference Planning

On July 11th, three days after the preplanning group had met with psychiatrist Robert Coles and two days after they had met with Kenneth Clark, Mary McGrory broke the story of the planning activity. Though the self-help emphasis of her column following the Howard speech was not as strong in this article, it was still present. She noted that in the Howard speech the President had "urged black Americans to forgive and forget and to look frankly at their own failures." Further, the President wanted to hand the civil rights movement back to Negroes and to enable them to speak out on the overwhelming problem that faced them — "the breakdown of the Negro family structure." So that the conference would not be just another rehearsal of Negro woes, followed by pledges of federal help, a staff of four of the President's brightest young men had been appointed for careful planning — Richard Goodwin, Harry McPherson, and Lee White of the White House staff and Daniel P. Moynihan. She wrote that these men would come up with specific proposals for presentation to the 500 or 600 delegates expected. Then there was mention of a series of two-hour conferences with individual sociologists, writers, psychiatrists, churchmen, and civil rights leaders. These sessions were to lay the intellectual groundwork for discussing specific questions of concern.

The following week, John D. Pomfret of *The New York Times* broke the first story to deal specifically with the contents of the Moynihan Report. Pomfret had specific White House authorization to read and write about the report but not to describe its authorship. Instead he was asked to write about a "White House study group" which was "laying the groundwork for a massive attempt to revive the structure of the Negro family." This was said to be the key to the next phase in achievement of Negro equality.

Pomfret's selections from the report gave a distorted impression of its content. There was a rather full presentation of statements concerning Negro family disorganization including both "fundamental" quotations — "the fundamental problem" is that of family structure and "the fundamental source of weakness of the Negro community is the deterioration of the Negro family." The report's section on the roots of the problem, however, was completely ignored so that there was no discussion of the effects of unemployment, low income, or of urbanization and past history. Finally, there was mention of Moynihan's point that ADC (Aid to Dependent Children) rates, no longer seem tightly related to the unemployment rate, but with an unfortunate misprint that suggested that since 1952 the number of aid cases opened has been going up despite the fact that the unemployment rate has been going down. Note also, that the reference here was to *the* unemployment rate rather than to *the Negro male* unemployment rate which Moynihan had used. Finally, there was a discussion of the fact that the White House study group had been meeting with experts to explore the dimensions of the problem. It was said that later the group would meet with a number of economists and experts in other fields. (So far as we can determine, these meetings did not materialize.) The programmatic ideas the group was said to have been considering involved (1) not denying welfare aid to families with an able-bodied man in the house, (2) coping somehow with the psychological impact on children of the lack of a strong father figure, (3) whether more education was the answer when children went from the classroom back into the slum and the broken home. Finally, the article noted that the initiative for the hoped-for breakthrough in civil rights has come largely from the Administration which was convinced that the problem and the need for fast action are great and that it must take the lead. This was a break with past patterns in that the Administration was no longer working as a broker for proposals put forward by pressure groups.

The Pomfret leak apparently triggered a decision to make the report available to those who asked for it. Within two days, the White House, in consultation with the Labor Department, decided to release the report as written. Apparently no special consideration was given to this decision; it just seemed a good idea. The White House felt it had a hot property but apparently was sufficiently ambivalent about the report to let Labor handle its release alone. No press announcement was to be made about its availability and no press release was to be prepared stating the government's conception of what the report contained. Pursuant to these decisions, on July 21st the Secretary's office instructed Labor's public information officer to arrange with the Government Printing Office for a supply of copies to be stocked at Labor and given to individuals requesting them. The initial order was for 500 copies; these were delivered in mid-August.

A few days later, in a perhaps unrelated background article, *The Wall Street Journal* reviewed the "new stage in civil rights" and after throwing cold water on demonstration tactics, poverty wars, and public works and commending the NAACP for limiting itself to the immediate task of helping enforce the newly passed laws announced that "promoting self-help must realistically appear as a large part of the ultimate answer.... Isn't the next task to enlighten even the most downtrodden Negro to the middle class outlook?" It warned that civil rights leaders could impede progress if "they meet the new stage with the facile answer of intensifying the militancy of the old."

Shortly, *The New York Times* editorialized on the subject of the Negro family, making reference to the study "recently released by the Department of Labor." Using a slightly longer selection from Frazier's prophecy of the experience of the Negro in "the city of destruction" had been vindicated in the ensuing twenty-five years. Paraphrasing the paragraph of the report that followed this Frazier quote, the editorial noted: "Whatever the index of social pathology ... it is apparent that the Negro family in the urban areas of this country is rapidly decaying." Although emphasizing the destructive effect of the slavery heritage, the editorial noted that viable Negro family structure did develop in rural areas "but it has not been able to withstand the pressures exerted by the great urban migration." Though some Negroes have established themselves in cohesive social units "because of the barriers imposed by poor education, discrimination and apathy, the ascent to middle class family stability is very slow." The President's White House Conference would consider these problems; something must be done but there were no clear prescriptions yet.

Then on August 9th, several days before the Watts outbreak, the full report was surfaced by *Newsweek* in a two-page article which provided a full summary of the report's main points and included three charts. The report was said to have "set off a quiet revolution in the basic White House approach to the continuing American dilemma of race." *Newsweek* was aware of the touchiness of the issue: "The Negro family problem was scarcely news to social scientists. But its very intimacy has excluded it from the public dialogue of civil rights; it reaches too deep into white prejudices and Negro sensitivities."

For the first time, Moynihan is listed as "among the authors" of the report; *Newsweek's* editor decided to do this although the White House apparently still preferred that the report be identified with it.

Unlike some of the earlier articles, *Newsweek* raised the issue of self-help only to suggest: "Yet the very size of the problem today imposes limits on what Negroes alone can do." Roy Wilkins was quoted as saying that "President Johnson has given a frank recognition to a big problem, a delicate problem . . . he has put (responsibility) at the white man's door and he's right." The article went on to note that though the report proposed no solution, "its findings suggest that jobs remain a principal part of the solution," though Moynihan's findings about recent trends of unemployment rates and ADC cases suggest that "the disintegration of Negro families may have fallen into a self-sustaining vicious circle." Therefore, conventional economic remedies were unlikely to be enough. Instead, Whitney Young was quoted as calling for an immense public works program and a massive "domestic Marshall Plan." What course should be followed was uncertain; therefore, White House staffers were studying the problem further and consulting with social scientists and Negro leaders for fresh ideas.

Explaining Watts

On August 16th, while sporadic sniping and arson continued on the last day of tthe Watts riots, *The Wall Street Journal* news roundup looked behind the riots to find that "Family Life Break-

down in Negro Slums Sows Seeds of Race Violence — Husbandless Homes Spawn Young Hoodlums, Impede Reforms, Sociologists Say." In a background article quoting sociologists, psychologists, and anthropologists (Frank Hartung, Sidney Copel,
Leo A. Despres, Philip Hauser, Seymour Leventman, and
Herbert Blumer), "a just released government study" was quoted
as indicating that in 20 percent of nonwhite homes no husband
is present. The article quoted no further from the Moynihan
Report but drew instead on interviews with social scientists,
an HEW study of ADC families, and population figures for Watts.
The article concentrated on the pathology of the ghetto dealing,
in addition to family disorganization, with problems of crime,
venereal disease, hopelessness, and so on. These were, in turn,
the result of high population density, dilapidated housing, unemployment, low income. The article ended with a quote from
Herbert Blumer:

The violence in Watts over the weekend was physical [but] the real
violence that brought it out was done to the social fabric of the community long ago — and continues to be done to it here and in practically every other big city in the country.

The next day in a very similar background article, Chalmers
M. Roberts in The Washington Post laid the riots to feelings of
"nobodiness and frustration" that result from the deprived lives
the Watts citizens are forced to live. Quarreling with the notion
of Watts as an area of separate homes, green lawns, palm trees
in backyards, Roberts noted that it was a ghetto nonetheless in
which few people own their own homes, many of the houses
are dilapidated, many of the residents illiterate, the unemployment rate probably well over 10 percent and job-hunting difficult because the industrial areas are far away from Watts. A
Negro psychiatrist, Dr. Harold W. Jones, was quoted as saying
that the rioters "see their insurrection as an opportunity to
achieve dignity and self-respect. It is as if they are saying, 'It's
better to be feared than to be held in contempt.' " Dr. Jones and
his colleague, Dr. Silber, were said to have agreed that "the
breakdown of the Negro family structure is a principal reason
for a lack of respect for authority." The two doctors were then
quoted as presenting essentially the same picture of family
disorganization as Moynihan had outlined.

On the same day, The New York Times presented its background article quoting historian Oscar Handlin and sociologists

Philip Hauser, Stanley Lieberson, Lewis M. Killian, and Melvin Seeman. Handlin seemed to belittle the riots as a racial manifestation, viewing them as mostly hooliganism. The other social scientists, however, took a broader view, emphasizing feelings of frustration and despair at the growing gap between Negroes and whites and between their own expectations and what they actually received.

On August 18th, by far the most influential news story connecting the report with the postriot atmosphere appeared. This was Roland Evans and Robert Novak's column "Inside Report" which was headlined simply, "The Moynihan Report." The article purported to tell the facts of an intense debate within the Administration on how to handle the Moynihan Report — "A much suppressed, much leaked Labor Department document which strips away usual equivocations and exposes the ugly truth about the big city Negro's plight." The report was said to bring up a taboo subject: preferential treatment for Negroes. The writers went on to say that Moynihan began working on his report because he was deeply disturbed by the big-city Negro riots of the summer of 1964. Their "inside" view of how Moynihan came to write the report continued: "He wondered, for instance, why in a time of decreasing unemployment, the plight of the urban Negro was getting worse — not better. His answer: a 78-page report (based largely on unexciting Census Bureau statistics) revealed the breakdown of the Negro family. He showed that broken homes, illegitimacy, and female-oriented homes were central to big city Negro problems." Secretary Wirtz was quoted as opposed to the release of the report because it would become grist for racist propaganda mills. Other officials believed "Moynihan's Report would stir up trouble by defining insoluble problems." Further, the Moynihan report data had been used by Theodore White, Newsweek, and UPI so that it had by now become more or less public.

The writers implied that Moynihan "leaked" his report over Wirtz's head to Bill D. Moyers, who was fascinated, thus producing the Howard University speech. "Using the Moynihan Report as a source, the President for the first time discussed the degeneration of Negro family life and called a White House Conference this fall to deal with it." Since then, experts and Negro leaders had been in and out of the White House to prepare for the conference. Evans and Novak's inside report, presumably based on White House sources, went on to say that the

White House planning group had found it easier to define problems than to solve them. For example, though they saw the basic need for male-directed discipline in the ghettos, they did not know how to get it. The heart of the problem, however, was tougher than that: "Moynihan believes that the public erroneously compares the Negro minority to the Jewish minority. When discriminatory bars were lowered, Jews were ready to move. But the implicit message of the Moynihan Report is that ending discrimination is not nearly enough for the Negro. But what is enough? Returning to the difficulties of preferential treatment and the fact that Administration officials hoped the White House Conference would not even mention it, the writers noted that the report inevitably led to posing this question. Therefore the internal debate on the report "is infinitely more than a mere intra-bureaucratic tiff. It may determine whether this country is doomed to succeeding summers of guerilla warfare in our cities."

This column seems to have been tremendously influential in the negative reaction to the report which was then beginning to build outside of the government. Its influence stemmed from the prominence of the writers whom many regard as having "the hottest column in Washington," one which exposes sensitive issues within the Administration and which provides authoritative "inside dope." Readers in Washington and New York could find their worst fears confirmed in the column. The government was seriously entertaining a wild report that placed the causes of ghetto problems in the Negro family and not in unemployment or any of the other institutional sources of deprivation.

In the main, Evans and Novak seem to have been correct in their statements about what was going on within the Administration. There was intense debate about whether the family thesis should become central to civil rights thinking; but Secretary of Labor had not stood in the way of the White House learning of Moynihan's ideas although others in his department were deeply suspicious of whether the report would lead to constructive results. However, the debate does not seem to have been carried on primarily in terms of preferential treatment or not, and Moynihan did not write his report primarily because he was disturbed about the 1964 summer riots (though he might well have believed that the report would be more likely to be attended to because of the fear of continuing riots).

In this context of presumably authoritative inside information, the one statement about the report's contents — that in a time of decreasing unemployment the plight of the urban Negro was getting worse because of the breakdown of the Negro family — was highly incendiary, misleading, and (from the response of Dr. Benjamin Payton) highly disturbing to those in the civil rights field. From the Evans and Novak column it would be impossible to tell that the brunt of Moynihan's argument was that underemployment and related poverty produced family breakdown. In short, the Evans and Novak column neatly reflected the growing pall over the report — the emphasis on the riots, on a controversy about a sensitive issue, and the isolation of the Negro family as a problem divorced from more traditional issues of employment, housing, education, poverty, and so on.

On August 24th, the President addressed the conferees of a White House Conference on Equal Employment Opportunities. He used the occasion to condemn the rioters of Watts and restated the main points of his Howard University speech, that ten years of private civil rights and federal activity had produced legislation guaranteeing equal rights but that this was just a key to open gates, not to provide the ability to walk through them. He mentioned that he had talked individually with Dr. King, Mr. Farmer, Mr. Roy Wilkins, and A. Philip Randolph about "the great meeting that we would have here later in the fall, because the cities of this nation and the Negro family are two of our most pressing, more important problems. Well, the bitter years that preceded the riots, the death of hope where hope existed, the sense of failure to change the conditions of life — these things no doubt lead to these riots. But they do not justify them."

After pledging more and better programs to deal with the employment, education, housing, health, and poverty problems, the President went on to extoll the success of the cabinet task force headed by the Vice-President which had so far produced 800,000 summer jobs for poor youth. This wasn't enough, but he was confident that they would reach the goal of providing 1,000,000 such jobs.

Then the President moved on to another preoccupation, that of foreign policy and the difficulties in Vietnam. He pledged that foreign difficulties would not mean neglecting the domestic problems of the deprived, but given the events of the following fall and winter one wonders if he was not expressing a concern as much as or more than making a promise. Moynihan's thesis still seemed very much alive in the White House, though the sharpness of the Howard speech was now diluted by preoccupation with domestic and foreign violence.

On August 23rd, a by-lined article by Jean M. White in *The Washington Post* bore the headline, "Report Finds Negroes' Family Life Crumbling." The article picked up the main ideas of the report and noted that "White House sources" say, "the Los Angeles riots reinforce the President's feeling of the urgent need to help restore Negro families' stability." The article summarized the main facts of Negro family disorganization and noted that "the study traces the roots of the Negro family breakdown back to the days of slavery . . ." For the first time, one particular quote dealing with the position of the Negro man during reconstruction was used: "Unquestionably these events worked against the emergence of a strong father-figure. The very essence of the male animal, from the bantam rooster to the four-star general, is to strut." This apparently was good copy since it was used over and over again in other articles that followed. Although the major emphasis of the article was on the fact of family breakdown and on its historical roots, the writer did, unlike Evans and Novak, Pomfret, and McGrory, include the report's statement that "failure to provide jobs for Negro youth has been the most conspicuous failure of the American social system in the past ten years" and also that the ratio of nonwhite to white mean income had fallen since the late 1950's.

On August 25th, an AP dispatch covered essentially the same points, although emphasizing rather more "a hard new look" at the report because of the Los Angeles riots. There was the same quote about the strutting essence of the male animal. The report was referred to as not officially public and the Department of Labor was said to be unwilling to indicate whether it would ever officially release the report. In this article, the emphasis on slavery and reconstruction as causes, and on illegitimacy, stood out. No mention was made of unemployment or urbanization as roots of the problem.

Though on August 21st the President felt constrained to condemn the rioters, by August 27th he was willing to tell reporters that there could well be riots in other cities where Negroes "feel they don't get a fair shake and justice is not open to them." In what Republicans felt was an effort to use the riots as a club over Congress to pass home rule for the District of Columbia, the President said:

Those of you here in the District of Columbia, I want to warn you this morning that the clock is ticking, time is moving, that we should and we must ask ourselves every night when we go home, are we doing all that we should in our nation's capitol, in all the other big cities of the country where 80 per cent of the population of this country is going to be living in the year 2000?

Later, meeting informally with reporters in his office the President emphasized that he

meant just what I said . . . we ought to face up to these problems. . . . before we have to suffer more serious problems and create additional problems. . . . We have to face up to the economic facts and meet them while we still have time to do it. . . . [In Los Angeles] we found we could not contain the disappointments and frustrations, and it took rather drastic action to get the situation back into focus. Now we have all the problems we had before, plus additional ones. . . . the scars of years of inaction reflected themselves. . . . there are complex problems and the solutions are neither quick nor easy, long-term answers must and will be found.

In his words and actions, the President neatly reflected the political bind in which he found himself after Watts. On the one hand, it was clear to him and his staff that "long-term answers" were required. Yet the political pressures to do something, to show some activity, required the appearance of immediate solutions. He appointed, therefore, a federal study group to draft a federal-state-local program for the Los Angeles area. This program involved essentially a concentration into the Watts area of already existing, but poorly financed and rationalized, federal programs. It is doubtful that the President, given the thinking his staff had exposed him to over the previous months, could really be very confident that this would make much difference.

On August 25th, an AP dispatch covered essentially the same vided some interested New Yorkers with further details on the report. In a story headlined "Report Focuses on Negro Family: Aid to Replace Matriarchy Asked by Johnson Panel," Herbers characterized Moynihan's report as a synthesis of published works reinforced by government statistics that contained little new information. He noted that President Johnson had accepted Moynihan's thesis, made it the basis for his Howard University speech, and the fall White House Conference. Although Moynihan was listed as playing a leading role, the White House sources from whom Herbers got his story characterized it as a report "prepared by a committee appointed by the President to help chart the government's course in race relations. The members came from several agencies of the government." Again, the quote

about the strutting bantam rooster, a quote on matriarchal structure, and mention of slavery appears. However, Herbers did not
confine his selections to those dealing with the historical past,
noting that "disintegration of the family . . . has been speeded
by poverty, isolation, and [urbanization]." This article also noted
that the report attracted new attention since the riots and that
"it pinpoints the causes of discontent in the Negro ghettos and
says the new crisis in race relations is much more severe than
is generally believed."

Several of these stories, then, apparently depended for their
information on White House sources and White House leaks. In
the main, the content of the articles lend themselves to the interpretation that the White House was primarily concerned
to use the Watts riots plus the report's thesis to generate a
sense of urgency about federal action in the area of civil rights
and a sense of the importance of the coming conference. Herbers'
article managed to do this in a way that was roughly consonant
with Moynihan's thesis and with the ideas that had begun to be
current in the White House over the course of the summer.
Evans' and Novak's treatment, on the other hand, forced the
issue (by its emphasis on preferential treatment and the "unexplained" family breakdown) in a direction that seriously em-
barrased any effort at "consensus building."

Finally, on the last day of August, New Yorkers were again
introduced to the report but in a context that related it to its
author's candidacy for the City Council President nomination.
Barry Gottehrer, in a *New York Herald Tribune* "Inside New
York" column headlined "Political Powderkeg," described the
report as an explosive and controversial one dealing with the
increasing plight of the urban Negro family and the government's
failure to cope with it. Mr. Gottehrer indicated that the report
"will explode into a major campaign issue in New York City's
mayoral race." Noting that the report was the basis for the
President's Howard University speech, that Moynihan worked
on the speech, and that it was a major factor in the President's
decision to call "a White House Conference on the Negro family" in the fall, he stated that Moynihan would make a speech
based on the report and an article to be published in *America*. He
suggested that "some top city Democrats feel Moynihan is making
a serious political mistake by doing so."

By the end of August, the main newspaper coverage of the
report in connection with the riots was over. September was

instead a month for the magazines. First off, in an article apparently unnoticed by his critics, Moynihan himself wrote about the Los Angeles riots in an article subtitled "Jobless Negroes and the Boom." He took up his argument with the aggregationist economists by noting that although the July employment statistics suggested that current economic policies which relate overall economic growth to lower levels of unemployment had been successful little seemed to have been accomplished for the Negro:

In July, amid this unexampled prosperity, the unemployment rate of adult Negro men went up sharply, from 5.7 per cent to 6.5 per cent. The unemployment rate for Negro women rose from 7.8 per cent to 8.8 per cent. At 9.1 per cent, the overall unemployment rate for non-whites is once again double that for the workforce as a whole. It is precisely those adult Negro males — the men who are trying to care for their families, play a part in their community, and provide an example for youth — who are getting worse off. [While over-all unemployment dropped 700,000, that of adult Negro men increased by 32,000.]

Moynihan went on to note that in 1964 the Area Redevelopment Administration conducted a survey of unemployed Negro workers in Watts:

Asked why they thought they were unable to get jobs, only 10 per cent of the males cited discrimination. Over half . . . felt it was because of their lack of skill or the lack of jobs. These are not matters which can be changed by civil rights acts, and they knew it. Surely it is possible by now for responsible persons in private life to recognize that in the midst of unexampled prosperity we are in fact presiding over a catastrophe.

He drew three conclusions:

(1) The United States has *two* unemployment problems. Massive general prosperity can conceal utter calamity in the Negro world.

(2) The training and education needs of Negro workers are even greater than we have thought. Plain old-fashioned discrimination could not account for the events of the last few months.

(3) The cities of the nation must begin insisting on national programs directed specifically to this issue. I do not believe there is a single serious social problem facing them of which unemployment is not one of the root causes. It is precisely because everyone else is so prosperous that urban leaders must insist on more attention being paid to those whose situation is just the opposite and for that very reason all the more bitter.

The New Republic first took notice of the report in its issue
of September 11th, commenting that "In the poverty jet set, [the
Moynihan Report] is all the rage." As were its daily journalist
colleagues, *The New Republic* was unable to resist the "strutting
male animal." In two and a half columns, the magazine managed
to touch on all of the main points of the report, emphasizing
particularly the finding and the implicit recommendation concerning Negroes in the armed forces, with which it was rather
unimpressed. Curiously missing from the story was any discussion of its impact in Washington on higher levels than the poverty jet set or the relationship to the Howard University speech
which other commentators had routinely noted.

On the same day, Richard Rovere's letter from Washington
in *The New Yorker Magazine* (dated September 2) provided the
most complete summary so far of the report's findings and discussion of its implications. Rovere started with a pointed and
perceptive version of the report, that the conference it stimulated
would be "aimed at developing a national policy to strengthen
the ego of the Negro male in the United States," but noted that
"the White House, of course, could not officially subscribe to
any such description of it." He characterized the report as "di-
agnostic, not prescriptive." Praising its candor, lucidity, insight,
and (for a government report) brevity, blending his own knowledge and perceptiveness with the contents of the report, Rovere
developed Moynihan's thesis with considerable detail and sensitivity. He was one of the few writers, for example, to extract
from the report this statistic: "the fundamental overwhelming
fact is that Negro unemployment except for a few years during
World War II and the Korean War has continued at disaster levels for 35 years." Again, better than any of the other reporters
he communicated Moynihan's notion of a vicious cycle and
avoided any connotation of a "mystery" about Negro family
breakdown.

Rovere managed to confront the reality of American standards by which Negro women seem to fare much better than
Negro men and at the same time to express his feelings that

There is something melancholy and distasteful about accepting standards such as these and measuring Negro achievement by them. It
implies a certain virtue or worth in categories that are perhaps
meaningful only in terms of pay scales. It attaches prestige to occupations that may be less honorable than occupations that have no
prestige at all. But it is this American society of 1965 — a society in

which there are many false values and in which squalor is by no means confined to the Negro ghettos — in which the Negro is seeking full and equal participation, and from which the Negro male is more systematically and humiliatingly excluded than the Negro female.

Rovere suggested that Administration thinking was moving in the direction of a "foreign policy" approach — "and aid and development program, an interior Marshall Plan, a long-term subsidy for the entire Negro community." He was not sure that even this President could get Congress to adopt such a program but he stated that there was good reason to believe the coming White House Conference would recommend it and "that the President, with nearly all his other legislative requests already satisfied, will put the full weight of his office behind it."

On September 17th, *Commonweal* took editorial note of the report, providing a brief summary of its main points and discussing the problem posed by the sensitivity of the issue. At this point, the editor knew that some weeks later he would be able to carry a full evaluation of the report by Herbert J. Gans. He suggested that liberal analysts have been reluctant to discuss the problems of the Negro family because "they can be used by racists to suggest the basic inferiority of the Negro and his inability to build a firm family foundation." To this he juxtaposed the Moynihan Report's contention that it was "absolutely essential" to confront these facts head-on and implied his own support for such a view.

In the September 18th issue of *America,* Moynihan wrote about his general interest in the family perspective in an article titled "A Family Policy for the Nation." In this article, he used some of the data on Negroes to illustrate his more general point that the country's tendency to think in terms of individual rather than family welfare had destructive consequences for poor families. He suggested that this was but one example of a general socioeconomic fact, that "many of the processes that are producing prosperity are also producing much of our poverty"; this was the "pathology of post-industrial society."

The United States was unique among industrial democracies in ignoring the family and concentrating instead on individuals without regard to their family status or responsibilities: "Most of the industrial democracies of the world have adopted a wide range of social programs designed specifically to support the stability and viability of the family." Such measures as family allowances, differential unemployment benefits depending on family responsibilities, differential wages depending on the family status of the wage earner, tax policies that take family size more realistically into account, all have been used by other countries to ensure family welfare.

He argued that the society had an interest in family stability and viability because the family performs important socialization and training functions for the society: "Family patterns can help or hinder efforts to bring people out of poverty and into the mainstream of American life." He did not wish to suggest that there was only one kind of adaptive family pattern but that there was a basic minimum of resources necessary for families to accomplish their functions adequately:

The stability and quality of family life are a prime determinant of individual and group achievement. This is not to argue for any one pattern — any more than to declare that there can be only one form of achievement. But what evidence we do have argues that social conditions ought to enable the general run of families to succeed in whatever arrangements fit their fancy.

The fact that American society does not operate to provide these conditions for many of its members is most clear with regard to the situation of Negro Americans, but this is only the latest in an historical series of failures to provide adequate resources for family welfare:

From the wild Irish slums of the 19th century Eastern seaboard, to the riot-torn suburbs of Los Angeles, there is one unmistakable lesson in American history; a community that allows a large number of men to grow up in broken families, dominated by women, never acquiring any stable relationship to male authority, never acquiring any set of rational expectations about the future — that community asks for and gets chaos. Crime, violence, unrest, disorder — most particularly the furious, unrestrained lashing out at the whole social structure — that is not only to be expected; it is very near to inevitable. And it is richly deserved.

Moynihan argued that as a nation we must "seriously and promptly address ourselves to the issue of what it takes for a working man to raise a family in an American city today, and then see to it that what it takes is available." This means that the nation must have a national family policy. In the beginning, this means that we must inform ourselves more fully about the condition of American families — to this end, Moynihan suggested that the President direct someone, perhaps the Secretary of HEW, to report annually to the Congress on the condition of American families and their many faceted situations. (Some months later, a new family post was created in HEW carrying the rank of Assistant Secretary.)

A story by *The Boston Herald's* Holmes Alexander on September 23rd provided some interesting insights into the report's reputation in official Washington. Alexander maintained that only twenty-five copies of the report were distributed to government officials. Alexander wrote that House Speaker McCormack was unable, though he hounded the office of Secretary Wirtz, to get a copy of the report in connection with Administration moves to have representatives sign a petition for the Washington Home Rule Bill. Similarly, the minority staff of the Labor Welfare Committee in the Senate could not get copies of the report as late as the second week in September.

The "secret" or "public" status of the report during August and September is a strange issue indeed. No announcement had been made of the report's availability; the press routinely referred to it as "still secret," as did many in the civil rights movement. The ambiguity of the report's status was physically embodied in its pages: the title page still carried "For Official Use Only," but on the back page was a GPO number and the statement that the document was for sale at a price of 45 cents! The perpetuation of the "For Official Use Only" tag (some copies carried a sticker indicating that this classification was lifted) was perhaps an oversight, perhaps a touch left in for drama. (It could have been removed however; two errata in the original report had been corrected before GPO printed its copies. In all other respects the GPO copies were identical to the original version — contrary to one rumor that some of the original had been deleted.)

In any case, there was little justification for Holmes Alexander's and others' reference to the report as "still secret"; once the report had a GPO number and price it was in the public domain. And Labor was distributing copies at a fast clip by mid-August; demand for copies built up then in response to the post-Watts press coverage. By the end of August several hundred copies had been distributed, about half within the government and half to the press and other outsiders. The demand was so heavy that on August 30th the Secretary's office instructed the public information officer to explain to those requesting more than one copy that it was possible to give only one to a customer.

Alexander's accusation that Senate and House members and staffs could not get copies was clearly inaccurate; the demand from Capitol Hill was great beginning about August 25th, and all requests were filled, including one from Senator Murphy, a minority member of the Senate Labor and Welfare Committee. While the demand for copies was high, and there was undoubtedly some delay in filling some of them (at the high point of demand there were more than a dozen requests a day), it seems clear that no knowledgeable person who wanted a copy should have been unable to get one. Indeed many ordinary citizens received copies in late August and September simply by writing for them — including one angry Florida gentleman who carried on a correspondence with the public information officer seeking to correct the slurs the report made on the character of white Southerners. By the end of September, well over half of the 2,250 copies delivered to Labor had been given out.

By September, the connection of the report and the Watts riot was no longer mentioned. None of the articles discussed so far brought it up. The emphasis had shifted instead to the planning for the White House Conference. On September 24th, *The Washington Star's* Richard Wilson, under the title "Gloomy Study Faces Parley on Negro," related the "still secret" report findings to Vice-President Humphrey's plan for the White House Conference. In Wilson's view, the report had not been released publicly because "its conclusions are so darkly discouraging." "Negro life is another world as little known to middle class Negroes as middle class whites and not understood at all by leaders such as Martin Luther King." Humphrey was said to propose that the conference develop "a direct and simple approach toward improving the physical and cultural environment in which Negroes live today," rather than where they should live in the future. But Wilson believed that matters were not so simple. Rather he saw the problem as "how to cause Negroes to help themselves, how to cause them to create for themselves in their own communities, an ordered society based upon a stable family structure." The complacent, satisfied, well-to-do Negro middle class had the primary responsibility for this. Wilson seemed to suggest that it was up to middle-class Negroes to take care of their own, thus echoing the "self-help," "they-should-pull-up-their-socks" theme initiated by Mary McGrory the previous June. *The Star,* consistent with its editorial policy, tended to systematically play down any need for greater federal involvement.

Finally, starting on September 24th and continuing through October, *The St. Louis Review,* newspaper of the Archdiocese of St. Louis, began a series of articles on the Moynihan Report by Stephen Darst. Significantly, the editorial note preceding the first article stated: "Since excerpts have been used in periodicals hostile to the Negro cause, *The St. Louis Review* has undertaken this series and will publish long excerpts to balance the picture" even though the report had not been released by the government. In addition, "The possibilities for changes in the direction of social legislation developed in our interview with Moynihan are explored for their effects on white families as well as Negro families."

In his first story, Darst stated that the report "written to be read only by the President of the United States and six other persons has created a sensation in political, intellectual and academic circles which could change the direction of social legislation for years to come." In two articles, Darst provided a very full summary of the contents of the report and in the third took up Moynihan's suggestion in the *America* article of September 18th that a family allowance system might be one element in increasing family stability of poor whites and Negroes.

It is perhaps not surprising that the Catholic press showed by and large the most consistent understanding of Moynihan's point of view and was the most responsive to its implications for the white as well as for the Negro poor. In its October issue, the *Catholic Family Leader,* publication of the Family Life Bureau of the National Catholic Welfare Conference, discussed the report and its relation to the White House Conference and notified its subscribers that it had stocked a supply of the now released report as well as reprints of Moynihan's *America* article for readers who were interested.

Taken as a whole, the effect of the press coverage of the Moynihan Report was to subtly exaggerate the already dramatic and sensational aspects of Moynihan's presentation and as a result to considerably deepen the impression that the report dealt almost exclusively with the family, its "pathology" and "instability," as *the* cause of the problems Negroes have. Only in the longer treatments of the report, or for the careful reader (which no journalist can count on) of some of the shorter articles, was there any clear communication of the vicious cycle with which Moynihan sought to deal.

We would suggest that most of the distortion that took place was the inevitable result of the way the press handles "social problem" reporting, with its tendency to think in terms of what is wrong with individuals rather than institutions and to concentrate on personal experiences and suffering rather than on the more impersonal forces behind personal experience. In only a few cases can the press treatment be said to be grinding an overtly conservative ideological ax (particularly the articles by Mary McGrory, Evans and Novak, and Richard Wilson). More typically the press treatment reflects the reductionist habits of journalists manifested in the dynamics of headline writing, the need for condensation of complex arguments (and the impatience with complexity because of this), the interest in "human interest" handles, and the desire for reader identification based on sympathy rather than understanding.

Newspapers as they presently operate are a poor medium by which to communicate about public policy, but they are nevertheless the principal medium; and the major participants in the controversy can be held responsible for knowing about these shortcomings and for trying to operate to counteract them. In the following chapter, we will examine the extent to which those who introduced the report to the public took realistic account of press handling of the complex and sensitive issues in first leaking and then publishing the report. In later chapters, we examine the extent to which those who opposed the report took account of the amusement-part mirror through which they saw it reflected.

In any case, with few copies of the report publicly available from which to judge its contents, those who were vitally concerned with the issue it dealt with tended to form a conception of what the report was about, what its "upshot" was that was to a greater or lesser degree not in accord with the facts. It is apparent that by the time they actually read the report many of its critics could no longer see it with fresh eyes but were instead heavily influenced by their exposure to the press coverage, particularly as this coverage tied the report to an official government "explanation" for Watts.

6

Public Statements About Sensitive Issues

We have examined Moynihan's strategy, its product, and the effect of that product within the Presidential Government, and we have analyzed the relevant press coverage from the time of the Howard University speech through the month of September. In the chapters that follow, we will describe the controversy that arose about the Moynihan Report and its central thesis. It is our view that the controversy, at least in its full public acrimony, was primarily a result of the nature of the press coverage of the report during the post-Watts time of poor communication and tenseness between the Administration and the civil rights movement. It may be useful, therefore, to pause and raise the question of how the controversy might have been avoided or greatly minimized by a different kind of public presentation of Moynihan's thesis. It is clear that the way the report's contents came across in the press did not have the kind of constructive impact that was possible and that the release of the report, which after all was prepared as an internal document, with no changes whatsoever served only to sustain and exacerbate the controversy. Perhaps by post facto analysis of how the communication might have been handled differently we can gain a better understanding of the nature of the controversy.

The Administration's public communication about the report was of two kinds: (1) there were leaks of the report to an increasing number of journalists starting in July, and (2) the report was available to the press and others in August. It is important to remember that the report was not prepared as a public document and that it was not the original intention of either its authors or of others in the government to release it. The report was released only after the controversy had begun and after Pomfret had written about it in July. The release of the report, then, was a result of leaking the report to certain reporters. That is, the pressure from the press for the release of the report could only have resulted from a prior leaking of the report so that it became widely known and so that the White House and the Department of Labor were in a poor position to maintain that it was really "for official use only." (Note that Evans and Novak in their column of August 18th, directly addressed themselves to the ambiguous status of the report as semipublic.)

Thus, the Administration initially had the option of keeping the report totally confidential, of not leaking its contents in any way. Given the controversy that in the end developed, perhaps that would have been the more constructive course. However, the motivation for the initial leaks of the report is fairly clear. Administrations are often in the position of wishing to have selective accounts of their thinking communicated by the press without revealing their views in full or being publicly tied to them. In this case, the Administration desired to show that it was doing something in connection with the problems of urban Negroes and that the Howard University speech was not simply a one-shot effort but was part of an organized strategy. Further, there was a desire to build up the importance of the forthcoming civil rights conference and to stimulate some interest and feeling of drama about it.

A very likely second motive clearly apparent in the articles of McGrory was the desire to have the Negro leadership assume more of the responsibility for the Negro community, thus coopting them as workers in the tandem for the consensus of the Great Society rather than as critics of it. After Watts, this latter motivation was probably strengthened since it would be convenient to have the civil rights leadership and Negroes more generally share the responsibility for the failure of society all too clearly communicated by the Watts rioters.

However, the way the report was handled by the Administration indicates that almost no attention was paid to the "sensitivities" of the civil rights groups and that little effort was made to avoid the appearance of waving a red flag before them. (We have no desire to justify the much discussed sensitivity of some Negro leaders on the question of family instability. In human terms, it is readily understandable; in political terms, it is a distinct liability which handicaps the flexibility and resilience of the civil rights movement. Nevertheless, it is a political reality that several individuals sought to help the White House to understand but which the Administration consistently ignored.)

The Administration was clearly aware that the report could be distorted, could be used as an excuse by whites for their own failings, yet, it apparently made minimal efforts to ensure against press reports that either contained or facilitated distortions and excuses. Apparently the process by which the report was leaked was rather lackadaisical. Certain reporters were given copies of the report and held brief conversations with one or more of the central figures involved. Minimal efforts seem to have been made to orient the reporters to the report and its implications in such a way as to avoid unconstructive results. Yet reporters are after all not too different from the general run of middle-class white Americans and share their ambivalence and conventional thinking about Negroes, including their reluctance to see the basic institutional sources of victimization and deprivation.

If one wished to make the point that family instability results from institutional sources of victimization and deprivation, then this point would have to be stressed very hard and reporters would have to be shown that there was something more to the situation than the titillating details of illegitimacy, emasculated men, and matriarchy. Yet the results in most of the press coverage suggest that this was not done. Most of the newspaper coverage played down the central role of unemployment, poverty, the wage system, and urbanization, which were Moynihan's main explanatory variables. Instead, the coverage concentrated heavily on symptoms giving a static picture as opposed to the dynamic one that Moynihan essayed.

We are left with the conclusion that the process of leaking the report was badly mishandled. Why this was so is not really clear to us. But we can suggest that there were several factors involved. Apparently, it was thought that the content of the report itself was not particularly important; rather it was the sense of drama and government concern that was important. The report was leaked because of a desire to show that there was government activity in this important area, because of a desire to create a sense of drama for the conference, and later because an explanation for Watts was needed that would satisfy the intense curiosity of the press and would have the effect of taking some of the heat off the White House.

A sympathetic observer might be tempted to conclude that the handling of the press in connection with the report was a result of ignorance rather than bad faith. However, ignorance itself is no excuse since it simply suggests how unimportant the White House thought these controversial issues to be. If the White House had seen important stakes for itself in how the press treatment developed, one can be sure that the staff would have been more energetic in guiding that press treatment. One need only think of the effort that goes into the handling of the press in connection with Vietnam, or the budget, or the question of a tax increase to be aware of the tremendous contrast. This greater effort at "managing the news" could have taken place either in July or early August before a controversy was apparent or, failing that, in late August or September when there could have been no doubt that the press coverage was making real trouble.

These issues are even more clear-cut when one considers the question of the decision to release the Moynihan Report itself. Granted that the report was released in response to pressure generated by leaks, one can still raise the question of why the original report was released at all. After all, the government now went on record in a formal, historically accountable way with a document which had been prepared solely as a basis for information and discussion within the government. Because the White House, and specifically the President, had become so closely identified with the report, they were committed to its style and content as a public document. Because the report bore the imprint of the Department of Labor, that department was committed in the same way. Yet apparently neither group was very happy about taking the responsibility for the report or its release; each seemed to want to leave it up to the other and to ignore the importance of a decision that was eventually to result in the government printing over 70,000 copies of a document which its author thought he was writing for fewer than 100 persons. Thus, though originally the White House had been anxious to identify the report as its own product (telling the press that the report was the result of the work of "a White House study group"), in the end the Department of Labor was left uncomfortably holding the bag.

This did not have to be. There was the possibility of issuing a different, reworked report that would have provided a better public face for Moynihan's thesis. This could have been done either in the form of a rather fully reworked document issued by the White House as background to better understanding the Howard University speech or as a more modest revision issued by the Department of Labor. Either one of these alternatives could have been accomplished with three or four days of hard work by available personnel.

The skeleton for such a document was already provided by the original report; modifications could have been readily put together from Moynihan's own drafts of documents for public release. There was Moynihan's *Daedalus* article, which avoided many of the pitfalls of the report; there were in addition drafts of most of the articles in the two subsequent *Daedalus* volumes on the Negro American, which could have been drawn on for ideas, data, and points of view. We think particularly of the article by St. Clair Drake, which follows Moynihan's in *Daedalus*. Drake copes with some of the complexities of the vicious circle with which Moynihan dealt by introducing the terms *direct* and *indirect* victimization:

> *Direct victimization* might be defined as the operation of sanctions which deny access to power, which limit the franchise, sustain job discrimination, permit unequal pay for similar work, or provide inferior training or no training at all. *Indirect victimization* is revealed in the consequences which flow from a social structure which decreases *"life chances,"* such as a high morbidity and mortality rates, low longevity rates, a high incidence of psychopathology, or the persistence of personality traits and attitudes which impose disadvantages in competition or excite derogatory and invidious comparisons with other groups.*

Further, in August Moynihan had completed his article dealing with Watts and unemployment and the *America* article on family policy. In addition, while in the government he had prepared

---

* St. Clair Drake, "The Social and Economic Status of the Negro." *Daedalus*, Vol. 94, No. 4 (Fall 1965).

certain manuscripts for public presentation of his thesis which would have been available for reworking the report.

Not only that, several experienced persons thoroughly familiar with Moynihan's ideas were available should the Administration have made a decision to produce a revised document for the public; most important among them were Richard Goodwin and Paul Barton as well as Moynihan himself.

Again, we must assume that the issue simply did not seem important enough to either the White House or the Department of Labor to go to the trouble of reworking the report. From the point of view of the White House, so long as the report was issued by the Department of Labor it seemed possible, and to some extent proved to be, to disassociate itself from the report if the controversy destroyed its usefulness. As we will discuss in somewhat more detail in Chapter 10, Moynihan and his report were considered expendable. ·

But let us assume that it could have been otherwise and ask the question, "What modifications of the report would have been necessary for a public document that would have (1) supported Moynihan's policy goals, (2) provided a more solid intellectual background for the President's Howard University speech, (3) served as a basic orientation to those parts of the coming White House conference dealing with problems of urban Negroes, and (4) represented a statement about the reality of Negro life in American society that the civil rights movement (given its own organizational needs and concerns) could live with and use as a basis for antagonistic cooperation with the government to develop more effective social and economic programs?"

First, we can get out of the way some of the minor stylistic factors in the original document which might have been edited out for a more public one. In his writing, Moynihan uses the word "fundamental" quite frequently as a more emphatic way of saying "important." In his report, he used this word four times — family structure is "the fundamental problem"; the deterioration of the Negro family is "the fundamental source of weakness of the Negro community"; the reversal of roles of husbands and wives is a "fundamental fact" of Negro family life; but also, "the fundamental, overwhelming fact is that Negro unemployment . . . has continued at disaster levels for 35 years." This set of "fundamental" quotations about the family was widely quoted and appear as much more accusatory in short press articles than in the report itself; the adjective could well have been avoided in a public document. Another example is the use of the word "failure." It is very easy to speak of "the failure of" Negroes — men, youth, and so on — to accomplish one or another kind of goal or skill that is important for successful adaptation to American society as it exists. Yet, in this context failure has the unfortunate connotation of individual responsibility rather than being a simple descriptive adjective. In both of these cases as in others, if one wishes to communicate the destructive consequences of institutions such as those of employment, education, community services, and the like these individual responsibility connotations of failure represent an interference.

In general, an editing of the report in terms of stylistic factors would have reduced some of the dramatic language in connection with less important issues like slavery and reconstruction while retaining it for the more important ones such as unemployment and poverty. This would have been a hedge against the tendency of journalists to pick up the more lively and dramatic language for direct quotes.

These are probably relatively minor issues, however, and there are more important ones to be considered. Moynihan's juxtaposition of the themes of liberty and equality does a great deal to clarify the shifting goals of the civil rights movement and to point up the inadequacies of the dominant legalistic approach to civil rights issues. However, in the public document the emphasis on a "next stage in the civil rights struggle" that would be directed not so much at combating discrimination as to providing social and economic resources, would have had to be handled in such a way as not to undercut the important and continuing civil rights efforts to deal with the reality of discrimination both in the South and in the North. In the original document, Moynihan pointed out in passing that Negroes would continue to experience discrimination for some time, but he did not stress this point because he wished to make a different one. A public report, however, would need to emphasize very strongly that there was no necessary contradiction between efforts to end discrimination and to increase socioeconomic resources but rather that the two strategies strengthened each other.

Next, a public report would have needed some statement explaining why the concept of family stability and welfare could be useful as a central reference point in evaluating society's workings with reference to Negroes and the effectiveness of present and potential government programs to redress the dis-advantages Negroes suffer. Such a statement was already avail-able from Moynihan's speech at the University of California conference on poverty in America (see pages 20–21). A clear state-ment that a focus on the family allowed one to evaluate the performance of the total society would have done much to reduce the impression that the original report "blamed" the family for the Negroes' disadvantaged situation. In this context it would also have been possible to point out that the adequacy of families to the task of socialization is crucial to the achieve-ment of equality, without seeming to point the finger of blame at Negro families rather than white society.

Moynihan sought at two points in his original report to remind his readers that one segment of Negro Americans, the middle-class segment, was experiencing progress and that his discussion of family instability and pathology did not characterize this seg-ment. However, in the public report these statements would have needed to be even more strongly emphasized in order to mini-mize the tendency to see the report as characterizing all of Negro life. Moynihan was aware of this need; thus, in a draft of a document he had prepared for a public audience, he had prefaced his discussion with a detailing of some of the areas in which there had been gains for more fortunately situated Negroes: in education, nonwhite professional employment, and the rate of increase in wages and salaries.

Buttressing this emphasis on differentiation within the Negro community with one segment experiencing gains and the other either absolute or relative losses, it would have been possible to devote somewhat more attention to variations in family sta-bility by socioeconomic level within the Negro community.

In the public version of the report, it would have been well to reduce the discussion of illegitimacy because of the inflam-matory nature of the issue with its inevitable overtones of immorality. For example, in one document Moynihan had avoided the use of the word illegitimacy and instead had referred to the fact that an increasing number of Negro children came into the world with "no fathers." In his *Daedalus* article, he had bypassed the question of illegitimacy almost entirely by dealing with the data in only two sentences of the article. Yet, while a complete omission in a revised document of any mention of the fact that over one third of the Negro children in the more disadvantaged segments of the community are illegitimate might have avoided some criticism, the issue was much too important simply to be swept under the rug. A careful treatment of the illegitimacy data might have strengthened the document and at the same time avoided the sensational uses to which the illegitimacy sections of the original report were put.

Probably more important than any other revision would have been a reorganization of the "roots-of-the-problem" section of the report so that it would begin with the current sources of Negro socioeconomic disadvantage and relegate the discussion of slavery and reconstruction to a note on historical background. In his version of the report which Moynihan himself prepared for publication — the *Daedalus* article — the emphasis on employment was central to the argument he built. Thus, immediately after discussing the twin ideals of liberty and equality, Moynihan wrote,

From the very outset, the principal measure of progress toward equality will be that of employment. . . . For the Negro American it is already, and will continue to be, the master problem. It is the measure of white *bona fides*. It is the measure of Negro competence, and also of the competence of American society. Most importantly, the linkage between problems of employment and the range of social pathology that afflicts the Negro community is unmistakable. Unemployment not only controls the present for the Negro American; but in a most profound way, it is creating the future as well.

In short, a "roots-of-the-problem" section that moved from the present back into the past would have been most likely to avoid some of the distortions apparent in the press treatment of the original report.

Such an emphasis would have kept the focus where it belonged, that is, on the current operation of institutional forces which prevent Negroes from achieving equality, and would have highlighted the policy implications that Moynihan had in mind.

In this connection, it probably would have been necessary to forgo the point that so intrigued Moynihan in his *Daedalus* article: whether or not the direct link between economic opportunities (as measured by the ups and downs of the employment rate) and family stability has become attenuated. While it may be appropriate in a journal like *Daedalus,* directed primarily at an intellectual audience, to raise the question of whether or not various kinds of family and community disorganization are immediately responsive to changes in the economic situation, such a query would tend to vitiate the burden of the main

argument Moynihan sought to advance in the report. (It is interesting that in the report itself, prepared for policy-oriented presidential executives, Moynihan devoted much less attention to this
issue than he did in the *Daedalus* piece prepared for a less
action-oriented audience.) In the long run, the issue that Moynihan raised is one that requires a careful and thorough sifting of
the facts, which apparently are not now readily available, before the true situation and its policy implications can be
determined.

Although too sanguine a version of the adaptive functions of
the "matriarchal family" would hardly have assisted in building public support for more effective federal policy to strengthen
the Negro family, a revised report might well have taken account
of the ability of some matrifocal families to withstand the pressures of the world around them and also have noted that until
the socioeconomic situation in which poor Negroes find themselves changes, matrifocality is a necessary, perhaps inevitable,
adaptation.

Finally, a public report would have been much strengthened
had it included a discussion of some of the policy implications of
the facts present, as Herbert Gans has observed in his *Commonweal* article (see pages 445–457). While the Administration may
not have wished to have to commit itself to concrete programs,
a general discussion of the direction in which the report's findings pointed would have helped to allay the anxieties of those
who feared that the report would lead to an emphasis on psychiatric social work and family-life education approaches. (We
can find no evidence that at any time anyone in the Administration thought of the report as implying this.) Because of their
generality, the implications that Moynihan himself communicated to the White House could have been presented in the revised report without in any way prematurely committing the
Administration to specific programs. Indeed, the Howard University speech had suggested most of them. From various materials that Moynihan had prepared for public presentation
it would have been possible to produce a concluding section
which indicated that the current plight of Negro Americans was
the result of a whole series of national actions which had
been allowed, consciously or otherwise, to work their effects on
Negro Americans — the national policy first of permitting slavery and later of acquiescing in segregation and discrimination,
of accepting levels of unemployment that are all but unknown

in other industrial democracies and of allowing a rapid urbanization of the Negro population without developing programs to cope with the attendant problems. From this analysis of the situation the general outlines of the solution follow quite directly — programs must be developed that provide for employment, more effective income maintenance, housing of better quality and more integrated housing, family planning, and so on. (If the White House was nervous about committing itself to programs it was not sure it could deliver, there would certainly have been nothing unusual in a Department of Labor document that argued along the lines just suggested.)

Such a report would probably not have elicited universal praise from those who in the end criticized the actual report. However, a revised report along these lines probably would not have precipitated a public controversy such as did in fact develop, nor would it have destroyed Moynihan's thesis (as embodied in the Howard University speech) as a platform from which the Administration could argue for concrete programs. There would have instead been enthusiastic support from some parts of the civil rights movement, grumbling and indifference from others, or a grudging willingness to use such a revised report as authority for negotiation with the Adminstration about a variety of programs (much as Benjamin Payton sought to use the Howard University speech before its close connection with the Moynihan Report made that impossible — see pages 233–244).

Such could have been the response of the Administration to the need in the summer of 1965 for some public airing of the issues that Moynihan raised, or to a later need for a statement of Moynihan's argument that would not sustain a needless controversy. This, of course, is relevant only if one assumes that the Administration's interests were not served by the controversy; we have suggested earlier and will argue in later sections that at least some of the needs of the Administration were well served by the controversy and that therefore there was little incentive for a careful handling of the original document. As events evolved through the balance of 1965 and into 1966, however, the question of whether or not a suitable public version of the report was communicated became increasingly irrelevant as the Adminstration's energies shifted from domestic programs to perfect a Great Society to programs for an Asian war, with attendant preoccupations with domestic inflation, labor shortages, and the like.

7

Opposition in the Permanent Government

Arthur Schlesinger, Jr., has identified four branches of government — the Legislative and Judicial plus the Executive branch which Schlesinger says must be broken into "Permanent Government" and the "Presidential Government." Much has been written about the tension between the "Permanent Government," made up of the thousands of career civil servants who are Washington's permanent residents, and the "Presidential Government," made up of the President and his appointees.* The tension between these two branches of the administration is perhaps inherent in any government in which the lower civil servants remain in their jobs through changes of administration.

The changing policies of new adminstrations must be carried out by the permanent bureaucracy, which often has a vested interest in maintaining the existing programs. Reinterpretation and dilution of policy, lack of implementation, as well as a general stagnation and conservatism in the Permanent Government are

* Arthur Schlesinger, Jr., *One Thousand Days* (Boston: Houghton Mifflin, 1965).

frequent complaints of the Presidential Government. Bureaucracy may be effective in the sense that specific rules are followed as it carries out its task, but it becomes pathological when these rules take on meanings that are independent of their functions toward organizational goals. Undoubtedly, one of the stronger, although implicit, rules in the civil service is that one should not directly criticize his presidentially appointed superiors. When this rule is carried to its extreme, it results in the suppression of complaints and criticism and leads to inefficiency.

The tensions between the Permanent Government and the Presidential Government were made manifest when the Moynihan Report began to take shape. In fact, there is little question that the first uneasiness toward, indeed criticisms of, the Moynihan Report occurred within the government (in fact, in the Department of Labor) rather than in the civil rights movement or among social scientists.

Opposition in the Labor Department

Moynihan, it will be remembered, was brought into the Department of Labor with the "New Frontier" as a special assistant to Secretary of Labor Goldberg. With Goldberg's move to the Supreme Court and Willard Wirtz's appointment as Secretary of Labor, Moynihan was given a presidential appointment as Assistant Secretary of Labor heading the Office of Policy Planning and Research. Moynihan was the first head of the Office of Policy Planning and Research, an office that was created at the same time he was appointed Assistant Secretary of Labor (he was the youngest assistant secretary in the government). The Office produced several policy papers like *The Negro Family* dealing with matters that were not routine issues of Department of Labor functioning, as well as others more directly related to its ongoing programs.

With the decision to write this specific report, Moynihan also made some decisions regarding the kinds of hypotheses and questions he wanted to explore in the research. He began the work by simply requesting that persons on his staff and in the Bureau of Labor Statistics obtain certain types of data for him. It takes little experience with empirical data to perceive the kinds of conclusions and assumptions that are involved in a piece of research from looking at the specification of questions. The people providing Moynihan's data were experts in the collection and analysis of statistical data. No doubt some of them knew more about the techniques and the quality of data that Moynihan was using than he did himself. When Moynihan asked for figures, for example, on the rate of illegitimacy or broken families among Negroes it was relatively easy for all the staff assistants to imagine the nature of the conclusions that were being drawn.

We have been told by one member of the Permanent Government that "Moynihan's use of the figures was criticized by people who worked it up for him, and he knew this." Thus the uneasiness about the report began even before it was written. The published report no doubt verified many of the early suspicions held by members of the Permanent Government. Many outsiders have referred us to Labor Department civil servants for information about what is wrong with the report.

The criticisms these experts made of the report's treatment of data were not that the data as such were inaccurate but rather that the selection of data was not in accord with their understanding of the situation. Thus, they felt Moynihan did not include enough comparisons with whites using economic and educational controls, that he did not include data contradicting his conclusions, and that the conclusions themselves were overly dramatic and not cautious enough. This is a common difference of perspective between presidential appointees and the Permanent Government. The technicians of the latter often argue against the phrasing of policy documents, and the presidential appointees reply that they have the political charter to make such judgments and decisions, not the career functionaries. Moynihan made a conscious *political* judgment to deal exhaustively with the respects in which the Negro situation was getting worse, not better, because he felt the Administration should be informed of the dangers inherent in the social transformation taking place, with Negro expectations rising faster than improvement in actual conditions.

It should be noted that there were senior members of the Permanent Government who supported Moynihan's analysis as both scientifically adequate and politically relevant. Two important facts about them should be noted, however. First, none of these experts were brought into the various planning activities abortively initiated during the summer of 1965; in short, the potential Permanent Government support for the thesis was not mobilized. Second, once the controversy reached public proportions these experts felt no further constructive purpose could be served by supporting the report; from their point of view the controversy precluded using the report as a basis for stimulating sensible over-all policy planning on domestic issues or a break with previous bureaucratic rigidities which limited such over-all planning.

The problem of bureaucratic authority and change was further exacerbated. Moynihan was using data in a manner that his subordinates believed was inappropriate, but these civil servants could do little more than indicate to their superior what they felt to be the limitations of the research. More blatant criticism, or going around Moynihan to someone with greater authority, would be unheard of and could well cost them their jobs once the report became government policy.

Therefore, one can see the problem for the civil servants who feel they have legitimate criticisms of a policy paper such as the Moynihan Report, but who are in a position in which it is impossible for them to directly and effectively criticize the report. They see the document as one having real potential for affecting national policy—and this was verified for them by the President's use of the report in the Howard University speech— but even though they may be qualified critics they are unable to use a direct and open route to voice their criticisms.

Solutions to this dilemma, which is intense for those civil servants who are concerned about the consequences of their work, must take more subtle forms. Their concern with direct criticisms is indicated by the fact that even though many of the Permanent Government people we interviewed were critical of the report, many were very explicit in saying their criticisms must be kept off the record — Moynihan was an official of the Department of Labor and it would be inappropriate for them to criticize his work. We should bear in mind that these interviews took place more than five months after Moynihan had resigned from the department.

In the case of the Moynihan Report, three strategies were used by the Permanent Government to solve their problems with respect to criticizing the report and defending their interest in maintaining present administrative programs in the areas of labor, civil rights, and poverty. One of these is that of writing an independent or separate document which clearly contradicts the report but is not a direct polemic. [For example, Moynihan is mentioned in the body of only one of five papers generally considered relevant to the controversy.) The second strategy is that of going outside of the government and obtaining support from more autonomous people who may criticize the report with impunity. The third and most widespread strategy involves conversation, rumors, and verbal analysis communicated where it will do the most good.

Getting "The Word"

It was in this latter way, through informal communication networks, that "the word" first went out about the report. Like any major organization, but writ large, a great deal of the important communication in Washington takes place through informal channels — through hall talks at meetings, at lunch, chitchat on the telephone, and parties and dinners of all kinds. For example, one member of the Permanent Government told us how he had heard from "the chief of my division that, 'Now the Negro family is becoming disintegrated.' I got him to borrow a copy of the report. Only through the pressure of one of his staff members, me, was he pushed to read the report." Because of the numbers of people and status levels involved these networks are highly variegated, but there are enough linkages that if something is really important it moves from one informal network to another.

In the case of the Moynihan Report and the building controversy, there were two large groups of people involved, each making up somewhat independent networks. One was the network of the welfare establishments including most particularly persons in the Departments of Labor, Health, Education, and Welfare, and the Office of Economic Opportunity. In addition, there was the network of people involved in civil rights, a smaller somewhat more intensely interacting group. The overlap between these networks was such that over the summer and early fall the somewhat different (and at times conflicting) objections to the report were readily communicated back and forth, reinforcing each other.

Communication in the informal network performs the function of combining "inside dope" with whatever is being said in the newspapers. The nature of word-of-mouth communication tends to round out, smooth out, and sharpen whatever subject is being bruited about. The Moynihan Report qualified as an exciting subject for a number of reasons. First of all, the Howard University Speech by itself was an important topic of conversation. Whenever the President makes a speech, those in the government with whose bailiwick he seemed to have been dealing must start thinking to themselves, "What are the implications of the speech for me, for my responsibilities? What was he really trying to say, what's behind it all?" (Moynihan: "The president has the power to bless; if he talks about a subject he can make it respectable for discussion.") The Howard University speech was obviously a major presidential utterance but it did not go in any straightforward way to programs that were well-established or to prospective ones that had been fully discussed and described. The speech could bode well or ill for almost any kind of civil rights or welfare program. The fact that the President himself indicated that the government did not know all of the answers and therefore was calling a White House Conference suggested that the programmatic implications of the speech were very much up in the air.

Another illustration of the power of presidential utterance will perhaps clarify this point. In his State of the Union Message of 1964, the President had included one sentence dealing with the necessity for more government action in the area of international and domestic population policy. On the basis of that one sentence, public servants concerned with population matters in a wide range of government agencies (from the State Department and AID to the Welfare Administration and NIH) took heart and began to probe more vigorously the limits of what the government might be able to do. Similarly, private groups outside the government also began to approach the government with more optimism and confidence about the possibility of getting government action. This presumably was exactly what the President wanted; he did not want to offer a program from his office, but he wanted the government to become more active in this field. As part of the rumor market in the population and family-planning network, it also became "common knowledge" that HEW Secretary Celebrezze was a major bottle-neck in getting more effective government action in this area. The combination of the President's statements and the renewed vigor of a wide range of Permanent Government subordinates in his department made the Secretary's position a very ticklish one.

What then, was "the word" about the Moynihan Report? Very shortly after the President's speech there was apparently a good

deal of conversation in the cocktail circuit to the effect that the
Moynihan Report provided "the real story" for what the President was trying to get at. Thus one government official, who
could well have believed that he was entitled to receive a copy
of this confidential report, told us, "Late in June all sorts of people started telling me that in order to really understand the
President's Howard speech you had to have read the Moynihan
Report and that it was a very powerful document. So I began
to wonder what is in this Moynihan Report?" The conversation
about the report in connection with the speech emphasized that
the White House was being very much influenced by it, that it
was not an ordinary civil rights document but pointed in the
direction of big changes of an unspecified kind.

As some of the reactions to the report also began to spread
through the circuit, insiders heard more and more about shortcomings. The word went around that it was technically poor,
that it had not been properly respectful of all of the available
data, and most specifically that even specialists in Moynihan's
own Department of Labor took exception to it. The upshot of
this kind of talk, that is, that the report was technically incorrect, apparently moved into knowledgeable civil rights circles
and was very willingly received there because of some of the
other concerns that civil rights people had.

In the civil rights network, there was less concern with the
report's adequacy technically or with the emphasis on crisis and
the need for a major change in government civil rights activity
(after all, that was what civil rights people wanted). There was,
however, considerable nervousness concerning the emphasis on
the Negro family and fear that this might be used, or might
merely seem likely to be used and therefore create controversy,
to blame Negroes for their own problems and to emphasize
dead-end self-help programs. There was also the fear that the
report might lead to programs designed to deal directly with
family problems rather than to more basic changes in discriminatory patterns or socioeconomic deprivation. *The fact that for
as much as two months this report was not available to key
people in the civil rights network served to heighten their
anxieties.*

Finally, a more ominous and directly personal note crept into
the bundle of ideas that became "the word." While none of
those who published criticism of the report said so, others were
willing to suggest that Moynihan was really "anti-Negro," a

"subtle racist," an apologist for the white power structure and so on. He seemed to fit the specifications for the newest villain of the civil rights movement, "the white liberal." As the controversy spread outside of the government, this view gained ground, particularly among those who did not know Moynihan and those most unsympathetic to his emphasis on socioeconomic rather than antidiscrimination measures. The fact that Moynihan had had few contacts over the years with the civil rights movement, being identified more with the Democratic party politics, made such attributions easy—he was unknown quantity to many of those most directly involved in the issues about which he had written.

The poor reputation the report began to earn in the informal communication network played into a number of organizational concerns and anxieties always present in a large government establishment where one program's bonanza can well mean starvation for another. Probably most central here was the fact that the report was clearly a document of the Presidential Government. It had been written for the White House and seemed to be available only to those with good connections with the Presidential Government. As such it was bureaucratically a "wild" report in that minimum control had been exercised to avoid stepping on the toes of the various departments concerned with the issues it raised. The Permanent Government reaction was in a sense instinctive; whatever the report said, it was said by an "outsider" who could not be expected to pay attention to the organizational requirements of the Permanent Government.

Since Kennedy's election, the Permanent Government had on numerous occasions been confronted with situations in which outsiders, either members of the Presidential Government or not even government people at all, seemed to be exercising considerably more influence on public affairs than those charged with government responsibility. Men with ideas of their own and with no bureaucratic loyalties had over the past five years increasingly put pressure on Permanent Government establishments to change their ways or their programs. In the general welfare area, the Office of Economic Opportunity was one result of this kind of ferment but it had now become a part of the Permanent Government itself.

The social science orientation of the report was perhaps important in this respect. Social scientists of all fields had found the government more and more open to at least listening to their ideas since Kennedy's election. Career government people often find themselves in the position of having these outsiders' views presented to them as authoritative when in fact they feel themselves both better informed and more experienced at dealing with the issues involved. While most social scientists who deal with the government have their primary relationships with members of the Permanent Government, an increasing number have established liaisons at higher levels than that or with those few Permanent Government officials who are more often found in the company of Presidential Government types than of their own kind.

Social scientists who have ideas to which they are strongly committed and which they wish to have the government adopt often find Permanent Government people overly cautious and conservative. For example, two of our informants, themselves rather anti-Moynihan Report, nevertheless described the anti-Moynihan segments of the Permanent Government with which they had dealt as "rather stodgy outfits." Though they did not like what Moynihan had written, they were in complete sympathy with his effort to shake up the bureaucracy. Another social scientist with a rather radical innovation he wished to persuade the government to adopt, commented that he was amazed at how easy it was to meet with cabinet officers and White House staff members to present his ideas and how open and willing to listen he found them.

The Kennedy years seemed to have begun the institutionalization of a kind of ready access for academic social scientists to higher levels of the federal government. The Permanent Government as an institution could not help but feel downgraded by this since until recently it had served as the main channel of communication between the social sciences and the top levels of government.

The welfare establishment was perhaps put on a spot by the Moynihan Report more than any other segment of the federal government. The report and the Howard University speech contained implicit criticisms of the way social welfare operates in the United States. In other writings and in speeches, Moynihan had made much more explicit criticisms along this line, and presumably his views were known to at least some of the persons involved in the informal communication networks. The welfare establishment is in a very difficult position because on the one hand it knows better than anyone else in the country how inadequate the national social welfare program is, and on the other hand it is charged with the responsibility for carrying it out and defending it against political attacks as either too much or too little. It is always in the position of maintaining, "Well things are bad, but they could be worse," and it is very easy when put on the defensive to shift this to the line, "Well things aren't so bad, look how far we've come." Moynihan's critique instead took the line, "Things are extremely bad, and it is inexcusable that we haven't done something about them."

In general, the welfare establishment's orientation to improvement tends to be that of perfecting existing programs so that they do a somewhat better job. The Presidential Government and the outside "experts" have the option of saying that the programs are inherently inadequate to the tasks with which they are supposed to deal. This was the not-so-hidden message Moynihan communicated in his report, that existing federal programs in labor and in welfare were inadequate to deal with the problems of urban Negroes and that new programs must be developed.

The welfare establishment is in an even more difficult position when it comes to civil rights issues. For years it has acquiesced to subtle and blatant discrimination and inadequate labor and welfare services to Negroes. While the ultimate responsibility for the patterns that exist lies at the higher levels of government, the operating levels are often left holding the bag and in their tight situation are inclined to minimize the extent of discriminatory treatment rather than own up to it and place the responsibility where it belongs.

Over many years, one of the most important ways of coping with this difficult situation has been to try to fuzz it over. Under the guise of civil libertarian reasoning, welfare organizations, both national and local, have tried to "wish away" race as a catagory; this has had the latent function of concealing the extent to which discrimination continues. One of the early civil rights activities of the Kennedy Administration was to try to reverse this trend so that at least the government could be informed about the extent to which Negroes were disadvantaged. Having this "color blind" point of view built into their ideology, it was relatively easy for welfare personnel to find Moynihan's intransigent emphasis on color reactionary rather than radical.

Part and parcel of this color-blindness is the general tendency of the welfare establishment to try to conduct "public relations" for the poor, the disadvantaged, and the victimized. Since they are not allowed to protect the interests of these people, at least they can protect their good name. But again one of the consequences of protecting the good name of the poor and disadvantaged is to gloss over the nature of their plight. Moynihan wanted his statistics to "bleed." The Permanent Government ideology avoids blood in order to save the reputation of those with whose welfare they are charged. The main villain often becomes the "stereotype" rather than the depriving life circumstance.

Thus, by its very existence as well as its contents Moynihan's report on *The Negro Family: The Case for National Action* seemed an attack on the adequacy of the welfare establishment's approach to Negro problems — its implicit message was that they had not cared enough even to really understand the problem. One Welfare Administration worker, commenting on HEW criticism, told us, "It's just that they're ashamed because they know they should have written it themselves."

As we will note later in somewhat greater detail, good public relations for Negroes which serves these latent functions for the welfare bureaucracy also meshes nicely with some of the needs of those in the civil rights area who are concerned to avoid the labels of "weak" or "pathological" or "unstable," not so much to preserve the good name of Negroes as to emphasize their power. Thus, in the case of the Moynihan Report the strategies of the two groups meshed but for quite different reasons—for the welfare establishment the report was too "alarmist," for the civil rights groups it was too "optimistic."

Finally, it should be noted that the Moynihan controversy developed in these ways through the informal communication channels of the government and out into the larger community of those who have to do with the government *because no effective counter-pressures were brought to bear by the Presidential Government.* Moynihan had left the government, was involved in a political campaign, and did not bring counter-pressure to bear. The White House was not involved in any initiatives that might have affected the growing controversy — either by dealing with it directly or by planning activities which would point out the particular direction it planned to go and therefore cut down on the speculation. The bureaucracies themselves were incapable of solving the problem. The welfare establishment was hamstrung by its history and by the necessity to defend existing programs, and the civil rights bureaucracy had expertise only in the legalistic approach to civil rights problems (although a few of its members were beginning to seriously explore the need for a shift to an approach that seeks to get at the basic institutional sources of the ghetto system).

Carrying the Criticism Outside

A second strategy used to solve the dilemma faced by members of the Permanent Government in disagreeing with the Presidential Government is that of going outside the government, frequently to the faculties of universities, and soliciting critiques. A close connection between the university and government has been specified by many writers who point to the constant interchange of personnel between Washington and the academic community. These official exchanges between the university campus and the government are of importance because they form the basis for informal networks that develop between the government and the campus.

Members of the academic community work informally with policy makers and seek to influence policy. Information on the Moynihan controversy shows that persons (the policy makers of the Presidential Government and members of the Permanent Government) call on members of the academy when problems such as "what to do about the Moynihan Report" occur. There is little question that a great deal of advice and information is exchanged, and while this affects policy decisions, these informal networks get little recognition. This is no doubt due to the fact that they are informal, and as we have found, they are extremely difficult to specify.

When a member of the Permanent Government wishes to criticize a report such as that written by Moynihan he may activate these informal networks by sending a summary of the report to his friends in the academy. During our interviews in Washington we were shown letters by university faculty criticizing the Moynihan Report. It appears that these letters were solicited by members of the Permanent Government, who had sent copies of the report to university faculty in order to obtain criticisms and who then used these letters within their bureaus as authority for rejecting the validity of the report.

Another indication of the use of the university by the Permanent Government is the nature of our interviews with the Permanent Government. These interviews resulted in our obtaining a great deal of statistical information on the Negro

American which we were told could be used in criticizing the Moynihan Report. In other words, we were given the statistics in order better to criticize the report in an "objective" or empirical manner. By making these statistics available to us it was assumed that our conclusions would result in statements critical of the report. Thus one civil servant, in a position which made it impossible for him to directly criticize the report, was asked what government people do when they are dissatisfied with a policy document but cannot publicly criticize it. After offering government data he felt cast doubt on the report, he replied: "Well, the only thing we can do is talk to people — we are not in a position to criticize him directly — and so it's up to you who are on the outside of the government, who have access to scholarly journals, to criticize the report."

The Permanent Government, and no doubt others, believe that policy papers written by the Administration are laden with values to the extent that they are no longer objective or scientific and therefore are not a valid basis for policy decisions. On the other hand, social scientists in the academy — unlike the policy makers — are thought to be objective and "value-free." Because of both their autonomy and the "myth of the objective scientist" the social scientist possesses a kind of power when he presents his "facts." The problem is that there are no "facts" in the sense of true descriptions of the world. As Gunnar Myrdal has pointed out, facts, as we know them in the social sciences are simply weak indexes of reality. Social scientists, as much as government administrators, attach differential significance and meanings to these "facts." The myth of the objective social scientist gives him more power than he would otherwise have. But it *is* a myth. Social science is, indeed, a "political" science.* And it is clear that the Permanent Government went to social scientists in the academy in order to use this leverage to support their interest in maintaining present or hoped-for administrative programs they felt the report challenged.

The Content of the Permanent Government Criticism

It is difficult to determine with any exactness the kinds of criticisms that were made of the report by this group during the summer and early fall. However, after it became clear later in

* Gunnar Myrdal, *An American Dilemma* (New York and London: Harper and Row, 1944).

the fall that the White House was not going to insist on the Moynihan thesis nor severely sanction reasonable criticism of it several public servants wrote documents which were made public or made speeches that seem to incorporate the main elements of the earlier, verbally communicated criticisms. We will examine these public statements as an approximation of the Permanent Government opposition.

Because we are not in a position to know in detail the kinds of criticisms leveled against the report during the summer of 1965, we fall back on these documents as a close approximation of those criticisms. In justice to their authors, it should be noted that these documents were published much later than the summer and that they do not represent a consciously formulated attempt or "plot" to discredit the report. At least one (by Myron J. Lefcowitz) was written without any cognizance of the Moynihan controversy; yet it too has been widely assumed by critics to be an attack on the report. However, quite aside from the fact that all of the authors were in a position to have heard Permanent Government criticism of the report during the summer and therefore to have taken it into account in the development of their own individual thinking about the issues the report raised, the documents have been considered by those unsympathetic to the report as attacks on it and from that point of view have become part of the anti-Moynihan literature.

There are at least five documents, all of which were written by government officials, that take issue with the Moynihan thesis with varying degrees of directness. In two of these papers, Moynihan is relegated to footnotes. Most of the papers or their content were made available at the White House Planning Conference; they were written and published during the height of the controversy; and the questions they raised are central to Moynihan's thesis.

The content of the papers varied considerably. Dorothy Newman's "Economic Status of the Negro," an agenda paper for the conference, largely consisted of a survey and summary of the statistical data that were relevant to the Moynihan argument and available to her in the Bureau of Labor Statistics. The paper by Myron J. Lefcowitz of the Office of Economic Opportunity, "Poverty and Negro-White Family Structures," compares the two racial groups while attempting to hold income constant. Elizabeth Herzog's "Is There a Breakdown in the Negro Family" (*Social Work*, February 1966) asks the question of whether or

not the "alarmist" tone of the Moynihan Report is justified and
to what degree the data in the Moynihan Report reflect racial
or economic characteristics. A speech by Mary Keyserling (of
the Woman's Bureau of the Department of Labor) to the Conference of the National Council of Negro Women criticizes the
report from the point of view of the Negro woman. Hylan
Lewis' agenda paper for the White House Conference largely
incorporates many arguments found in the other documents. We
will discuss the Lewis paper in more detail in Chapter 10.

Major Questions Raised by the Permanent Government

There are several major questions that were raised about the
Moynihan Report by the Permanent Government, both in these
papers and in our interviews and written communications with
members of the Permanent Government. While each of these
papers tends to emphasize a given question about the Moynihan
thesis, there is considerable overlap among these papers as
well as among the views expressed by critics in our interviews.

The main criticism of the Moynihan Report raised by members of the Permanent Government was that it was oversimplified. It is clear that Moynihan had written a very pointed argument and had not emphasized data that would reduce the impact
of his thesis. This critique took two forms. First it was said
that one cannot talk about "The Negro Family" as if it were a
completely homogeneous institution. There are great differences
among families both within and between social class. As Hylan
Lewis wrote in the agenda paper, "The family and family behavior among Negroes show great range and variability; especially overlooked and underrated is the diversity among low-
income Negro families. When these are overlooked for any
reason, there is danger that the depreciated, and probably more
dramatic and threatening, characteristics of a small segment
of the population may be imputed to an entire population."
This is indeed what Moynihan had done — emphasized dramatic and negative characteristics and as such had de-empha-
sized the differences existing within the Negro community.

The second aspect of the "oversimplified" criticism of the
report can be seen in such statements made to us as "Moynihan
refused to look at some data that were available to him." Indeed, the Permanent Government criticisms of the report seem
to say that Moynihan had data available to him that would

have reduced the drama of his argument but would have made it more correct. Reading these papers, one is left with the message that there are complications in the statistical data on economic status, urban and rural migration, educational level, and employment rates, such that it is extremely difficult to generalize about the Negro community, much less the family.

In addition to data that would have complicated the thesis considerably had Moynihan included them in the report, the critics felt there were also indications that the alarmist interpretation of "rapid deterioration" was quite inappropriate. While there was no denying that the nonwhite employment rate had continued to be much larger than the white unemployment rate, Dorothy Newman wrote that "gains in employment of non-white workers have occurred in the fields from which they have tended to be excluded, such as professional and technical jobs, the crafts, and sales and clerical occupations. The increases since 1961 were much greater than any three-year interval since 1954." In terms of income distributions again the criticism was that Moynihan had oversimplified the argument and that unlike what Moynihan reported, "The summary distributions and ratios reveal that there is, in fact, a gap, but that it has declined recently. For the rest, they tend to be misleading and certainly are not analytical enough for use in policy making." Newman then pointed out that while nationally Negro family income was about 55 percent of white in 1964, there was considerable regional variation in this ratio: in the North and West it was about 70 percent, while in the South it was less than 50 percent. In rural areas it is even lower — dropping to below 40 percent.

A similar argument was raised by Elizabeth Herzog and Hylan Lewis concerning Moynihan's emphasis on the alarming rise in fatherless families among Negroes. It was difficult to say that the data warrant the adjective "alarming." The data show gradual increases from 1949 (19 percent) to 1959 (24 percent). From 1960 to 1964, the proportion of female-headed families among Negroes showed no net rise at all, standing at 23 percent in 1964. (By 1965 it was 24.9 percent.) The total rise from 1949 to 1964 was about five percentage points, or about one third of a percentage point a year.

The same criticism was made of Moynihan's statement of the "alarming rise in illegitimacy." The data indicate that the number of illegitimate births has risen in the ten years between 1954 and 1964 from 176,600 to 276,000. Herzog wrote, "This is a tremendous number, and the more distressing since there has been no services explosion to keep up with the population explosion." But she added that "in terms of people's behavior, the only relevant index of increase in illegitimacy is *rate,* that is, the number of births out of wedlock per one thousand unmarried women of childbearing age." Between 1957 and 1964 the *rate* has "oscillated within about two points, at about the same level, rising or falling one point or less annually, but in effect representing a seven year plateau."

The argument that the present situation of the Negro in the United States is improving or at least that "there is no crisis" is amendable to the interests of the Permanent Government. The "noncrisis view" offered by Permanent Government critics suggested that "the best way to strengthen low income families, as families, is to give primary attention to building up the economic and social status of Negro men." (This is quite consistent with the argument and recommendations made by Moynihan.) The policy suggested by the Permanent Government was along the line that a number of noneconomic supports can and should be given to low-income Negro families, pending the time when fewer of them are fatherless. Such helps should include among other things, (1) aid for the overburdened mother in her multiple role as homemaker, child-rearer and breadwinner, and (2) effective male models introduced into the lives of children—girls as well as boys. (All of these recommendations are within the purview of present welfare programs.) This view suggests that in "the long run . . . what these families need most is jobs for Negro men — jobs with status, with stability, with future, and with fair wages. No one claims that this can be achieved easily, quickly, or cheaply; but many believe that it can and must be done." In the meantime, the implication remains that the present welfare interventions into intrafamily problems should be continued.

A third critique of the Moynihan thesis made by the Permanent Government that is related to the "oversimplified" critique was that Moynihan did not consider the effects of economic position and the differences between social classes. His comparisons between Negro and white often did not control for income level. While comparative data between these groups is not available as fully as one might wish, there appear to have been data available to Moynihan which he did not use. Several of the papers and statements in interviews by members of the

Permanent Government made the point that differences between Negro and white in family type and stability, education of children, and related pathologies are considerably reduced (but not eliminated) when one compares the two racial groups at the same income level. The conclusion of these comparisons was that although some differences could be noted, these appeared to be less important than differences between lower and higher income levels.

It is clear that many members of the Permanent Government, especially those working in the welfare establishment or the poverty program, support the latter conclusion and opt for a program "which will break into the poverty cycle" as opposed to a program that will break into the specific "cultural cycle" of the Negro. Those working for the poverty program are not interested in preferential treatment for Negroes but rather are interested in treatment of the poor — be they black or white. One of the implications of the Moynihan Report is that Negroes should receive special treatment; the Office of Economic Opportunity is interested in serving poverty not race.

From our interviews, it was apparent that keeping the War on Poverty out of the area of civil rights is a particularly useful political strategy since it avoids harsh confrontations with racist power. Thus by demonstrating that differences between Negro and white are largely accounted for by differences in income, one demonstrates that the attack should be on poverty not race.

There is a consequence of this argument which suggests that adequately controlled comparisons within different income levels would show that the differences associated with income outweigh those associated with color. One is not far from saying that color makes no difference and that it is the economic position that is the sole determinant. Simply because one factor accounts for a greater amount of the difference does not mean that the other factor should be forgotten. The results of these statements is that we will begin to forget that color does make a difference in American society. These critics made the same mistake that Moynihan made by his assumption that "we have gone beyond equal opportunity." Color does make a difference — not only discrimination but also culture makes a difference.

A knotty issue of methodology is bound up in the questions raised by the Permanent Government critics of the report. The basic methodological questions involve the proper grounds for imputing causality or noncausality. Recently Travis Hirschi and

Hanan C. Selvin have written about "false criteria of causality (and noncausality) in delinquency research," (*Social Problems,* Winter 1966) in a way that seems directly applicable to this line of criticism of the Moynihan Report. These authors take to task a 1960 HEW *Report to The Congress on Juvenile Delinquency* which argued that the following factors could *not* be considered "causes" of delinquency: broken homes, poverty, poor housing, lack of recreational facilities, poor physical health, race, and working mothers. The report examined research studies on delinquency and from this examination concluded that although very often there was a significant statistical association between these factors and delinquency, other considerations indicated that the factors were "concommitants" rather than causes. Hirschi and Selvin argue that the criteria for causality used to support this view are methodologically false and describe six false criteria the authors of the 1960 *Report to Congress* used. Many of the same criteria are used to argue against "race" as a factor in the problems Moynihan discussed. Our concern here, however, is not so much with the methodological issue; for this we refer the interested reader to the Hirschi-Selvin paper. However, these authors' conclusions as to the political effect of the methodological reasoning involved in these false criteria of causality apply with equal weight to the points at issue concerning the "noncausality" of the factors that Moynihan asserted were causes:

The implications of these standards of causality for practical efforts to reduce delinquency are devasting. Since nothing that can be pointed to in the practical world is a cause of delinquency (e.g., poverty, broken homes, lack of recreational facilities, working mothers), the practitioner is left with the task of combatting a nebulous "anomie" or an unmeasured "inadequacy of the home"; or else he must change the adolescent's interpretation of the "meaning" of events without at the same time changing the events themselves or the context in which they occur.

Mills has suggested that accepting the principle of multiple causation implies denying the possibility of radical change in the social structure. Our analysis suggests that rejecting the principle of multiple causation implies denying the possibility of *any* change in the social structure — since, in this view, nothing causes anything.

Another example of the strategy of what was considered an oblique attack on the Moynihan Report can be found in a speech made by Mrs. Mary Keyserling, head of the Women's Bureau of the Department of Labor, to the Conference on the Negro Woman in the U.S.A. (November 11, 1965). At that time, Mrs. Keyserling quoted and disagreed with Moynihan's statement in *Daedalus*: "It is in the perspective of the underemployment of the Negro father that we must regard the Negro mother as being *over-employed*." (Keyserling's emphasis.) The crucial point here is that Mrs. Keyserling did not make it clear whether she was attacking Moynihan, an erstwhile official of the Department of Labor, or the Moynihan Report, an official document of that department. Indeed she made it clear in our interviews that she was not attacking the entire report but rather specific parts of the report that lent themselves to interpretations detrimental to women.

Mrs. Keyserling's specific objections to sections of the Moynihan Report largely reflect the anxieties felt by women, particularly Negro women, upon reading the report. Her speech to the Conference of Negro Women reflected criticism over the summer and fall by those sympathetic to Negro women. First indications of these objections were in a letter by Dr. Pauli Murray criticizing the *Newsweek* article (August 9, 1965) that summarized the Moynihan Report.

Dr. Murray wrote that the implications of the *Newsweek* article did "a great disservice to the thousands of Negro women in the United States who have struggled to prepare themselves for employment in a limited job market which is not only highly competitive but which, historically, has severely restricted economic opportunities for women as well as Negroes."

She concluded her letter with the statement, "Since our current emphasis is on better education to get better jobs for all Americans it is bitterly ironic that Negro women should be impliedly censured for their efforts to overcome a handicap not of their making and for trying to meet the standards of the country as a whole."

Mrs. Keyserling and the women she represents objected to those parts of the Moynihan Report which implied that women would be taken out of their jobs in order to give the men full employment: as Pauli Murray commented, "the Negro males may be pitted against Negro females in a highly competitive instead of a co-operative endeavor." This concern is not too far from reality as Mrs. Keyserling pointed out in her speech by quoting the director of a work-training center in Washington, D. C., who stated, "We're not encouraging women. We're trying to reestablish the male as head of the house."

Mrs. Keyserling summarized her objections to parts of the Moynihan thesis with the statement,

But let us not fall into the error of believing that we solve an unemployment problem by trying to take one group of people out of the jobs they are now in and which they need desperately, in order to open employment opportunities for others. There must be jobs for all who need and want work. Particularly is this true in the case in point and might I add that the majority of jobs women hold unfortunately are not jobs that men want or will take.

Another implication, if not assumption, in the Moynihan Report is that the matriarchial family structure of the Negro lower class is pathological. Indeed the chapter "The Tangle of Pathology" begins with the question of matriarchy and then proceeds to compare the female-headed families with complete families. Women have objected to the Moynihan Report on the ground that the occurrence of the matrifocal family is not the desire or fault of women but rather it is a necessary path that they must take in adapting to and surviving in a slum. The clearest statement defending the women's point of view was made by Mrs. Dorothy Height, President of the National Council of Negro Women. Mrs. Height said, "Matriarchy is not a desire of women. Rather it is a matter of being forced to become a matriarch. You need recognition of the fact that women have saved the family in the crises of three hundred years, and there would be no family at all without what they have done. There are strengths in the family which should have been brought out by Moynihan."
A major part of the feminine attack on the Moynihan thesis is against the assumption that men should necessarily be the heads of families in American society. Indeed, Moynihan stated that he saw no inherent need for male dominance but that the norm in American society is such that the male is expected to be the head of the family. It is in this context that the matrifocal family was seen as deviant and perhaps pathological. Since the suffrage movement, women have been attacking this assumption and no doubt they will continue to do so. And the attack, of course, was both on seeing families that are matrifocal as pathological and on seeing employment as primarily the role of the male.
One feminist leader summarized women's objections with the following statement: "The assumption that Moynihan makes that leadership is necessarily male in our society is not correct. Rather

the leadership should be dealt to the qualified person without regard to their sex. We must develop a sense of partnership between male and female. The question is not how do you upgrade the male and how do you downgrade the woman."

In our view, most of the Permanent Government opposition can be seen as highly functional in terms of protecting the viewpoints and interests of the agencies involved and of the Permanent Government as a stratum in contests with the Presidential Government. However, it should be understood that this does not mean that each critic of the report responded in a self-consciously protective way or did not sincerely believe in the accuracy and relevance of his criticisms. Rather, the bureaucratic positions held by these men and women encouraged them to see reality in a different way from the way it appeared to Moynihan, or to academics, or to civil rights officials. But the net effect of the Permanent Government criticism, much of it showing high technical sophistication and intimate knowledge of the issues involved, supported the vested interests of less-than-adequate bureaucratic programs dealing with the problems of the disadvantaged.

8

The Civil Rights Reactions Build

Reactions to the Howard Speech

Civil rights reactions to the Howard University speech were very positive. Martin Luther King, Roy Wilkins, and Whitney Young had been called by the White House and read the speech before it was given. At that time, they had expressed their enthusiasm and anticipated other civil rights leaders' pleasant surprise on hearing the speech. For the first time, the government was taking a definite and positive initiative in the area of civil rights that was independent of establishing or enforcing laws and was not in reaction to pressure by the civil rights movement.

Robert Carter, general counsel for the NAACP said of the speech: "The President had an amazing comprehension of the barriers that are present in our society to the Negro's progress, and an amazing comprehension of the debilitation that results from slum living. He also demonstrated that he understood the problems of translating abstract generalities into a specific program." A spokesman for the Urban League said: "The Howard

University speech was largely taken out of Mr. Young's book, *To Be Equal*. The two men who had drafted the speech, used the book in writing the speech." Others said: "Johnson had been very strong in the area of civil rights, perhaps as strong as you can expect a President to be, but that was before the Howard speech. The Howard speech went beyond that and surprised everyone."

Government Civil Rights Reactions to the President's Speech

Any time the President makes a policy speech, appointees and serious civil servants all over Washington ask themselves: "What are the implications of that for me and my office?" If they have been working on some program or idea that is mentioned or related to the speech, they seem to immediately act by moving more vigorously and confidently.

Those most directly concerned with civil rights were not privy to the events before the speech. Neither the President's Council on Equal Opportunities nor the Civil Rights Commission were consulted before the speech and like other government civil rights offices neither had received copies of the Moynihan Report. The speech came as a complete surprise. The Howard speech is unique, not only in what it said but also in the fact that it did not "receive clearance." Both this speech and the "We Shall Overcome" speech did not go through the normal procedure of being passed through the hands of the Permanent Government for approval and revision before it was made by the President. These speeches are the products of the Presidential Government, indeed the White House staff alone, and it is not surprising that they are unique in their content.

Wiley Branton, its director, immediately became concerned about the implications the speech had for the Council on Equal Opportunities. He assumed from the beginning that the White House Conference would be considered to be primarily the responsibility of his office; thus he began exploring and questioning other persons in the Administration about the speech and the plans for the conference. Evidently he did not find anything out until the preplanning sessions at the White House. It was in these early sessions that Branton spoke out against the use of the phrase "the Negro family." Said Branton, "The phrase, 'the Negro Family' struck me in a psychologically bad way. I didn't like the way it was being used." Evidently there was considerable debate, with Branton saying that it should not be used and that it came out in a derogatory manner such that it contributed to the existing stereotypes and resulted in more harm than good.

Initial Civil Rights Reaction to Conference Planning

Civil rights leaders were also consulted about the coming conference. We have been told that the Urban League had been "asked very early about the planning of the fall conference." On the day of signing of the Voting Rights Bill, James Farmer and John Lewis were asked by the President for their suggestions. They were told, "We need to know what to do next to solve this problem." This was in the first week in August, a month after the academic consultants had begun talking in the White House. The President also indicated in his speech of August 20th that he had spent the first week in August, "at the White House visiting individually with Dr. King, Mr. Farmer, Mr. Roy Wilkins, A. Phillip Randolph and talking about the great meeting that we would have here later in the fall, because the cities of this nation and the Negro family are two of our most pressing, and more important problems."

The meetings of the leaders of the civil rights movement in the White House were quite informal, and did not represent "planning" for the conference. For example, one of the directors of the conference learned of the meetings between the President and the civil rights people from the newspapers. Even though he was meeting in the White House on the planning of the conference he never met when the civil rights leaders came. "There seemed to be no relationship between what we were doing and what was going on with the civil rights leaders."

Even though there was planning for the White House Conference going on during the first two months of the summer, one is left with the distinct impression that there was little coordination between these planning sessions and little coordination of those in authority. One government person has told us, "My complaint was, for example, if you're going to ask a professor to do research and write a paper you should give him the go ahead with authority. Suppose you get Joe Blow to write a research paper and someone upstairs changes his mind and says, 'No, we don't want that.' The biggest complaint that I have about the conference was the administration of the conference. No one could speak with authority. It was like some comic play."

In addition to the speech and newspaper stories concerning the academic consultations going on in the White House, rumors concerning the Moynihan Report and the White House Conference were being spread through the Washington cocktail circuit. Even though many people had not seen the report until September, the stories about the report began moving through the cocktail circuit in the early part of the summer. Frank Reeves, now Professor of Law at Harvard University, tells us that persons outside the government often find out information about things going on within the government before government people who are directly connected. According to the cocktail circuit early in June, the report was supposedly a complete summary of "the Negro in our society, very broad and very detailed." One can readily imagine the uneasiness that developed in the civil rights organizations by the end of July. They had been brought into the White House separately and lackadaisically, but not with academicians who, according to the newspapers, were having a major role in the planning of the White House Conference. In addition to this, the Washington cocktail circuit as well as newspaper stories were referring to the report on the Negro American that was evidently having a great influence on the Administration thinking in the civil rights area. But the report was still an internal document and not available to them.

It was during this time that civil rights leaders began asking their contacts in government civil rights agencies about the report. But the government civil rights people had not yet been able to get copies. It was, of course, quite embarrassing for government civil rights experts to be told by persons outside the government about the Moynihan Report, but even more embarrassing when they were unable to answer the questions raised by civil rights leaders. The atmosphere of secrecy and tight security built around the report no doubt added to the developing uneasiness in the movement.

Apparently the White House was engaged in the process of "leapfrogging" not only the private civil rights agencies but its own civil rights agencies as well. From the point of view of both civil rights types, the results of the efforts of the "White House study group" touted in the press were being kept unclear to them. Even after the report itself became available to them, there was no meaningful liason between the "study group" and the civil rights people.

Concern with the White House Conference, the Howard speech, and the Moynihan Report was suddenly interrupted by the Watts riot. There is no question that the lack of activity concerned with the White House Conference during the month of August was largely a result of the Watts riot. Persons in government agencies as well as the civil rights movement were distracted by the Watts riot. But while Watts distracted attention from the Moynihan Report, the ultimate effect was to exacerbate the anxieties that had begun to develop. The report took on special meanings and importance in the context of the riots.

The Moynihan Report was connected to the Watts riots by coincidence of timing (*Newsweek,* August 9th), and after Watts the report was also used to explain the riots. We have in our files eleven articles that appeared in the two weeks between August 16th and September 1st which relate the Moynihan Report or the breakdown of the Negro family to the Watts riot. Because of the newspaper coverage, the Moynihan Report was taken as the government's explanation for the riots.

Watts gave the Moynihan Report new meaning. It made crystal clear the malaise that was felt by the civil rights movement and the government earlier in the year. It is difficult to say which of these two groups was more shaken by the riots. Members of the civil rights organization have told us that the government was shaken and that they themselves were not. On the other hand, members of government have pointed their finger in the opposite direction. The question of who was more disturbed is of little importance in that it is clear that Watts renewed the convictions of both that something new must be done.

For the Johnson Administration, Watts made explicit that a substantial minority of the American population — that minority which was the most urbanized — was not to be included in consensus politics. The urban Negro was in direct conflict with law and order.

The riot meant, for the Johnson Administration, that the poverty program had done little to solve the problems of the urban poor. The fact that little money had been spent in the Watts area (no doubt contributing to the riots) did in fact save the Administration some embarrassment over the success or failure of the poverty program.

As noted in an editorial in *The Economist*, progress reports on the implementations of the Civil Rights Acts of 1964 — which appeared a week following the riots — only underlined the irrelevance of these laws to the problems facing the urban northern Negro.

To the civil rights movement the Watts riot only amplified what they had known in the spring. Watts made explicit the failure of the movement. "Civil rights organizations have failed," commented James Farmer, National Director of CORE just after Watts, "No one had any roots in the ghetto." And Bayard Rustin said, "We must hold ourselves responsible for not reaching them . . . Roy [Wilkins], Martin [Luther King] and I haven't done a damn thing about it. We've done plenty to get votes in the South and seats in the lunchrooms, but we've had no program for these youngsters." One civil rights leader described the irony of the conversations he had witnessed between SNCC workers and Harlem youths. "The SNCC workers were trying to convince them to come and join the demonstration and march with them, but these guys were telling the SNCC workers to come and ride the subways and 'We'll really show you how to get whitey.' "

For civil rights leaders, Robert Carter's comment on the Moynihan Report — "It taught us things that we already knew but were not thinking of" — could well be applied to the Watts riot. Watts made clear the alienation of the urban Negro from the civil rights movement.

9

After Watts the Issue Is Joined

The newspaper accounts of the report had used the document as an explanation of the Watts riot and as the government's proof that something was being done about the northern urban Negro. Also the newspapers left the distinct impression that the family question was to be central to the White House Conference. The report, by mid-September, had taken on an image that was rather different from the written and originally published form, and the reactions to the report were largely reactions to the image derived from the newspaper coverage. In addition to these factors, it must be remembered that the report was still widely regarded as a confidential or internal government document. This vacuum only added to the distorted image — there was nothing to correct whatever distortions were made.

It was in this vacuum that the debate around the Moynihan Report developed. With no official word from Washington concerning the report's relationship to the White House Conference and few copies of the report in hand, full reign was given to the controversy.

194

More than one government civil rights expert warned the White House, with increasing urgency, that civil rights leaders were becoming greatly concerned at the newspaper and rumor-mill statements that the conference would be "about the family." As often as these concerns were expressed, and the dangers inherent in the way the family emphasis was being handled were emphasized, the White House response seemed to be that the civil rights organizations had been adequately informed about the contents of the conference and that there was no need for special communications on this matter, or for clarifying press releases. As one outside observer commented, "They just didn't work on their problem, even after they were told about it."

The early concern about the report is reflected in a letter written on August 27th by Herbert Gans to Richard Goodwin of the White House staff. Gans wrote:

I think the emphasis [on family difficulties] is all to the good, if not overdone. There is danger, however, that it may result in a wave of social work and psychiatric solutions intended to change the Negro female-based family to a middle class type. Such solutions could maintain the already overly paternalistic and manipulative way with which we have been dealing with the problems of the Negro, and more important, they could deflect attention away from the economic causes of the Negro problem. Whatever the ravages of slavery, the female-based Negro family today is a result of current unemployment among Negro males, and secondarily, of the pattern of social welfare, especially ADC, which as you know encourages women to reject (or hide) their men, and in both cases, downgrades their familial role and power. These two causal factors ought to be emphasized in the forming of new programs.

At this time Gans had not seen the report, nor was he aware of the building controversy; it was John Herbers' *New York Times* article that disturbed him.

Adding to the growing concern within the civil rights movement were the events that took place aboard the presidential yacht, the *Honey Fitz*, on September 15th. Earlier in the fall, Vice-President Humphrey had suggested to one of his staff that it would be a good idea to get together with civil rights leaders under informal circumstances in order to foster communications between the government and the movement. The Vice-President's staff arranged an afternoon ride on the *Honey Fitz* and invited several leaders of the civil rights movement including Clarence Mitchell of the Washington NAACP, Floyd McKissick of CORE,

Whitney Young, Martin Luther King, Andrew Young of the SCLC, along with the Vice-President and several of his staff.

We have collected several accounts of the boat ride, all of which are not consistent. One thing that is clear is that it did not turn out to be the relaxing evening on the Potomac the Vice-President had expected. Instead, "they almost turned the boat over." Evidently, an argument began over enforcement of the voting rights bill. The civil rights leaders suggested that nothing new was needed in the area of civil rights; if the government would simply implement the laws that were presently on the books then much of the problem would be solved. Specific discussion centered on the voting rights bill and the federal registrars. Evidently the government had not sent federal registrars to some areas of the South where civil rights leaders felt they should be sent and several times Southern activists had collected persons to register and found no registrars available. In response to this argument, one of Humphrey's assistants pointed out that one of the reasons for fewer federal registrars was a news release sent out by the NAACP which hailed the success of voting registration in the South. He emphasized that it was difficult for the government to move in this area when the NAACP was telling the public of the success of the registration drive with the present number of registrars.

But more important for our purposes, we understand that one of the Vice-President's staff also attempted to answer the demands of McKissick and Mitchell with the question of *"What about this Moynihan Report: the problem is more than just getting people registered to vote."* Civil rights leaders replied, "Let's get back to the specific issues of now!" As McKissick explained to us: "Many of the students in the South had made personal sacrifice in order to get people out to vote. But when we did this, when we got masses to go, there were no registrars. That made us waste a whole damn summer of work. And then they go turn to the Moynihan Report."

Although we have no indication that the boat ride had a direct relationship to the coming White House Conference or the President's reorganization of the civil rights organization a week later, it is clear that the boat ride took on significance in that it was one of the few communications between the government and civil rights organization during September. The implication taken away from the meeting by some participants was that the government was not going to further implement the registration drive and,

more than this, that the Administration was using the Moynihan
Report as its excuse not to move more rapidly on the implementation of laws — indeed, that it had invented a new problem and
now was using this to avoid further action on the old one.

It is difficult to determine after an event such as the Moynihan
controversy the opinions held by persons in the center of the
controversy. Thus, it is difficult to say now exactly what people
were feeling in September. It is clear that concern about the
Moynihan Report grew during this time. Perhaps one of the best
reflections of the attitudes and anxieties in civil rights circles is
the critique of the Moynihan Report written by William Ryan.
(This critique will be discussed in detail in the next chapter).
Ryan had been associated with Boston CORE for some time. He
became concerned about the Moynihan thesis when he read the
Newsweek article that appeared just prior to Watts. He immediately began talking to friends in local and national civil rights
circles trying to get their feeling about the report. He had no
contacts with persons in the government. Says Ryan, "I was outside that sphere. All I knew was what was in the newspapers. I
understood the report was the basis for the White House Conference and this of course magnified my concern." He began
writing the critique in September and distributed it in the first
week of October.

We find the following major ideological objections to the report
reflected in the Ryan critique. First, Ryan stated his concern that
"this document will be the basic working paper for the President's
White House Conference in November. This conference may be
considered the first step toward achieving a consensus about the
programs to help the 'disorganized' Negro family." Ryan then suggested that the reason "*the report can be read in such a way as
to imply the present unequal status of the Negro in America
results not from the obvious causes of discrimination and segregation, but rather from a more basic cause, the 'instability' of the
Negro family. It is further implied that corrective measures should
be focused on increasing the stability of the Negro family, rather
than merely on eliminating discriminatory patterns in American life.*"

Ryan directed a great deal of his attack against a new ideology
that he felt was developing in some circles. "Unemployment, the
new ideologists tell us, results from the breakdown of Negro
family life; poor education of Negroes results from 'cultural
deprivation'; the slum conditions endured by so many Negro

families is the result of lack of 'acculturation' of Southern rural migrants."

Ryan's concern with this new ideology was, we believe, a justified one. One of the most influential books on education in the slum, *Slums and Suburbs** by James Bryant Conant, concluded with the statement that a "considerable degree of what a school should do and can do is determined by the status and ambition of the families being served." Despite Conant's later modification of his view, this conclusion to a study comparing the slums with suburban schools no doubt results, if accepted by school boards in the country, in an acceptance of the continued miseducation of slum children. Rather than recommending compensatory education for the slum children, Conant, again reflecting the ideology of maintaining the present status relationships, suggested and prescribed vocational education for slum children. The ideology that accepts the present social structure because that is the way things are has been challenged by civil rights advocates since the first emancipation movement. Now social scientists and educators with the status of Conant and Moynihan seemed to be giving "scientific" support to the status quo.

Ryan was also concerned that "the popularization of the Moynihan Report — if not the document itself — will provide fat fodder for this new racist ideology, tempting Americans to construct one more version of the Puritan myth that riches and poverty are both deserved."

Indeed this happened on a very small scale. We have copies of a document written by Albert C. Persons, *Riot, Riot, Riot,** that was sold at public newstands in the South. Moynihan is quoted in this document, although completely out of context and in quite a distorted manner: "The report finds that 'the single most important social fact in the United States today' to be the 'massive deterioration of the family and its institutions' in the Negro American world." Indeed, the Moynihan Report had been used to support the old racist ideology. However, the racist use of the report, feared by some in the White House as well as by civil rights activists, never materialized on a large scale. Indeed, some southern newspapers criticized the report, and the Administration for issuing it, on the grounds that it blamed white people for Negroes' family problems rather than Negroes themselves.

* James Bryant Conant, *Slums and Suburbs: A Commentary on Schools in Metropolitan Areas* (New York: McGraw-Hill, 1961).
* Albert C. Persons, *Riot, Riot, Riot* (Birmingham, Ala.: Esco Publishers, 1966).

Ryan concluded his critique with the concern that "we are in danger of being reduced into de-emphasizing discrimination as the overriding cause of the Negroes' current status of inequality."

In early October, there developed several major criticisms of the report based largely on the fear of the possible political implications and the effect the report would have on governmental policy. First, the report seemed to overlook the problem of discrimination and place the blame for Negroes' deprivation on the Negro community rather than the white community and thus was used to justify the status quo. It might be used by Southern racists to support the racist doctrine that the Negro is indeed inferior and segregation must be maintained. It could be used by politicians as an excuse to halt further government efforts in the area of civil rights. Indeed the government had used it on the *Honey Fitz* to parry the civil rights leaders' attack on the Justice Department for not sending more federal voting registrars. Finally the report apparently was to be at the center of the White House Conference "To Fulfill These Rights." It was feared that the conference was going to be used by the government to achieve a Johnsonian consensus about what programs were needed to help the poor.

Indeed, by October the vacuum of no convincing official denial of these rumors resulted in a seeming reversal of the Howard speech — the same report that "caused" the President to call for additional bold steps in the area of civil rights and urban poverty became in the public mind the government excuse to do nothing but achieve consensus.

Civil Rights Reactions to the Moynihan Report

It was in this context and largely in response to the growing newspaper coverage (and the three critiques of the report by Ryan, Benjamin Payton, and Herbert Gans) that the civil rights leaders heard about and responded to the Moynihan document. Some told us in January that they had not yet read the entire report. Others referred us to the Ryan article, while others suggested that we write the Protestant Council of New York for Payton's criticism. It is clear that the civil rights organizations read and were influenced by these critiques. James Farmer's articles appearing in the *Amsterdam News* in December clearly reflected the Ryan critique. But it is also clear that civil rights reactions to the Moynihan Report were not homogeneous. As with other stereotypes, the assumption that everyone in the movement would react similarly is simply incorrect.

Perhaps the most straightforward criticism of the report was made by John Lewis of SNCC. The report, according to Lewis, "takes too much for granted." It begins with the assumption that the problems of discrimination and racism have been solved. Perhaps the assumption is more true in the North than in the South, but it is difficult to accept the assumption that discrimination is no longer a problem. (Indeed the report did begin with the assumption that "we have gone beyond equal opportunity." If this assumption were accepted by the American public as used by the government on the *Honey Fitz,* then a great deal of support for the civil rights movement would be lost.)

Floyd McKissick, the new director of CORE, said of the report:

My major criticism of the report is that it assumes that middle class American values are the correct ones for everyone in America. Just because Moynihan believes in the middle class values doesn't mean that they are the best for everyone in America. It dosn't mean that they are good for everyone. Moynihan thinks everyone should have a family structure like his own. Moynihan also emphasizes that negative aspects of the Negroes and then seems to say that it's the individual's fault when it's the damn system that really needs changing.

Clarence Mitchell of the Washington office of the NAACP objected to the report because it "implied that it was necessary for the improvement of the Negro community to come from within." Mitchell added, "it's funny how newspapers always run big stories when the Negro community starts to run its own clean-up campaign." It is clear that if attention were directed toward clean-up campaigns this would reduce the number of demonstrations oriented toward conflict with white power and segregated institutional structures.

Bayard Rustin criticized the report by suggesting,

It was first of all incomplete. It left people with the view that this was a complete and perfectly true picture of the Negro families. But then it gave no suggestions for correcting measures. Secondly, the report accentuated or exaggerated the negative. One important point that must be made is that what may seem to be a disease to the white middle class may be a healthy adaptation to the Negro lower class. Also, Moynihan posed as a great scholar of the Negro family and this was a mistake. He left out a great deal of what E. Franklin Frazier has done. Finally, we must talk about the poor family, not simply the Negro family. Poverty is a problem. It is amazing to me that Negro families exist at all.

Rustin concluded with the comment, "I don't agree with the criticisms of Moynihan that he is a racist. I think the racist argument is kind of silly."

It will be remembered that the Moynihan Report had two elements in it — one the implication that the pressing problem of the Negro in the North is within the Negro community itself, the second that equality of results must be achieved before racial peace is restored. In addition to the criticisms made of the Moynihan Report, many persons in the movement saw it as did Robert Carter of the NAACP. Carter said,

I could not understand the great shock that people were expressing over the report. Moynihan, it seemed to me, was making a comment on the results of discrimination in our society. It's an old story and not a startling discovery and not new. These things that he points out — the pathologies of the ghetto — are a result of discrimination. The interesting thing is that the American public often knows things but often this knowledge is not meaningful to them and then something like the Moynihan Report comes out and they learn them again.

Carter went on to say,

It seems to me that if you're going to reform the Negro male and the Negro family, we cannot do anything without changing the social conditions surrounding the ghetto. It is impossible to do anything without changing the social pathology of discrimination. It is difficult to begin talking about the weakening of the Negro family structure in an industrial society. We look at the middle class or upper middle class family structure and we can see that it is also weakening.

Then Carter added a very perceptive comment,

The real costs of doing what must be done in order to improve the structure of the Negro family are great. You're going to have to step on a lot of people's toes and a lot of changes are going to have to be made. My question is, is the Administration really prepared to do these things? President Johnson's speech, to me, was not an artificial abstraction, but rather was very good. The problem is whether or not he is now willing to carry out what he said he would do.

Norman Hill of the AFL-CIO said of the report, "Perhaps I am in a minority or expressing a minority point of view, but I liked the report. It told me that wide economic changes in the social structure were needed in order to solve these problems." Nevertheless, Hill observed that "there were things in the report that could create problems for civil rights activists." Similarly Whitney Young said,

My book, *To Be Equal,* identified the same pathologies in the Negro ghetto. And I called for an urban Marshall Plan, just as the Moynihan Report implies. I think that the title *The Negro Family* was tragic in that as a result it has stigmatized an entire group of people when the majority of that group of people do not fall into the category of the Negro family that Moynihan describes. Moynihan did not point up that comparable data on low income whites would show very much the same thing. It just happened that there are more poor Negroes than there are whites. Also one can't talk about the pathologies of Negroes without talking about the pathologies of white society. If Negroes are sick socially, then whites are sick morally.

Mr. Young and Michael Harrington prefaced their remarks about the Moynihan Report with the statement that "It was written as an internal document and not written for the public." Harrington suggested that Moynihan had written the document for "shock purposes" and perhaps for that reason he emphasized the negative aspect of the Negro community and did not elaborate the view that much of the behavior of the poor is an adaptation to the environment of the slums.

Martin Luther King, in a speech made on October 29th in Westchester County, New York, summarized his reactions to the Moynihan Report succinctly with the statement,

As public awareness [of the breakdown of the Negro family] increases there will be dangers and opportunities. The opportunity will be to deal fully rather than haphazardly with the problem as a whole — to see it as a social catastrophe and meet it as other disasters are met with an adequacy of resources. The danger will be that problems will be attributed to innate Negro weaknesses and used to justify, neglect and rationalize oppression.

Some persons in the movement had upon reading the Moynihan Report focussed on the dangers that were involved in the document; others had focussed on the opportunities.

Civil Rights and the Government

One of the major complaints that we have received in our interviews with the members of the civil rights organizations was that during the summer and fall of 1965 there seemed to be little communication between the officials of the movement and the White House. There was considerable confusion as to who in the White House was the liaison between government and civil rights organizations. One leader complained that the "President depends on people who don't know how the Negro feels to give him advice on civil rights measures. What is needed is a man who has contacts in the Negro community and is also close to the President. The problem with the present advisers is that they don't have contacts among the leaders of the Negro community."

If the ride on the *Honey Fitz* is any indication, there was indeed little communication between the White House and the civil rights organizations. This is perhaps a major factor contributing to the Moynihan controversy. Several leaders of the "movement" have told us that there was no contact between the time of the Watts riot and the first week of October when A. Phillip Randolph was appointed Honorary Chairman of the Conference. Many of the civil rights leaders did not know about Randolph's appointment until it appeared in the newspapers! As one told us, "The whole thing was a bit of a mess. We could not find out who was running the conference."

Finally, in the middle of September, a meeting of civil rights leaders was held in New York. "People were there from the NAACP, SNCC, CORE; Roy Wilkins was in Europe, therefore he was not at the meeting. We decided at that time that we must get into the planning of the conference." One leader who went to Washington to tell the government how the civil rights leaders felt said that "In response, they seemed to have delayed even more. As far as we could tell there was no one running the conference."

From "Great Society" to Vietnam

Indeed, little was being done to plan the conference between late July and the end of September. Thus one civil rights leader said, "It wasn't that we were being kept out of the planning, it's just that nothing was going on." It is difficult to understand why the White House group allowed this hiatus to develop and why they refused to effectively deny that this conference was about the family — perhaps because they considerably underestimated the complex intellectual and human-relations task involved, certainly because Watts took up so much of the energy of those who were involved in the planning, and very likely because the White House was finding itself increasingly preoccupied with the Vietnam situation. As one highly placed government man has observed about the fate of the Howard speech agenda from June to January — "You know, there are less than twenty men in the government who can get something new done, and they really have to work and fight to do it; with Vietnam building up they just had to drop this other thing." Toward the end of the year this relationship was much clearer — "Every time a helicopter goes to Texas there goes another poverty program" — but already in September and October decisions were being made which both absorbed the energies of the President and his staff and made ever more unattractive a heavy commitment of resources to the "New Reconstruction" which Moynihan had called for (instead we got "Great Society" programs for Vietnam).

A brief review of the Administration's Vietnam activity in the summer of 1965 may be useful here. Although the United States escalation had started some months earlier, until the early summer Vietnam still seemed a minor involvement. Early in June, however, following a bombing pause in May, the government began to acknowledge that U.S. ground forces were now engaged in combat "in defense of key installations" (June 6th). A few days later it was announced that U.S. forces would participate in combat if requested to by the South Vietnamese army, and by the end of the month it was announced that U.S. troops had engaged in offensive action for the first time.

July and August, the most crucial months for the development of the Moynihan controversy, were also crucial for the Vietnam escalation. In July authoritative sources indicated that up to 150,000 additional men had been programmed for Vietnam, and the President was considering a possible reserve call-up, higher draft calls, an increase in the defense budget and other "new and serious decisions." Toward the end of July, Johnson began a much publicized "sweeping survey" of the U.S. position in order to formulate new policies. On August 5th, he asked Congress for an additional $1.7 billion for fiscal 1966 to support the war (by the end of the year the war had added $4.7 billion to the 1966 budget and an addition of $10.5 billion was projected for fiscal 1967).

Starting in June, then, and continuing into the next year, the escalation of troops, materiel, and money commitments was steadily rising from month to month — troop projections increased from less than 50,000 in May to 150,000 in July, to 200,000 later in the year, and finally to over 400,000 in January. Small wonder, then, that White House manpower, energy, and imagination were not available for a major move in the civil rights area.

The distractions and preoccupations with Vietnam are illustrated by an experience of one expert during July. He had been called to the White House to meet with one of the President's assistants and then with the President himself. Instead he was shunted to a different set of aides because both the man he had been scheduled to see and the President were at that time fully involved with Vietnam matters.

Thus the demands of Vietnam, both external and internal political ones, distracted the White House from any central involvement with new civil rights programs of the order suggested by the Howard University speech. There was first a diversion of intellectual resources and presidential attention. Beyond this, there would certainly have been a disinclination to invest time and energy in working out the new multibillion-dollar social and economic programs so clearly suggested by the Howard speech at a time when new multibillion-dollar Vietnam war commitments were being made. By the end of the year, when such programs were being suggested by civil rights leaders, those in the White House were even more sharply aware that multibillion-dollar domestic programs were out of the question — the problem was rather that of somehow not cutting domestic spending and thus laying the Administration open to accusations of opting for guns rather than butter.

Already in the summer the White House had upped the number of children in the Head Start program as a way of shifting attention from Vietnam to a domestic poverty program. Similarly, the Office of Economic Opportunity budget was increased the following January and paid for by less conspicuous cuts in other domestic programs.

One astute observer of Washington civil rights events has called this sequence of events an example of the "benign Machiavellism" of the Johnson Administration. The evidence of disorganization in the conference planning and White House relations with the movement would not appear to support such a conclusion. Yet sometimes manipulative goals can be served as well by failure to plan as by planning — it could well be that the failure to treat the conference as the important event it had first seemed and the related failure of following through served several functions. First of all, it strongly disorganized the civil rights forces who in the end managed to bring about a show of unity only in opposition to the Moynihan Report, not in effective demands on the Administration. This further deepened the public and government image of the movement as inadequate to the demands of the next stage of the civil rights struggle, as was also "proved" by Watts.

For a government that wanted to move vigorously on social and economic reform to benefit Negroes, the Moynihan *Report* provided a strong justification. For a government that wanted to "cool it," to avoid action that could no longer be afforded without having to take the blame for inaction, the Moynihan *controversy* provided an ideal distraction. The White House, above the conflict, could look at the disarray in the ranks of those who might bring pressure for costly programs and relax; the heat was directed elsewhere. Thus much later in the year, one official of a national civil rights organization, not noted for his effectiveness otherwise nor for any other role in the controversy, told a government official: "We're going to get that guy (Moynihan)." Asked what good "getting" Moynihan would do, he replied: "Well, we've got to get somebody and I guess Moynihan is it." A strategy of "getting Moynihan" would obviously distract from "getting" the White House in the sense of either pressing for expanded federal commitments or protesting the lack of action.

The Development of the Conference

After the meeting on the *Honey Fitz,* Johnson reorganized the government civil rights organizations. As a result of the changes on September 24th, the civil rights responsibilities of the Attorney General and the Secretary of Labor were broadened. The Civil Rights Commission was given new fact-finding chores and the Commerce Department's Community Relations Service was to be transferred to the Justice Department. Two existing organizations, the President's Council on Equal Opportunity and the President's Committee on Equal Employment Opportunity, were abolished.

We have had several indications that there was considerable disorganization in the Administration's handling of the conference planning. One high government source said,

I was totally disturbed with the uncertainty and the delay in getting the conference going. There was no one in charge of the conference. They never gave anyone the authority. Finally, someone suggested putting the conference off until the spring. I kind of agreed with this, but they then said that they couldn't do this because the President had said in his speech that there would be a fall conference. But there was just not enough time left to make it a fall conference. It was then that some-

one suggested that if they were going to insist that there should be a
fall conference, they should set the date and make it a planning session.
This was the course of action that they finally adopted.

There have been some indications that in the summer the
President had assigned conference planning to the "Vice-President's people," but about the time of the President's operation
someone on the White House staff told him that nothing was
being done. It was at this point that the President began to act.
One government source said, "As far as I can tell [until then]
the President was not aware of the fact that there were problems
around the administration of the conference."

It must be remembered that the President is a person who has
the habit of delaying decisions. Whether this is intentional or
for the drama of surprise, it is clear that he has a pattern of
waiting. Humphrey's candidacy for the Vice-Presidency was announced at the last minute; Robert Weaver's appointment to the
Housing and Urban Development Department came long after it
was expected; Johnson waited until very late to call a White
House Conference on Equal Employment, as required by Title VII
of the Civil Rights Act of 1964.

One observer of Senate Majority Leader Johnson remembered
that "Johnson was a man of detail. He would not let a single
detail go by without some decision being made on it. He would
write a list of votes and count the votes very carefully before a
bill went up on the floor."

It has also been said that the President is a man who does not
like other people to get him in trouble, that he sensed that the
White House Conference was getting out of control, and because
of this he became concerned with its administration. It was feared
that the conference might be getting out of control in two ways.
First, it was possible for the conference to become a forum on
Vietnam, with more and more civil rights leaders joining the
critics of government policy in Vietnam. Second, the White House
apparently began to be concerned about what the conference
would develop as programs: might not the conference come up
with recommendations that they were unwilling or unable to
carry out?

On October 4th, the President announced the date for the coming conference and appointed its chairmen. It was at this time
that the final planning and arranging for the conference began.
The earlier sessions in the White House with social scientists did
not make specific plans for the conference; there was no con-

tinuity between the two except for the fact that some of the White House staff were involved in both.

On October 13th, there was another shifting of responsibilities around the conference staff. Several persons including Hylan Lewis and Norman Hill were brought in as consultants to the staff. At this time, several civil rights leaders wrote memoranda making recommendations for the coming conference. The conference staff then had a month to make the arrangements for the conference. One of the conference staff described the situation:

There was not enough time to hold a full-fledged conference and the brainstorming session seemed to be a good idea. Secondly, there was concern with what the conference would produce; that is, there was some concern that it would get out of hand. During the short time between the appointment of a conference staff and the conference, it was necessary to organize the conference, get a staff of secretaries and so forth. Because we didn't have time it was necessary to take people from other agencies in government.

There is little question that the conference was put together quite quickly. One indication of this was that invitations were sent out only a week before the conference was held.

The invitation list was created or selected by bringing in persons from the church, labor, business and race groups. The problem was to select two hundred people from all over the country who represented these groups, who are experts on race relations, and at the same time not leave some out who should have been invited.

The invitation list was checked by the White House and quite a bit of control kept over who came to the conference.

One member of the Permanent Government who worked on the conference planning described the situation:

It was the biggest mess I have ever seen. People did not know what they were doing. We put things together very quickly. We would make decisions and then they would change them saying, "they won't like this," or "they think that we should do that," or "they will react such and such." We never did during the entire time find out who "they" were. I assumed it must be someone in the White House, somewhere up there. It was like Alice in Wonderland and Kafka combined!

Another member of the staff said, "We were continually having to change our decisions; decisions on who would come to the conference, how the program would be run — the number of people who would come. No one ever knew who had the final decision making or who had the final approval of whatever we did."

It was widely believed that until late August and early September the conference was going to focus on the family perspective. It was during this time that persons from the civil rights organizations were coming to government civil rights officials and asking about the family question.

The decision to have eight panels including one on the family had been firmly established when Carl Holman of the Civil Rights Commission, accompanied by Berl Bernhard, Harold Fleming, and Clifford Alexander, met with the civil rights leaders on October 21st in New York. This was the first of two meetings between leaders of the civil rights organizations and the government conference staff.

At this meeting, the civil rights organizations argued that the conference should be limited to three subjects — jobs, protection of civil rights workers, and implementation of the 1964 and 1965 Civil Rights Act — and that it should not deal with the family in any manner whatsoever. The civil rights opposition was not homogeneous. For example, James Forman of SNCC disagreed with other leaders and said, "Look, after all it's not our conference, it's the President's conference and he's going to have a say in who comes and what's discussed." There was also considerable discussion about who should come to the conference with many of the civil rights leaders, particularly SNCC, saying that there were local grass-roots groups who had ideas that should be presented. The government indicated that the conference would not focus on any particular theme, it would simply generate ideas along whatever lines the participants wanted. At this time, the conference was to be limited to fifty delegates.

There was a second meeting between civil rights organizations and government held on October 30th in the Indian Treaty Room of the Executive Office Building. At this meeting, the government was represented by Lee White, Clifford Alexander, Carl Holman, Berl Bernhard, Morris Abram, William Coleman, Harold Fleming, and Joseph Califano, the President's "trouble-shooter." From the civil rights movement, there were Ralph Abernathy, Whitney Young, Jack Greenberg, Roy Wilkins, James Farmer, Bayard Rustin, Marion Barry, Dorothy Height, Rev. Walter Fauntroy, representatives of SNCC, and "someone from the National Council of Churches."

The government presented its proposal of eight panels or workshops; and even though it was understood that the family panel would center on the paper written by Hylan Lewis — a non-Moynihan approach — there was considerable discussion about the family. The government maintained that the family panel was only one of eight workshops and all were equally important, that there was no reason to single out one and eliminate it. It was following this meeting that SNCC submitted a list of sixteen "grass-roots" people, fourteen of whom were finally invited to the conference. By this meeting, the number of delegates had risen from fifty to one hundred and fifty.

This was the last of the formal meetings between leaders of the civil rights organizations and the conference staff. There were other individual meetings and phone calls between leaders of the "movement" and the conference staff.

From the early part of October and the first meeting of civil rights leaders in New York before they were contacted by the conference staff to the weeks just prior to the White House Conference, the civil rights concern over the Moynihan Report subsided. Perhaps the best indication of this development of a strategy of ignoring the report was CORE's *Charge to the White House Conference.* This document, we have been told by CORE officers, went through three successive revisions, each of which moved further and further away from a major emphasis on attacking the Moynihan Report. In the middle of October CORE held a meeting with its recently formed research advisory staff made up of social scientists such as Herbert Gans, S. M. Miller, and Frank Riessman. This meeting was devoted in its entirety to a discussion of the Moynihan Report. By the end of October, word had spread within the movement that Hylan Lewis was writing the agenda paper for the family session, and that the family would be discussed in only one of eight sessions of the conference. It was understood that Lewis' paper would *not* be "Moynihanian." CORE adopted the strategy that "one should not rock the boat when the seas were subsiding." Further argument about the family issue was unnecessary since it was clear that it was no longer central to the conference and further debate would only draw attention to a matter that they wished forgotten. The final draft of the CORE charge included only one statement referring to the Moynihan Report: "and most recently, in a new and all embracing canard, we hear about the 'pathology' of the Negro family instead of the sickness of America." Thus CORE had largely forgotten the Moynihan Report before the White House Conference and turned its attention to the development of its own strategies to aid in incorporating the Negro in American society.

The National Council Of Churches and Its Pre-White House Conference

During the early fall, there began a parallel development that had the effect of increasing the controversy over the Moynihan Report, yet unlike the civil rights organizations those involved did not slow down when the civil rights organizations changed strategy and began neglecting the Moynihan thesis. These were the church-race groups of the Protestant Council of the City of New York and the National Council of Churches.

The church's involvement in the Moynihan controversy was spearheaded by Dr. Benjamin Payton, who in the summer of 1965 was Director of the Office of Religion and Race of the Protestant Council and Anna Hedgeman, Director of Special Events for the National Council of Churches' Commission on Religion and Race. Since that time, Payton has been promoted to the job vacated by Robert Spike, Director of the National Council of Churches' Commission on Religion and Race. Payton became concerned about the Moynihan Report when he read John Pomfret's article in *The New York Times* (July 17th). At that time, he tried to get a copy of the report and was able to do so "through devious means." He began writing his critique of the Moynihan Report during Moynihan's campaign in New York. It was after he had completed one draft that he received a copy of the critique written by William Ryan. (Ryan released his paper on October 8th.) Payton did not release his critique until after the New York primary on September 14th. "I did not want people to say that I was looking for a way to keep Moynihan from getting votes; I wrote the paper for much more important reasons." (Anna Hedgeman was running against Moynihan in the New York primary. Both lost.) Payton distributed his critique of the Moynihan Report on October 14th, a month after the primary election. He mailed out several hundred copies of the report including copies "to persons I knew in universities. I wanted sociological critiques of the Moynihan Report done as soon as possible. You see I wanted to develop an alternative framework to the Moynihan thesis."

Included with the copies of the critique was a letter suggesting that "Pre-White House Conferences" for metropolitan areas across the country be organized with the explicit participation of as wide a range of persons and groups as is possible. Payton erroneously included in his critique the statement, "Although it has not even been made public yet . . . ." The article was a vigorous attack on the report, coupled with an effort to substitute "metropolitics" for "family stability" as the important issue. Yet one is left with the impression, after reading the newspaper articles, the Moynihan Report, and the Payton critique, that it was the newspaper articles about which Payton was writing. He was attacking the public image of the Moynihan Report rather than the report itself.

On November 9th under the leadership of Dr. Payton's office, a New York Pre-White House Conference was held. The news release describing this conference said that "Approximately one hundred leaders of New York City civic, religious and civil rights organizations" attended. A three-point resolution, prepared by the steering committee prior to the meeting, was adopted by the delegates.

The three-point resolution began with the statement:

Appreciation to President Johnson for the very able leadership he has provided in the struggle for racial justice in America, and our hope that the much needed initiative he is providing in the form of White House Conference on civil rights will not be weakened or distorted by the very agenda of that conference. *It is our position that the question of "family stability" be stricken entirely from that agenda and be approached through an economic and urban analysis of needs in the critical area of jobs, housing and equality integrated education* [emphasis ours].

The group suggested that the analysis should deal with the extent to which federal funds are being used to maintain segregation and other forms of discrimination in violation of federal laws and should consider means for the protection of individual civil rights.

The second part of the resolution called for another White House Conference in 1967 "as a follow-up to the one now being planned for June of 1966." The third part of the resolution asked:

. . . that the major efforts in this whole process, bench-marked by the White House Conferences, be devoted to preparation of "An Economic Development Budget for Equal Rights in America"; one that establishes priority expenditures for jobs and job training programs, housing and slum rehabilitation, health and welfare facilities and institutional needs for creating quality integrated education.

The news release concluded with a quote from Dr. Payton's critique of the Moynihan Report which he said was "plagued by

the simplistic logic which holds it together, the inadequate empirical evidence it utilizes and the erroneous premise upon which
it is based." The statement that "Although it has not even been
made public yet, the report has already had an impact upon the
civil rights movement and upon more general American politics
that is quite deadening and utterly misleading" remained in the
news release of November 9th.

Thus the church group, rather than "cooling it" as did the civil
rights organizations, called a pre-White House Conference on
Civil Rights to resolve that "family stability" be stricken from
the record.

One government civil rights man described the New York
meeting in the following manner. "It was like someone who gets
all steamed up for a fight and then finds out there is nothing to
fight for, but because they have their body sugar up so high they
have to go ahead and fight anyway." This man gave the church
more credit than others; his statement implied that the church
group knew of the détente between the conference staff and the
civil rights organizations.

Other civil rights leaders, including ones highly critical of the
report, denied involvement in this church move:

As far as the churches are concerned, we have not been involved with
them. My guess is that they leapt off the deep end as far as the Moynihan Report is concerned. You know they came out saying that they
didn't want the family at all as far as its being discussed at the White
House Conference. I think that this is the wrong and incorrect tactic —
that it only feeds into the hands of critics who say, "You're afraid to
talk about yourself, or admit things about yourself."

Indications are that there were few if any contacts between
the church groups and the civil rights organizations during the
fall of 1965. Somehow the informal networks between the government and the civil rights organizations did not include the
church. Robert Spike was regarded as one of the ten most
powerful men in civil rights, and his organization had spearheaded the increasing involvement of the Protestant Churches in
direct action civil rights work (particularly in the Delta Ministry
and Selma). The church groups had played a crucial role in the
passage of the 1964 and 1965 civil rights' bills. Yet, his organization was not included in *all* of the planning meetings between the
White House Conference staff and the movement, nor in the
civil rights organizations' strategy change with regard to the
Moynihan Report. Though Spike himself had good White House

contacts, the efforts of his organization and of the closely related New York church group did not seem to mesh with those of the civil rights organizations in their negotiations with the Conference staff. None of the civil rights "Big Six" leaders were listed on the coordinating committee for the Spring 1966 pre-White House Conference and none spoke at the November pre-White House Conference.

Our interviews with leaders of civil rights organizations indicate that the church groups are on the edge of the informal networks of the civil rights organizations. Their influence in the area of civil rights seems largely because of their own push, money, and manpower rather than because they are established as important members of the civil rights movement. One well-informed respondent said of the church, "They are always on the make. They try to be more militant than anyone else." Another commented, "The Commission on Religion and Race is carrying out a very interesting experiment; they are trying to create social change through press releases."

Whatever the motivation and/or lack of communication, it is clear that the Protestant Council's involvement in the conference agenda issue was a tempest in a teapot after the main storm was over. With regard to the Moynihan controversy, however, the involvement seems crucial to the controversy becoming a full-fledged public issue.

The Philadelphia and Detroit Meetings

In addition to the meeting held by the church groups in New York, there were at least two other "pre-White House" meetings held in the early part of November. One of these meetings, held in Detroit, has been kept out of the press and its participants have been particularly close-mouthed about it. One participant said, "We stayed up until five o'clock in the morning arguing over the conference." Evidently people from the more radical civil rights organizations and one government representative were present. As best we can tell, the meeting was primarily concerned with the Moynihan Report, the question of whether or not it would be central to the planning conference, and whether the conference would be boycotted by some civil rights people. One participant reported that it "was the consensus of the group that . . . somehow the Moynihan Report was establishing that the Negro family had degenerated to the point where it could be truthfully said that the American Negro was, in fact, . . . somewhat less than human."

The other meeting was held in Philadelphia, where militant grass roots Negro leaders from across the nation met with conference staff members on November 5th. According to the *Congressional Quarterly* (November 12, 1965), there was some conflict over this meeting, specifically between Julius Hobson of Washington, D. C., head of the Organization for Black Power, Jesse Gray, Leader of the 1963 Rent Strikes in New York City, and members of the White House Conference staff. Evidently Hobson was not invited to the Philadelphia meeting because of his "radical left wing position" and Gray because he had little mass support. The *Congressional Quarterly* reported that the Organization for Black Power met in Philadelphia, after the Philadelphia meeting, and voted to boycott the White House Conference.

The Philadelphia meeting was called by the conference staff at the suggestion of William T. Coleman, a Negro lawyer from Philadelphia and co-chairman of the planning conference. The militants to be invited were selected by two or three prominent Eastern and Midwestern militant leaders. This meeting was to function to educate Coleman, who knew little about the problems of lower-class Negroes. One participant described the meeting by saying that the local Negro leaders were both eloquent and vivid in communicating their understanding of what ghetto life was like and brought it to life for the conference people. There was a good deal of criticism and suspiciousness by the local people because they felt that they would not be invited to the planning conference and that the calling of the Philadelphia meeting was simply a way of cooling them out. There was considerable criticism of the Moynihan Report (although few if any of them had read it). One objection to it was not on the ground that it was inaccurate but that it was just one other case of whites telling Negroes what they were like and how they ought to live. One local leader was concerned that a family session would discuss birth control which he regarded as a subtle form of genocide; he felt white people did not want Negroes to become a larger proportion of the population.

The important point about the Philadelphia meeting is that although it did not have a direct effect on the coming planning conference, it did give the conference staff a chance to communicate with local civil rights leaders who in the opinion of some of the staff were "in closer touch with the real situation than some of the national groups."

10

Intellectual Commentary on the Report

The intensive coverage that the report received in the news-papers through August and September generated in turn more serious treatment in unpublished papers and in articles in various journals of opinion. It is important to note that this intellectual activity was tangential to the negotiations being carried out between the government and the civil rights groups and that the articles which were widely distributed on a private basis or published appeared *after* the civil rights organization had struck a more or less acceptable compromise with the government on the organization and content of the conference. The intellectual critique did, however, play an important role in sustaining the controversy and providing content for it as the White House Conference drew near.

A preview of the issues dealt with in these critiques was provided in a perceptive piece by Christopher Jencks in *The New York Review of Books* of October 14th. Himself obviously rather skeptical of the report's tone, Jencks provided a summary of the main themes of critiques that later came to light:

Moynihan's analysis is in the conservative tradition that guided the drafting of the poverty program . . . The guiding assumption is that social pathology is caused less by basic defects in the social system than by defects in particular individuals and groups which prevent their adjusting to the system. The prescription is therefore to change the deviance, not the system.

He noted that some academicians and intellectuals "have been irate, and to my mind somewhat paranoid, about the report." These critics felt that there was "nothing inherently wrong with martriarchial families . . . and that picking on the Negro family for improvement is a subtle form of racism." It appeared that emphasis on the family was a way for the Administration to escape responsibility for other race problems and that concentration on the family could be seen as "a first step toward 1984." Jencks felt that this latter concern "seems to derive largely from a fear that the government will try to impose sexual continence and fidelity — virtues which almost all critics think greatly overrated." He suggested that if it were true that Negro lower-class families were matriarchial by choice it would be unreasonable for the government to try to alter this, but there was "considerable reason to suppose that they eagerly adopt more patriarchial middle class norms whenever they can," and that, therefore, the government ought to help them do so. Jencks concluded, "Indeed, if the new emphasis on 'stabilizing' the Negro family means giving Negroes a free choice between living as they do now or as the white middle classes do, it is hard to think that even the radicals will oppose it." But oppose it a great many radicals and others not so neatly pigeonholed did.

It is tempting to relate criticism of the Moynihan Report to ideological issues of radicalism versus conservative liberalism (a position many critics and allies would characterize as Moynihan's). It is true that all of the published critics of Moynihan would consider themselves more "left" than he; and that some of them identify themselves as part of either the "Old Left" or the "New Left." But, the same could be said for many of his public defenders. Broader ideological positions certainly informed some of the criticism, but it is our view that the main issues in this case are not so easily typed as radical versus conservative but rather exist at the less abstract level of organizational needs (in the case of the civil rights movement) and definitions of short-run tactical interests (in the case of some of the Permanent Government and outside social science critics). Many of Moynihan's "left" critics are themselves deeply involved in attempts to modify the way the government operates with respect to Negroes and the poor generally — they are engaged in "reform-mongering" rather than radical politics and are as dedicated as Moynihan himself to the idea that the executive establishment is amenable to program innovation under some circumstances. These critics would not have attacked a report "in the conservative tradition of the poverty program" which coincided with their own definition of their interests; they would have swallowed their ideological distaste and used the report as an argument for their programs.

One is similarly tempted to characterize some of the opposition to the report, particularly from some Permanent Government critics and a few civil rights objectors, as conservative vis à vis Moynihan's subdued welfare socialism (or welfare capitalism, as you please). Again, however, the opposition seems to us to stem from organizational threats to their existence and tactical requirements rather than from ideological positions.

Herbert J. Gans in Commonweal

On October 15th *Commonweal* Magazine published an article by Herbert J. Gans that still stands as the only thorough analysis of the report's social science base and political implications. It will be remembered that in August Gans had been concerned about the press coverage of the report and had written Richard Goodwin of the White House staff to express his concern. Afterwards, having read the report itself, Gans sought to put the issue in perspective — partly to offset the potential dangers he saw in the way the report was being used by the press and partly to attempt to head off the total rejection of the report by civil rights people which he saw building. At the time, however, he had not read the two most influential critiques to the report, those by William Ryan and Benjamin Payton.

Following a careful summary of the report's findings, Gans expressed his concern that because the report did not offer recommendations there was the danger, now that it had become public, of "the hasty development of programs that do not address themselves to the basic problem . . . . The vacuum that is created when no recommendations are attached to a policy proposal can easily be filled by undesirable solutions, and the report's conclusions can be conveniently misinterpreted." While Gans recognized a close interpenetration between the forces that victimize Negro families and the crippling results of this victimization, he was concerned that the report's emphasis on this latter theme "and the inherent sensationality of the data" will result in too much attention going to the disabilities and not sufficient attention going to the causes. He noted that the findings could be used by right-wing and racist groups to support their claim of Negro inferiority, that politicians may argue that Negroes should help themselves overcome "their" shortcomings, that the report could lead to a "clamor for pseudopsychiatric programs" which emphasized counseling and therapy, and finally that the report could be used to justify a reduction of efforts in the elimination of racial discrimination and the War on Poverty.

Gans then argued that our knowledge of the effects of lower-class Negro family structure was not as solid as we might wish nor as the report sometimes implied. Given this uncertainty and the much greater certainty of the primacy of economic deprivation Gans concluded that "it would thus be tragic if the findings . . . were used to justify demands for Negro self-improvement or the development of a middle-class family structure before further programs to bring about real equality are set up."

Noting that the conclusions and recommendations of the White House Conference will be crucial in this, Gans went on to suggest what he believed were some of the recommendations called for by the findings of the Moynihan Report. In a programmatic statement that was reminiscent of Moynihan's own internal recommendations, Gans emphasized jobs (both public works programs and an expanded program for subprofessionals in service areas), income maintenance programs ("governmental wage supplements," longer-term unemployment compensation related to family size, etc.), a realistic housing program which provided new housing outside the ghetto and desegregated existing housing, and more men to work with children in "the female dominated environment in which Negro boys grow up." Then Gans recommended "a thorough research program" on the Negro family to determine exactly the nature and the extent of the problem that Moynihan posed.

Gans ended on a pessimistic note. He emphasized the deep resistance to carrying out the kind of massive federal program he believed the report indicated: "The economic, social and political changes required to provide equality are drastic, and both the white and the Negro middle class — not to mention the white lower class — have a considerable investment in the status quo which condemns the poor Negro to membership in a powerless, dependent and deprived underclass." In order to counter these forces Gans believed that federal and local officials

must be supported — and pressured — by professional, religious and civic groups dedicated to racial equality. Also, the civil rights movement must begin to represent and speak for the low-income Negro population more than it has done in the past, for if the Negro revolution and the social peace of which Moynihan speaks are to be won, they must be won by and for that population.

"In the desert of compassion" that characterized societal attitudes toward poor Negroes, Gans concluded, "the Moynihan Report is a tiny oasis of hope, and if properly interpreted and implemented a first guide to the achievement of equality in the years to come." *

Gans had sought to establish a point of view which he thought worth saving from newspaper treatments overly titillated by family pathology and from civil rights critics determined to bury the question of Negro family welfare as a subject of public discussion or policy guidance. But it was far too late for that. Most of the civil rights groups had expressed their uneasiness about public discussion and seemed to have succeeded in avoiding any important emphasis on the family at the conference. Meanwhile two critics of the report had prepared documents that were to prove to be highly influential in legitimating a total discrediting of the report, at least so far as the public use of it for policy justification was concerned.

William Ryan's Savage Discovery: Privately Circulated and in The Nation

The November 22nd issue of The Nation carried an article, "Savage Discovery: The Moynihan Report," by William Ryan, a Boston psychologist active in a number of community psychiatry and mental health programs. Ryan distributed about fifty copies of his unpublished paper to people he knew and later complied with one hundred or more requests for copies from others. A longer version of the paper appeared in the NAACP's Crisis. On October 8th, several hundred copies of Ryan's document had been sent by Anna Hedgeman of the National Council of Churches

---

* Some of these quotations are from the longer, unpublished version of the Gans article; see Chapter 16C for this version.

to various political figures (the White House, congressmen, senators) and private organization leaders who might be concerned with these matters. Hedgeman had also brought Ryan's paper to the attention of Benjamin Payton, who was at the time also working on a critique of the report.

Ryan had read *Newsweek's* summary of the report in August and after discussing it with others in the movement and discovering that they were as concerned as he, he decided to undertake a written critique of the report which he prepared early in September and passed along (through James Breeden, a Boston cleric then on Robert Spike's staff) to Mrs. Hedgeman and Dr. Payton and to CORE's national office. The critique found willing and interested eyes in these places because of the already-existing concern about the report, and was particularly welcome because Ryan sought to criticize the adequacy of Moynihan's use of social science material as well as the apparent policy implications. Our interviews in New York, Washington, and elsewhere indicate that Ryan's article was widely regarded among critics as a definitive social science critique of the report. Because of its singular importance as the best-known critique of the report, we will consider its contents in detail, particularly in connection with its social science reasoning (other critiques have relied less heavily on a social science viewpoint).

In his article, Ryan saw as the report's main conclusion, "Negro family instability is the basic cause of Negro inequality and 'pathology' that are reflected in unemployment statistics, census data and the results of sociological research." In a slashing attack, Ryan went on to state that the report has "serious shortcomings," "draws dangerously inexact conclusions from weak and insufficient data; . . . encourages (no doubt unintentionally) a new form of subtle racism, . . . and seduces the reader into believing it is not racism and discrimination but the weakness and defects of the Negro himself that account for . . . inequality." He considered the report to be "irresponsible nonsense!" or more charitably not to have proved its contention and to contain "damnably inaccurate simplicity [which is] surely heresy."

Ryan took as his main target for detailed analysis Moynihan's treatment of illegitimacy statistics. He said that Moynihan used illegitimacy statistics as "the prime index of 'family breakdown.' " He considered Moynihan's implicit hypothesis to be that "The values of Negro culture . . . are such that there is little commitment to the main components of family organization — legitimacy, marital stability, etc. The *implicit* point is that Negroes tolerate promiscuity, illegitimacy, one-parent families, welfare dependency, and everything else that is supposed to follow." (Our emphasis.) Ryan then undertook an analysis of the differences in illegitimacy ratios for Negroes and whites which sought to demonstrate that these differences are due exclusively to inadequate access to means for avoiding being publicly labeled as an illegitimate child.

At this point, it should be noted that Ryan's criticism was somewhat tangential to Moynihan's use of illegitimacy data. Moynihan used the illegitimacy differential as one of two proximate causes for the fact that almost one fourth of Negro families are headed by females. In his discussion of Negro family breakdown, he took up first the question of the high rate of marital breakup; second, illegitimacy; and then moved on to demonstrate that Negro families are much more often headed by females. The "implicit" hypothesis Ryan attributes to Moynihan could hardly be discerned in Moynihan's own treatment of the data. To the extent that he considered why the high illegitimacy ratios exist he did so in terms of the correlation of illegitimate births with nonwhite male unemployment rates and income. Thus Ryan complained that "fully 22 per cent of the large and dramatic charts and graphs concern illegitimacy," (referring to four of the eighteen charts) but did not note that two of these four charts concern variation in illegitimacy ratios by socioeconomic status.

Having established Moynihan's implicit hypothesis, Ryan proceeded to demonstrate that other factors beside "a careless acceptance by Negroes of promiscuity and illegitimacy" accounted for the differential. He attributed the difference in illegitimacy rates to differences in reporting, shotgun marriages, abortion, contraception. All of these factors, and some others, are clearly involved as causes of the differential, but only the first bears directly on Moynihan's use of the data since Moynihan was not concerned to explain illegitimacy by something peculiar to Negro values, but rather to demonstrate its effects in terms of fostering female-headed households.* How the differential comes about is

---

* We are indebted to Ira Reiss of the University of Iowa and John Gagnon of Indiana University and the Kinsey Institute for technical consultation on the following discussion; they are however in no way responsible for any of the shortcomings of that discussion.

not central to his use of the data except in the case of underreporting.

Underreporting. Most social scientists seem to agree that there
is significant underreporting of illegitimate births and that there
are probably some class and race biases in this, but no one seems
to know or to have any informed guesses about the extent of this
underreporting or the distribution of the bias. Even if the actual
white rate were twice the reported rate, there would still be a
four to one differential. However, there seems little reason to
believe that white illegitimate births are underreported to that
extent. First of all, there seems little reason to believe that there
is more than a very small difference in the underreporting of
white lower class illegitimacies compared to Negro illegitimacies.
It is primarily at the middle-class level that underreporting occurs.
The Kinsey studies on pregnancy, birth, and abortion certainly
would not sustain an interpretation that the underreporting is of
this order.

While there are no data on which to make a judgment concerning the problem of underreporting, there is only very little data
to judge the other issues Ryan raised and this small amount of
data comes primarily from the Kinsey researchers, who do provide information on "shotgun marriages" and abortions as well
as on rate of premarital conception and premarital intercourse.
Using what little data there are, we will try to assess the importance of these various factors for the light it may shed on the
issues Moynihan and Ryan raise.

Shotgun Marriages. Ryan asserted that conceptions resulting in
marriage before birth are "less frequent among Negroes because
of the man's financial insecurity." If true this would tend to
support Moynihan's argument that economic deprivation produces female-headed households.

However, the Kinsey data lend no support to this view. With
education controlled almost exactly the same proportions of
Negro and white women who have a premarital pregnancy marry
before the birth of the child. This would mean that without controlling for education a *higher* proportion of all Negro women
with premarital conceptions are likely to marry before birth of
the child than of whites (primarily as a result of white use of

abortion, the second factor which Ryan mentioned). It would appear that about one quarter of pregnant non-college-educated women of both races marry before the birth of the child as opposed to 10 percent or fewer of college-educated women of both races. Since a higher proportion of white women than Negro women attend college it follows that the over-all ratio will show that more pregnant Negro girls marry than pregnant white girls.

Evidence contrary to the Kinsey findings, however, comes from a study by William F. Pratt of marriages and illegitimate births in the Detroit metropolitan area. Pratt's study is more recent and based on a large sample of marriage and birth records. It suggests that of all conceptions before marriage *which eventuate in birth* (i.e., excluding abortions and miscarriages) in about two thirds of the white cases the woman marries before the birth of the child, compared to only about one quarter of the nonwhite cases. It was on this study that Ryan drew for his conclusion that "shotgun" marriages are more common among whites. Since Pratt's study does not include illegitimate conceptions that do not eventuate in birth, however, it does not give us direct findings on the proportion of shotgun marriages in the two groups. If, however, one assumes that the ratio of abortions and miscarriages to live births is the same for Pratt's Detroit group as it was in the Kinsey studies one can estimate the proportion of women who become pregnant who have shotgun marriages. With this assumption, at least, there is no marked divergence between Pratt's findings and those of the Kinsey studies. Although Pratt's study (with this assumption about abortion) does suggest more white shotgun marriages than the Kinsey studies, the difference is quite small.

Abortions. In the case of abortions, Ryan was clearly dealing with an important factor. According to the Kinsey study about three times as many non-college-educated white girls who become pregnant premaritally have induced abortions as Negro girls of the same educational levels (the proportion among college-educated girls of both races are the same). However, spontaneous abortions (miscarriages) afflict low-income Negroes much more than whites. (In his longer, unpublished memo Ryan included spontaneous abortions in his estimate). Although the Kinsey data here are incomplete, the results suggest that about twice as many

Negroes as whites at the noncollege levels abort spontaneously. Combining the two sources of abortion then results in a ratio of about two to one with education controlled, and slightly higher with education uncontrolled. Clearly, a significant proportion of the illegitimacy ratio differential is due to the fact that whites are more likely to have abortions of one kind or another than are Negroes.

Premarital conception. By this method, Ryan argued that the "illegitimate conception" rates of whites and Negroes are closer to a two to one ratio. On this point, the Kinsey data provide some information. Ryan suggests a 2 to 1 difference in premarital conception rates, but the Kinsey studies suggest that the ratio is on the order of 3 to 4 to one with education controlled, and of course, higher than that without educational controls. For example, comparing high-school-educated girls, by the age of 20 some 7 percent of whites and 35 percent of Negroes have had a premarital conception experience; comparing the same women at the age of 25, some 11 percent of whites and 41 percent of Negroes have had a premarital conception experience. In order to make an accurate over-all assessment of the differential experience with premarital conception, we would have to have a balanced sample and one that takes into account age at marriage; but this is not available. The Kinsey results do suggest, however, that Ryan's two-to-one ratio is entirely too low.

Contraception. Ryan then asserted that there is differential access to contraception in the two groups and that this has an effect. While it is certainly true that over-all whites as a group are much more inclined to use contraception than are Negroes as a group, no one knows the extent of this differential in connection with *nonmarital* intercourse. It is very likely that the extent of use of contraception by whites, particularly lower-class whites, before marriage is greatly exaggerated. At least this would be the conclusion one would be led to by examination of the way married white men and women talk about the use of contraception early in marriage — they very often indicate relative unfamiliarity with the practice. While popular journalistic treatments and a few social scientists have argued that the use of contraception in premarital intercourse is on the upswing among whites of all classes, there is no solid data to support this view. Since such a discovery has been announced periodically for the past 30 years, there is some reason to believe that it is a myth.

Frequency of intercourse.   Nevertheless, Negro women who have premarital coital experience are much more likely to become pregnant than white women. For example, in the Kinsey studies at the high school level 50 percent of Negro women with intercourse experience had a premarital pregnancy by the age of 25 compared to only 25 percent of white women. Part of this difference may indeed be due to the fact that the white women and men are more inclined to use contraception, but at least a third to a half of the difference is accounted for by the fact that, again according to the Kinsey study, even among those who had premarital intercourse, the Negro girls had intercourse more often than their white counterparts. A part of the differential for those exposed by premarital intercourse to the risks of pregnancy is due to a greater frequency of intercourse in the Negro group.

Premarital intercourse.   By this point, Ryan felt that he might have sufficiently accounted for the difference in rates to conclude that it is possible that the "illegitimate intercourse" rates are about the same among Negroes and whites. Such little evidence as exists on this question, however, is solidly against such a conclusion. The qualitative data from community studies of working-class white and Negro areas would suggest that there is a great deal more sexual involvement at younger ages in Negro communities than white communities. Similarly, the Kinsey studies show marked differences in exposure to premarital coitus. For example, for non-college-educated women, at the age of 15 some 10 percent to 15 percent of white girls have had premarital intercourse compared to over half of Negro girls; by the age of 20 about a third of white girls compared to 82 percent of Negro girls have had intercourse. In most areas examined so far, the differences between white and Negro girls at the college level has been minimal. Here, however, there is still a marked difference. By the age of 20, about a quarter of college-educated white girls have had intercourse compared to almost half of Negro girls. The work of Ira Reiss on premarital sex attitudes strongly reinforces the conclusion that regardless of social-class status Negro girls are more likely to be involved in premarital intercourse than white girls. Reiss finds that even with class differences controlled, Negroes are more accepting of premarital coitus for themselves than are comparable whites.

Postmarital exposure. There is an additional factor which accounts for the observed differences in illegitimacy ratios that Ryan does not mention. Kingsley Davis had described a rather marked change in the nature of illegitimacy over the past 15 years. The proportion of illegitimate births that are first births has declined considerably for both whites and nonwhites, the proportion of second to fourth births has increased slightly, and the proportion of fifth and higher-order births has increased a very great deal. In 1947, white illegitimate births were more often first births than were Negro illegitimate births but this was even more the case in 1962. Thus in 1962, the ratio of Negro to white illegitimate first births was 5 to 1; that of illegitimate second or higher-order births was twelve to one. In 1962, fully 60 percent of Negro illegitimate births were not first births (compared to only 37 percent of white illegitimate births).

Clearly, one of the reasons why Negroes have more higher order illegitimate births than whites is that at any one time a higher proportion of Negro women who have once been married are no longer married. Phrased in another way, as a group Negro women, despite the fact that they marry at roughly the same ages as whites, spend a higher proportion of their fecund years in an unmarried state (because of death, divorce, etc.). Therefore they are exposed to the risk of illegitimate conception for a greater proportion of their fecund time than are white women. This "cause" of higher illegitimacy ratios clearly fits with Moynihan's thesis; the connection is in line with his views about the effects of unemployment and poverty on marital disruption rates. (This factor probably looms largest in the difference observed in the report concerning variation in illegitimacy rates by male unemployment and family-income level.)

The relative weight of the factors. We can summarize this discussion of factors affecting the illegitimacy rates of whites and Negroes in the following schematic presentation, but due to the inadequacies of the data it is impossible to apportion the variance accurately among the different factors.

Factors making for higher Negro illegitimacy relative to white illegitimacy	Factors making for lower Negro illegitimacy relative to white illegitimacy
Major Factors	*Major Factors*
Greater resort to induced abortion by pregnant, unmarried whites	Higher spontaneous abortion rate among Negro women.
Greater frequency of coitus by those Negro women who have non-marital coitus	
Higher proportion of Negro women having non-marital coitus	
Higher proportion of fecund years spent by Negro women in a non-married status	
Minor Factors	*Minor Factors*
Greater use of contraception by whites in non-marital intercourse	Subfecundity of Negro women due to poor health and nutrition
Higher rates of marriage by white women premaritally pregnant	
Underreporting of white illegitimate births	

None of this, of course, need sustain the hypothesis that Negro illegitimacy is a sole result of slavery and Reconstruction. But it cannot be maintained that there are no differences in the sexual behavior of whites and Negroes, and these differences cannot be explained as a simple and direct result of discrimination (though it is not at all difficult to trace the causal chain back to the victimized position forced on Negroes by the present society as well as the past one).

Having considered findings concerning illegitimacy Ryan turned to those concerning ADC and adoption. He noted that Negro women seldom have any choice about whether or not to keep their children since the services of adoption agencies and maternity homes are mostly for white mothers. Moynihan had also noted: "In a typical pattern of discrimination, Negro children in all public and private orphanages are a smaller proportion of all children than their proportion of the population although their needs are clearly greater."

It is interesting that so much of the outrage about the Moynihan Report seems to be due to the fact that he dealt with illegitimacy statistics. Certainly in many of the newspaper accounts a sensitive reader will note veiled accusations of immorality — to say nothing of Theodore White's treatment of the same subject in his

Making of the President, 1964, where the accusation is much more blatant (as in the use of terms like "biological anarchy" and "zoological tenements"). While it is difficult to expect the reality of lower-class sexual behavior and the resulting illegitimacy to stimulate anything in conventional middle-class people (white or Negro) but dismay and a sense of appalled concern, those interested in civil rights are only being realistic when they in turn become concerned about the possible destructive uses that may be made of such facts.

However, one has a right to expect that intelligent social observers will deal with the problem by taking it out of a Puritan, moral-immoral dialogue and placing it in the context of social causes and social costs both from the point of view of the wider society and of the individual involved. Illegitimacy statistics are a way of quantifying the facts that a great many Negro children are born into situations in which they are not wanted and are then required to live in homes which do not have whatever advantages present and legitimate fathers may bring. Second, this statistic is a convenient way of suggesting the burgeoning welfare costs that may be expected to continue so long as a more effective government policy is not developed to encourage families headed by men. A realistic assessment of these burgeoning costs is one way for the government to come to an understanding that a refusal to develop more realistic job, wage, and income maintenance policies is in the long run uneconomic.

Having taken up what he regards as the most serious errors in the report, Ryan discussed more generally the nature of the evidence brought forward in support of Moynihan's thesis. He did not like the descriptive character of the report, characterizing it as "retailing stale and well-known sociological facts." While the facts are in a sense well-known, whether or not they are stale depends on one's point of view. Moynihan believed that the facts were not well-known or well-attended to at the higher levels of the administration to whose attention he wished to bring them.

Ryan summed up what he believed to be valid in Moynihan's presentation as follows:

What these cool correlations mean, when translated from census data to the lives of human beings, is that poor people tend to live in slums, to be oppressed and exploited and mistreated, and to experience enormous amounts of social, economic, mental, and physical suffering as a result. The disproportionate share of the poor are Negro and they experience a vastly disproportionate share of this suffering . . . . Poor

Negro families — that is, half of all Negro families — are bitterly discriminated against and exploited, with the result that the individual, the family and the community are deeply injured.

Despite the fact that Ryan could phrase to his own satisfaction essentially the same points that Moynihan was making, he did also have a genuine disagreement. That is, he was unwilling to accept the notion that family instability is in any sense a cause of the "tangle of pathology" of the ghetto. In doing so, he underemphasized the full range of elements that Moynihan put into his model — a deprived position in the institutional system producing family instability which in turn is a fundamental cause of other forms of pathology. There were, as we have seen in the discussion of press coverage of the report, good reasons for comments on the report that stressed the central role of economic and educational deprivation, and the role of discrimination in these, but to do so it was not necessary to distort the full range of Moynihan's ideas.

Along the same lines of his criticism of Moynihan's treatment of illegitimacy data, Ryan considered as an error in fact the report's discussion of the greater proportion of crimes against persons committed by Negroes. He did not like Moynihan's use of arrest and conviction rates to sustain this interpretation. In making this criticism, he failed to note that Moynihan himself had pointed out that the data are unquestionably biased against Negroes who are arraigned more casually than are whites. But the Report went on to say that the bias was not strong enough to overcome the fact that Negroes are disproportionately represented among those who commit crimes against persons and that "the overwhelming number of offenses committed are directed toward other Negroes: the cost of crime to the Negro community is a combination of that to the criminal and to the victim." Few Negroes who live in slums would disagree with this statement. Actually there is a typical pattern of discrimination which could well operate in the opposite direction from that which Ryan claimed. That is, police have been traditionally rather lackadaisical about crime in the ghetto. It may well be that, particularly in connection with crimes against persons, Negroes are less likely to be arrested than whites because the police regard such crimes as unimportant. We should not forget that Negroes in ghettos have two kinds of complaints against police, one involving their brutality, lack of respect and hostility, and the other involving their lack of interest in and ability to protect residents from the depredations of those around them.

Ryan considers it a "fantastic error" that Moynihan states: "The white family has achieved a high degree of stability and is maintaining that stability. By contrast, the family structure of lower-class Negroes . . . is approaching complete breakdown." He notes Moynihan's error in not pointing out that the white illegitimacy rate has shown a greater increase than the Negro illegitimacy rate (but this zooming white rate still accounts for only 3 percent of white births and fewer than 2 percent of white women ever have an illegitimate birth). Ryan would rather maintain that American families in general are crumbling because of a white divorce rate that has "zoomed almost 800 percent in less than 100 years." Such a view seems to be a popular rejoinder among some of the report's critics. Yet most sociologists regard the increased divorce rate over the past century as in part of a result of prosperity which allows desertion (the old "poor man's divorce") to be turned into divorce. Similarly most family sociologists, noting the high rate of subsequent remarriages of divorced couples, are inclined not to regard the century's divorce rate as an index of serious family disorganization. Finally, since about the mid-1950's the white divorce rate has been decreasing somewhat, suggesting that whatever reorganizations of family life were indicated by the previous increase in divorce are in the process of being consolidated. In discussing divorce, Ryan also failed to note that the data which Moynihan used indicated that at any one time more married Negro women currently have the marital status of "divorced" than white women. This is principally because of a lower remarriage rate, which in turn can be seen as a fairly direct result of the unpromising economic prospects of the men who might be available for remarriage to divorced Negro women.

There is, of course, no reason why there should not be serious discussion of the travail of the middle-class suburban couple, nor why these travails should not provide material for the enjoyable sport of *épater le bourgeois*. However, the costs of the sport should be borne by its middle-class objects and by the intellectuals who engage in it and not by the lower-class family, Negro or white, from whose plight it tends to distract attention. That it does indeed distract attention can be seen in the popularity of this rejoinder to Moynihan's thesis, a rejoinder that has been popular not only among civil rights and social science critics but also among some Administration officials from whom this group would like to get action on Negro problems. Thus one highly placed Administration person responded when Moynihan first approached him with the subject of the plight of the Negro family, "Well, the whole American family has busted up."

Ryan believed that there was a new ideology which "would make it seem that unemployment, poor education and slum conditions result from family breakdown, 'cultural deprivation,' and lack of 'acculturation' of southern rural migrants." Elements of such an ideology certainly exist and appear from time to time in the press, in the conversations of middle class people who want to "go slow" on integration and occasionally in an unthinking manner of presentation of social science findings. But the proper defense against "savage discovery" is not to deny reality but rather to see it in perspective. Ryan wished to keep the tension developed from the fact that Negroes are disadvantaged because they are miseducated in segregated slum schools, because they are the last hired and the first fired, because slum landlords neglect their property and because there is a criminal shortage of decent low-income housing. But he was unwilling to come to terms with some of the effects of living in this kind of an environment.

Ryan presented as stereotypes of the new ideology "the promiscuous mother who produces a litter of illegitimate brats," "the child who cannot read because . . . his parents never talk to him," "the 'untenantable' Negro family . . . that is reputed to throw garbage out of the window." Yet behind these stereotypes there are people whose adaptations to slum life have resulted in ways of behaving that *are* destructive of their possibilities for taking advantage of any new opportunities that might come their way. There are women who have many illegitimate children and even more that have one or two. There are children who find it difficult to learn in school because their life at home does not provide them with the kinds of experiences that maximize their chances of doing well at school, and there are families who throw garbage out of the window, thereby getting themselves in trouble with their neighbors and others. Just because these things are true, it is not necessary to conclude that "segregation and discrimination are not the terrible villains we thought they were." To the contrary, segregation and discrimination *are* the terrible villains we thought they were precisely because they have these kinds of effects as well as other effects on the people who must live in a segregated world.

Payton's Critique

As has been described in the previous chapter, the then director of the Office of Religion and Race of the Protestant Council of New York had prepared in September a critique of the Moynihan Report and distributed it widely, both in New York City and elsewhere, about the middle of October. This paper, combined with the Ryan critique, served as the principle intellectual basis for the resolution passed by a Pre-White House Conference in New York on November 9th requesting that the question of "family stability" be "stricken entirely from the agenda" of the White House Conference. We have discussed in the last section some of the effects of this line of action on the part of the Commission on Religion and Race of the National Council of Churches and the Office of Religion and Race of the Protestant Council of New York. Here we will examine the intellectual issues raised by Payton's original document and by his subsequent article in *Christianity and Crisis*.

Payton titled his original document, "The President, the Social Experts, and the Ghetto: An Analysis of an Emerging Strategy in Civil Rights." In his paper, Payton attempted what he believed was a desperately needed "clarification . . . regarding the validity and implications of the 'Moynihan Report,' the predictable outcomes for civil rights of a strategy based upon it, and the implications for American politics in general when the relationship between politicians, social experts and private citizens takes the particular shape produced in the aftermath of that report." Payton's over-all evaluation of the report seemed to be as follows:

Too neatly rounded out of the assumptions, limited data and interests of one social expert . . . , the symmetry of the report is flawed only by the simplistic logic which holds it together, the inadequate empirical evidence it utilizes, and the erroneous premises upon which it is based. Although it has not even been made public yet, the report has already had an impact upon the civil rights movement and upon more general American politics that is quite deadening and utterly misleading.

He indicated that the report came to highly questionable conclusions, of which the most important are:
1. Since unemployment is decreasing, Negro riots cannot be attributed to lack of jobs for Negroes.
2. Therefore, the riots are caused, not only by discrimination and an inadequate supply of economic opportunities but past exploitation, particularly that under slavery. Therefore, it is not poor housing, education, job status but "litters of illegitimate Negro

teenagers, husbandless Negro women and Negro men . . . insufficiently acculturated" to standards of family stability that make for problems. "In short," wrote Payton, "an all but totally pathological set of relationships internal to the Negro community: these, assert the 'Moynihan Report,' are the real causes of the recent riot."

The connection with two *New York Times* news stories (July 19th and August 27th) and the Evans and Novak column of August 18th was clear in the issues Payton defined. He picked up from Evans and Novak the emphasis on Negro riots and the characterization of the report as based on census bureau statistics, from *The New York Times* the emphasis on the importance of slavery, and from both the emphasis on illegitimate children, husbandless Negro women, and men who will not stay married. From Payton's characterization one would not know that Moynihan had not mentioned the riots in his report.

The prime influence on what Payton wrote would seem to be the press coverage that he cited rather than the report itself. Following this summary of Moynihan's findings as he saw them, Payton sought to demonstrate that Moynihan's conclusions regarding unemployment among Negroes are based on "inadequate empirical data." He was concerned to demonstrate the incorrectness of what he believed to be Moynihan's contention that Negroes shared in the general gains in the total employment picture and also in income. Yet Moynihan was arguing that a 2-to-1 Negro-white unemployment ratio had persisted since 1940: "The fundamental, overwhelming factor is that *Negro unemployment,* with the exception of a few years during World War II and the Korean War, has continued at disaster levels for thirty-five years." Indeed, a month before Payton distributed copies of his paper, Moynihan had characterized unemployment as a key factor in the Watts riot. It is ironic that Payton attempted to demonstrate the invalidity of "the optimistic Moynihan Report" by citing July 1965 Negro unemployment rates (in Chicago and Rochester, New York), thus seizing on exactly the same month that Moynihan used in his *Reporter* article to demonstrate that Negroes do not necessarily benefit from sharp increases in employment opportunities.

Then Payton sought to set right what he believed to be Moynihan's incorrect statements concerning Negro income:

In general — *Moynihan to the contrary and notwithstanding* — it has been demonstrated that since the 1950's, the relative gains made by

Negroes have been steadily worsening. According to Herman P. Miller, one of our most competent authorities on income statistics, "White-non-white income differentials are not narrowing." On the contrary: "During the last decade . . . it shows some evidence of having widened." This is the important and harrowing fact that social experts, policy makers and private citizens must come to terms with [emphasis ours].

With respect to the Moynihan Report, such a statement was carrying coals to Newcastle. Moynihan had used the same data that Miller had used to make exactly the same point. He had noted in the report that outside of the South, "the ratio of non-white to white family income in cities increased from 57 to 63%" in the 1950's but had then begun a decline which persisted through 1963. More important, in every region of the country except the South, Negro-family income relative to white-family income had declined from 1960 to 1963.

Having successfully demolished the thesis he incorrectly characterized as Moynihan's, Payton then summarized Ryan's criticism of Moynihan's treatment of Negro-white illegitimacy differentials. After reviewing and endorsing Ryan's criticisms, Payton concluded that it was clear "that the argument of the 'Moynihan Report' is quite specious." He argued that matriarchy and illegitimacy are "themselves mere symptoms of other more basic problems" and that instead what is central to the plight of urban Negroes is "insufficient jobs and job training programs; inferior segregated education; inadequate and unsafe housing conditions." The problem is a "socio-economic system that does not provide enough of the goods and services required to live a minimally decent life, and that discriminates on the basis of race and social class considerations in the distribution of such items." (As with some of Ryan's views, what Payton said was not particularly different from the argument that Moynihan advanced except that Moynihan went on to argue that the effects on the family of lack of resources are such that family disorganization, in turn, influences the ghetto situation in an unconstructive way.) Payton supported this point by a quotation from Richard Cloward dealing with the dynamics of poverty in which Cloward observed that . . . "we have robbed men of manhood, women of husbands, and children of fathers. To create a stable monogamous family, we need to provide men (especially Negro men) with the opportunity to be men and that involves enabling them to perform occupationally." Again this is exactly the point that Moynihan was making. Ironically, Moynihan had also quoted Cloward's (and

Robert Ontel's) assessment of some of the difficulties of the Mobilization for Youth project. In that quotation, Cloward and Ontel had noted problems posed in their efforts to engage slum youth in meaningful contacts with the occupational world by the youth's lack of self-confidence and a sense of competence. The point in that case was that the effect on the individual of growing up in a depriving situation was such as to make it difficult for him to take advantage of the opportunities that Mobilization for Youth was trying to provide.

Having demolished the thesis of Moynihan as reported in the newspapers without really seriously addressing himself to Moynihan's views as reflected in the report itself, Payton went on to argue that the problem is not "family instability" but "metropolitan instability." He presented a rather straightforward discussion of the problems of incoherence and planlessness in metropolitan areas and the destructive and discriminatory effects metropolitan incoherence has on the situation of Negroes. Here again the views he advanced were not at all in conflict with the ones that Moynihan had offered and quite closely paralleled some of Moynihan's points about the growth of de facto housing and school segregation. One would not be hard put to connect Payton's interest in "the metropolitan area as a racial problem" with Moynihan's interest in family instability; as a matter of fact, many observers have seen both problems as parts of one ball of wax. Yet Payton insisted that they are diametrically opposed approaches to the same problem. He considered taking the issue of family stability as a major one — "not a 'great departure' on how 'to fulfill these rights,' but an initiative of a very low order consisting in a gross, if not insulting, reversal of priorities."

Since it would be very difficult to explain Payton's animus toward Moynihan's report on intellectual grounds, we must look elsewhere. In the latter part of his paper, Payton discussed what he believed to be some of the political implications of the Moynihan thesis, particularly of the fact that it seemed to have been adopted by the White House as a basis for planning the White House Conference. It is apparent that it was Payton's expectations concerning how the Moynihan thesis could be used, combined with his personal preference for a metropolitan planning approach that excited his hostility. That is, it was not so much that there was an inherent conflict between his social science views of this situation and those of Moynihan as that Payton was suspicious of how the Administration was handling civil rights problems and had made a choice for a strategy based on metropolitan planning and administration of programs. He found little support for this approach in the report.

Having to his own satisfaction demolished Moynihan's argument, Payton took the Howard University speech as a specific instance of presidential use of social experts. He wrote, "that President Johnson reached to significant social experts . . . is evident from the quality of the speech." (Yet, if he paid as close attention to the newspaper coverage of the report as his outrage about the report seemed to suggest, Payton should have known that the only social expert President Johnson reached to was the self-same Moynihan.) Of the speech Payton wrote, "The President sketched . . . an approach to the question of civil rights that promised to lift the whole issue to a new level of discussion, and provide a more meaningful framework within which action might be planned for its resolution." He went on to characterize the speech in an extremely flattering way, referring to "an impressive array of technical data," "imaginative ethical insight," "incisive social analysis," "a devastatingly clear rationale."

Payton was not unique in finding it difficult to relate the inspiring and forward-looking character of the Howard speech to the press coverage of the conference preplanning with its emphasis on Negro family instability. He asked, "What kind of political action does this portend? Was the decision to limit the conference an explicit political decision or covert political judgment masquerading as merely the technical judgment of a social expert?" He suggested in passing that he suspected that the emphasis on family stability was designed to justify "new family welfare legislation." Then, Payton embarked on a straightforward analysis of the importance of more rational metropolitan government, and the use of resources in metropolitan areas in such a way that Negroes are not systematically disadvantaged by the way cities work.

One other theme of Payton's critique expressed a very widespread objection to the Moynihan thesis. Payton quarrelled with the pathological emphasis of the report and argued that such an emphasis makes it very difficult to understand where the new vigor of Negro rights groups stems from. This is more than a mere intellectual critique, since it goes to the heart of a very important political issue which Payton stated in the course of some comments on Gunner Myrdal's approach to civil rights problems: "The political and programmatic result [of overemphasis on weakness of the Negro community] is that although Myrdal is able to appreciate the need for *federal* political action, he is quite unable to appreciate the need for local community action on the part of *Negroes themselves." In essence, then, the Moynihan thesis is seen as deeply embarrassing to those who wish to build Negro political power, since emphasis on pathological processes within the Negro community tends to vitiate the claims of those who would maintain that Negroes have succeeded in amassing some power and are on the road to amassing greater power.*

Curiously, however, Payton's program (as reflected in a position paper developed by his Pre-White House Conference planning group early in 1966) was not particularly different from Moynihan's program as reflected in his recommendations in the May 4th memorandum to the President except that Payton placed his proposals in the context of metropolitan programs and Moynihan implicitly placed his in the context of federal programs. It is therefore not so much the content of the remedy but the mode of administering and controlling these programs that separated them. Payton wanted local administration and presumably was willing to run the risk of conservative white political control in order to have the opportunity for the local Negro power to assert itself and to participate in the control. Moynihan, on the other hand, wished to short-circuit these problems with federal action directed by an Administration determined to end the political embarrassment as well as the injustice of Negro inequality.

Much can be said in support of each of these strategies. There are ample reasons for doubting the ability of the federal government to move in a really vigorous way to end racial injustice by compensatory programs, but there are equally good reasons for doubting the ability of Negro power groups to effectively ward off conservative white establishments (no matter how impressed one is with the political changes that have taken place in the ghettos of big cities during the past few years). Such issues are well worth debating, but not in the context in which Payton places them when he suggests that those who, like Myrdal, underemphasize the political potentialities and vigor of Negro communities are "probably . . . subtly affected by the virus of racial bias."

The document we have been discussing, though not published, proved to have been quite influential in sustaining the mood of suspicion and criticism about the report and about the direction the conference planning was going. We have noted that several weeks before the document was actually distributed the decision to downgrade sharply the role of family discussion in the conference had been made and had been communicated to the major civil rights groups, but apparently not to the church groups that Payton represented.

It is unclear why Payton prepared what he regarded as a major critique of the report with so little attention to its contents. He has explained (for example, at his face-to-face confrontation with Moynihan in the family session of the White House Planning Conference — see Chapter 10) that he referred only to newspaper articles rather than the report itself because it was his understanding that the report had not been made public at the time he wrote his document. However, at the time his paper was most widely distributed (in mid-October) the report had indeed been made public and many people had managed to obtain copies of it from the Government Printing Office. Quite aside from that, Payton's reluctance to quote directly from the report and his reference to only three short newspaper articles are difficult to understand given the very wide and much fuller coverage of the report during the two months previous to the distribution of his paper. The *Newsweek* article of August 9th contained much more detail about the report than does Payton's article, as did the September 11th Richard Rovere article in *The New Yorker* and the *St. Louis Review* summary. Herbert Gans, writing at the same time as Payton, seemed to feel no responsibility to guard the contents of a report that had been widely leaked for months, nor for that matter did William Ryan on whom Payton relied for his major technical criticisms of the report. One is left with the impression that Payton was simply not interested in criticizing the report per se but rather in getting at what he felt to be extremely pernicious press treatment and White House political strategy.

This emphasis continued in a published article by Payton, "New Trends in Civil Rights," which appeared in the December 13th issue of *Christianity and Crisis*. Although in some ways quite different from the unpublished version, omitting some points and adding a new section on " 'Equality,' the Problem of Definition," Payton still engaged the public issues the report had generated more than the report itself.

In this article, Payton began with a review of the "unusual kind of perplexity and frustration" which had settled recently over the civil rights movement. He saw two tendencies in discussion about civil rights strategy, one of which emphasized the

importance of continuing to struggle to knock down discriminatory barriers and the other of improvements within the Negro
community that would enable Negroes to take advantage of the
equality of opportunity that is now available to them. Payton
regarded those who emphasize the barriers within the community
to ability to take advantage of equal opportunity as guilty of
fostering "but new masks for the old face of prejudice, new
rationalizations for persistent refusal to share power and position
more equally with Negroes." Those who wish to concentrate on
continuing discriminatory barriers on the other hand were seen
as realistically dealing with "deeper resistances that continue in
complex and often devious ways from the present into the future."

It is clear that he regarded Moynihan as representing the
"Negro improvement" school rather than the "continuing anti-
discrimination" school. This was good polemical style since it
managed to maintain the surface unity of the civil rights movement, but it failed to note the honest and serious concerns that
most civil rights leaders express from time to time concerning
the relative balance of these two approaches. As a matter of fact,
no major civil rights group, with the possible exception of SNCC,
had not been deeply preoccupied with both of these concerns
from time to time over the past several years. The problem Payton
was dealing with is really that of how the civil rights groups can
go about their business, making use of their opportunities in the
most effective possible way, in an atmosphere of publicity that
tends to push them toward rigid positions and to be extra sensitive to any evidence that the civil rights movement is going to
allow whites to disavow their guilt and their perfidy. As with
criticisms of the report, Payton's militancy seems to go more to
the press issue than to the hard choices that civil rights leaders
struggle with.

Payton then took up a criticism of Moynihan not contained in
his original paper. He discussed Moynihan's emphasis on the
criterion of equal results as a demand of the civil rights movement and characterized it as "an awkward and impossible goal."
Instead he said that the issue was one of "equal chances." One is
strongly tempted to regard this as simply a semantic battle of no
consequence. In a very real sense, Payton and Moynihan were
talking about the same thing. The problem is that simple terms
such as "equal opportunity" and "equal chance" do not capture
the full human reality which we intuitively bring to bear in our
evaluation of situations as just or unjust. With the concepts of

"equal results" or "equal chances," we seek to get at situations in which barriers to the achievement of a satisfying life exist. Moynihan wished to draw attention to the fact that equality of opportunity must be a lifelong situation rather than one of just the moment.* In other words, Moynihan wished to draw attention to a time dimension in equality. This is the same reality that Payton emphasized by drawing on R. H. Tawney, who observed that equal opportunity "obtains in so far as . . . each member of the community, whatever his birth or occupation or social position, possesses in fact and not merely in form, equal chances of using to the full his natural endowments of physique, of character and of intelligence."

Apparently Payton was not originally so disturbed by Moynihan's emphasis on equal results. In his original paper, he made no mention at all of Moynihan's treatment of the subject and did include a quote from the President's Howard University speech emphasizing the importance of "not just equality as a right and a theory, but equality as a fact and a result." This was part of the President's "devastatingly clear rationale" for embarking on a new stage in the civil rights struggle. Payton seemed now to fear that Moynihan was assuming that Negroes do in fact enjoy equal life chances but will not or cannot take advantage of them. Yet in fact there seems to be little difference between the two of them on the question of what equal life chances involve, with Moynihan using presumed "equality of opportunity" to emphasize the fact that simply stopping discrimination does very little to produce equality for those who do not have the ability to achieve in terms of their goals. Both Payton and Moynihan end up at the same point; in Payton's words: "A 'special effort' is required precisely in order to produce equal life chances."

* Thus, in another context he had written:
  More and more we are finding it is possible to take one group of young persons, with a full range of talent and abilities, and feed them, house them, care for and teach them so well, that they all end up much more capable persons than they started out.
  And we are finding that it is possible to take an exactly similar group of young persons, and hardly feed them, and barely house them, and not care for them, and miseducate them. And they turn out much less capable persons than they were at the beginning.
  If at the end of this process you give each group an equal oportunity to take the same set of examinations, or to compete in the same market place, you do not get equal results. You get unequal results. That is what the principle of equality is all about. Equal opportunity is not enough. Equal means that persons born with equal abilities will grow up with equal abilities.

Moynihan's emphasis on equal results probably comes in part from his adopting the perspective of a political executive and seeking to address such executives in terms that would be meaningful to them. Whatever the philosophical basis of the concept of equality, the operational basis tends to be exactly that of equal results. The approach of civil rights groups in recent times has been to demonstrate the absence of equality by demonstrating that equal results do not obtain. One examines test scores in schools; by determining that Negroes do not score as well on the tests as whites one thereby demonstrates that the school system does not provide them with equal life chances. One follows closely shifts in occupational distribution to determine whether or not movement is toward or away from equality. One observes income distribution of the total groups or people with similar qualifications to determine whether Negroes are moving toward more equal life chances or less.

From the political executive's point of view, then, what is relevant is the equal results. If the political executive is ever to get rid of the problem, ever to have less heat on him because of it, he can expect to do so only by bringing about situations that produce more equal results. It would avail him little to argue that the social system really provides equal life chances but somehow does not produce equal results.

Having discussed the question of equality, Payton moved on to cover some of the same issues covered in his initial memorandum. He was obviously still heavily influenced by the press coverage of the report. Thus, he said of the report, "While acknowledging a relationship between the rate of employment and family stability, the burden of the report seeks to demonstrate" that unemployment no longer explains such things as the rise in ADC cases. This hardly seems fair comment on a report that devotes seven pages to the socioeconomic cause of family instability and only a paragraph to the fairly recent emergence of a more complex, less direct, cause-and-effect relationship, although it was fair comment on most of the news coverage of the report. It does, however, touch on a widely noted ambiguity in Moynihan's thesis.

Payton noted that the report as dealt with in the press had led to "facile 'explanations' of the urban riots of 1964–65" and had provided ammunition for those hostile to the Negro's cause. This is certainly true but the implication seemed to be that therefore what Moynihan said was incorrect. Such a view would seem to be extremely naïve. These is almost nothing that can be said in truth about the situation of Negro Americans which cannot be turned by persons sufficiently motivated into a criticism or even into a strategy for blunting the Negro drive for equality. Thus the emphasis on building more solid community strength and political power can be seen as a "self-help" activity in which Negroes take care of their own and whites need no longer worry. It can be used to legitimate a view that Negroes are entitled to no more than their political power can earn them. And so it goes. If social scientists and civil rights functionaries allow themselves to be distracted by purposeful misunderstanding, or even more subtly motivated misunderstanding, they will soon get themselves in the situation of not being able to advocate any course of action.

Rather surprisingly, now that he had had an opportunity to re-examine the report and his own analysis, Payton continued the blatant error of characterizing the report as "much more optimistic about the employment situation among Negroes than are other observers." This hardly squares with Moynihan's characterization that "Negro unemployment . . . has continued at disaster levels for thirty-five years." Payton retained his reference to the fact that Negro income has worsened in relation to white income, still without noting that Moynihan made exactly the same point. One is left to conclude that Moynihan had not seriously discussed these facts.

Payton then concluded his brief discussion of the report with a précis of Ryan's critique of illegitimacy statistics and introduced his view that "metropolitics" should be the focal point of efforts to mobilize larger resources to deal with Negro inequality.

Within the confines of a brief article Payton then outlined his view that the problems of metropolitan areas must provide the background for any effort to solve Negro problems although he no longer presented this argument in the context of the President's Howard University speech. This would be exceedingly awkward for him since by now the fact that Moynihan provided the impetus for and wrote that speech had become even more widely known.

In connection with his emphasis on "metropolitics," Payton noted that in New York City the church race groups had taken the initiative in preparing "an economic development budget for equal rights" which would emphasize the importance of housing and slum rehabilitation, education, job training and job-creation programs, and health and medical facilities. One is again struck by the needless quarrel with Moynihan since the same kind of programmatic recommendations grew out of his efforts and, as in the case of Moynihan's work, Payton emphasized that the effect of such mobilization of resources would be to benefit not only Negroes but "all of the disinherited who have been robbed of their birthright of freedom and equal opportunity."

The Christian Century Editorial

The Alice in Wonderland character of much press commentary about the report was by now well entrenched. In an editorial entitled "The Moynihan Report," the Christian Century (December 15, 1965) sought to examine "sound" and "unemotional" reactions to the report while eschewing less responsible criticism, treating the report as a serious document deserving serious commentary.

After a brief summary of the report, more reminiscent of the newspaper coverage than of the report itself, the editorialist noted with approval the criticisms by Payton including the Ryan analysis of illegitimacy. The editorialist's view of the report contained a number of remarkable distortions. Moynihan was said to maintain "that the pathology of the Negro family was caused principally by a ruthless slavery system which created among Negroes a matrifocal society and a consequent denigration of the Negro male image" and "that the current forms of matriarchial society among Negroes are produced and maintained primarily by causes remote in the American Negro's history." It is almost beyond belief that a well-informed and sophisticated writer could read the report and draw these conclusions from the fact that out of forty-eight pages of text, two and a half pages deal with historical factors *were it not that these "facts" about the report's content were already so well established by the time the report itself became available to readers.*

The second major conclusion the writer attributed to Moynihan was "that Negro delinquency and unemployment are produced in major part by the deterioration of the Negro family." The editor, fortunately, corrects this error of Moynihan. "Indeed we could reverse Moynihan's argument and say that until the Negro male is fully, productively and securely employed he cannot emerge in the family as a strong father figure and claim for himself the dominant masculine role expected of the male in western culture." Or, "reversing Moynihan's arguments," Negro delinquency will remain high as long as Negroes live in slums and that the Negro family, "more the victim than the villain," suffers multiple blows from the society.

Having thus set the records straight about the proper relationship among the variables with which Moynihan dealt, the editorialist took up Moynihan's recommendations concerning establishment of a national policy to further the stability of the Negro family and argued that not only would this be a difficult goal it would be an impossible one. If based on the writer's conceptions of what Moynihan had implied in discussing family stability (that it was a cause unto itself uninfluenced by other institutional systems), this conclusion is correct, but the writer went on to argue essentially what Moynihan had in mind as the proper role of the federal government. The writer notes: "The federal government cannot directly approach Negro family life in a creative way. Family life is a product of traditions multiplied by the societal climate. The federal government can do something about the climate — about jobs, housing and education. Only by these avenues can it get into the Negro home in a creative way."

The *Christian Century* editorial provided a fitting epitaph for the report. It should become, the writer argued, merely "secondary resource material" for the spring White House Conference. It was a well-intentioned (not really "racist" or "facist") but a thoroughly mistaken effort to develop national policy. Now that its errors had been properly exposed, the nation could go about dealing with the issues Moynihan had ignored — jobs, housing, and education!

11

Confrontation at the Conference

Though the Moynihan Report had stimulated the White House to call the conference, by the time the scaled-down planning sessions convened in the middle of November the report had acquired such a history of controversy that it was far more an embarrassment to all concerned than anything else. When the planning staff had finally gotten rolling a scant month before the date set for the conference, they had been confronted with a very sensitive situation. Although the basic outlines of the conference had been set, there still remained the question of how to deal with the family issue. There had been strong pressures to do away with the session on the family entirely and these pressures had met equally strong resistance from the White House. Five of the sessions were devoted to standard categories of civil rights concern which had been institutionalized in Civil Rights Commission reports some years before — voting, education, employment, housing, justice. In addition, there were three sessions which did not have this kind of history, one on health and welfare, one on the community, and an unwelcome guest, the family.

In order to head off direct intrusion of the controversy into the conference proceedings, its planners chose very carefully the chairman of the family session and the chairmen of the two closely related ones of education and health and welfare. These must be men who were trusted by civil rights groups, men who could by no stretch of the imagination be considered tainted by the brush of "subtle racism." As chairman of the family section, the planners chose Hylan Lewis, Professor of Sociology at Howard University, and a man with a distinguished record of research into Negro family life. Civil rights activists were reassured by this choice and understood that the tone of the family session would be, if anything, anti-Moynihan. (We do not mean that they were told this by the conference staff, but at least some civil rights leaders took this understanding away from their meetings with the conference staff.)

The conference planners were in an extremely ticklish position. On the one hand, they had to continually disavow any intention of making the family the basic theme of the conference or even making consideration of family stability and instability one of several major concerns. On the other hand, the conference was convened under the authority of the President's Howard University speech which had spoken of the special nature of Negro poverty and of family problems as central to this special nature. Too vigorous a repudiation of Moynihan could be taken as a criticism of the President, no repudiation as part of a government plot to do in the movement.

In short, when the conference met there had developed a heightened irritability and sensistivity on the part of those involved in civil rights, both in the government and in the movement. The government's irritability was suppressed and hidden from public view, but the impact of Watts and the Moynihan controversy had thrust the movement's vulnerability into the public eye. As one long-time observer of the movement commented:

I think there was a real intensification of Negro sensitivity after the rioting in Watts. The change was sudden and dramatic. Immediately after the rioting there was a whole series of mea culpas on the part of almost all the civil rights leaders: "We are guilty, we have failed, we have established no contact with the people in the ghetto." All of which, of course, was true. Sometime in the early fall, however, there was a total shift . . . . In good measure, this probably was a delayed defensive reaction to the anti-Negro hostility and discussion aroused by the rioting, and in part it certainly reflected a suspicion that the Johnson Administration might be trying to shift the burden of responsibility from the government to the Negro community. But it seems to me that there is no question that the old mood of the "movement" changed, and changed radically in a very short time: the fact that Whitney Young felt obliged to write a column critical of at least part of the Moynihan report — a column that had a defensiveness about the problems of the ghetto that was completely new to Whitney's writing — seems to me *prima-facie* evidence of a shift.

What I am saying, in effect, is that I think the movement took a very long backward step during or because of the Moynihan controversy, reverting to the most rigid and ancient formulation, which pits self-improvement as the polar opposite to the drive for civil rights, rather than seeing it as simply one crucial part of an overall program. The insistence on seeing things always in "either-or" terms rather than in "both-and" terms is, I think, terribly self-destructive.

The Agenda

The deeply felt wish of all who had had to struggle with this problem was fittingly expressed at the opening session of the conference when Berl Bernhard, its executive director, amused the participants by saying, "I want you to know that I have been reliably informed that no such person as Daniel Patrick Moynihan exists." Indeed, though it subsequently turned out that Moynihan was alive and kicking, he seemed in danger of being buried in paper. The agenda paper for the family section was the longest of the eight agenda papers (although the housing paper came close). In addition, there were numerous other documents providing background on the subject of the Negro family, all having more or less the effect of blunting Moynihan's sharply focused argument. There was a thirty-eight page document on the economic status of the Negro prepared by Dorothy Newman, Assistant Economic Consultant of the Bureau of Labor Statistics; this document was accompanied by forty-three charts and eighteen tables. There was a paper by Jack Lefcowitz of the Office of Economic Opportunity discussing "poverty and Negro-white family structure" and emphasizing the fact that the race difference in various family-related variables are much reduced when economic controls are introduced. Against the vast array of reprints, tables, and charts, the Moynihan Report seemed puny indeed.

The agenda paper itself represented a careful attempt to shed light on the situation of Negro families, particularly poor Negro families, and to discuss some of the issues without fanning the controversy. It was prepared by Hylan Lewis with the assistance of Elizabeth Herzog, a social scientist in the U.S. Children's Bureau (HEW), assisted by Bonita Valien, Alvin Schorr, Marian Chase, and Jack Lefcowitz.

Though it did not contain any direct attack on the Moynihan Report or its main thesis, the agenda paper was inevitably read as a critical response to the report. The main thrust of the agenda paper was to argue against Moynihan's view that the Negro family was undergoing massive deterioration, was "crumbling." Thus, the agenda paper noted that the increase in female-headed Negro families from 18.8 percent in 1949 to 23.2 percent in 1962 represented an increase of only 4.4 percent in more than a decade, or less than one third of a percentage point per year. Further, that increase had stopped in 1959, and since that year there seemed to have been a rather stable plateau. Similar points were made with respect to illegitimacy. The illegitimacy *rate* (that is, the proportion of unmarried women who have illegitimate children) had been in a stable plateau since 1957 (though the agenda paper failed to deal adequately with the fact that since 1957 the proportion of Negro illegitimate *births* had increased by 14 percent while during the same period the proportion of white illegitimate births had increased 50 percent).

For the agenda paper authors, then, the increase in these two indices of family disorganization did not amount to "crumbling," while for Moynihan they did. Noting that the advocates of the rapid deterioration view and the "plateau view" both agreed that there were important disparities between the family stability of white and nonwhite groups and that there is a need for strong and prompt intervention, the agenda paper went on to say that "Differences lie: (a) in interpreting the current situation as a crisis versus a long term manifestation, and (b) in the attitudes of alarm and hostility that may be held with regard to an erupting crisis, as compared with the problem-solving approach that is more likely with regard to a long-continued situation."

This is, of course, exactly the area in which Moynihan's strategy had differed from that of other government social scientists. Moynihan felt that it was necessary to add drama to "well-known facts" in order to effectively compete for the attention of the Chief Executive and his staff and felt justified in calling a 25 percent increase in the proportion of female-headed Negro families an index of crumbling family stability — he felt such an increase in the unemployment rate would certainly generate a great deal more concern at the highest levels of government than seemed to have been generated by a comparable increase in female-headed households.

The agenda paper also discussed the question of the legacy of slavery for Negro family forms. The issue was joined by opposing the presumed influence of slavery to the influence of socioeconomic factors that can operate on whites as well as Negroes. The agenda paper noted that when indices of family stability or instability are controlled for socioeconomic status, race differences are considerably diminished, although they still exist. Therefore it was difficult to argue that slavery by producing a cultural heritage is therefore an influential factor in the situation of the Negro family today.

The balance of the agenda paper took up in detail some of the complexities involved in the situation of Negro families; it examined the conflicting social science evidence on the effects of broken homes, of the absence of the father, of the fact that women may have both to work and head families, of the difficulties of obtaining proper day care for children whose mothers work. It discussed the situation of the mother of an illegitimate child and of the child himself and the literature on child rearing and the lifestyles of the poor in general and the Negro poor.

The general effect of this thoughtful and scholarly treatment was to downgrade considerably the significance of Moynihan's treatment and to replace Moynihan's action-oriented tone (despite the lack of specific programmatic suggestion in the report) with an emphasis on "understanding." In this regard, it should be noted that the family agenda paper was by far the most scholarly of all of the agenda papers for the conference. The others were much more directly oriented to programmatic action.

As a result of this approach, in the body of the agenda paper discussion the only programmatic emphasis that was apparent was in the health and welfare area — the need for day-care centers for working mothers, for better services to illegitimate mothers, for birth control — exactly the kind of emphasis that the civil rights groups had feared would be derived from the Moynihan Report. However, that such a conservative emphasis was not the intention of the planners of the family session was indicated by a suggested set of agenda topics which prefaced the scholarly portion of the paper. Here there was more emphasis on the contribution of employment programs, income maintenance, more male influence in schools and communities, better schooling, and the like — all more in line with the direction Moynihan had sought to reinforce by his report.

The Experts Discuss

Despite the tense situation which the controversy had posed for the conference planners and which they had sought to cope with by the various means just discussed, the actual deliberations of the family panel were minimally affected by the presumed dangers of Moynihan's approach. That is, the discussion tended to concentrate quite heavily on the belief of most of the participants that family stability for poor Negroes, as for poor whites, would not be achieved until Negro men had stable employment, until income maintenance plans were worked out that provided decent income for workers whose wages were insufficient or for female-headed families where the mother could not work. There was similarly strong emphasis on education programs that offered decent opportunities to Negro children and provided them with meaningful models of masculinity.

The emphasis on "social work approaches" to family stability, so feared by critics of the report, was a distinctly minor theme in the sessions. Much of the discussion revolved around exactly the criticism that Moynihan had made of the welfare bureaucracy; that is, the tendency of the government to try to supply substitute family services rather than to provide families with the resources that would allow them to perform necessary functions on their own. It would have been difficult indeed to muster more than a few voices in favor of programs of family counseling and education, or other kinds of remedial programs that avoided the necessity for basic institutional changes in the economic, educational, and housing spheres. But no one mentioned the report.

In The Halls

All of this, of course, did not mean that the Moynihan controversy disappeared at the conference. Although it was apparently not the case, as some press reports and civil rights gossip suggested, that there was a great deal of discussion of the report in the various panels of the conference, it does seem to be true that the report provided one of the main subjects of conversation in the halls and over the dinner tables. While a few individuals with unimpeachable civil rights credentials sought to argue against the general negative evaluation of the report and to argue its merits, the general tone of the informal conversation had been well symbolized by Bernhard's comment at the opening session. Those who did speak out against the attack on the Moynihan report argued not only that the report was accurate but even more strongly that the nature of the attack constituted the "introduction of McCarthyism into the movement."

One long-time student of the movement observed that the anger about the report expressed during the conference reflected a new mood that had been developing for some time:

This new mood reached its climax at the November conference. There was a total refusal by most of the Negroes [I heard] to discuss *anything* that might remotely imply that there was anything whatsoever that Negroes, individually or collectively, should be doing or needed to do. [One leader's] formulation, which was repeated *ad nauseam,* was that race is entirely a white man's problem that could only be solved by white men, and that it was intolerable that the government had all these white men sitting around discussing "our problem." They simply refused to discuss anything but what the government ought to be doing. They even refused to discuss the question of how Negroes might mount more effective political pressure to force the government to institute the programs they were demanding. The high point of that discussion came when [a local leader] explained "I have all the effective power I need; it's just that the mayor won't listen to me."

Confrontation

Moynihan himself was a participant in the family panel, but he felt so compromised by the controversy that he spoke not at all on the first day and only twice on the second day. At first he sought only to explain how he came to write the report, what his strategy was, and that his basic intent was to point up the effect of the social and economic situation of Negroes on their family life and the feedback effect of family disorganization on that situation, but not to introduce a new factor to explain away the society's failure to accord Negroes a decent status. Also, he wanted to deny the rumor that the conference was originally going to be only about the family and said that in the original preplanning session of the previous summer the plan had involved a series of panels much like the ones that were finally set up.

Apparently, Moynihan at this point had not seen Payton's paper, although he knew of its existence and of the fact that it had been used as a basis for a resolution by a New York group asking that the subject of the family be stricken entirely from the agenda of the conference. During the second day, however, someone gave Moynihan a copy of Payton's critique and he read it quickly. Late in the morning session of the second day of the conference, Moynihan rose to speak about Payton's article on "a point of personal privilege." He spoke directly to Payton, also a participant in the family session. Moynihan had great difficulty believing that Payton had read his report since he could see little relationship between what it said about the report and what he felt he had written. He was particularly concerned that the report had been taken as playing down the importance of social and economic remedies and after restating his thesis asked the assembled group.

Do you see that the object of this report was not to say that jobs don't matter, but rather that jobs matter in the most fundamental way? That housing matters in a profound way, not because it is pretty but because of the lives of children. . . . [and that] we can measure our success or failure as a society, not in terms of the gross national product, not in terms of income level, and not in the prettiness and attractiveness or peacefulness of our people, but in the health, and the living, loving reality of the family in our society.

In his response, Payton indicated that he had been outraged by Moynihan's Report and that he was still unwilling to accept Moynihan's explanation that at the bottom of this whole matter of Negro family stability are inadequate jobs and unemployment. Quoting from the report he noted Moynihan's statement that the deterioration of the Negro family is "the fundamental source of weakness of the Negro community at the present time" and that in his conclusions Moynihan pointed to the fact that since 1960 the previous close relationship between Negro unemployment rates and new ADC cases no longer obtained. Payton felt that this added up to a view "that the Negro family is now probably so pathological that even the provision of jobs won't do it." Further he felt that Lewis' agenda paper did not point to the alarmist conclusions which Moynihan himself had pointed to. As a result, despite the fact that Moynihan's instincts were clearly good ones, because of these errors "conclusions have been made and have become very widespread which have done the Negro community a fundamental harm, and I do hope you will find it possible to believe that."

After three other participants had spoken — one asserting that this was no minor controversy because several of the more militant local organizations had seriously considered boycotting the conference in order not to seem to legitimate the report, and two others in support of the general validity of Moynihan's thesis — Payton was asked to read a quotation from E. Franklin Frazier which Moynihan had used to conclude his report and to indicate in what way he felt Moynihan was saying something that was different from Frazier. That particular Frazier quote (after discussing the effects of family disorganization on Negro children and youth) concluded, "the mitigation of this problem must await those changes in the Negro and American society which will enable the Negro father to play the role required of him." Payton felt that this quotation clearly indicated that Frazier recognized the key role that economics plays in creating a stable family. If Frazier were alive today his programmatic suggestions would probably be in terms of new jobs and new job training programs. Moynihan on the other hand, Payton felt, did not make clear this connection with the economic structure.

Several of the other participants then noted that the report had been written as an internal government document and that Moynihan could not have foreseen the very tense post-Watts situation in which it would receive wide publicity. Others noted that anyone who deals with such a touchy and sensitive issue is taking on the likelihood of trouble no matter what he says and that this is simply an occupational risk of experts in this area.

The confrontation had been dramatic, but did little to clarify matters. Moynihan felt he had given primacy to the economic position of Negro men in explaining family instability; Payton felt he had not. Moynihan felt that it was legitimate to also raise the issues of the feedback effects and of the situation getting worse because of the tangle of pathology; Payton felt that such an emphasis did fundamental harm to the Negro community.

The Press and the Conference

Newspaper discussions of the report had died down considerably during October. With the conference, however, the report again became salient. On the opening day of the conference, *The Washington Post's* Jean White headlined her story, "Family Report Sparks Debate." Briefly reviewing the history of the report and characterizing it as saying that "family breakdown is seen largely as a heritage of slavery," she noted that the conference agenda had been "broadened" to include seven other study topics beside the family. She observed that Hylan Lewis' agenda paper "challenges the main thrust of the Moynihan report" by arguing that the most important thing is to provide jobs, better education, and the like for Negro men who can then provide for their families. The press, then, expected the continuation of the controversy within the conference, and spotted the agenda paper as an official conference document discrediting the report. The reporter did not indicate the source of her information concerning the agenda paper, but since the article was written before the conference opened one can assume that it was leaked to her by someone on the conference staff.

On the following day, however, Jean White's reporting of the first day's events made no mention of the family because there was harder news than that. She dealt with the President's announcement that he was authorizing a study of de facto segregation in the nation's schools, and with a confrontation between civil rights leaders and government officials on the education and housing issues. (Word had leaked that the President was not going to sign an executive order outlawing housing discrimination because the Attorney General had said that it was unconstitutional.) Also, many of the civil rights leaders were angry at the President's reversal of Education Commissioner Keppel's decision to withhold funds from the Chicago school system. Finally, A. Phillip Randolph, honorary chairman of the conference, had proposed a hundred-billion dollar "freedom budget" to abolish Negro ghettos in the cities. He had called for a vast public works program to provide jobs and to build needed institutions and housing.

Reporting of the second day's events similarly emphasized the angry feelings of civil rights activists about the Administration's lack of action on immediately pressing questions. An effort was made by Clarence Mitchell, Washington Director of the NAACP, to get the final plenary session of the conference to adopt a resolution urging the President to take immediate steps to protect "the lives and safety of Negroes and civil rights workers in the deep south," but he was ruled out of order by Chairman Randolph. The education panel of the conference had passed a resolution (something the conference planners sought to avoid) urging the President personally to adopt a policy of "tougher enforcement of school desegregation, North and South"; the Willis-Keppel-Daley fiasco rankled deeply. Civil rights leaders were concerned that the bills of 1964 and 1965 were becoming meaningless because of a failure of nerve on the part of the Administration in enforcement.

However, the Moynihan controversy had not gone unnoticed. *The Washington Star's* Mary McGrory headlined her story, "Moynihan Conspicuously Ignored: The 'Non-Person' at the Right's Parley." Quoting Bernhard's *mot*, she noted that Moynihan was hardly given an expert's welcome at the conference and went on to review Payton's unpublished critique and Ryan's *Nation* article. Two days later, *The Washington Star* carried an article about conflicting views of the report at a Catholic University conference on inner-city research with participating priests apparently arguing both for and against the report. A few days later, on November 23rd, Whitney Young referred to the report during a speech in Washington. Earlier, in an October article in the *Amsterdam News*, Young had endorsed the main thesis of the report — that is, that there was a great deal of family disorganization in the Negro community and that it stemmed from social and economic deprivation which in turn stemmed from patterns of discrimination. Now, however, he was concerned about the invidious interpretations of the report and noted in his speech that America "can no longer discuss the pathology of Negro society without discussing also the pathology of the white society that permits that pathology to develop." At a subsequent press conference, he disagreed that the Negro family was now deteriorating, saying in essence that white society had never allowed a strong Negro family structure. He felt that perhaps the report "may have rendered us a service in that it started us talking" about the weaknesses of the Negro family.

On November 24th, Evans and Novak entered the scene for a second time. Not ones to mince words, they headlined their Inside Report "Civil Rights Disaster" and noted that "one high policy maker in the Administration grumbled bitterly that the Negro leadership knows only how to put its hand out to Uncle Sam. White intellectuals who had come to Washington to discuss Negro social disorganization were stunned by the demagoguery." Evans and Novak suggested that the government's judgment of the conference was that it was a failure. The gap between the movement and the Administration was wider than ever; "a carefully planned effort to inject a new realism regarding the plight of the Northern Negro was a failure" because of "shrill cries of Negro militants," the unwillingness of Negro leaders to discuss reality and the inclination of leaders simply to ask for money. At the conference, there was only "a tired rehashing of old slogans." The villains seemed to be people like Bayard Rustin, "who has never disguised his doctrinaire socialist view," Floyd McKissick (shortly to become the head of CORE) "who insisted that to alleviate the Negroes' plight, the 'capitalist system' must be changed" and Lawrence Landry (of Chicago's ACT) who "complained publicly that the conference was dominated by 'whites and Jews.' "

That Evans and Novak were not alone in their soundings of the White House response became apparent the following day when John Herbers headlined his new analysis, "Parley Said to Displease White House: Subject of Families Rejected or Ignored." Apparently the President was both angry and hurt by what went on at the conference, as is his wont when opposed. The White House was said to be disappointed and bewildered because (1) the conference rejected or ignored the subject of family stability, and (2) rather than a consensus on procedure to bring Negroes into the main stream of American society there was "a torrent of criticism that the Administration had not done all it could to enforce civil rights laws." The White House sources were disappointed because their ideas about Moynihan's thesis as a starting point to justify to white America the need for new kinds of assistance were rejected by the civil rights leaders. Though many ideas were discussed at the conference, "there was no new 'handle,' no suggestion for winning the 'understanding heart' that President Johnson has said is needed for Negroes to become first-class Americans." Therefore the ideas would receive consideration, "but mostly it's back to the drafting board for the White House."

On November 29th, Newsweek told essentially the same story of what had happened at the conference, also noting the harsh lobby talk about the report: "The report was 'a complete insult,' gruffed one militant in a group of self-styled 'bomb-throwers' who held an angry rump session in a first floor hotel room."

On November 29th, Joseph Alsop, a new entry among commentators on the Moynihan controversy, spoke in his column of the disappointment of Administration officials with the rejection of the report and the behavior at the conference. The Administration felt that the civil rights leaders had no practicable programs

to offer: "Injustice is the theme, not what can be done about it."
Later reports were to suggest that this dim view of the conference's accomplishments was shared by the Justice Department,
including the Attorney General. One such source was quoted as
saying, "It was a disaster — an outpouring of shabby campus style
politicking, bickering and talking for effect."

Late in November, Michael Harrington had tried in his column
to bring the matter into perspective. He argued with Evans and
Novak's "misinformed revelation." Defending Bayard Rustin
against the accusation that he was a "doctrinaire socialist," Harrington pointed out that Randolph's freedom budget was in line
with programs that had been seriously considered by many un-
doctrinaire policy makers including the late President Kennedy.
Then, he dealt with the essence of the Moynihan controversy:

> In the midst of all this innuendo there is, however, a serious
> confusion: that either one discusses the dislocations of Negro family
> life or one talks about employment, the slums and job generation.
> . . . Unfortunately, the report has been more widely quoted than read;
> and some of the attacks upon it have been unfair in the extreme. Evans
> and Novak come to the rescue by taking the worst caricatures of the
> report as the valid interpretation of it: that Federal policy should
> ignore jobs, housing and schools and, after having dramatized how
> depraved Negro life is, should tell the black ghetto poor to improve
> themselves. If these columnists think they are thus being a friend of
> Daniel Patrick Moynihan . . . he needs no enemies.
> But, as the Moynihan report itself makes plain, unemployment and
> under employment are fundamental to the problem of the Negro family.
> . . . White America has imposed family problems upon many Negroes.
> The only way to deal with them is through a freedom budget which
> generates jobs and destroys the environment of racial poverty. Evans
> and Novak have got everything wrong.

With Evans and Novak, Moynihan may not have needed
enemies but they were there. A good many of the civil rights
leaders, frustrated by the conference talkathon, the abundantly
evident disinterest of the Administration in vigorously following
up the Howard University speech, and the press leaks indicating
that the Administration felt the conference was a disaster because
the civil rights people had been badly behaved, felt their worst
fears about the Moynihan Report had been confirmed.

James Farmer in two columns in the *Amsterdam News* attacked
the report as providing "the fuel for a new racism," containing
statistical facts, "misread, misinterpreted and warped into a

series of conclusions that could make Robert Shelton into a holy prophet." He saw the report as blaming the Negro community and family for the deprived position in which they found themselves, thus allowing "a massive academic cop out for the white conscience." Farmer was disturbed that much of what Moynihan had written in his report was a rehash of things civil rights people have been saying all along. Finally, he noted that "recently" Moynihan had broadend the conclusions of his report, indicating that "he has agreed with our contention that improved job, housing and education options are essential in the fight to stop community erosion. These late refinements, however welcome, serve to confirm the haphazard judgment at work when the unqualified report was originally issued." (This would tend to confirm Herbert Gans' observation the previous October that the lack of inclusion of Moynihan's recommendations in the printed report served to stimulate unnecessary hostility to it.)

Farmer's militant critique of the report was somewhat belied by his actions of about the same time in that he resigned as head of CORE, effective the following spring, in order to head a national program to deal with illiteracy and other difficulties of Negro and white poor people. The program was to be financed by federal and private funds. The juxtaposition of Farmer's vigorous efforts to discredit the report and his resignation to head this kind of improvement-of-the-poor program led one close Moynihan partisan to observe, "I wish him well in his new job and I hope he has occasion to write a report someday!"

The heat of the Moynihan controversy was hardly subsiding, given the continued press interest, civil rights outrage, and Moynihan's own vigorous defense (see pages 260–265). These pressures apparently led the Department of Labor to seek to further disassociate itself from the report. For the week of December 27th, the Department issued a press release providing excerpts from an interview with Secretary of Labor Wirtz conducted by Paul Niven as part of a National Education Series TV program on "the President's men." The press release excerpted a portion of that interview in which Niven had asked Wirtz about the Moynihan Report. Wirtz seemed to be saying that perhaps the report reflected an overemphasis on "the breakdown in Negro family life." He sought to broaden the context by talking about the problems of every poor family, not just Negroes. Secretary Wirtz went on, "I rather think you'll find earlier emphasis . . . on the economic need for jobs, the broader need for education . . . rather than any exclusive attention directed at the family as such." The Secretary also sought to broaden the issue by emphasizing that poverty and its attendant problems, though proportionately more frequent among Negroes, strike a larger total number of whites than Negroes and went on:

My own approach is to think that we ought to seize — and we will seize — upon the civil rights revolution as a concentration of our interest on the whole area of disadvantage. I think it will be one of the grand developments of the century if the nation's whole conscience is pricked by the fact of this one racial protest group . . . and we answer it not in terms of meeting the Negro situation but in terms of meeting the whole disadvantaged situation.

Some months later on another television program, the Secretary referred to the report as "not an official Labor Department" document.

By year's end, then, Administration voices on the subject of civil rights were considerably blunted compared to the Howard University speech of six months before. For example, in a year-end article on how the President assessed 1965 (based on "high White House sources"), Ottenad of the *St. Louis Post Dispatch* characterized the President's feelings as . . . "in the struggle for civil rights, the quest for liberty and equality has ended and the much more difficult search for true fraternity has started. . . . the new search, to give Negroes fraternal and meaningful association with their fellow men, is the next crucial struggle he foresees." Apparently the President was particularly encouraged because the Watts riot was the only widespread outbreak of racial violence of 1965! In June, "liberty" had been almost achieved and the next struggle would be for "equality." By the end of the year, "equality" had also been achieved and now the problem was that of "fraternity." Surely this was an Administration achievement of the first order; the struggle for equality had been won in only six months!

Moynihan's Counterattack

Over the late fall, Moynihan had learned that there was an increasing amount of criticism of his report by people in the civil rights movement. But it was only at the conference itself that he learned the extent and deep-felt character of the opposition to it. At this point, Moynihan discovered that he had two problems. One involved the defense of the accuracy of what he had said and the validity of the programmatic goals toward which he felt these pointed. The second involved his stature as a public figure and a political man of some importance.

Concerning the first question, the report was after all a tactic toward a goal, and from this point of view he could simply let the report and its thesis die and at a later date come up with a different formulation of essentially the same issue in an effort to get the kind of sharply focused public commitment he felt necessary to move beyond palliative programs.

Indeed, he was strongly urged to do this by many within the government and some outside. As one of the outsiders commented, "We need some kind of handle on this problem, but I guess the report isn't the right one." Presidential Government officials urged Moynihan not to attack his critics; by doing so he would only magnify them and make them heroes. A Permanent Government man deeply involved in efforts to stimulate major federal programs to cope with Negro disadvantage wrote Moynihan urging him to try to bury the controversy that had become so apparent at the conference:

I'm really sorry that the press and everybody else took off after you the way they did . . . It is all too easy to become a scape-goat for something that you really didn't intend to do . . . [after the report was written] as events evolved, the situation — at least the political situation — changed quite radically. Rather than being the hero, having stimulated the government into action, you became the villain.

With careful evaluation, and in the long run it will be evident, that many of the points you made are accurate and could, in fact, be documented further. Your critics have raised many questions about it, some quite accurately, but all too many of them are being used for the political advantage of themselves. Sadly, I sense that in some of the new leadership groups there is no real interest in the Negro by these leaders; and they are using an attack on you for their own political advantage rather than to clarify the issue.

I hope that you, in your heart, can honestly feel that, though you were and are fully associated with the report as written for January, 1965, given all the conditions of that time, however, as of November–December, 1965, the issues are different and therefore you would dissociate yourself with the report as being immediately relevant as of today. At this point you can again turn to the Negro leaders and say, "Together we can look at these issues and come up with a different and perhaps more appropriate and more full report." After all, that was all you were driving for in January; to get a more thorough evaluation of the problem. I think this you can do.

From the Administration's point of view, of course, were Moynihan to pursue these lines of action, a great deal of the heat generated about the issue would go away and the government would find it easier to try to rebuild an accommodation with the civil rights movement.

From the point of view of Moynihan as a public and political figure, however, the matter was not so simple. As a person he was acquiring the reputation of being a "subtle racist," a man who had provided, perhaps innocently, rationalizations for continued discrimination and segregation; in short a "white liberal" of the worst sort. As one not-so-sympathetic observer had commented, "Moynihan is one of a new breed, a social science politico and like all politicos he is expendable." If Moynihan had still been a member of the government he probably would have had to accept this fate, but he was now a private citizen and had the option of trying to save his reputation as a public figure. By that old political standby, a mail count, he knew that he was in good position to do this.

Therefore Moynihan responded vigorously to approaches of newsmen and magazines now that the conference was over. He had turned down one network TV appearance before the conference (at the request of its staff) in order not to fan the flames of the controversy, but when a second invitation came he accepted it.

Beginning with his responses to reporters' queries at the conference itself, Moynihan sought to correct what he felt were the misconceptions of the report and its intentions. He was now in the position of filling in the part of the record that was missing in the published report, particularly that part that had to do with what he felt were the report's programmatic implications. He followed these interviews with an article of his own in The Washington Post of November 28th which the Post titled with quaint irrelevance, "Moynihan Was Treating Negro Family as People." In addition to summarizing the report's thesis, he sought to correct two of the main misconceptions about the report:

It cannot be too much emphasized that these conditions are in no way associated only with Negroes. The most important point is that the conditions reported in the Negro family are the classic conditions of a lower class city population plagued by unemployment, bad housing, low income and powerlessness . . .

The idea has arisen that to raise the subject of family life is somehow to downgrade the issues of employment, of housing, of discrimination. Surely, just the opposite is, or ought to be, the case. . . . The object of the [report] was to show the direct connection between such statistical abstractions and the human tragedies of life in the slums.

Ten days later, Moynihan made himself available to *Newsweek's* interviewers for a background story on the report, its critics, and the conference. Again he sought to show the relevance of the report, with its emphasis on the family and on the tangle of pathology, to the development of national programs of employment, housing, and education. *Newsweek* sought to counter the strong criticism of the report and the implication that it sustained racism by quoting Kenneth Clark: "It's kind of a wolf pack operating in a very undignified way. If Pat is a racist, I am. He highlights the total pattern of segregation and discrimination. Is a doctor responsible for a disease simply because he diagnoses it?"

About a week later, Moynihan discussed with John Herbers of *The New York Times* his hope that the federal government would adopt a national family policy. By this time, he knew that this was one of the recommendations that had come out of the staff work on the deliberations of the family panel at the White House Conference.

Then, on December 12th, Moynihan appeared on *Meet The Press*. The brunt of his response to questions by the reporters seemed to be to deny their suggestion that the controversy about the report had achieved such proportions that the Administration could no longer use it as a basis for national policy. For example, reporter Novak sought to get him to admit that the criticism had had an impact on the Administration and upon President Johnson. Moynihan replied:

Well, you would have to ask the President but certainly there has never been a man in American history who has been so forthright and stalwart and staunch on this subject. In speech to the opening session of the White House Conference he said, "We will go beyond opportunity to achievement." I believe he means that. He's backed up everything he's said in this area and he has a report from our conference which suggests that a national family policy should be the primary objective of the administration. He has the report and he certainly will respond to it.

Whatever the inclinations of the Administration, Moynihan sought to keep them committed to the line adopted in the Howard University speech.

Further he sought to reassert his thesis of a vicious cycle in such a way that it highlighted the importance of national programs to do away with poverty. Correspondent Valariani asked whether it was true that his report dealt more with symptoms than causes, that the disease was really discrimination and segregation. Moynihan replied:

That is the largest part of the issue, yes . . . I was trying to show that . . . unemployment . . . ended up with orphaned children, abandoned mothers, with men living furtive lives without even an address. And unemployment had flesh and blood and it could bleed, that's all I was trying to do. But let's not make any mistake on this; that having done that to people and done that to their families . . . that hurts people, that deprives them of opportunities. Not to have a father and not to have a mother — you've lost something that helps you in life. And so this process feeds back into the cycle so we can't act as if the family were just a result, it is also an effect and strong families produce strong people.

Life Magazine in its year-end double issue had chosen to present the situation of the American city. As part of this series, there was a long article on a Negro slum area in Cleveland. In the background part of that article, by Paul Welch, Moynihan's report was fitted in with case material from families living in one slum building.

In these various ways, Moynihan managed to restate his thesis in a way that he felt counteracted the distortions it had acquired as a topic of public discussion. But whatever this may have done to clarify the intellectual issue and the public discussion of it, he could not put the report back in the position it had enjoyed in the early summer.

Somewhat surprisingly, a defender of Moynihan turned up at the black nationalist extreme of the Negro movement. Daniel Watts editorialized in the December Liberator, the publication of adherents to Malcolm X, that Moynihan was the only participant in the planning conference who had a possible blueprint for action:

The so-called American Negro is obsolete.

On November 17th and 18th, there came to the District of Columbia, an assemblage of 200 odd delegates, not to join in the wake of the passing of this product of white America's phantasy, but in trying to resurrect him. The cast of characters included the Self-annointed One, Madame Socrates of the Civil Rights movement, Pullman Porter Chief, White House-Court Jester (the curly hair one) the lesser "no-bility" including the usual *I used to be colored myself, Black Anglo-Saxons,* or *I know your problem, I was born on the lower east side,* and last but not least the white liberal (usually a powerless individual in his own community, but one who turns to the Black community, and uses our plight to enhance his new found high paying position as chief analyst and explainer of the race problem to the white power structure).

Not one of these so-called leaders, would be capable of stopping a riot in Harlem, or an uprising in Watts, Los Angeles. And yet they were there, naked and exposed, without power, stating the case for a people they know not, and cared even less about. The one man at the conference possessing a *possible* blueprint for meaningful change, was Daniel P. Moynihan, author of *Beyond the Melting Pot* and the unreleased but very much leaked, *Moynihan Report.* Needless to say, Mr. Moynihan was avoided like a plague. Any recommendations that threatened the uncle tom's vested interest in maintaining the status quo, [discrimination] was treated as something alien, in fact not part of the game of hustling *the man* for more *guilt* money."

Aftermath

Throughout the winter of 1966, the report was from time to time the subject of comment or controversy, but for the most part the full-scale battle was over; and after Moynihan's counterattack there remained only a series of potshots and skirmishes.

For example, on January 25 the *Detroit Free Press* reported a discussion of the report at a meeting sponsored by the Jewish Labor Committee in which it was condemned by Wayne State University sociologist Arthur Lipow as a "distorted . . . disgraceful . . . ideological rationalization to avoid the basic problem of Negro Americans." Lipow's characterizations of the report did not go unchallenged. According to the *Free Press* "most of the audience, which included top civil rights leaders in Detroit, were openly hostile to Lipow's analysis. One Negro woman charged him with being blind to harsh realities of the situation of many Negro Americans. . . ."

Whitney Young criticized the report in his news column "To Be Equal" (*St. Louis Argus,* January 28, 1966) saying that it had been written in a manner which suggested that it described all Negro families. He also repeated the earlier criticism by those who pointed out that Moynihan did not give comparative statistics for white families at the same income level and did not qualify the very problematic data that he used; for instance, Negro crime rates. Yet Young included in his critique the statement:

The real message of the report, obscured by the unfortunate emphasis on the distorted figures, is that unemployment among Negroes, twice the white rate and affecting perhaps 25 per cent of Negro men, has effects which go beyond the economic, harming the social fabric of family life. The poverty and unemployment which afflict disproportionate numbers of Negroes in the United States take a tremendous toll from the man who is jobless, the housewife who is forced into the labor market to make ends meet, and the child denied the atmosphere he needs to grow up properly motivated."

There were three intellectual critiques of the Moynihan Report during this time, two appearing in the March–April (1966) issue of *Dissent,* by Laura Carper and by Frank Riessman. The third by Bayard Rustin in an article attacking the McCone Report (*Commentary,* March 1966).

Carper attacked the report first for its ideological basis and its implication that "*50 percent* of the Negro population is incapable of profiting [from the poverty program] because of a psychological distemper." She objected to Moynihan's conclusion concerning the sudden change in the relationship between ADC and employment: "Presumably, the negative correlation after 1962 shows or suggests that giving the Negro male a job will no longer insure or help insure family stability. The conclusion is that something more is needed." Carper suggested that "The negative correlation is due to an inconsistency between youth unemployment rate and the unemployment rate of the nonwhite male population as a whole and to an important change in policy on the part of the welfare authorities. As a staff member of the (welfare) department informed me, 'It is our policy to give everyone a chance now.' "

She criticized the Moynihan Report for its lack of understanding of the nature of oppressed people: "If one eliminates the positive social function of a cultural constellation, if one ignores the meaning personal relations have to the people involved, if one, in short, uses science to depersonalize, what emerges is always pathology. For health involves spontaneous human feelings of affection and tenderness which the Moynihan Report . . . cannot encompass."

She continued, "I am seeking to show that matriarchy within the larger social context of what the report calls patriarchy is common to the way of life of poor people. And further, that people living under oppression always develop social formations which appear to the surrounding oppressive culture to be excessive or pathological."

Riessman's primary objection to the Moynihan Report was that it was *"a one-sided presentation of the consequences of segregation and discrimination.* That damage has been done to the Negro as a result of discrimination cannot and should not be denied. But the Negro has responded to his oppressive conditions by many powerful coping endeavors. He has developed many ways of fighting the system, protecting himself, providing self-help and even joy. One of the significant forms of his adaptation has been the extended, female-based family."

Riessman noted that in psychiatry it is recognized that mental health and mental illness can coexist in the same individual, and that this concept has important implications "for social action because it draws attention to the need for concentrating on the health-producing aspects of an organism or group."

Bayard Rustin in his critique of the McCone Report (*Commentary,* March 1965) identified several basic similarities between it and the Moynihan Report. First he noted that both depart from

the standard government paper on social problems. [The McCone Report] goes beyond the mere recital of statistics to discuss, somewhat sympathetically, the real problems of the Watts community. . . . It never reached them, however, for, again like the Moynihan Report, it is ambivalent about the basic reforms that are needed to solve these problems and therefore shies away from spelling them out too explicity.

Rustin also argued that both the Moynihan and the McCone Reports contain ambivalences such that both liberals and conservatives use the report. The liberals point out that radical changes are necessary and the conservatives happily point to the Negro's characteristic pathologies. "On the other hand," Rustin added, "both sides have criticized the reports for feeding ammunition to the opposition."

The spring of 1966 also produced defenses of the report. The most notable of these appeared in *Muhammad Speaks* (April 8, 1966). There it was noted that like a recent U.S. Government publication "White-Non-White Differences in Health, Education and Welfare," the Moynihan Report gives "substance to some of the Honorable Elijah Muhammad's contentions and claims." The article consisted primarily of quotes from the report with little editorializing, but the implication was clear. The Muslims reacted positively to the report as an indication of the consequences of the treatment the Negro has received in the United States. The article concluded by suggesting that "the most significant statement in 'The Negro Family: The Case for National Action,'" is "The only religious movement that appears to have enlisted a considerable number of lower class Negro males in northern cities of late is that of the Black Muslims: a movement based on total rejection of white society. . . ."

Moynihan sought to answer many of his critics in his last defense (Look, May 17) by writing, "There is no such thing as The Negro Family. There are only families of Negro Americans — nearly five million of them — living almost every kind of life in every part of the nation and world, and in just about every condition." He emphasized that in this article he was talking about a particular segment of the Negro population — those families living in poverty with one or both parents missing. The article emphasized three points that were made in the original report. Moynihan evidently still felt that they were not only true but also important to say.

First he observed that in a large "number of these families, the father is absent not because he is dead but because, in a deep sense of the word, our society has never let him come alive. Either the family never really existed or, if it did, it broke up when he left." Appalling statistics testify to "the ordeal of the Negro father, hounded by discrimination, unemployment, bad housing, low pay."

Second, he asserted that the absence of the father makes a difference in the development of the child. He cited several social scientists who have compared children of complete and incomplete families, demonstrating the effects of an absent father: "A five-year-old boy needs a father. If he has to live without one, he has been cheated. It does not matter whether he goes on to become a Supreme Court justice or a brain surgeon. He has been cheated. A just society is one in which children are loved and protected and taught by parents who are able to support them in dignity and independence. That is what a large part of life is about."

Finally Moynihan argued that "America has not paid enough attention to the factors that are causing the disintegration of many Negro families." He noted that many of the present welfare programs were drawn without regard to their effects on the family — indeed some required the father to be absent if the family is to receive aid.

The article closed with explicit demand for action to be taken. "The United States," wrote Moynihan, "has a clear opportunity and an unmistakable responsibility to do something to help provide Negro Americans with the basic conditions of family stability: full employment; decent housing, with apartments large enough for the large families many Negroes have; better-than-average education to do a tougher-than-average job. Perhaps, most of all, a family income for men with family responsibilities . . . ."

The debate over the Moynihan Report was addressed directly by Bayard Rustin in an article, "Why Don't Negroes . . ." (*America*, June 4, 1966), that was distributed at the spring White House Conference.

Rustin first made it clear that he felt that "it is unfair to charge Moynihan with being a racist, open or covert, and that, as a matter of fact, he was trying in his report to insist on the social and economic dimension of the race issue — for example, in his showing that prolonged unemployment tended to disintegrate the white family structure and to place particularly difficult psychological burdens on the male. The Negro family, Moynihan shows, has lived in a depressionlike atmosphere ever since the 1930's, and the result has been a predictable breakdown."

Rustin's major criticism of the report was that the data were present in "a form guaranteed to promote confusion. An inter-office memo on one aspect of a problem, it was taken by many, both friends and foes, as a comprehensive statement." As a result, it was possible for some to use the report as a basis to say that the first step was for the Negroes to get their own house in order.

He also criticized the report for focusing on the negative aspects of Negro life and not considering the degree to which what are regarded as problems or pathologies from a middle-class point of view can be seen as the poor's attempt to adapt to a pathological environment.

Using Abram Kardiner and Lionel Ovesey's study, *The Mark of Oppression,** Rustin traced the now well-known pattern of family disintegration as a result of unemployment and discrimination. He ended his discussion of the Negro family by arguing that it is the economic position of the Negro male, rather than his self-image and self-esteem that is the determining factor.

That is why A. Phillip Randolph has proposed a "Freedom Budget," a multi-million dollar social investment to destroy the racial ghettos

* Abram Kardiner and Lionel Ovesey, *The Mark of Oppression: Explorations in the Personality of the American Negro* (New York: World Publishing Co., 1964).

of America, house the black and white poor decently and create full and fair employment in the process. His approach is fundamental if we are serious about reconstructing the Negro family and allowing the Negro male to be head of the household.

By the end of the spring, Moynihan was being dropped as "the person to attack." Attention of intellectuals concerned with civil rights as well as civil rights leaders turned toward the developing White House Conference. In February, the President announced the appointment of the Conference Chairman, Honorary Chairman, and the Conference Council, but there were very few reports describing the Council's deliberations. No doubt a great deal was going on informally among Permanent Government members, civil rights leaders, and the White House staff, but without additional interviewing these events cannot be discussed here. We believe it can be safely assumed that like the planning session the decisions were made by a relatively small group. Yet quite unlike the fall planning session, these decisions did not become public as they were being discussed, and neither controversy nor notoriety developed.

12

"To Fulfill These Rights":
Non-Moynihanian

Berl Bernhard's statement to the fall planning conference that he had been reliably informed that no such man as Daniel Patrick Moynihan existed characterized even better Moynihan's relationship to the full-scale White House Conference, "To Fulfill These Rights." Moynihan was present, but silent, and his paper on the Negro family had been consigned to oblivion. Even though there was a room full of literature on the problems of fulfilling the rights of Negroes, *The Negro Family: The Case For National Action* was absent.

Included in the room of literature was a compilation of Department of Labor statistics on *The Negroes in the United States: Their Economic and Social Situation.* Included in it was a very extensive bibliography on the Negro in the United States. While the bibliography contains fifteen references to Department of Labor documents, there was no reference to the most notorious — *The Negro Family: The Case For National Action.* In a fashion very consistent with our analysis of the permanent bureaucracy, the polemic was hidden; as one conference delegate said, "That thing on the economic status of the Negroes doesn't say so, but once you get through that long introduction and start looking at the tables you can see that it's a polemic against Moynihan."

Evidently the decision to remove the topic of the Negro family from the agenda of the White House Conference had been made in the early part of the year *before* the President appointed the council for the June conference. According to one member of the council, it had never considered the question of whether or not the Negro family would be discussed in the conference. He expressed confusion when we asked him about the Moynihan Report and the subject of the Negro family. Even though he had heard about the Moynihan Report, he had not read it, and *no copies had been given to the council.*

The family was the focus of Johnson's Howard University speech; there had been a panel in the planning conference devoted to the subject of the family; yet, the report of the planning session that was given to the council in February evidently did not include the discussion from the family panel.

The document that had been central to the Howard University speech had faded into official oblivion. The White House had moved a long way from Johnson's statement at Howard University that,

Unless we work to strengthen the family, to create conditions under which most parents will stay together — all the rest: schools, and playgrounds, public assistance and private concern, will never be enough to cut completely the circle of despair and deprivation.

At the spring conference, Cliff Alexander of the White House staff was asked why the subject of the Negro family had been dropped. He replied, in the conversation-stopping manner characteristic of many high Washington officials, that "The family is not an action topic for a can-do conference."

This was not the desire of all those present. Dorothy Height, President of the National Council for Negro Women, said at a press conference during the first day of the conference,

Those of us who are aware of the problems of the Negro family look to this conference with the hope that something will be done about the family in the ghetto. Very few Negro families have the protection of white children. We need to implement services in the community that will protect the Negro family.

But the subject of the Negro family was rarely mentioned by the conferees. Roy Wilkins explained to a reporter:

The Negro community resents, without logic, the efforts to focus attention on the Negro family, as if it were a moral criticism of themselves. They regard it as a diversionary matter to the real issues—housing, employment, job training and justice.

The White House Strategy — Programmed Consensus

With a brief review of the social context of the civil rights movement and the experience of the White House during the previous year of efforts in policy making in civil rights and with what little knowledge we have about the decision making that took place in the spring of 1966, it is possible to make some inferences as to the strategy developed by the White House for the spring conference.

The poverty movement began during the Kennedy Administration at a time when Kennedy was stimulating radical critiques of American society and his economic advisors were pointing out that the economy could not progress with 20 percent of the population not spending money. The poverty movement from the outset was government policy. There was little question about its goals and objectives.

The civil rights movement began outside the government and has been political since the outset. Debate, conflict, and criticism of government has characterized the civil rights movement since its outset. The government has always had control of the poverty movement and has never had control of the civil rights movement.

Even with their ideological and power differences, in 1965 there were pressures toward merging these two movements. Such a merging on substantive issues, such as removal of slums, improved housing, more and better jobs, was welcomed by some members of both groups as it became clear that neither movement could achieve its goals without the other. But beneath the "happy marriage," the basic ideological orientations of the two movements produced conflicts not comfortable for the Johnson consensus (dramatically represented by a demonstration outbreak at a recent poverty conference). The government, particularly under the Johnson Administration, had adopted the ideological stance of consensus. The White House Conference was programmed to reach consensus. One member of the council said in defense of the "Council's Report and Recommendations," "It's not bad when you are trying to reach a general consensus." On the other hand, the civil rights movement has adopted the ideological stance of conflict. The White House Conference can be seen as an example of the interaction of these two divergent ideological bases of planned social change.

We have suggested that the Moynihan Report fitted almost perfectly into the government's needs to "leapfrog" the movement and to rechannel the civil rights movement away from the mere passage and implementation of legislation into the area of social and economic change, thereby reducing the conflict with the movement by co-optation. But ideological movements do not change so readily. The focus on the family as the government's policy base in the area of civil rights obviously did not work. Not only was it found that the civil rights movement did not want to focus efforts on the Negro family but it was also seen that the money required to ensure family stability was more than the government was willing to spend. Yet what was learned in 1965 — that the next stage of the movement would involve social and economic changes and that if Johnson was to reach a consensus he needed to co-opt the civil rights movement — remained true in the spring of 1966. The problem then was one of the government asserting an "independent" policy in the area of civil rights that would be accepted by the movement and would therefore take the lead away from the movement's leaders. How could it assert itself and co-opt the movement at the same time?

In February, the President announced the appointment of Mr. Benjamin Heineman, Chairman of the Chicago and Northwestern Railway, as the chairman of the conference. Prior to this, Mr. Heineman had little to do with civil rights. Also appointed were A. Phillip Randolph as Honorary Chairman of the conference and a Conference Council of some thirty persons. Eight of the council were associated with industry and big business; seven were leaders of the civil rights movement; the remaining half were government men, lawyers, judges, labor leaders, and scholars.

The small social science representation on the council and among the delegates to the final conference indicates another change away from the President's Howard University speech. There Johnson had said that the delegates would be "scholars, and experts, and outstanding Negro leaders — men of both races — and officials of the government at every level." (There was no mention of the businessmen who came later to dominate the council.) The fall planning session was attended by scholars, civil rights leaders, and government officials; indeed, the panel discussions were dominated by scholars and experts.

This cannot be said of the final conference. Delegates were primarily local civil rights leaders, a few national Negro leaders and even fewer scholars and experts. There were several rather well-known social scientists and writers who were strikingly absent. Social scientists such as Frank Riessman, Urie Bronfenbrenner, Herbert Gans, Arnold Rose, Marvin Wolfgang, Nathan Glazer, Charles Grigg, and Lewis Killian and authors such as Michael Harrington and Charles Silberman were not present. All were present at the fall planning conference.

The conference had changed in character from one dominated by scholars and experts to one which was supposedly "representative of American civil rights interests." This change of character of the delegates is only one indication of the entire redefinition of the White House Conference. The fall planning session was designed to study the problems carefully and to begin to suggest solutions. Six months later, the government felt it knew enough about the problems and that the conference did "not have to spend a great amount of time defining the problems with which we must deal; they have been described, analyzed, and discussed at length in many forums and in the preparatory stages of this conference."

Thus the government seemed to have backed away from its earlier practice of using social science consultants in developing a meaningful and effective strategy against the Northern slums. In a very real sense, the social scientists had already served their purpose insofar as they had legitimated the government's stance in this area. Social scientists had dominated the fall planning conference, and some of them were listed as consultants to the council for the spring conference. If the heated debates of the fall planning conference were any indication, their presence at the spring conference would only threaten the peace of the meeting. Social science had legitimized the "Council's Report and Recommendations to the Conference," and a social science attack on the report would be quite embarrassing.

The council's principal job was the production of the central document for the conference, the "Council's Report and Recommendations to the Conference." This 104-page document contained a wide range of recommendations focusing on the areas of Economic Security and Welfare, Education, Housing, and Administration of Justice. (Of course there was no mention of the Negro family.) It was further legitimated, based on the fall planning conference, by the consultation of social scientists and leaders of the civil rights movement who were members of the council and was the principal tool in using the White House Conference to reach the goal of consensus politics.

The recommendations were to be read by the delegates to the conference prior to the meeting, and the business of the conference was to be the discussions, criticisms, and additions to these recommendations. Then, after the conference was over, the council, with the aid of government staff people, was to study the transcripts of the conference discussions and rewrite the recommendations. The final document would then be presented to the President. This group, behind closed doors, away from the press and critics of the government, would be able to assess which of the recommendations would be the best, and the government would not have to take the risk it had taken in 1965. The Administration would have "feedback" on all its recommendations, and Johnson would know the kind of policy that would be acceptable and could further co-opt the movement.

This plan for the White House Conference was defended by Mr. Heineman as the most democratic format that was possible, given the meeting of 2,400 persons for two days. Heineman said in defending the council's decision not to allow resolutions to be voted on during the conference:

After considerable discussion by the Presidentially appointed council consisting of a broad representation of persons interested in civil rights, it was concluded at that time that taking of formal votes would not be in the best interest of this conference. This was true for several reasons. The report consisted of broad, complex and numerous recommendations. The conference was open to suggestions, proposals and comments by any conferee. Everyone should be given an opportunity to speak. To establish this session with 2,400 persons on a parliamentary basis would be undemocratic in itself. This is true because it would not allow people to make their views known.

A fair and desirable substitute is to make a complete stenotype transcript of the proceedings, all of which would be considered in the draft of recommendations to the President.

With such an arrangement persons who are not familiar with parliamentary procedures and are unskilled in competitive debate would have an opportunity to participate in the conference.

With such an arrangement it is true that everyone at the conference would have a chance to speak and that the government would get feedback on its recommendations. But there is a real question of how "democratic" the conference was, particularly with respect to decision making. If one makes the (incorrect) assumption that the Administration called the conference so persons interested in civil rights would have a determining part in the formation of national policy in civil rights, the format of the conference was hardly democratic.

Floyd McKissick of CORE said that the conference had been rigged and later changed his mind and said it was a hoax. Delegates told reporters, "We came for a dialogue and we are going to get a monologue."

It was suggested by many of the delegates that the list of delegates had been carefully screened so as to eliminate any "bomb throwers" from attendance at the conference. Many said that no grass roots activists were invited to the conference. Southern grass roots were represented, and a number of "grass roots" people were there from the North — the most verbal from Watts and Harlem. Activists such as Julius Hobson of Washington ACT or Jesse Gray, organizer of the New York Rent Strikes, were not invited. But Lawrence Landry, leader of Chicago ACT, was. There were several delegates who came to the conference without invitations and after some pressure on the conference staff were able to pay the $25 registration fee, and obtain delegate badges.)

The conference staff must be seen as walking a very thin line between maintaining reasonable order and control over the conference and at the same time not meeting objections with direct conflict. Conflict would itself produce additional conflict. The organizers had to compromise to maintain control. Allowing persons who had come to Washington on their own into the conference is one example of this strategy. Perhaps a clearer example is the change in the resolution policy. Floyd McKissick had let it be known he was going to present a motion at the first general meeting of the conference that resolutions be made and voted upon in the conference committee. The National Council of Churches passed out a mimeographed sheet supporting such a move immediately before the opening session. The council, hearing McKissick's demands, had moved after a night of deliberation to compromise and allowed resolutions to be made during the last committee meetings. By changing the rules, the council avoided direct conflict with the more militant delegates and therefore maintained control over the convention.

Resolutions were made only during the last part of the last session. (It should be pointed out that several delegates objected to taking up the entire time of the last committee meeting to make resolutions. They wanted to talk about the scheduled subject.) Some of the committees required their members to draw up the resolutions and turn in a written copy to a "Resolutions Committee." These committees then reviewed the resolutions and selected those that were finally presented before the committee. One resolution on preferential treatment was rejected by such a committee and not presented to the group. The delegate who had turned in this resolution was not recognized by the committee chairman when he discovered that his resolutions were not going to be presented. Later, when talking to the chairman, he was unable to find any reason for its rejection other than "You didn't start your paragraph with 'Whereas be it resolved!' "

There are many ways in which one can say that the conference was open and free, and likewise there are ways that the conference was tightly controlled. It is true that anyone could stand up and say anything in the committee meetings. Also, the council did back down on the policy of "no resolutions from the floor" and allowed resolutions to be made during the last meeting of the panel. But perhaps most important is the fact that control over the federal policies that result from the White House Conference are at least two steps away from the delegates of the conference. First the transcript from the committee meetings will be screened and then a set of recommendations will be sent to the President. The President still has the alternative of rejecting any proposal he wishes. As one member of the conference staff said, "The President doesn't have to do a thing that they recommend unless he wants to."

The Panel Discussions

The group of 2,400 delegates were broken into 12 groups of 200 which were to discuss the recommendations from the council or anything else that came up. As far as we were able to discern these twelve groups were randomly chosen so that each committee had considerable variation in orientations and involvement in the movement. Each committee was more or less representative of the conference at large.

Unlike the fall planning conference, the committees were not chosen on the basis of their interest in a special area, nor did they discuss only one area. Rather, each committee discussed the four areas covered by the council's recommendations. Everyone had their chance to talk about Housing, Economic Security and Welfare, Education, and the Administration of Justice.

The committee of delegates were assigned a chairman who remained with them for the entire conference. The chairman's job was to recognize delegates who wished to speak, control the audience, and ask members of a panel of experts to respond to questions, criticisms, or suggestions made by the delegates. The panels of experts were federal and local government men, as well as social scientists and other professionals specializing in the areas being discussed. The panels rotated from one committee of delegates to another depending on the subject matter of a given three-hour period.

Unlike the planned format of the conference, however, there was little discussion of the "Recommendations of the Council." The discussion and comments were about the problems of individual delegates' communities or neighborhoods. Rarely did the discussion follow a "theme" or a single issue. The committee discussions consisted of a series of separate statements with little continuity. Each delegate would stand up and say what he had to say about his problem without considering what previous speakers had said. There is little question why Vietnam was not an issue for most of the delegates. As Whitney Young suggested to a reporter, "These people are more concerned about the rat tonight and the job tomorrow than they are about Vietnam."

Because of this, there was a tremendous range of topics and complaints made. For example, in a typical sequence a lady from the South stood up to say, "What are you going to do about the lily white unions who run the railroads in the South. Our men are trained but they can't break into those unions." She was immediately followed by a man from a northern urban area who suggested that a major reason for the lack of employment was that transportation was inadequate, "Men cannot work because they have no cars to get them to the jobs."

A similar pattern of separate statements characterized a committee discussing housing. A Negro minister told of how his church in Philadelphia had bought land and obtained loans sufficient to build semiprivate housing. He said in concluding, "We pulled ourselves up by our boot straps and prevented the slums that were cropping up around us from involving us, too." Then a minister pointed out that the national real estate organizations have attempted to co-opt the National Council of Churches into accepting their *voluntary* compliance to housing integration and were now fighting the housing legislation in Congress. Then a Negro from Alabama rose to suggest that there was no problem of segregated housing in the South, there the problem was *housing of any kind*. He ended his statement with

We've gone about as far as we can without getting into the streets and raising hell for what's supposed to be ours. Looks like this conference isn't going to be any good for us. Black folks are going to stop thinking that they are inferior, they have ideas of their own, and they're going to get what's due them out of life. Some of the people that I know can count the chickens without going outside. When the wind blows they fall against the side of the house — inside. We need housing in the South. People in Washington need to come down to Alabama and see how people live — I mean, survive.

This was characteristic of the tone of militancy that was made explicit several times in the committee meetings by southern "grass roots" Negroes.

Perhaps most explicit was a lady from Mississippi who said,

We want action. We are tired of promises and want action now or else we're going to have Watts all over the country. We in the South are ready. We have been in slavery. We want our freedom just like everyone else wants theirs. We want you — Washington — to do something now. It is time to do something and stop just talking about it. Will action take place or not?

This was in a committee meeting that was discussing education and desegregation of public schools. This lady was complaining that her school district was segregated but that the government had done nothing toward cutting off federal funds from the school board. The committee chairman, in response to this statement, noticed in the back of the room Mr. David Seeley, the assistant commissioner of the Equal Education Opportunity Program of the Office of Education. The chairman called on Mr. Seeley to answer the question saying, "Mr. Seeley, did you hear that?" Mr. Seeley went to the microphone to say that he had come to the meeting to listen and not to talk and that, "Yes, I heard it." As he returned to his seat he said under his breath, "But no action."

Seeley's comment was characteristic of the government stance at the conference. For the most part the panel of government experts defended the council's recommendations; rarely did they admit to the importance of the delegates' suggestions or criticisms. Even more rarely did the panel criticize the document.

Most characteristic was Seeley's way of avoiding direct conflict with the delegates.

There was no interchange of ideas. There was no real dialogue. The government had presented its recommendations; now the delegates were presenting theirs. Conflict and debate cannot be said to characterize these meetings. On the surface it was, as Mary McGrory said, "A real peaceful session." Yet the feeling that emerged from listening to these committee discussions was a sense of futility, senselessness, hopelessness, and powerlessness. Knowledge that they were going to make resolutions on the last meeting of the conference did give some feeling of significance. Several times this was mentioned, and occasionally the chairmen warned their committees: "What we are doing is important. We've got to be serious and think about what we are doing. Tomorrow afternoon you have to vote on resolutions." Perhaps the meetings would have seemed even more senseless had the council not changed its policy and allowed resolutions.

One indication of the feeling that pervaded the committee meetings was the low attendance. By the second meeting, for example, there were only 75 persons in one committee. During the second day, this number dwindled to 54 and, in two other committees, to 61 and 55 delegates. This is to be compared with the 200 delegates who were assigned to each committee. Only in the last session when resolutions were being made did attendance pick up again; and even then there were, for example, only 81 delegates in one committee and 75 in another.

Part of this low attendance at the committee meetings can be explained by the fact that all the delegates were not interested in all four problem areas. As one delegate explained, "There are people here who came to talk about education or housing and are not interested in discussing the welfare program."

Yet the feeling that was dominant was expressed by a delegate from Bogalusa, Louisiana, who told a reporter: "The Negro people in Bogalusa will be peeved. They spend $500 to send me to this big show, this come-on, this waste of time. I hoped I would come back and tell them some kind of action would be taken immediately."

From the point of view of many delegates, the least important part of the conference was the panel discussions. Far more important was the informal activity outside the committee meetings in the halls. At any time during the entire conference, the hotel lobby was filled with conference delegates. This is where one could find the leaders of the movement. The importance of this informal activity became especially clear as one observed attempts to engage in a conversation. Hardly more than one sentence could be exchanged before someone walked up and interrupted the conversation to talk about old times or new problems.

In a very real sense, the most important part of the White House Conference was in these informal meetings rather than in the planned program. The conference became a national convention of civil righters, and in the characteristic form of conventioners they came to talk to their friends rather than to attend the official meetings.

We have suggested that the government attempted to control the conference in order to prevent an outbreak such as occurred at the poverty meetings held earlier in the spring. The government had protected itself and continued to protect itself from any direct conflict with dissident members of the movement. Such programmed consensus has its consequences, particularly when working with a group whose ideology stems from years of conflict with power structures.

Only those delegates who came to the conference and attended the committee meetings can be classified as following the consensus program. This consists of less than half the delegates attending and only national leaders such as Whitney Young, Bayard Rustin, and Roy Wilkins.

Those who came to Washington but spent most of their time outside of the meetings talking to their friends represent an implicit rejection of the official program. Floyd McKissick represents still another step toward the rejection of the programmed consensus. McKissick not only directly criticized the convention but was aware enough of the dynamics of government politics to realize that his influence could be increased by going outside of the official channels of the conference to the press. Newsmen need something dramatic to write about, and something going on outside of the establishment's program made relatively exciting stories. McKissick was able to use the press to his advantage and thereby increased his influence.

The Administration recognized this threat to its consensus and brought out its big guns for defense. As *The New York Times* John Herbers observed:

At this point the Federal apparatus went into operation. President Johnson made an unscheduled appearance at the dinner Tuesday night and won a warm reception by reiterating dedication to the movement and by taking the unusual action of introducing a speaker, Solicitor General Thurgood Marshall, a pioneer Negro leader.

The next morning Arthur J. Goldberg, United States delegate to the United Nations, and other Cabinet members came to the conference. The working sessions were laced with Federal officials. The session at which Mr. McKissick presented his Vietnam resolution, which was soundly defeated, was chaired by a Goldberg assistant, James M. Nabrit Jr.

The picketing outside of the hotel led by Julius Hobson, Jesse Gray, and Dick Gregory was covered by the newspapers and television, but it had little or no influence on the conference. Many of the delegates did not know it was happening until they went to their rooms and hurriedly turned on the news "to see what was happening at the conference." These actions along with the SNCC boycott of the conference, represent the extreme rejections of the President's consensus. Even though they represented a minority of the Negro community (the delegates upheld James Nabrit's ruling that McKissick's anti-Vietnam resolution was out of order by a ten to one margin), they represented a new mood that was growing in the movement.

By excluding the possibility of organized debate and conflict on the substantive issues that were discussed at the conference and excluding the delegates from full participation in the decision making, the White House was able to fulfill its obligation to have a White House Conference "To Fulfill These Rights," but it left many delegates who attended the meetings with a feeling that they had wasted their time.

Exactly one year had elapsed between the Howard University speech and the spring conference. During that year the nation had learned that it was at war, and that the civil rights initiative the speech seemed to represent was not going to develop. To some observers the Howard speech seemed likely to be the last major domestic policy address the President would make until the Vietnam war was over; in July 1965, the President had gone to war, although it took the rest of the nation some months to really understand that fact.

Several weeks after the spring conference, an event occurred which neatly symbolized the dead end into which the report and the Howard speech had run. Representatives of the White House Conference Council met with the President to present their report of the conference deliberations. According to one of those present, the President spoke with them for one hour. *Approximately 4* minutes of the time was devoted to the subject of civil rights, and for 56 minutes the President harangued his council about Vietnam, the importance of the war, and the stupidity of domestic "doves" and of foreign diplomats who run off to Hanoi and Washington trying to make peace through compromises.

The Council's Report and Recommendations

When one considers the fact that the "Council's Report and Recommendations" to the conference delegates was written by a group dominated by businessmen appointed by the President, it is a surprisingly liberal document. There was little added to it during the two-day conference. In a very real sense, the President had fulfilled his objective of leapfrogging the movement. As one delegate told a reporter, "It looks to me that we're going to have Mr. Johnson as our leader whether we like it or not." It would be difficult to maintain from studying the recommendations, especially after noticing the names of Martin Luther King, Roy Wilkins, Whitney Young, Floyd McKissick, and John Lewis among its authors, that the President was backing away from the new stage in civil rights or the war against poverty.

In the Howard speech, after announcing the coming conference, Johnson pledged that the fulfillment of the rights of Negroes "will be a chief goal of my Administration, and of my program next year, and in years to come. And I hope, and I pray, and I believe, it will be a part of the program of all America." The conference as it was originally described emphasized its role to generate ideas and programs that the Administration could carry out. It was hoped that the result would be a revitalization of the present government bureaucracy dealing with the problems of urban slums.

The expectations for the spring White House Conference were that it would look critically at the federal government's role in the area of poverty and civil rights and as a result the government would change many of its present welfare practices and establish new and stronger agencies toward the implementation of civil rights laws.

The council's recommendations did contain suggestions for changes in the welfare establishment and for increased federal effort in the areas of civil rights and poverty, but it also included recommendations that reinforced, rather than challenged, the present welfare establishment with its dedication to individual treatment rather than institutional change. Also there were many indications that responsibility for action was to be given to local and state governments rather than assumed by the federal Administration.

The Welfare Establishment Survives

Generally the document placed emphasis on the economic roots of the Negro problem. The largest section dealt with "Economic Security and Welfare," and many of the recommendations dealt specifically with changes in the economic stability of the Negro. The most radical of these was the suggestion of guaranteed employment for those workers who could not be placed in, or promptly trained for, regular employment.

Yet the section containing recommendations dealing with public assistance and welfare programs suggested little change. The principal suggestion was for the establishment of a federal standard for public assistance. Moynihan's earlier recommendations that the government take the responsibility for guaranteeing a minimum income for all people was considerably tempered. The council wrote:

There should be explicit acceptance of the *government's responsibility for guaranteeing a minimum income* to all Americans. This involves (a) making available "last resort employment" to those willing and able to work but who cannot find jobs, and (b) utilizing an improved public assistance system to provide income to needy persons who are unable to seek employment because of age, physical or mental disability, family responsibilities or other reasons; and who are not adequately protected by social insurance programs."

While this was one of the more radical statements in the section on "Economic Security and Welfare" it was based on the same assumption underlying the present welfare establishment: one must either work, if he is able, or be completely unable to work before he is to be considered worthy of receiving a decent income.

The welfare orientation of the council's recommendations is particularly evident in the recommendations dealing with youth, where the emphasis was on counseling services.

The recommendation that employment services be federalized would no doubt reduce the amount of discrimination by employment agencies and does have important implications for giving unemployed Negroes access to and knowledge about employment opportunities. But an additional recommendation fit perfectly the predilections of the labor and welfare establishment.

An *individualized approach to disadvantaged workers* should be adopted to meet the especially difficult employment and training needs of the hard-core unemployed. This should include the *establishment of Human Resource Development Centers* described under Recommendation I. Such Centers, located in major cities, should provide intensive and individualized services. The Center's services should include diagnosis of need, intensive and prolonged counseling; referral to health and welfare, or other assistance to workers with especially severe unemployment problems; referral to training; specialized job placement assistance; and continuing contact with counselors to solve human relations and other problems which may interfere with performance on the job.

As Herbert Gans had written to the White House staff nine months earlier, "such solutions could maintain the already overly paternalistic and manipulative way with which we have been dealing with the problems of the Negro, and more important they could deflect attention away from the economic causes of the Negro problems." To a large degree, his fears had come true. The welfare establishment had considerable influence on the "Council's Report and Recommendations." The Permanent Government has been successful in warding off real change in its policies. We, too, can not help wonder with James Tobin why "personal attitudes which doomed a man to unemployment in 1932 or even 1954 or 1962 did not handicap him in 1944, 1951 or 1956."

"Spin Off" — Get the Heat Out of the White House

No amount of legislation, no degree of commitment on the part of the national government, can by itself bring equal opportunity and achievement to Negro Americans. It must be joined by a massive effort on the part of the States and local government, of industry, and of all citizens, white and Negro.

From the President's Message to Congress
April 28, 1966

This statement by the President provided a major guideline for the White House Conference. In addition to suggestions for action on the federal level the council's report contains many recommendations indicative of a developing governmental policy. News columnist Joseph Kraft has labeled the decentralization of government's domestic efforts as "spin-off." He observed that the "mere composition of the council (dominated by businessmen and industrialists) suggested that, if the Federal Government had a role in securing civil rights, the main burden fell on the private and semi-private sectors of the economy."

The "Introduction" to the council's report made the direction of this policy of emphasizing the efforts of the private sector quite clear. The council wrote:

The need for additional legislation, adminstrative changes, and executive leadership at all three levels of government has been extensively treated; the proposals in this category and the Conference reactions to them will be transmitted to the President and will be made available to state and local public officials.

But the Conference would fail in its purpose if it did no more than that. Governmental action, however forceful and creative, can not succeed unless it is accompanied by a mobilization of effort by private citizens and the organizations and institutions through which they express their will. Indeed, the role of government itself is in large part determined by the presence or absence of such citizen efforts.

That is why the major emphasis of this Conference must be on immediate, practical steps to enlist in this cause the great mass of uncommitted, uninvolved Americans [emphasis ours].

While there are few specific recommendations on how to enlist "the great mass of uncommitted, uninvolved Americans," the Council's Report does contain a number of suggestions which clearly indicate that the developing federal policy in civil rights, as in other domestic problem areas, would be that of decentralization, if not withdrawal of federal efforts.

Running through the document was a strong emphasis on local coordination of government and private civil rights efforts. This was most notable in the largest section of the report, "Economic Security and Welfare," which begins with a proposal to "Establish Metropolitan Jobs Councils in All Major Urban Areas, to Plan, Co-ordinate, and Implement Local Programs to Increase Jobs."

The local orientation of this first recommendation by the Conference Council was quite explicit. The report stated that

Membership of the Councils should include representatives of business, organized labor, metropolitan governments, education and training institutions and other appropriate community organizations. Each Council should be free to develop its own organization and sources of funds, including foundations, business and labor contributions, and government grants.

The section on "Education" which contained very extensive recommendations for federal action, began with the "warning" that

State and local governments, if they are to preserve control and development of education in their own hands, must take a new approach to revenue needs. *States must commit themselves to a public policy of equalization, educate their citizens on revenue needs, and devise formulas in allocation of financial and human resources that will remedy past inequities.*

Also:

Individual local school districts must also take the initiative in achieving equality of educational opportunity.

The "spin-off" policy could also be seen in the conclusion of the "Education" section where the council wrote:

The only truly viable solutions will arise from communities which treat the issue as a whole, and devise connecting and continuous plans to carry them towards the goals simultaneously — in short, "workable programs."

State administrative and financial reforms are crucial. Federal sanctions against unconstitutional and inhumane conditions, federal investment, and experimental leadership are equally vital. *But the heart of the educational change, as with its social and economic framework, lies in the commitment of each community to higher goals* [emphasis ours].

And the community commitment involves much more than modification of policy and program by government and school systems. It depends on a broad base of cooperation, and the active participation of religious institutions, business and labor organizations, civic and community groups, social and fraternal society, private foundations, and individual families and citizens.

Perhaps the best example of "spin-off" is contained in the section of the report covering "Housing." There the Council outlined four goals: (1) freedom of choice; (2) an adequate and expanding supply of new housing for low- and moderate-income families; (3) racially inclusive suburban communities and new towns; and (4) revitalization and integration of existing ghetto areas. In each of these areas, the Council's Report delineated the responsibilities of the federal government, the state government, local government, private groups, and individual citizens. The "Housing" section stated in its concluding pages,

The recommendations in this report include many examples of the type of local initiative which might be undertaken. However, taken separately they do not constitute a program. Before significant change is likely to occur it will be necessary to develop a broadly based community effort through which many groups can be persuaded, assisted, and guided in carrying out specific projects which collectively would constitute a program.

While it will take time to develop the organizational machinery for achieving the four housing goals listed in this report, a start can be made in any community at any time. Outlined below is a broadly sketched model for a metropolitan area program to work toward the goals set forth in the report.

Only the section of the report on Administration of Justice can be characterized as directing primary responsibility to the federal government in the protection of Negroes and civil rights workers from intimidation, obtaining equal justice for Negroes, and improving police–minority-group relations.

The Council was very much aware of this strategy of "spin-off." The "Conclusion" that began with the remarks of the President just quoted included the statement:

We will need new Fededal legislation and more executive action. Every section of this Report deals with these needs as well as the necessity for better enforcement of present laws and more realistic funding.

There is no question that much remains to be accomplished by our national government.

But these recommendations should not blind us to a central issue. It is that the national government's response to the compelling cry of the Negro American for justice and true equality has not been matched by state and local government, by business and labor, the housing industry, educational institutions, and the wide spectrum of voluntary organizations who, through united effort, have the power to improve our society.

It remains to be seen whether or not the White House Conference will generate the support and action from previously unmotivated, inactive or reactive, groups. The Administration must have been aware of the history of previous failure to change inaction by local government through exhortation. Yet it seemed to assume that now that there had been a White House Conference, local, state, and private efforts would begin on a full scale. We doubt it.

There is little question that Joseph Kraft was accurate in maintaining that the federal government had recently discovered that the American system was too complicated and diverse to be managed solely from the top. Johnson's waning popularity on the Gallup ratings could also have contributed to this subtle republicanism.

Though Joseph Califano, a White House aide, had sought to justify the "spin-off" policy by asserting that under modern conditions the federal system requires "joint action at the local level through groups of governmental units and of citizens," one expert on the civil rights movement was probably more accurate about White House motivations when he observed of the conference:

It seems to me that the move away from the position of the Howard speech is now complete. The "Council's Report and Recommendations to the White House Conference" strikes me as an incredible hodgepodge of every idea that has been advanced so far, with no analytic structure underlying it. I have the feeling that the White House has now lost its desire to legislate, too: the report recommends so much, in such vague terms, that it strikes me as a prescription for inaction. Certainly the White House has moved away from any position that might arouse criticism from or by the civil rights movement — which means moving away from an attempt to develop bold or new approaches.

It will be remembered that from the time of the Howard speech on, and particularly after the "disaster" of the planning conference, some Administration spokesmen had complained that the movement "knows only how to put its hand out to Uncle Sam." The stage management of the spring conference was sufficiently expert to prevent this issue from being too much out into the open; rather than attack the movement, the Administration strategy was to ignore anything that contradicted the emphasis on "spin-off," and to maintain that the delegates shared the belief that the federal government does not have the lion's share of responsibility for programs to solve civil rights problems. Thus, by the middle of the first day of the conference, a newsman could report the following conversation with Berl Bernhard, general counsel of the conference:

Most heartening, Bernhard said, was his feeling that the delegates seemed to have become convinced that the federal government cannot be saddled with the whole task of solving all the nation's civil rights problems, but that the solutions can come only from a sharing of the responsibility by all segments of society.

Yet, in fact, the major refrain of the conference delegates was that the federal government should take more and more responsibility for civil rights problems; the dominant form of delegate comments involved simply the explication of specific problems and the request or demand that the government do something about them.

The Johnson Administration is not noted for its attachment to a philosophy, as opposed to strategy, of government. The idea of "spin-off," of local responsibility, and of the importance of coordination (which may well be a bowdlerized version of the long-range policy planning which Moynihan and others in the government had argued for) should probably be viewed more as a political tactic than as a new-found White House philosophy. So long as the Vietnam war, or other intense and expensive foreign adventures last, the White House will find attractive ideas about domestic society that direct responsibility away from the Administration, and ones that privatize domestic social problems. There was little in the actions of the President before the summer of 1965 that would lead one to believe that he was so little interested in federal initiative and involvement as this new view would suggest. In any case, it became clear at the spring conference that the White House had mastered the rhetoric and tactics of encircling and leapfrogging the civil rights movement as a national force, though it had lost its will, and probably its ability, to use its new position to begin any major domestic reform that might significantly improve the situation of Negro Americans.

13

Conclusions and Implications

We have discussed in the past chapters some significant interactions among the points of view and personnel of three institutions, the federal government, the civil rights organizations, and
social science. We will discuss in this chapter some of the more
important implications for these three institutions and their
interrelationships that can be derived from a close examination
of the events of the Moynihan controversy.

The Government, The Civil Rights Organizations and the Negro

1. The most central and significannt question raised by the
Moynihan Report and by the actions of the Administration in
connection with it have to do with *the establishment of an independent federal government stance with respect to the situation of the Negro American.* We have noted that it was Moynihan's intention to encourage the establishment of a government
policy in this area and that his activities fell on fertile ground
in Administration thinking — the desire to "leapfrog" the move-

ment rather than try to keep up with it. In the past the federal government had simply responded to the pressure of events and to civil rights representations. While it is perhaps generally true that governments tend to respond to pressures more than to establish independent lines of action, the civil rights situation is a rather extreme case of this. In most other areas of domestic policy the government has a more independent policy which it pursues while accommodating to various pressures. The government should have an independent policy in this area and not simply be responsive to the pressures of private groups. Whether Negroes are accorded justice by American society should not be a simple function on how effective their leadership is at interest group politics. The President can well maintain, if he wishes, that he has legitimate right to such a role by virtue of the fact that the votes of millions of individual Negroes helped elect him and that these individuals look to him and the government he heads to act in ways that will help them realize their goals.

However, the fact that the government has not had such an independent role in the past and that civil rights organizations have developed their strategies on the assumption that the government will do nothing unless it is forced to, and then will only do what it is told to do, means that any shift toward a more independent government role will require corresponding shifts in the way the civil rights organizations deal with the government. It will mean that positive communication will have to assume a two-way flow rather than simply a one-way flow, with the civil rights organizations receiving and evaluating the initiatives of the government as well as pressuring the government to lend itself to initiatives proposed by the movement. In this respect, the civil rights organizations will have to assume some of the functions (with their attendant expertise and negotiating skills) that other lobbying groups such as business, labor, health, and welfare organization, now have in relation to the government. While the role of "creative protest" certainly will not diminish for a considerable length of time, the considerations that go into deciding what is and what is not a productive protest will involve new elements. In short, the task of the civil rights organization will become a more complex one.

None of this will come about, however, unless the government makes more than a pro forma decision in favor of an independent government role in civil rights. That is, it is not sufficient to announce and symbolize a decision to truly represent Negro citizens. The government's decision to lead rather than follow in the much heralded next stage of the civil rights struggle is meaningful only if the government puts forward a program. It was clear that Moynihan had such a program in mind and it seemed that the Administration was on the verge of developing such a program. However, it was quite clear that an effective program would require major federal expenditures. The more intimately the Administration officials understand the problems Moynihan put on their desks the clearer it will become to them that the back wages due the Negro community dwarf any current domestic program. Since it will not be politically feasible, nor indeed just, to seek to satisfy the legitimate needs of the Negro community without at the same time satisfying those of the communities of white poor, the price tag is large indeed.

Given such considerations it seems quite likely that the Moynihan controversy was but a minor element in the slowness with which the Administration followed up the Howard University speech. As the prospective costs of the Vietnam war became clearer and clearer over the summer and through the fall, the prospect of doing anything of a significant nature on the domestic front became less and less attractive. We feel, although the evidence here is highly inferential, that distractions and preoccupations concerning Vietnam had a great deal to do with the seeming disorganization of the government's response to the controversy as it built up and with the similar disorganization which occurred in putting together the White House Conference "To Fulfill These Rights."

The controversy was, then, a kind of lucky break for the Administration since it served to distract from and conceal the fact that the Administration was not really ready to assume the independent role it had reached for at Howard University. The civil rights organizations were at the same time given a breathing spell before learning how to cope with a more vigorous, initiating, federal posture.

2. Whether the government assumes an independent role or not, but especially if it does, a very real question is raised concerning the adequacy of the presently existing liaison mechanisms between the federal government and the civil rights organizations. At present, except for emergency situations this liaison seems practically nonexistent, at least at the higher levels of government. Because the federal government has not wanted to

become deeply committed to the Negro cause, it has tended to be quite standoffish in its relationships with the civil rights organizations. On the other side, with the very deep doubts they have about the sincerity of the federal government, civil rights people have not labored very hard to cultivate such relationships. The result is that the government really knows very little in depth about the thinking of civil rights organizations and *seems to operate as much on the basis of what can be learned from the newspapers and magazines as on the basis of close and continuing contact.* Even as "diplomatic relationships" the relationships between the civil rights organizations and the government would be considered poor, much less when considered within the framework of normally existing relationships between various sectors of the society and the higher levels of the Administration.

The government, probably at the White House level, needs much more extensive liaison with the civil rights movement than it now has. But, it probably will not tolerate this until it is ready to make some major permanent commitment in this area. While the government's position should be independent, it should not be blind. There is some evidence to suggest that the White House seriously underestimated the "veto power" of the civil rights movement on the direction of the Administration's civil rights policy. While it is true that the civil rights organizations have relatively little power to seriously damage the Administration politically or to force it to do things it does not want to do, the moral of the Moynihan controversy would seem to be that the movement does have the power to discredit federal *initiative* when it wishes. (Some of the civil rights organizations perhaps need to learn not to confuse this negative power with the positive power to pressure the government to do something that it is reluctant to do.)

3. The whole question of federal initiative in the civil rights area, whenever it is meaningfully embarked upon, will raise very real issues for the civil rights organizations. Over the years federal policy has moved in the direction of initiating *federal programs* relatively free of local control. Indeed those to the left of center generally work for a maximum degree of federal control and a minimum degree of local control in order to assure uniform national standards and to keep federal control out of the hands of state and local, generally more conservative, government. But the civil rights movement where it has been most effec-

tive, has been heavily local in its orientation, and there seems some inclination on the part of the more vigorous civil rights groups to ground their strategy in a local base.

Therefore a very likely source of conflict between the federal government and the civil rights groups, in addition to those having to do with the question of how much payoff for individual Negroes, will concern the organizational requirements and ambitions of the political organizations Negro leaders are building. The recent popularity of self-sufficient "black power" as a slogan and embryonic strategy within the movement is very intimately connected with this issue. Leaders of such local power groups are likely not to be as impressed with programs controlled from Washington as they are with ones controlled at the local level. It may take vigorous negotiation on the part of any federal administration to argue the merits of programs that are not channeled through local power groups.

The strategy of self-sufficient black power is a strategy of despair that assumes that nothing can be accomplished unless it is forced or blackmailed out of the white power structure. This may well be true, but if it is not true there is still the danger of its becoming a self-fulfilling prophecy if two conditions are not met: that is, (1) if a better government liaison is not created with these highly varied civil rights organizations and (2) if civil rights organizations do not develop a broader intellectual mastery of the many legal, social, and economic factors that operate together to produce the situation of caste victimization.

4. The civil rights movement and government response to it has historically had a highly legalistic focus — the target was discrimination, and discrimination was embodied in laws, in highly developed practices of segregation and discrimination, and in "the cake of custom." The history of the past ten years has taught us that while we cannot "legislate morality," we can at least legislate somewhat less blatantly immoral behavior. However, as formally institutionalized barriers are wiped away, we are increasingly confronted with the needs of Negroes for *resources* rather than simply for a change in the *rules*. Though the inadequacy of the resources available to Negroes through their lifetime may well be a result of discriminatory patterns, it does not necessarily follow that the strategies developed to attack clear and present discrimination and segregation are necessarily the most effective ones to attack the results of discrimination. Many different kinds of changes in the way our society operates

will be necessary if Negroes are ever to achieve equality. Many of these are the same kinds of permanent changes that are necessary if we are to do away with all kinds of poverty and disadvantage. Others are tactical changes that may be required to undo the effects of discrimination and disadvantage. Many are changes that should be made on their own merits quite aside from their effect of reducing Negro disadvantage or poverty generally — for example, the provision of better services in the public sector which in turn can be made to provide decent jobs for those unemployed or underemployed. As yet only a few persons in the civil rights movement (Bayard Rustin is the best example) seem to fully appreciate the leverage that can be gotten by programs that are not primarily antidiscrimination. Yet it seems certain that these will be the kinds of programs that will loom largest in any federal initiative in this area — if Moynihan had not existed someone would have had to invent him.

The Government and Social Science

1. The central issue raised by the Moynihan Report for the government social science relationship is that of the political use of social science findings. That is, the Moynihan Report is not basically a research report or a technical document; it is a polemic which makes use of social science techniques and findings to convince others. It was designed as a persuasive document because Moynihan felt that the social science data he could bring to bear would have a persuasive effect. Provided certain conditions are met, social scientists should be pleased that social science is used in this way since there comes a point in the policy-making process where the simply technical- and research-oriented approach is no longer adequate to the task.

One of the problems of this kind of persuasive use of social science has to do with the fact that the rhetoric of persuasion is generally considerably simpler than the rhetoric of scholarly or research discourse. The suitable criteria for evaluating a persuasive document are not that all its i's are dotted and all its t's are crossed but that it select some crucial issues and present them in such a way as not to belie a fuller and more balanced intellectual discussion of them. It is our view that the Moynihan Report does not violate this standard although we recognize that some other social scientists would disagree. That is, from our point of view, considering the particular goal toward which Moynihan was working — that is, to persuade top Administration officials that there was a crying need for action, and that such action might reasonably take as its focus the possible payoffs of new programs for increased family welfare — the document was both adequate to its task and not seriously distorting of the reality with which it attempted to deal. This is particularly so since Moynihan sought not to provide a full range of programs to deal with the problem but only to get the problem established as a highly priority item in the domestic agenda.

Having said this, however, we must look at some of the dangers involved in such a persuasive document. The greatest danger is that the part will be taken for the whole. That is, the sharply focused persuasive argument can be taken as presenting the "whole truth." Yet no persuasive document directed toward catching the attention of high officials can hope to do that. Therefore the period of following through once the initial goal has been achieved becomes crucial. If the policy-generating process stops with that one document, or if the document comes to be used for purposes other than that for which it was designed then the danger of unconstructive uses is considerably increased. Moynihan intended that there would be very careful follow-up of his document not only at the conference which the President announced but also by government working parties and fact-gathering groups. This, however, did not happen. No working party was appointed and what fact-finding efforts have gone on have been more in reaction to the controversy than to the report itself.

2. The other central issue raised has to do with that of audience. It is clear that any document is prepared on the basis of an assumption about the nature and needs of the audience for whom it was intended. Moynihan's report was prepared as an internal government document, intended for a very small audience. That Moynihan did not believe that his approach in that document was applicable to a public document is apparent when one contrasts the report to his *Daedalus* article. The *Daedalus* article avoids many of the sensitive issues that the the report deals with. The question then arises: Why was the report leaked, and why was it released?

If Moynihan had written the same document in his private capacity, it could not possibly have caused the same kind of controversy. The controversy resulted primarily from the fact that the document had the government imprimatur. Moynihan gave considerable thought to the design and phrasing of his report for the official audience he had in mind. Apparently no one involved gave comparable thought to how a document should be designed to accomplish the same goals but for a different audience — newspaper reporters and the public. As the Howard University speech makes very clear, it is quite possible to take exactly the same ideas and to cast them in a form that is publicly acceptable but that must be *done*, the job will not do itself.

Apparently newspaper men were expected to do this job for the government, yet with the benefit of hindsight we can see that this was too much to ask of most of them. It would seem reasonable to conclude that the document should never have been leaked or only with the most careful briefing of those to whom it was leaked, and that it should not have been publicly released until it had been rewritten with the public audience in mind. It seems very likely that no one in the government really wanted to release the report but that the extensive leaking of it forced their hands. In this respect the White House staff committed the cardinal error that Neustadt has described of allowing events to control them rather than their controlling the events.*

We have suggested one alternative interpretation of the leaks and the release of the report. Some of the press treatment, citing "White House sources," gives one the impression that at least some officials were inclined to use the report not so much to validate increased federal programs to provide Negroes with resources as to validate a "self-help," "no federal hand-outs" view. From such a point of view, the leaking of the report in the particular way it was done was a much more rational political strategy since it both communicated the self-improvement notion and also had the latent function of creating a controversy which distracted attention from Administration inaction. We have noted the possible role of increasing Vietnam costs, first in terms of the energy of the White House staff and then in terms of money, in encouraging such a strategy shift.

3. It has been argued against the Moynihan Report that a more technical, balanced, and less dramatic document would not have run into the difficulties that beset the report. This is probably true; but it is also true that such a document would have had no persuasive effect on political leaders. The Permanent Government preference for undramatic documents is perhaps functional within

* Richard Neustadt, *Presidential Power* (New York: John Wiley & Sons, 1960).

the confines of the Permanent Government but hardly elsewhere. If documents are to influence political men, they must capture political and moral sentiments; if they are to capture public sentiments, they must in some way adopt a public rhetoric much as Michael Harrington's *The Other America** laid the public groundwork for renewed discussions of poverty. As far as persuasiveness with "men of action" is concerned, the more careful style may well protect the self-conception of a writer, but it is likely to accomplish little else. To depart from this style is certainly a risk for a government official, but government needs risk takers as much as it needs steady souls; indeed, in an area of such entrenched intransigence as the civil rights problem it needs risk takers considerably more than it needs steadiness.

4. Probably the most direct relevance of the Moynihan controversy for a better understanding of government/social science relations has to do with the fact that it emphasizes the great need of government for social scientists who are directly concerned with policy-related issues rather than with data gathering or other established and routinized functions. (The government does, indeed, have some highly competent and imaginative social scientists in positions which bring them into meaningful contact with policy makers, but it has far too few of them.)

Also the government has no regularized way of making use of social scientists at the policy-making nexus. The tendency is rather for social scientists to pull together data and reasoning which are then consistently watered down and fuzzed over as they make their way up through the Permanent Government apparatus. A few career civil servants have managed to break out of this system by their own initiative and intellectual style and to form educational and consulting relationships with policy makers, and on much rarer occasions to occupy a policy-making position themselves. In addition, of course, the government does make use of outside consultants from time to time, but unless this use is carefully thought through the impact is often relatively negligible. Moynihan sought to fulfill all of these roles himself because he was very much aware of how underrepresented social science thinking was in the Presidential Government; he knew that he was one man trying to do a job that might better be done by several. Yet in this case Labor's response was "once burnt, twice shy." It did not appoint an assistant secretary to fill Moyni-

* Michael Harrington, *The Other America: Poverty in the United States* (New York: Macmillan, 1962).

han's policy-planning position but instead allowed that position to lapse.

The Civil Rights Organizations and Social Science

1. The most central issue in this area has to do with the extent to which private organizations like those of the civil rights movement have the resources to make use of social science information in pursuit of their policy goals — particularly those relating to the government, which shows increasing ability to make use of this kind of information. As Melvin Webber has observed, information represents political and economic capital, "information like money, yields power to those who have it. And, like money, the way it is distributed will determine which groups will be favored and which deprived." There are two aspects to any problem of consumption, in this case the consumption of social science information. One involves the *ability* to consume and the other the *willingness* to consume.

2. Civil rights organizations are generally quite poor in terms of the availability of specialized staff members; they are action organizations. Where the issues of policy and tactics are fairly clear-cut, this lack of staff poses minimum difficulties; but as the movement seeks to deal with more complex social situations and with issues affecting the total system rather than with particular instances of discriminatory practice, its small staff has a competitive disadvantage vis-à-vis the institutions it seeks to change.

In the case of the Moynihan Report and the issues it raised, the inadequacies of staff of the civil rights organizations were very apparent. While a very few officials of the civil rights organizations are extremely knowledgeable about what social science has developed concerning the situation of Negro Americans, as organizations they were not in a good position to evaluate the report, to examine its general validity or to determine the opportunities and threats which the government's adoption of Moynihan's point of view might present for them. Clarence Mitchell's "gut reaction" was much more typical. Though some social scientists have been served in an informal way as consultants and advisers (for example, Robert Coles and Thomas Pettigrew), there does not seem to be any regularized system within the movement for applying social science thinking to the operational problems the movement has. Compared to many other kinds of lobbying and pressure groups, the civil rights organizations appear as "stripped for action."

Some social scientists and some officials of the movement have recognized the disadvantage this represents and have made efforts to overcome it. One of the most hopeful signs in this direction was the Social Science Advisory Committee to CORE which functioned briefly over the fall of 1965. It was composed of some of the most knowledgeable men in the country in the area of poverty and race; the committee made available to CORE a kind of thinking not ordinarily available to civil rights organizations. The payoff of this kind of activity is apparent in "The CORE Charge to the White House Conference," by far the most sophisticated document presented there by an organization. Similarly, in Dr. Benjamin Payton at least one civil rights organization has a social scientist in a position analogous to that Moynihan had in the government and, therefore, has the opportunity to make more direct operational use of social science.

3. The second aspect of the consumption of services has to do with the willingness to consume them. Even if there is the possibility of acquiring the staff resources, there is still the question of whether the organization will want them. There is always a tension between the action orientation of line members of an organization and the intellectual orientation of its staff members. The ideology of the civil rights movement has become very heavily action oriented, and its members' conviction that they "understand" all that one needs to understand and need only bring to bear the willingness to act has also grown. In such a climate the tolerance for complex ideas and "sociological gobbledygook" is quite low. It is certainly no accident that in general the correlation between the sociological sophistication and the "conservatism" of the various civil rights organizations is very high. The generally conservative reputation sociology has acquired has probably served to discourage those in the movement from seeking close consultation. Yet, as the movement addresses itself more and more to the problems of the ghetto, this intellectual gap will pose greater and greater threats to the success of the movement.

There are signs that some civil rights organizations are attempting constructive initiatives in the direction of closing this gap, particularly the development of the A. Phillip Randolph Institute in New York under Bayard Rustin and the year-long effort initiated by Martin Luther King to examine issues of social science and civil rights policy under the direction of Robert Green of Michigan State University.

Without a greater commitment on the part of civil rights organizations to make use of social science, they run the risk of
creating a "mindless militancy" to cope with the ghetto; without
a similar commitment on the part of social scientists they run the
risk of perpetuating the irrelevance of their activities to significant social issues. If the federal government ever actually succeeds in establishing an independent role in the civil rights area,
failure to make extensive and sophisticated use of the social sciences will put the civil rights movement at a very great competitive disadvantage in bringing to bear countervailing power and
proposals.

The Social Sciences and the Situation of Negro Americans

During the 1920's and 1930's the social sciences, particularly
sociology and psychology, assumed the task of destroying the
intellectual foundations of racism and white supremacy. Before
that, the social sciences, along with biology, had been deeply
implicated in sustaining racist ideology; but in the relatively brief
span of twenty years these disciplines completely reversed the
intellectual status of racist views. From the early 1940's to fairly
recently, however, studies in the area of race went into a long
and somewhat unnoticed decline. Despite the historic 1954 Supreme Court decision and the social changes that seemed likely
to follow it, few social scientists turned their attention to a renewed interest in the subject. Only as a result of the civil rights
revolution of the late 1950's and early 1960's did civil rights
subjects assume the importance they had formerly had as areas
of applied social science efforts.

1. The position of social science in the current situation is
markedly different from that of the earlier time. Before social
science addressed itself fairly exclusively to white concerns, white
stereotypes, white cupidity. Whatever social scientists said they
had to worry only about reactions against and attacks on their
work from the conservative white world. And they could define
their position as morally unambiguous since they knew that they
were attacking the citadels of discriminatory power. In the present
situation, however, the social scientist works on these problems
in the context of a vigorous contest between the new, highly
vocal, civil rights movement and the old white power structure.
Therefore, there is a double sensitivity to his works. Whereas
before almost anything he said that cast doubt on the validity of

white stereotypes was unambiguously a contribution to the civil rights cause, now what the social scientist does is examined for its subtleties, for the implications its particular construction of reality has for the strategies of the movement as well as for the strategies of the white world. Therefore it is possible for social science products to challenge the beliefs and intellectual justifications of both of these contenders. The Moynihan Report and the social science research on which it was based seemed to have done this.

Social scientists like to believe that their primary commitment is to "truth," however ambiguously their philosophies require them to regard that concept. In their pursuit of adequate comprehension of the reality of the lives of Negro Americans and the forces which play on them, they are likely to come increasingly into conflict with established and preferred views on the part of highly varied white power groups on the one hand and civil rights groups on the other. They have the task, then, of guarding their autonomy against the pressures of all of these groups that may wish to dictate the nature of the problems considered, the findings developed, and the implications drawn.

2. Perhaps the major threat to the autonomy of the social scientist in this area is not, however, his reaction to outside pressures for conformity to the established view of one or another group but rather the conflict between his own ideological position on civil rights and his commitment to a search for truth. Social scientists, at least most of those involved in research in the civil rights area, generally think of themselves as strongly committed to the goals of the civil rights movement. Their thinking about civil rights is often influenced as much by the heroes of the movement as by the social science literature. Therefore, they themselves are in the same position as members of the movement when confronted with data that challenge the simpler sloganized ideologies of the movement.

This is but a very sharp case of a general problem that social scientists face in going about their work. In order to do worthwhile research, social scientists must place themselves in positions which make them vulnerable to having either or both their theoretical views and their more simply human views of social reality upset. From time to time, all social scientists commit the error of glossing over data that are alien to their conceptions. One particular form this takes in the study of Negro Americans (or the poor or other disadvantaged groups) is that of reluctance to face facts that call into question the sympathetic image the researcher wishes to maintain.

Alvin Gouldner has suggested that this glossing over of some data or "resistance to hostile information" indicates a *"lack of awareness"* by the social scientist. Gouldner suggests that:

It is not the state of the world that makes information hostile, but the state of the world in relation to a man's purpose. The knowledge and use of information inimical to one's own desires and values is awareness (and, perhaps, some part of wisdom, too). Awareness is access to hostile information born of a capacity to overcome one's own resistance to it and cannot, therefore, simply be "retrieved" without a struggle — as can information. Since such resistance is always based in some part upon the pain or fear of knowing, the struggle to overcome resistance and to attain awareness always requires a measure of valor.*

It should be noted that such resistance to hostile information is a form of "gut reaction." Few social scientists, for example, would admit to a personal, conscious view that having an illegitimate child is "immoral." But, the reactions of a great many social scientists to the use Moynihan made of illegitimacy data would suggest that they are struggling with such a view within themselves which they project on the larger public. They seem to be saying, "It's not that *I* think there's anything wrong with having an illegitimate child, it's just that conventional people do and therefore we ought not to talk about this." Similarly, if the social scientist deeply wishes to believe that something new and constructive can come from the depriving experiences Negro Americans have, it is often very difficult for him to face life as it is actually lived in the ghetto.

Seymour Krim in an article, "Ask for White Cadillac," reprinted in Williams' *The Angry Black,* captures very nicely this issue of our ability to withstand alien truths:

To ask for credit for trying to tell the truth, however, is the naivest kind of romanticism when you finally realize that the balance of life is maintained by cruel necessity. Truth is a bitter mirror to a humanity limping with wounded pride toward the heart's blind castle of contentment; those who would fool with it must be prepared for the worst, for in their zeal they are lancing the most private dreams of the race." †

---

* Alvin W. Gouldner, *Enter Plato* (New York: Basic Books, 1965).
† John A. Williams (ed.) (New York: Lancer Books, 1962).

3. But the obligation of the social scientist to *learn* and *know* the facts about the situation he is studying regardless of how uncomfortable those facts may be for him carries with it also the responsibility to communicate what he has learned, even though he is aware that what he communicates may become highly controversial and may prove to be an embarrassment for those with whose cause he is identified. A secret science is no science at all, as nuclear physicists have so vigorously argued. Social scientists close to policy matters often feel strong temptations to argue against this view. Long before the Moynihan controversy, we had heard, for example, some of the Permanent Government persons involved in the Moynihan controversy argue about the desirability of publishing sensitive findings along the following line: "How do you know that the constructive effect of research will outweigh the damage to the reputations of the people studied? Our science isn't that good yet. Maybe all that will happen is that we will strengthen prejudice and provide rationalizations for bigotry."

This is a knotty issue and one which perhaps can only be resolved by an act of faith. If you believe that in the long run truth makes men freer and more autonomous, then you are willing to run the risk that some people will use the facts you turn up and the interpretations you make to fight a rear-guard action. If you do not believe this, if you believe instead that truth may or may not free men depending on the situation, even in the long run, then perhaps avoidance is better because it seems to us that a watered-down set of findings would violate other ethical standards, would have little chance of providing practical guides to action, and thus is hardly worth spending time and someone else's money for.

At the level of strategy, however, this concern for the effect of findings on public issues sensitizes the social scientist to the question of how research results will be interpreted by others and to his responsibility to anticipate misuses; from this anticipation, he can attempt to counteract the possibility of misuse. That is, though we do not feel a researcher must avoid telling the truth because it may hurt a group (problems of confidentiality aside), we do believe that he must take this possibility into account in presenting his findings and make every reasonable effort to deny weapons to potential misusers.

Though the social scientist has the responsibility to try to guard against the misuse of what he has to say, he should never have the misapprehension that he can completely guard against such uses. Instead, if he is to do useful research at all he must take that risk — and it is a dual risk. Partly he takes the short-run risk of damaging those whom he studies and whom he wishes to help. He can minimize this risk by trying to make his research policy relevant (particularly to the extent that it is directed to a non-social science audience), by pointing out the policy directions he believes that his findings suggest. He must recognize that he also takes a risk in terms of his personal reputation; in the words of one of the White House Conference participants, becoming a subject of controversy is simply "an occupational hazard."

4. Further, social science as a whole, as well as the individual social scientist, has a responsibility not only to study significant problems and to report findings to policy implications accurately but also to be sensitive to the way these findings are used, particularly to whether or not they are used in ways that seem illegitimate given the findings. Though the social scientist cannot be held responsible for the misuse of his work (assuming he has taken precautions to make clear what he regards as legitimate uses), he does have a responsibility at least to pay attention to the uses to which his work is put. Social science generally has a responsibility in this way to monitor the persuasive or technical applications of social science and to comment upon these uses in a vigorous and meaningful way.

5. More generally, with respect to the growing and by-and-large desirable application of social science to policy-related issues, most particularly by governments, social scientists have a responsibility to examine and to comment. It is not enough when social scientists do "basic research" (often an implicit claim to being "noncontroversial" research) and let somebody else apply it. Social scientists have a responsibility for monitoring this application and for making public comment upon it. In short, the social scientist has a particular blend of the citizen's responsibility to evaluate the actions of his government and the intellectual's responsibility to bring to bear his skills in such a way as to inform the public of the uses and misuses of power. This is one of the ways that he minimizes the risk to which he puts the objects of his study, though not necessarily the risk he himself runs.

However, in the social sciences, professionalization processes often generate pressures against the fulfillment of these responsibilities or actually foster sanctions against a sense of responsibility for the policy implication of social science. As one of the participants in the controversy observed:

People who think in policy terms are few, and so are departments which are hospitable to them. Sociology is still a theoretically oriented discipline; few people do research to solve policy dilemmas. Second, there is still strong sanction against social scientists getting involved in policy controversies, which is part of the sanction against popular writing by academics. Anyone who writes books that are popular outside the social sciences is distrusted, and if the books create controversy and thus become more popular or at least more visible in the mass media, a mixture of jealously and professionalism get the writer into trouble.

6. Though the great need for more vigorous exercise of this responsibility is clearest with respect to the federal government, and secondarily with respect to local governments, because these organizations wield the greatest power, the responsibility does not end there. An ideologically much more uncomfortable responsibility is that of critically examining, from social science's special perspective, the activities of those private groups who participate in the policy-forming and decision-making process. To the extent that private organizations such as the civil rights organizations have a role in the formation of public policy, they are responsible not only to themselves and to their members but to the public at large. They are, in short, accountable to the public, though perhaps in a more restricted sense than is an elected party or official. And one of the functions of the social sciences, along with journalism and intellectual pursuits generally, is to further public accountability in a society whose complexity makes it easier for people to avoid their responsibilities.

7. One could hardly maintain the view that social scientists fulfill their responsibilities in this regard as well as they should, although the current mood of the discipline would seem to indicate at least renewed recognition that such responsibilities exist. Assuming that there is a willingness to fulfill these responsibilities, we can ask in what kind of position the various disciplines are to fulfill them. That is, to what extent is the knowledge base of the disciplines sufficient for the task of evaluating the activities of policy-making groups? Obviously the social sciences have a long way to go, although there seems to be increasingly the conviction both within the discipline and on the part of outsiders that social scientists have something to offer that represents an improvement over the ordinary sources of policy formation.

Nevertheless with respect to any policy area there are important gaps. An examination of the Moynihan controversy points to some rather glaring ones that implicate not only academic social science but also the government as a source of basic data.

At the purely academic level, what is most noticeable is that the "Frazier problem" raised over thirty years ago is still not solved to the satisfaction of those acquainted with it as researchers or to the satisfaction of all policy makers. While the general formulation of the problem — that the socioeconomic system constrains the family in ways that lead to disorganization and that family disorganization then feeds back into the system to sustain and perpetuate social and economic disadvantage — is reasonably well accepted, the application of this view to policy guidance in any particular respect is highly problematic. And indeed this is what the controversy (to the extent that it has an intellectual justification) has been all about. It was to this fact of uncertainty about the details of the family-disorganization process that Herbert Gans pointed when he counseled against too enthusiastic use of ideas about the effects of female-headed households.

Unless social scientists as a group are willing to devote a great deal more attention to this kind of problem, they will never be in a position to sustain fully their view that they have an important role to play in the decision-making process.

8. Such considerations also feed back into the general question of the relationship between the government and social science. For example, a few years ago (and to some extent even today) there was a great deal of reluctance on the part of government agencies supporting social science research to support research that dealt specifically with Negro Americans. It was feared on the one hand that southern congressmen would take exception to spending money in this way, and on the other hand that singling out any particular ethnic group for study somehow represented a violation of the civil libertarian point of view, perhaps even a violation of the Fourteenth Amendment. It was sometimes suggested that although the main interest of a study might have to do with Negroes, it would be better to design the sample in such a way that one is studying "just people."

9. The question of the adequacy of our knowledge at the level of basic data gathering implicates both the social sciences and government. Why should it be that illegitimacy data are in such poor shape that there can be a controversy as to whether or not

the data are even good enough to be used in testing hypotheses or establishing the validity of a general line of reasoning? If the data are really as bad as that, why does the government collect them at all? Or if the data are not as bad as that, why has it been that the agencies involved have not been prodded and given the necessary resources to collect decent data?

Further, why should it be that although little evidence supports Ryan's views, it is almost impossible to test the validity of his views about the dynamics of the Negro-white differential in illegitimacy rates? How is it that a social science which regards itself as reasonably mature does not have at its fingertips sufficient data concerning the question of underreporting, marriage when pregnant, contraception, intercourse rates and the like, to provide an accurate explanation of the differential? Again, the interests and the anxieties of both the social scientists and the funding agencies are implicated.

10. We have noted that the welfare establishment's policy of trying to be "color-blind" has had the very serious unanticipated consequence of making it difficult to know what is going on. The most dramatic example of this in the Moynihan Report has to do with Moynihan's use of new ADC cases as a dependent variable in connection with unemployment rates. First, he had to use *total* new ADC cases *because no breakdowns by race were available*. What kind of "good public relations" logic justifies such a policy?

Further, several of Moynihan's critics have expressed doubt about Moynihan's reasoning concerning the lack of association since 1960 between Negro unemployment rates and new ADC cases. They have expressed doubts, but they have not been able to prove that the other factors they suspect may be involved are in fact involved. Why not? Why is it that the government's statistics are kept in such a way that it is not possible to determine readily whether the lack of association is due to a change in the situation of Negroes or to a change in the way the programs are run or the statistics compiled?

11. It would seem that the government does have a special responsibility for reorganizing its data-gathering procedures and for storing data in such a way that they can be readily retrieved to answer such questions. This, of course, is a general problem with respect to all kinds of government data, not just those concerned with the situation of Negro Americans.

With respect to this latter problem, however, we feel that the government has a special responsibility to do a better job of pulling together at some central place available data on the Negro American as well as other ethnic groups. Perhaps we need an information center with this kind of responsibility so that it would be possible to acquire more readily the kind of data that may be needed for policy formulation and also the kind of data that are needed to resolve some still-open social science questions concerning the situation of various ethnic groups in the country. Social scientists tend to reason comparatively; they have done so with respect to the situation of Negroes, as with other ethnic groups. If they are going to make the best use of the comparative method they need much better supplied centers for such information than now exist. Were such a center established now it could prove invaluable for charting the success or failure of the various federal and private programs that undoubtedly will be launched in the years to come to cope with the problem of disadvantage in American society.

12. Finally, social scientists will have to come to terms with the difference between their rhetoric and the rhetoric of public policy formation and debate. This latter rhetoric is a simpler one and the tendency is for social scientists to seek to force the rest of the society to change its ways rather than learn how to operate within those ways. But a retreat to scientism in which one avoids sharp formulations is an avoidance of responsibility or sometimes a way of purveying a hidden polemic rather than putting one's polemical cards on the table.

The problem, then, is not that of avoiding the simple rhetoric of public debate but rather learning how to use and evaluate that rhetoric in such a way that the central questions of policy relevance and "accuracy-sufficient-for-the-need" are meaningfully engaged.

An Open-Ending

This is as far as we can take the story of the Moynihan Report controversy, and as much as we have been able to learn from it. The questions raised by Moynihan are still open, the fate of his effort to modify the national agenda is still unknown, and the social science issues his controversy touched still unresolved. We will conclude therefore with two quotations by men much involved in the issues we have discussed. The first is the last published statement by E. Franklin Frazier on the subject of the effects of Negro family disorganization. The second is a view concerning the proper relationship of the institutions of government and the family offered by Nathan Glazer in the pre-Watts summer of 1965, at a time when the Moynihan Report was obviously much on his mind.

Frazier:
General Effects of Family Disorganization on Negro Community

The widespread disorganization of family life among Negroes has affected practically every phase of their community life and adjustments to the larger white world. Bcause of the absence of stability in family life, there is a lack of traditions. Life among a large portion of the urban Negro population is casual, precarious, and fragmentary. It lacks continuity and its roots do not go deeper than the contingencies of daily living. This affects the socialization of the Negro child. With a fourth to a third of Negro families in cities without a male head, many Negro children suffer the initial handicap of not having the discipline and authority of the father in the home. Negro mothers who have the responsibility for the support of the family are forced to neglect their children who pick up all forms of socially disapproved behavior in the disorganized areas in which these families are concentrated.

Without the direction provided by family traditions and the discipline of parents, large numbers of Negro children grow up without aims and ambitions. The formal instruction provided by the public schools cannot make up for the deficiency in family training. In fact, much of the Negro child's lack of interest in education is attributable to the fact that it is unrelated to the experiences in the family. Moreover, the lack of employment opportunities for Negro youth helps to encourage the aimlessness and lack of ambition among Negro youths without a normal family life. Thus family disorganization and social and economic forces in the community unite to create a sense of irresponsibility among Negro youth. Out of such an environment comes the large number of criminals and juvenile delinquents in the cities of the country.*

Glazer:

But when we put together the terms "government" and "family," when we place in juxtaposition the most public and formal part of our social life and the most intimate and concealed part, we obviously must pause and consider what *are* the relationships, what should be the relationships, between the government and family?

---

* E. Franklin Frazier, *The Negro in The United States* (New York: Macmillan Company, Revised Edition, 1957), pp. 636–637.

We know how such relationships have developed. Government has taken on responsibility for economic prosperity; it has taken on responsibility, too, for seeing that every part of society, every group and class, shares in the prosperity. Now then, if we assume that certain conditions for sharing in that prosperity must be set — the condition of minimal education, of responsibility in work, of the achievement of limited skill — and if we then find that certain familial and social settings are not conductive to the achievement of these minimal conditions, then government becomes responsible in some measure for what goes on in the family.

There is another route by which government becomes related to family, which affects today many more Negro families than this route based on a governmental assumption of responsibility for a generally shared prosperity. Government much earlier took on a responsibility to see that no one who could not earn sufficient income starved; this then required an elaborate system of rules and regulations to determine what was a family, what was insufficient income, what was a minimal standard of living, etc. In effect, the establishment of a welfare system places today perhaps one-quarter of Negro children under the investigative and regulative eye of government and inevitably deeply influences a substantial part of Negro family life.

Through the responsibility for welfare, then, and through the newer responsibility to maintain general prosperity, government is involved with the family. But this is a hazardous involvement. Do we know enough about family life and the significance of any kind of intervention within it to sanction a large effort to restructure or reform the lower class of Negro family? I doubt it. In the nature of the case, this is an area in which not all knowledge can be or should be used for public policy. There are parts of the society that are more legitimately subject to government intervention than the family — the economy, the educational system, the system of police and courts and prisons — and we may hope to influence the family through these institutions. We are now all enamored with the possibilities of social engineering. And yet there are limits to the desirable reach of social engineering.*

---

* That Moynihan's work was the impetus for these thoughts is suggested by the paragraph that follows:

Daniel P. Moynihan, Assistant Secretary of Labor under Presidents Kennedy and Johnson, once reported to me a meeting of high government officials dealing with the crisis of the low-income Negro in the United States, falling ever behind the better educated middle class, white and Negro alike. He proposed as one immediate measure that might improve matters restoring two mail deliveries a day — in effect, creating fifty thousand new jobs in the postal service and perhaps fifty thousand new fathers of families for a community where they are too few. I think E. Franklin Frazier would have liked this form of social engineering, which left the structure of the Negro family to each family, but which set conditions that we know produce the opportunity for stability, better education, and higher income. Nathan Glazer, "Foreword" to E. Franklin Frazier, The Negro Family in the United States (Chicago: University of Chicago Press, Revised and Abridged Edition, 1966), pp. xvi–xvii.

The Government's Response to the Report

A. AGENDA PAPER NO. V: THE FAMILY: RESOURCES FOR CHANGE — PLANNING SESSION FOR THE WHITE HOUSE CONFERENCE "TO FULFILL THESE RIGHTS," NOVEMBER 16–18, 1965

Hylan Lewis

[Editors' note: Professor Lewis wishes to acknowledge that this agenda paper was a staff product prepared with the major collaboration of Elizabeth Herzog and the invaluable assistance of Bonita Valien, Alvin Schorr, Marian Chase, and Jack Lefcowitz. See pages 248–251.]

Summary

This planning session has a concern for the influences on contemporary family life, especially family life among Negroes. It is assumed that the aims of the working session are to propose policies and programs for the immediate future as well as long-term directions and programs. The agenda paper refers to some of the issues and some of the facts having to do with

1. The effects of low income on family life
2. Family composition among Negroes — its characteristics, factors influencing it, and its consequences
3. Plans and programs aimed at strengthening family life, especially among the low-income population.

Among the issues: the nature and extent of family disorganization among Negroes, the reasons given for it, the outlook for it, and of course what to do about it.

The measures of family disorganization most frequently used are the incidence of families headed by females, illegitimacy, and the attributes and behavior of the disadvantaged male. The nature of the prognosis and programs proposed are heavily conditioned by whether the indications of "family breakdown" are seen primarily as a heritage of slavery or as responses to current conditions.

Among the facts:

Over-all, two-thirds of Negro families include two parents. The increase in the proportion of female-headed households has been less than five percentage points in 15 years, with no rise in the last five years. The evidence is that Negro-white differences in family structure diminish when controlled for income and that differences by income are more striking than differences by color; that factors attributable to the effects of inequities in housing, employment, health, and education account for a large amount of the difference between the figures for Negroes and whites.

The family and family behavior among Negroes show great range and variability; especially overlooked and underrated is the diversity among low-income Negro families. When these are overlooked for any reason, there is danger that the depreciated, and probably more dramatic and threatening, characteristics of a small segment of the population may be imputed to an entire population.

Family and personal strengths, resiliencies and demonstrated capacities for change found at all levels are a prime resource to be taken into account in planning programs aimed at strengthening family life among Negroes.

Questions

1. What are the goals for *all* families?

   Are there special goals for different categories of families?
   — e.g., Negro families? Negro low-income families? Negro
   families in urban ghettos? urban problem families? rural problem families?

2. What is the most important single thing that needs to be done
   now to improve the quality of family life generally? For low-
   income families?

3. What should be the general objective with regard to low-
   income Negro families:

   (a) to propose a model to which all families should conform?
   (b) to offer the kinds of economic and social supports that
       seem best suited to allow families to work out their own
       forms and functions?

4. Among the Federal Government's efforts to strengthen the
   family which programs seem to be moving effectively in needed
   directions — i.e., programs such as the following:

   Aid to Families of Dependent Children
   public housing, and other Federal aid to housing
   day care
   vocational training and rehabilitation
   employment counseling and services
   training and use of non-professional aids
   family counseling and education
   medical and survivors' insurance
   foster family and group family care
   social and protective services for children
   federal aids to education

The Family: Resources for Change

. . . the family is rooted in human nature — in human nature conceived not as a bundle of instincts but as a product of social life; . . .
the family may take protean forms as it survives or is reborn in times
of cataclysmic social change; and . . . we can predict with some assurance the persistence of the family but not the specific forms which
it may take in the future.[1]

The viability of families, especially low-income families, is
critically relevant to our national design and commitment "to

fulfill these rights." The purpose of this agenda paper is to serve the working group's examination of stresses and potentials for contemporary families. The discussion is cued to "outside" as well as "inside," and to contemporary as well as historical, factors affecting the course and quality of family life, particularly among low-income Negroes. The aim is to focus attention on the policy and program implications of current family facts and issues. The agenda paper has been prepared with these goals of the planning session in mind:

(1) the proposal of directions and long-term programs that seem most promising for eliminating or reducing the factors that make for family stress and instability, and for maximizing the realization of family potentials

(2) the proposal of some specific programs, services or activities to be accomplished within a stated time.

It is through the family that the individual enters into the privileges and liabilities bestowed upon him as a citizen. And it is through the family that the effects of his citizen status first impinge on his inner circle and his inner self. The family acts, not merely as conduit, but rather as agent, reagent and catalyst. It defines the child's world for him; and it, initially, defines him to himself.

The functions of the family are discussed chiefly in terms of what it does for children, and the emphasis is accurate. Yet the viability of the family depends on the satisfactions and supports it offers to adults, since it is they who determine whether a family unit survives or dissolves. Moreover, what the family can offer to its children depends on the psychological, social, physical and economic status of the adults who preside over it.

It is often claimed that the United States is a child-centered country and, like most claims, this one is occasionally challenged. If we were child-centered, ask the challengers, would we be spending on education only a fraction of what we spend for defense? Would our most family-labeled program, Aid to Families of Dependent Children, have focused for so many years on the sex morality and employability of the mother, with so little official regard for the care of children while the mother works?

I. Contemporary Family Forms

A major issue in any discussion of the Negro family is the higher proportion of female-headed households among Negroes

CHAPTER FOURTEEN

compared with whites.[2] The genesis of such families is, by some, attributed to slavery. Others reject or place little emphasis on slavery as an explanation, as compared with current conditions. For example, it has been suggested that

. . . not enough is known about . . . present family forms and functions and about the behavior patterns which are distinctly urban products with a dynamic and history of their own. The forms, as in the case of the family headed by the female, may be the same but the context in which they fit and function has probably changed in important details.[3]

In one sense, the disagreement about the influence of the slavery heritage on current family forms and practices appears largely academic. We are dealing with the problems and potentials of today, as they are manifested today. Although historical influences may affect kind and degree of potential for growth, it is not necessary to agree on underlying causes in order to perceive present problems and build upon present potentials.

In another sense, the controversy is not academic, for it colors opinions about the nature and extent of differences and similarities between Negro and white families at very low income levels. Those who emphasize the historical influence point to differences; those who emphasize post-slavery influences point to similarities between the two.

The habit of analyzing data by color rather than by income level has tended to support the slavery-specific hypothesis. Since a much larger proportion of Negroes than of whites are on the lowest income levels, what look like statistically significant differences between Negroes and whites may actually be differences between socio-economic levels. [See Figures 14.1a and 14.1b Ed.] But if the figures are presented only in one way, the other possibility is obscured. Studies of prenatal care, for example, indicate that in effect one is comparing the prosperous with the poor in all three of the following comparisons: white mothers with non-white mothers; married mothers with unmarried mothers; all mothers who do with all mothers who do not obtain prenatal care.[4]

The Lefcowitz paper compares a variety of qualities for Negroes and whites who are poor and for Negroes and whites who are not poor.[5] In effect, Negro and white comparisons are made after a rough standardization for income. These data suggest that

1. When controlled for income, Negro-white differences in family structure diminish. Differences by income are more strik-

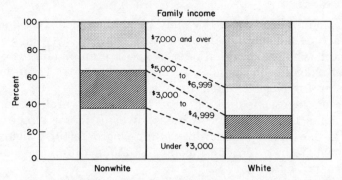

Figure 14.1a. Two out of five nonwhite families had incomes below $3,000 in 1964.

Source: U.S. Bureau of the Census.

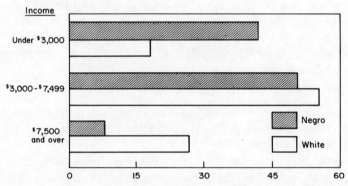

Figure 14.1b. About half of the Negro and white urban families* had incomes of $3,000–$7,500. But most of the remaining Negroes had lower incomes whereas most of the remaining whites had higher incomes.

* After taxes, 1960–1961; includes single consumers.

Source: U.S. Department of Labor, Bureau of Labor Statistics.

ing than differences by color.

2. When Negro and white children with similar incomes are compared, differences between them in educational achievement diminish and the differences by class appear more striking than the differences by color.

3. There is far more difference in employment status by income than by color.

4. The relative position of men with respect to women, economically and educationally, is the same for whites as for nonwhites.

In short, some differences diminish and others disappear. On the other hand, even within income classes, some striking differences remain, differences that may be attributed to two qualities. First, a time-consuming, sophisticated analysis may be required to discern what quality that overlaps with ethnic status is operating. For example, the number of children born per 1,000 mothers is greater for Negroes than for whites. However, the migration pattern of Negroes is different from whites and rural background, like income level, appears to be a powerful factor affecting fertility. If one could standardize white-Negro fertility figures for rural background and for income, would a difference continue to appear?

A second quality that creates difference between Negroes and whites is, obviously, the impact of discriminatory treatment. If the rate of home ownership is higher for whites than for Negroes, even within income classes, can there be any doubt that discrimination by real estate and financing firms is responsible? As another example, the mortality rate of young Negro men exceeds that of white men.* Obviously, this increases the incidence of Negro broken families.

We may come to three general conclusions:

1. Plainly, and overlooking the fact that most Negroes are poor, there are more female-headed families among Negroes than among whites.

2. Poverty accounts for a large measure of this difference. If the qualities of poverty were removed from statistical comparisons, figures for Negroes would move much closer to those for whites.

3. Locatable factors emerging in general from discrimination — health, housing, employment, and so forth — account for a large measure of the difference between figures for Negroes and for whites.

Opinions differ about the rate of increase in the proportion of female-headed families.[6] Some, citing the increase in the proportion on nonwhite families headed by women, from 1949 (18.8%) to 1962 (23.2%), see a headlong deterioration, a rapid "crumbling" of the low-income Negro family. Others point out that the rise from 1949 to 1964 was 4.4 percentage points in all (that is, less than one-third of one percentage point a year); that it was gradual

---

*At ages 25–30, 7 per 1,000 white males and 16 per 1,000 Negro males are likely to die. These figures are not adjusted for income. White young women can marry-up into a comparatively large pool of non-poor white young men. The relative opportunity for Negro young women has been much smaller.

from 1949 (18.8%) to 1959 (23.6%) and that from 1959 to 1964 it has remained relatively stable. They conclude that there exists a plateau, or perhaps a gradual but not acute increase in the over-all proportion of broken homes among low-income Negroes.

Those who hold the rapid-deterioration view urge strong action to halt an accelerating breakdown. Those who hold the plateau view urge strong action to remedy adverse conditions that have existed far too long. There is consensus between the two schools of thought with regard to the existence of a long-standing disparity between white and nonwhite rates, and the need for strong and prompt intervention. Differences lie: (a) in interpreting the current situation as a crisis vs. a long-term manifestation; (b) in the attitudes of alarm and hostility that may be held with regard to an erupting crisis, as compared with the problem-solving approach that is more likely with regard to a long-coninued situation.

The Father — Present and Absent

The two-parent family is modal in the United States, which is to say that it is the norm for American Negroes. [See Figures 14.2a and 14.2b. Ed.] Over-all, two-thirds of Negro families include two parents. At the upper income levels the proportion rises and at the lower income levels it falls. Nevertheless, it is useful to re-

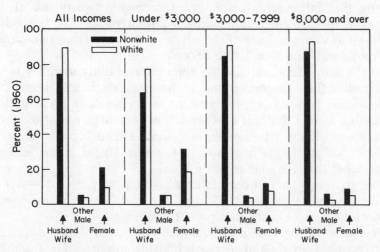

Figure 14.2a. All families at all income levels. Most families have male heads, but female heads are more prevalent among nonwhites.
Source: U.S. Bureau of the Census.

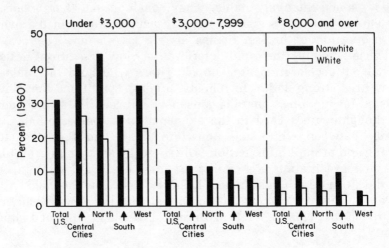

Figure 14.2b. Families with female heads. The proportion of female family
              heads falls sharply with rising income. It is most prevalent
              among the poorest families in large cities and in the North.
Source: U.S. Bureau of the Census.

member that when we speak of the female-headed household we
are talking about a minority, even among the poor. The fact that
family composition is especially flexible among the very poor
means that, although at any given moment, two-thirds of the
Negro families in the urban slums include two parents, individual
children at various times of their lives may move from two-parent
to one-parent homes and vice versa.[7]

At the same time, outside the slum areas, family stability is the
rule rather than the exception. In focusing on family homes, as
Erikson has pointed out, the present father tends to be forgotten.
Forgotten also is the fact that we know very little about him. We
do not even know whether there is evidence to support an occasionally voiced impression that the stable Negro home is more
patriarchal that the stable white home.

The great majority of our children — some 87 per cent — live in
a home with two parents. Most of the rest live in a one-parent
home, and in most cases that parent is the mother.

Few would deny that a harmonious two-parent home offers the
best prospect for a child to reach his full potential. On the other
hand, a substantial minority of American children, over six and a
half million of them, live in a home headed by a woman. It is

reasonable, therefore, to review current assumptions about the one-parent home and what it means for the developmental prospects of the children who grow up in it.

It has been our habit to view any deviation from our modal family pattern as an aberration. A number of research findings have tended to reinforce this habit. The question may be raised, however, whether a form that includes so many children and has produced so many effective and apparently happy adults, deserves a less negative status. Perhaps the time has come to recognize the one-parent family as a family form in its own right.

Among reasons urged for reassessment of the one-parent family as a family form in its own right are the following:

1. The one-parent family is with us and shows no sign of becoming less frequent. [See Figure 14.3. Ed.]

2. There is reason to believe that children in such families are adversely affected by the negative assumptions which cluster around it.

3. Through time and space the family has absorbed a vast array of different forms and still has continued to function as the family.

4. The modal American family may not be as functionally two-parent or as "patriarchal" as is sometimes assumed.

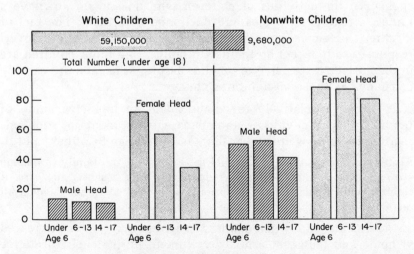

Figure 14.3. Over 80% of the nonwhite children living in families headed by females and 40–50% of those in families with male heads were poor in 1963.

Source: Mollie Orshansky, "Who's Who Among the Poor," *Social Security Bulletin,* July 1965.

5. Analysis of research findings concerning the one-parent family fails to support a sweeping indictment of its potential for producing children capable of fruitful and gratifying lives.

1. The first proposition is supported by a vast array of statistics. The march of these figures is reminiscent of figures concerning the working mother. Not many years ago, conferences were discussing whether mothers should or should not be permitted or encouraged to work. At present, the main focus of discussion is rather, what kinds of daytime care or other supervision should be established to help the working mother fulfill her dual role. (A subject which is touched upon at somewhat greater length below.) In any case, although there is hope that effective economic and social measures can reduce the frequency of one-parent homes, it seems unlikely that the numbers will be drastically reduced in the very near future.

2. With regard to effects on children of popular assumptions about the one-parent home, the evidence is chiefly presumptive. Specialists in child development provide persuasive discussions and data bearing on the growth of positive and negative identity. There is no lack of evidence that children are alert to the classifications implicit in questions at school about father's occupation, in social differences between mothers who do and do not have a spouse, in the activities of children who do and do not have a father to take them places and do things with them. The fact of a father's presence or absence is ineluctable; the subtle or overt responses to that fact on the part of adults and other children are in themselves responsive to popular assumptions, and are capable of change as those assumptions change.

3. Although relatively few have made an intensive study of family forms through time and space, most students of problems relating to families are aware that, as Witmer and Kotinsky put it:

All the evidence points to the infinite capacity of the family to change — to change its composition, to redefine the way it shares the care of children with other social institutions — and yet to retain its over-all responsibility for them.[8]

4. The extent to which children in two-parent homes are reared at home and taught at school by women, during their formative years, has been the subject of extensive comment. Without assuming that this is to their advantage, some raise questions about the extent to which it reduces the contrast between children in one-parent and in two-parent homes.

5. Correlation between undesired behavior or attributes and the one-parent home has been a repetitive research finding. The broken home has been reported as associated with emotional maladjustment, poor school achievement, juvenile deliquency, and illegitimacy. However, when data are controlled for socio-economic status, such correlations often fade out. The relationship is more often apparent in studies that have not made a point of such control. Its occurrence is too frequent to require documentation here. Its absence under adequate statistical controls is less familiar but is reported in a number of studies.[9]

In this connection it is sometimes pointed out that studies which claim adequate controls also have shown children doing better in warm, stable one-parent homes than in two-parent homes with tension and friction. If such findings are trusted, the implication may be an underlining of the need to offer to one-parent homes the kinds of support that would enhance the mother's ability to be a competent, unharried and undefeated mother.[10]

The proponents of the views summarized above do not by any means advocate the one-parent family as the most desired type. What they do advocate is: (1) recognition of the one-parent family as an existing and fairly common form rather than a sick form or a strange deviation from normality; (2) recognition that a sound one-parent home may be better for a child than a torn and strife-ridden two-parent home; (3) devising of ways to enhance the ability of parents without partners to provide a sound one-parent home.

The choice, unfortunately, is not necessarily between a warm, stable, adequate two-parent home and a one-parent home. No one would hesitate to prefer the former for any American child. To avoid the separation of the parents does not, however, insure for the child a "good" or "adequate" home. Evidence available so far does not justify the assumption that any two-parent home is better for a child than any one-parent home; or that the intactness or broken-ness of the home is, in itself, the variable that determines whether or not a child will reach his full potential. As in so many cases, it is an extremely important variable, the net effect of which depends on a number of other important variables. And as in so many cases, the net effect can be helped or hindered by community attitudes and supports.

The relatively frequent dissolution of marriages among low-income Negro families is generally attributed, by students of the subject, to the disadvantaged economic position of the Negro male and the consequent downgrading of his role and status within the family, his own self-esteem, and his readiness to struggle with continuing and insuperable family responsibilities.[11] A new determination to improve the economic status of Negro men co-incides with a widening of information about and access to the means of birth control. Some see in this convergence a likelihood of mutual reinforcement. A man with a stable income is more ready to accept the responsibilities of family head than one whose economic position is precarious. At the same time, the responsi-bilities of a family head are more manageable if the size of the family can be planned. The most optimistic prognosticators add that marital stability is likely to be enhanced by the convergence of male ego satisfaction, female respect for him as a breadwinner, and ability of each to give and to receive sex satisfactions with-out fear of undesired pregnancy.

Early indications suggest that in general people will reach out for services when they believe the services will meet a felt need, and specifically that birth control information and assistance can increase the interest in receiving prenatal health care. "Our ex-perience so far in the maternity and infant care programs gives us hopeful indications that the institution of family planning services more than doubles attendance at postpartum clinics and, in some programs at least, seems to have a favorable influence in attracting women to prenatal clinics early as word gets around that the services are available." [12]

The Present Mother

In a fatherless home, the mother carries a multiple burden: as head of family, as breadwinner, as homemaker, as mentor, com-forter and caretaker of children. Some psychologists hold that, during the first two years of a child's life, the father's presence is more important for his psychological, physical and economic help to the mother than for his direct effect on the child's well-being. (This assumes, of course, that he does give such support.)

The one-parent mother of very low income is likely to be either a working mother or a relief recipient. In either case she is likely to be more fatigued, less healthy physically and more subject to depression than a prosperous mother. If she is "on relief," she and her family may be living on less than a subsistence budget —

although recent modifications in welfare practices and policies may bring about some modification of this situation.

If she is a working mother, the same comparisons would hold, plus the problem of arranging supervision for the children while she is out of the home. Mothers without husbands are far more likely to work than other mothers with children under eighteen; and nonwhite mothers are more likely to work than white mothers. They are also likely to receive lower pay.

The effects on children of having their mothers work outside the home are hotly debated. Research findings show strong convergence on three conclusions: (1) that almost no generalization holds true for all working mothers or all their children; (2) that many popular assumptions about working mothers and their children do not stand up under challenge; (3) that the mother's working, in itself, is only one among many factors impinging on children, and may well be a secondary factor.

Primary factors appear to condition its impact on children and family life in three chief ways:

(a) The type of arrangements made for the child's care and supervision during the mother's absence. These are partly the result of attitudes, assumption and behavior, which affect the child whether the mother works or not. But to a large extent they are the result of resources available to her.

(b) The way the child perceives and reacts to the mother's absence. This is also a result of basic factors — including his own special needs — which again affect the child in any case.

(c) Parental attitudes and behavior, including specific reactions to the mother's outside work. These, once more, are largely the product of basic factors which would affect the child in any case, although in special instances the working mother situation may have a secondary influence on their impact and interaction.[13]

The conclusions listed above have been reported by a number of independent investigators. They leave unanswered a good many questions that cannot be discussed here. They also drive home a realization that the very mothers most likely to have no option about working outside the home are the ones least able to arrange for adequate supervision of children while the mother is out of the home.

Some of their problems were highlighted by studies conducted in the late fifties and mid-sixties. The Children's Bureau and the

Women's Bureau contracted with the Bureau of Census in February 1965 for a new survey to obtain information on the child-care arrangements of one specific group of working mothers: those women who worked 27 weeks or more in 1964, either full- or part-time and who had at least one child under 14 years of age living at home. There were 6.1 million mothers in this group. These mothers had a total of 12.3 million children under 14, one-fifth of all U.S. children in this age group. The number of mothers in the labor force with children under six numbered 3.6 million.

A number of different child-care arrangements were reported:

Almost one-half of the children (46 per cent) were cared for in their own homes, usually by a father (15 per cent) or by another relative (21 per cent) and less frequently by a nonrelative (10 per cent). For 5 per cent the relative caring for the children at home was a child under 16 years of age.

Care in someone else's home (15 per cent) was reported much less frequently than care in own home and was equally divided between care by a relative and by a nonrelative.

Group care (in day centers, after school centers, etc.) was reported for 2 per cent of the children but this type of arrangement also varied by age, being 4 per cent for children under 3, 7 per cent for children 3 to 5, and 1 per cent or less for children 6 years of age or older.

Eight per cent of the children in the survey were expected to care for themselves, an arrangement that varied by age, amounting to 1 per cent for the children under 6, 8 per cent for those 6 to 11, and 20 per cent for children 12 or 13 years of age.[14]

The picture is not reassuring, especially if one considers that the "latchkey" children for whom no arrangements are made are probably over-represented among the lowest income families, that the proportion of children in group care remains very low, and that some of the arrangements reported are sketchy in the extreme. Studies of children under the AFDC program show a larger proportion of children with no daytime care arrangements. It should be added that some of these studies also have revealed great concern on the part of some mothers about the lack of child supervision, and ingenious arrangements by a few of them to have the children report regularly by telephone.

Children and Daytime Care

In recent years, new and systematic efforts have been made to increase the quantity and quality of day-care facilities for children of working mothers, and new legislation has given impetus to these efforts. Nevertheless, the 1965 figures suggest a large gap to be filled.[15]

Although research results indicate that outside employment of the mother does not, in and of itself, affect children adversely, a good many believe that it is better for children to be in their own homes with their own mothers during the first two years. Even if present measures do not demonstrate adverse effects, they say, we are not able to tell whether the own mother's care would be better for them. This discussion, invoking "the Bowlby thesis" on the one hand, and, on the other, accounts of the many "fulfilled" men and women who were raised by nurses and governesses, will probably not be resolved in the near future.

Meanwhile, new controversies are flaring about the need of preschool children to obtain training for school adjustment and achievement of a kind believed not to be provided in their own homes. Should day care centers offer, not only custodial care and opportunities for socialization, but also cognitive enrichment to enhance school readiness? The hotly debated and many-faceted subject of preschool care for children of low income families is equally pertinent to discussions of education and discussions of family life. It includes consideration of what mothers offer to children and what a specific mother offers to a specific child under specific circumstances, as compared with what trained and responsive day-care attendants or nursery school teachers can offer. It includes questions about whether cognitive enrichment is being sought at the expense of social and emotional development; of whether nursery school cooperativeness is cultivated at the expense of independence and coping abilities; of whether the intellectual gains reported after preschool training are stable, or fade away under the impact of unfortunate school experiences in over-crowded classes, with split shifts, and teachers often hampered by inadequate teaching or by their own unconsciously acquired habits.[16]

Closely linked to problems of preschool and later education is the role of the parent in his child's schooling. There is ample evidence that low-income Negro parents have high educational aspirations for their children; and that they (like the rest of the American public) see education as the magic key to wealth and happiness. It is equally clear, however, that they tend to view themselves as having no role in the child's education, aside from housing and feeding him while he goes to school. The school is seen as a foreign and fearsome place, where a parent goes chiefly when summoned because his child has failed in his work or gotten into trouble.

There is a widely accepted dictum that small children cannot be helped toward school readiness and social competence if their parents are not involved. Many programs are based on this principle, some very ingenious and apparently effective. Nevertheless, on-the-spot visits often reveal that glowingly described programs in fact are able to "reach" very few parents, at great cost and investment of staff. The great breakthrough in parent and family life education has yet to be made, at least for the low income groups. Pending it, the question remains whether one must assume that any child whose parent is unable or unwilling to be "reached" is himself beyond the reach of programs designed to open up for him the way to the kind of life that most people in this country consider a good life.

The use of nonprofessional aides in nursery schools and day-care centers is urged as one means of combatting both the problem of parental involvement and the problem of insufficient adequate male models. Some centers for daytime care of children from low-income families encourage the mothers to serve as aides, thus increasing their involvement, giving them practice in enhancing intellectual stimulation and interpersonal response, establishing them as active collaborators in the school program, and — in some instances — augmenting their income a little. Some of these centers strive to promote active school-home partnership by arranging for parents to visit the schools their children will later attend and to become acquainted with the teachers in whose classes the children will be.

Some success has been reported in the use of teen-age boys as nursery school aides, including "delinquents" and "near-delinquents." The children respond with eager warmth to these "big men" in their lives. The youthful "big men" in turn, appear to derive great pleasure and profit from the response of the children, who treat them as responsible adults and thus evoke warmth, responsibility and enhanced self-respect.

Recently some parents whose children are in a preschool enrichment program met with the teachers to express their concern about the lax discipline in the school. Children were not smacked when they failed to obey adults, and were not scolded if they were "ugly" to each other. The teachers explained that they were trying to instill inner controls that would continue to operate when the children were too old to spank, and when so many low-income parents feel their children have moved beyond parental control. After considerable discussion, both parents and teachers expressed satisfaction.

The observers, however, were left with a number of questions that echoed concerns expressed by others: Are the children being "socialized" in a way that will be a disadvantage to them in their own neighborhoods?

Are the school and home environments incompatible in a way that will be detrimental to the children and to family cohesion?

Will the encouragement of spontaneity and autonomy in the nursery school equip them badly for the atmosphere of the usual public schoolroom?

Is the cognitive being stressed at the expense of other elements?

Births Out of Wedlock

A number of statements frequently made about births out of wedlock are supported by evidence which — even allowing for vagaries of national reporting that including over-reporting and under-reporting, as well as lack of reporting from some 15 states — still affords solid support for these particular generalizations.

It is solidly established, for example, that numbers of births out of wedlock have increased strikingly in the past twenty years and that rates have tripled since 1938. Rates are far higher among Negroes than among whites. In fact, the majority of children born out of wedlock are nonwhite, although only 12 per cent of the population are nonwhite.

There is also ample and unchallenged evidence that illegitimacy rates are much higher among the poor than among the prosperous. If further evidence were needed on a virtually unchallenged generalization, figures on rates in high and low income tracts should be sufficient. Pakter and associates, for example, found that the proportion of births out-of-wedlock in relation to total nonwhite births varied from a high of 37.5 per cent in the Central Harlem district to a comparative low of 8.9 per cent in the Pelham Bay district.[17] It is difficult to say to what extent differences should be ascribed to greater use of contraception and abortion by the nonpoor, to more frequent marriage because of pregnancy among the nonpoor, to higher fertility rates among the poor and among nonwhites, and to differential reporting.

A few points, also based on available figures, are less recognized and publicized. Some of these relate to the increase in rates of illegitimacy, by which is meant the number of births out of wedlock per 1,000 unmarried women of child-bearing age. The rise in *rates* (as differentiated from *numbers*) has been relatively steady over several decades, and has paralleled to a considerable degree changes in birth rates generally. This rise represents a long-term trend and not a sudden upsurge. Moreover, in the last six years reported (1957-1963) the rates have oscillated at about the same level, rising or falling one or two points or less, but in effect representing a six-year plateau. Thus, the current picture is a rise in numbers and a leveling off in rates of nonwedlock births.[18]

The rates for teen-agers have increased *less* than the rates for other age groups over the past twenty years, and in the last eight years reported their rates have remained relatively constant. The rates for those fourteen and under have not increased since 1947. The population explosion has multiplied *numbers* in that age group, but rates have remained constant. True, the figures derive from estimates, but this is true of all figures on unmarried mothers and there is as much reason to trust one part of them as to trust another part. Thus any recent increase in the magnitude of problems relating to births out of wedlock is attributable to increase in population rather than to changes in the way people are behaving.

The figures just cited refer to all births out of wedlock, since rates for white and nonwhite are not available separately. Until recently, rates were undoubtedly increasing faster among nonwhites than among whites. Recently, however, nonwedlock births have increased faster among whites than among nonwhites.[19] This minor shift in relative rate of increase does not, of course, alter the large and long-standing difference between white and nonwhite illegitimacy rates nor answer the question noted above, concerning it.

Although rates of illegitimacy have not increased during the past six years, numbers have multiplied, reaching 259,000 in 1963. Unfortunately, social and medical service have not kept pace. It has been estimated roughly that probably less than one-third of our unmarried mothers receive social services near the time of the child's birth. Presumably still fewer receive them at other times.

No careful observer asserts that the insufficient services we do have are distributed evenly or efficiently. With regard to social services, it has been estimated that in 1961 about one unmarried mother in six received services from a public or voluntary child welfare agency.[20] Three-fourths of the mothers served by such agencies in 1961 were white, although the majority of the children born out of wedlock in that year were nonwhite. From this we can estimate that nearly one-third of the white unmarried mothers and less than one-tenth of the nonwhite were served by public or private child welfare agencies.

On the whole, the unmarried mothers served by voluntary child welfare agencies, maternity homes and family service agencies tend to be of higher socio-economic status (including somewhat higher education) than the average for all unmarried mothers in the United States. They also tend, as do those served by public agencies, to be younger and more likely to place their children in adoption. About 70 per cent of the white babies born out of wedlock and less than 10 per cent of the nonwhite are legally adopted.

Failure to receive services does not necessarily mean that service has been sought and refused. On the contrary, a major deterrent to receiving social services is that the unmarried mother-to-be sees no need of them. It should be added that her definition of her needs and her conception of the kind of help social agencies give seldom coincide with agency definition. Moreover, if all unmarried mothers did seek agency help, the agencies would be unable to cope with the demand.

In the case of medical services, problems of eligibility and of arranging for care bulk far larger than with social services, and many women — married or unmarried — wait until they are in labor in order to obtain emergency service because they are not eligible to receive prenatal care. Far too few mothers, married or unmarried, receive adequate prenatal care and many receive none at all. However, still fewer unmarried than married mothers-to-be receive such care.[21]

Those who have studied the problems of low-income Negro unmarried mothers on the whole subscribe to the belief that the most effective way to describe nonwedlock births in this group would be to improve the economic situation of the low-income Negro male. Census tract data and special studies show that as income increases rates of nonwedlock birth, like the frequency of female-headed homes, decrease.[22]

How illegitimacy rates will respond to dissemination of birth control information and devices remains to be seen. Some predict that, after moderate delay, there will be a radical decrease in the number of births out of wedlock. Those who question the prediction hold that among low-income Negroes a positive value attaches to having a child, both as an affirmation of masculinity or femininity and because children are prized in themselves. This view, in turn, is countered by reminders of nonwedlock children left in hospitals by mothers who do not want to keep them. It seems reasonable to assume that given the information and materials they need, at least some unmarried women will take steps to avoid pregnancy. It is possible also that the possibility of family planning would encourage men to enter and maintain the continuing obligations of marriage — the more so if, at the same time, their own economic stability is improved.

Recent changes in policies with regard to AFDC are also cited as a possible influence in decreasing illegitimacy rates. Among other features, these changes modify the "man in the house" rule, which is said to discourage marriage, on the one hand and, on the other, to encourage over-reporting of illegitimacy through fear of losing the relief check if it is known that there is a stable relation with a man.

The often-heard statement that no stigma attaches to illegitimacy among low-income Negroes usually carries the implication that no stigma means no penalty, and that this means it doesn't matter whether one is born in or out of wedlock. This implication runs contrary to abundant evidence. To be born in wedlock and to have your children born in wedlock is a decided social plus, and a gratification.

The plus value of regular marriage is stronger than the minus value of no marriage. The lack of marriage is by no means a matter of indifference. Some low-income mothers pray for boys in order to avoid "trouble" for their daughters, and when trouble comes there is grief and anger, even though you stick to your own, take care of your own, and never turn them away. There is also a revulsion against forcing a marriage between a girl pregnant out of wedlock and the putative father, unless they really love each other. The question is — is an unhappy marriage more desirable than an out-of-wedlock birth? A girl may wait until she is "sure she loves him" — even though the assurance comes after the baby is born.

Both national statistics and special studies make it clear that women move in and out of married and unmarried motherhood, so that many families include both legitimate and illegitimate children. The pattern is familiar also among middle- and high-income whites, although with them it is more usual to have one illegitimate child (which may or may not be placed in adoption) and then marry and have children only in wedlock.

Attitudes toward illegitimacy and toward marriage are clearly linked with the economic position of the Negro male. A male head of house who is not a bread-winner and provider is a hazard to the happiness of the marriage, and his loss of economic status is so great a hazard to his intra-family status that he may decamp, either to protect his own ego or to make his family eligible for support from AFDC. Recent changes in the AFDC program are aimed against the second reason for family desertion.

One reason why it is difficult for middle-class observers to fathom attitudes toward sex and marriage among the poor is failure to recognize that values may be honored by people who do not adhere to them in daily life. This discrepancy between what one believes and what one does may arise from conflict between different sets of values observed by the same individual, and different hierarchies of values held by different nations, socio-economic classes, or individuals. Food and shelter for self or family may rank higher than scrupulous honesty; avoidance of an unhappy marriage may rank higher than legitimate birth status, and the value hierarchy may be constant in an individual's life or may change according to the situation.

Rodman posits the "value stretch," which he describes as broader among the poor than among the prosperous. The very poor, he says, "share the general values of the society with members of other classes, but in addition they have stretched these values or developed alternative values, which help them to adjust to their deprived circumstances." [23] Thus, the "lower-class value stretch" refers to "the wider range of values, and the lower degree of commitment to these values, to be found within the lower class." Some commentators raise question whether the "stretch" is wider among the low-income groups than among those with middle or high incomes, or merely more perceptible to middle-class observers. The behavior of the prosperous with regard to taxes is mentioned in this connection, as are sharp business practices, sexual infidelity, and the frequent placing of career advancement before the needs of family or country. No one has devised an accurate measure of stretch-difference. It seems clear, however, that on all socio-economic levels people can consciously believe in certain values, even while they continue to act as if those values did not exist.[24]

Child-Rearing Practices

A number of differences between the poor and the prosperous with regard to child-rearing practices have been described, and attempts have been made to relate some of them directly to school achievement, social satisfactions and later vocational adequacy. Among the differences frequently cited: The poor are less likely to encourage a child's interest in exploration, discovery, inquiry; they are more likely to reward inactivity and passivity as attributes of a "good child"; they are less likely to enhance and reward development of verbal skills through precept and approval; they are more likely to display repressive and punitive attitudes toward sex, sex questioning and experimentation, and a view of the sex relationship as basically exploitative; they are more likely to rely on authoritarian methods of child rearing; they are more likely to discipline by corporal punishment, harshly and inconsistently applied.

Little challenge is raised against these generalizations, although many are quick to point out that some of them are almost inevitable in crowded dwellings where adults are harried, depressed and fatigued.

Some other generalizations about child-rearing practices, as about attributes of the poor generally, arouse more objections. Some of the objections relate to the investigators' use of "culture-bound instruments"; some to the claim that the traits involved are direct products of the "reality world" in which both parents and children dwell. These kinds of challenges have been raised against statements that children are reared to low esteem of selves and parents, present time-orientation, impulse gratification, fatalism, emphasis on "keeping out of trouble" rather than positive achievement, lack of goal commitment.

Objections are raised also to implications that some of the attitudes and psychological sets listed in the preceding paragraph are basic traits rather than responses to immediate environment; and that they apply globally to an income category or neighborhood. For example, a study of child-rearing practices among low-income families in Washington, D. C. reports that the amount of diversity among low-income families is overlooked and underrated in popular and scientific thinking.[25] In addition, the study supports the following propositions:

1. The life chances and the actual behavior of low-income families are not to be confused with the cultural values and the preferences of families so classified.

2. A great deal of behavior among low-income urban families reflects a straddling of behavior and of goals associated with deprivation and poverty on the one hand, and of behavior and of goals associated with higher socio-economic status and affluence on the other hand.

3. Among a considerable proportion of low-income urban families observed, failures to conform in overt behavior to the so-called middle-class values are due less to any lack of recognition of, and affirmation of, middle-class values than they are due to such factors as (a) lack of money to support these values, (b) a process of diminution in the will to do so, and (c) a lessened confidence in their own, and especially their children's, life chances in the present and future.

4. Most parents in low-income families tend to show greater conformity to and convergence with the ascribed standards of parents of middle and upper income in what they indicate they want than in their actual behavior.

5. The range and the specifics of the child-rearing concerns of low-income parents approximate closely the range and the specifics of child-rearing concerns ascribed to upper- and middle-income families. The specifics of child rearing concerns and the priorities attached to particular concerns vary from family to family.

6. The amount of family income and the evenness of its flow makes a significant difference in child-rearing priorities acted upon by parents.

7. Major priority among families with low income tends to be given to meeting basic physical needs — food, clothing, and shelter.

8. The need to invest a significant proportion of energies into meeting basic physical needs on inadequate income can result in a kind of compartmentalization of child-rearing concerns.

9. With few exceptions, low-income parents do not approve of the circumstances in which they now live or in which their children are being brought up.

10. A major aspiration of low-income parents for their children is to see their children do better in life — especially in jobs, education, and family behavior — than they have been able to do themselves.

11. Many low-income parents assess their own child-rearing performances in terms of whether they have made advances over the child-rearing circumstances and performances of their own parents.

12. The economic and social roles wished of, and expected of, the low-income male as husband and father by wives, mothers, and children are not different from those of the middle and upper classes, but his abilities — and the family and community consequences of his inabilities — to fulfill these roles are different.

Some Familiar Generalizations

A great many generalizations are made about the poor, often without differentiating among various categories of people and life styles found on the lower income levels. [See Figures 14.4 and 14.5. Ed.] In general, the ill-defined group referred to as "the poor" does not include the stable, respectable working class. Nevertheless, certain characteristics are reported in inverse relation to income from top to bottom, (e.g., education, physical and mental health, regular employment, adequate housing, privacy, membership in organizations).[26] Some of the attributions come from

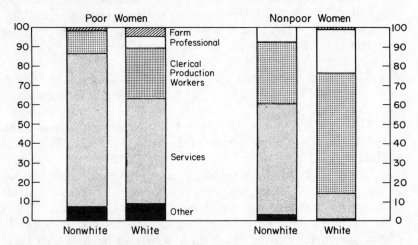

Figure 14.4.   Among white as well as nonwhite poor* women, most were in service occupations; among the nonpoor the majority of the nonwhite were still in services, but the majority of the white were craftsmen, clerical or production workers.

   * Poor by Social Security Administration criteria, based on a 1963 income of $1,580 a year for a nonfarm single person under 65 ($1,470 aged 65 and over), to $5,090 for a nonfarm family of 7 or more persons. The poverty line for single persons and families living on a farm was put at 60 percent of the above.
Source: Office of Economic Opportunity.

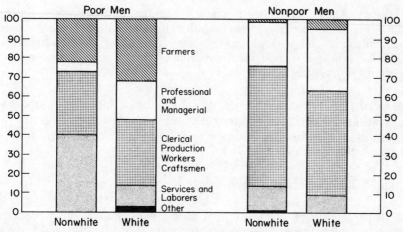

Figure 14.5.   Among poor* men, the largest proportion of nonwhite were in
farm, service and laborer occupations; the largest proportion
of white were in crafts, production or clerical work. Among
the nonpoor, there are few in farming and the bulk of both
nonwhite and white workers are in crafts, clerical or production work.

  * Poor by Social Security Administration criteria, based on a 1963 income
of $1,580 a year for a nonfarm single person under 65 ($1,470 aged 65 and
over) to $5,090 for a nonfarm family of 7 or more persons. The poverty line
for single persons and families living on a farm was put at 60 percent of
the above.
Source: Office of Economic Opportunity.

studies based on inadequate breakdowns, so that in our studies
as in our life, class distinctions become blurred.

The term "culture of poverty" is used by Oscar Lewis in a
dynamic sense to express the interplay of circumstance and attitude. There is no special issue when the term is used in this way.
Issues arise when the term is used to mean a world outlook or
style of life that has become a thing in itself. At this edge of the
term, there is an implication that the source of such a world
outlook lies in other people — parents, peers — who hold the
same attitudes and that the attitudes persist, whatever their relation to reality.

Many of the attitudes and much of the behavior of persons
enmeshed in "the culture of poverty" are a response to facts of
life. One author writes about the effects of prolonged malnutrition:

. . . various functional changes occur. These functional changes are
manifested clinically by symptoms usually placed in the neurasthenic

syndrome. They include such common complaints as excessive fatiga-
bility, disturbances in sleep, inability to concentrate, "gas," heart
consciousness, and various queer bodily sensations . . . Occurrences
[of these symptoms] as a manifestation of tissue depletion of certain
nutrients is undoubted.

As for drive and ambition, a study describes "depression, apathy,
and lethargy" as consequences of malnutrition. The tendency to
blame others rather than one's self has also been attributed to
inadequate nutrition.[27]

The following effects have been attributed to poor housing:

. . . a perception of one's self that leads to pessimism and passivity,
stress to which the individual cannot adapt, poor health, and a state
of dissatisfaction; pleased in company but not in solitude, cynicism
about people and organizations, a high degree of sexual stimulation
without legitimate outlet, and difficulty in household management and
child rearing; . . . relationships that tend to spread out in the neighborhood rather than deeply into the family.[28]

The ways in which some of these effects are produced are almost
self-evident. Poor health is a consequence of the effects of poor
housing in contributing to accidents, to respiratory and skin diseases, and so forth. Poor health has its attitudinal and behavioral
consequences, of course. The effects of crowding are possibly less
apparent but are felt through their effects on privacy, on time and
opportunity for communication, and on the tendency to live out-
of-doors. Living in congested neighborhoods, where tenants are
transient and physical hazards are real, produces in many a constant sense of loneliness, helplessness and anxiety.

With regard to the higher level of aggression attributed to the
poor, one report comments that, in encouraging their children to
fight back, slum dwellers show a realistic perception of the social
problems in their neighborhoods. This view receives support from
a low-income father who said of his son: "I . . . knock the hell
out of him, 'cause he can't be no sissy and grow up in this here
jungle."

One frequent generalization made about the poor is that they
have less belief in their control over their own destinies than the
prosperous — less sense of autonomy. And to this, another com-
mentator responds — why wouldn't they?

Perhaps the most frequent generalization of all is that the poor have a shorter time perspective than the prosperous, that they are present-oriented rather than future-oriented. A number of challenges to this one have been heard lately, especially with regard to the Negro poor. Those who question the blanket accuracy of the present time-orientation generalization, add that in many instances future time-orientation just doesn't make sense for many of the poor. Nevertheless, they claim, when it does make sense to people of any income level, they plan for the future.

Many of the middle class have been recruited from the poor, many of the poor have middle-class tastes and preferences. Time orientation may not be a culture trait or a unitary trait. It may be rather a multiple and realistic response to the multiple aspects of life as it presents itself, with future-oriented planning and performance where that makes sense, and present-oriented response where the future is unpromising and unpredictable.

It has been argued from cases and from large-scale but partial experiences (e.g., moving poor people into public housing, which rapidly turn into slums) that the attitudes and behavior — however they began — persist well beyond the need for them. Virtually all evidence lies in a contrary director, that upward mobility is accompanied by change in values. The difference between the impression and the evidence may depend on whether a shorter or longer time span is considered or whether one element of reality (housing) or several (schools, nutrition, job opportunity) are changed.

There is abundant evidence of resources for change among Negro families, particularly among children. Dr. Robert Coles writes:

. . . I was constantly surprised at the endurance shown by children we would all call poor or, in the current fashion, "culturally disadvantaged."
What enabled such children from such families to survive, emotionally and educationally, ordeals I feel sure many white middle-class boys and girls would find impossible? What has been the source of the strength shown by the sit-in students, many of whom do not come from comfortable homes but, quite the contrary, from rural cabins or slum tenements? Why do some Negro children — like the ones I have studied — behave so idealistically and bravely, while others go on to lives of uselessness and apathy, lives filled with hate, violence and crime?[29]

References

1. Ernest W. Burgess, Preface to E. Franklin Frazier, *The Negro Family in the United States* (New York, 1957).
2. Office of Policy Planning and Research, U.S. Department of Labor, *The Negro Family: The Case for National Action* (March 1965), pp. 9 ff.
3. Hylan Lewis, "The Changing Negro Family" in *The Nation's Children*, Vol. I (New York, 1960), p. 126.
4. Elizabeth Herzog and Rose Bernstein, *Health Services for Unmarried Mothers*, Children's Bureau Publication No. 425, Welfare Administration, U. S. Department of Health, Education, and Welfare (Washington, D. C., 1964), p. 32.
5. Jack Lefcowitz, "Poverty and Negro-White Family Structure," unpublished paper, Research and Planning Division, Office of Economic Opportunity (1965).
6. Office of Police Planning and Research, U.S. Department of Labor, *The Negro Family: The Case for National Action* (March 1965), pp. 9 ff.
7. The section entitled "The Father — Present and Absent" is part of an unpublished manuscript by Elizabeth Herzog, Children's Bureau, Welfare Administration, U. S. Department of Health, Education, and Welfare.
8. Helen Leland Witmer and Ruth Kotinsky, *Personality in the Making* (New York, 1962), p. 209.
9. Ivan F. Nye, *Family Relationships and Delinquent Behavior* (New York, 1958). Clark Vincent, *Unmarried Mothers* (New York, 1961).
10. Ivan F. Nye, "Child Adjustment in Broken and in Unhappy Broken Homes," Marriage and Family Living, Vol. 19 (1957); and Virginia Wimperis, *The Unmarried Mother and her Child* (London, 1960).
11. E. Franklin Frazier, *The Negro Family in the United States* (New York, 1957). St. Clair Drake and Horace R. Cayton, *Black Metropolis* (New York, 1954). Thomas F. Pettigrew, *A Profile of the Negro American* (Princeton, 1964). Hylan Lewis, "The Changing Negro Family," in *The Nation's Children* (New York, 1960). Office of Policy Planning and Research, U. S. Department of Labor, *The Negro Family: The Case for National Action* (March 1965).
12. Katherine B. Oettinger, "This Most Profound Challenge," U.S. Department of Health, Education, and Welfare, Welfare Administration, Children's Bureau (1965). Address before the Fall Conference on Public Family Planning Clinics, Hotel Roosevelt, New York, New York, September 9, 1965.
13. Elizabeth Herzog, *Children of Working Mothers*, U.S. Department of Health, Education, and Welfare, Welfare Administration, Children's Bureau Publication No. 382 (1960); reprinted 1964. See also Alberta Engvall Siegel, Lois Meek Stolz, Ethel Alice Hitchcock, and Jean Adamson: "Dependence and Independence in the Children of Working Mothers," *Child Development* (1959) Vol. 30, pp. 533–546.
14. U.S. Department of Health, Education, and Welfare, Welfare Administration, Children's Bureau and U.S. Department of Labor, Women's Bureau, *Child Care Arrangements of the Nation's Working Mothers — a preliminary report* (Washington, D. C., 1965), (Processed) pp. 1–4.
15. Kathryn Close, "Day Care As a Service For All Who Need It," *Children* (July–August 1965), pp. 157–160.
16. Kenneth B. Clark, *Dark Ghetto* (New York, 1965); S. M. Miller and Ira E. Harrison, "Types of Dropouts: 'The Unemployables,' " Presented at the Annual Meeting of the American Orthopsychiatric Association, Wash-

ington, D. C., March, 1963. (Syracuse University Youth Development Center, Syracuse, New York).

17. Jean Pakter, et al, "Out-of-Wedlock Births in New York City: I— Sociological Aspects," American Journal of Public Health, LI (1961).

18. The section entitled "Births Out of Wedlock" is based on the following papers: Elizabeth Herzog, "The Chronic Revolution," Journal of Clinical Pediatrics, to be published December, 1965 or January, 1966; "Unmarried Mothers: Some Questions to be Answered and Some Answers to be Questioned," Child Welfare (October 1962); Hylan Lewis and Elizabeth Herzog, "Priorities in Research on Unmarried Mothers," in Research Perspectives on the Unmarried Mother, Child Welfare League of America, Inc. (New York, 1961).

19. National Center for Health Statistics, Public Health Service, U.S. Department of Health, Education and Welfare: Vital Statistics of the United States, 1963: Vol. 1, Natality.

20. Hannah M. Adams, Social Services for Unmarried Mothers and Their Children Provided through Public and Voluntary Child Welfare Agencies. Child Welfare Report No. 12. Children's Bureau, Social Security Administration, U.S. Department of Health, Education, and Welfare (Washington, D. C., 1962).

21. Elizabeth Herzog and Rose Bernstein, Health Services for Unmarried Mothers, Children's Bureau Publication 425, Welfare Administration, U.S. Department of Health, Education, and Welfare (1964).

22. Paul H. Gebhard, et al., Pregnancy, Birth and Abortion (New York, 1958).

23. Hyman Rodman, "The Lower-Class Value Stretch," Social Forces, Vol. 42, No. 2 (December 1963), pp. 205–215. See also Hylan Lewis, "Culture, Class and the Behavior of Low Income Families," prepared for Conference on Lower Class Culture, Barbizon Plaza Hotel, New York City, June 27–29, 1963.

24. William J. Goode, "Illegitimacy in the Caribbean Social Structure," American Sociological Review, Vol. 25 (1960). Elizabeth Herzog, "Some Assumptions About the Poor," Social Services Review (1962). Oscar Lewis, Children of Sanchez (New York, 1961). Hortense Powdermaker, After Freedom: A Cultural Study in the Deep South (New York, 1939).

25. From Hylan Lewis, "Culture, Class and Child Rearing among Low Income Urban Negroes," prepared for inclusion as a chapter in a forthcoming volume, Arthur Ross (ed.), Jobs and Color, to be published by Harcourt, Brace, and World. The paper is based on materials from a 5-year project, "Child Rearing Practices Among Low Income Families in the District of Columbia," sponsored by the Health and Welfare Council of the National Capital Area, and supported by NIMH Grants, MH 278-5.

26. Seymour Martin Lipset, "Democracy and Working-Class Authoritarianism," American Sociological Review, Vol. 24:4, pp. 482–501 (August 1959). Elizabeth Herzog, "Some Assumptions About the Poor," Social Service Review, Vol. 37, 4 (December 1963).

27. J. Jolliffe, "The Pathogenesis of Deficiency Disease," A. Keys, "Caloric Deficiency and Starvation," and F. F. Tisdall, "The Relation of Nutrition to Health," in J. Jolliffe, F. F. Tisdall, and P. R. Cannon, Clinical Nutrition (1950).

28. Alvin L. Schorr, Slums and Social Insecurity, Division of Research and Statistics, Social Security Administration, U.S. Department of Health, Education, and Welfare, 1963.

29. Robert Coles, "There's Sinew in Negro Family," The Washington Post (October 10, 1965).

B. IS THERE A "BREAKDOWN"
OF THE NEGRO FAMILY*

Elizabeth Herzog

[Editors' note: This article, by the Chief, Child Life Studies Branch, Division of Research, Children's Bureau, Welfare Administration, Department of Health, Education, and Welfare, was published in Social Work, January 1966. Much of the content is similar to Agenda Paper No. V, of which Miss Herzog was a co-author. See pages 178–184.]

Much has been said of late — and often with great heat — about the Negro family. Despite prevailing consensus on a number of points, controversy has been generated with regard to other points because one man's fact is another man's fiction. Some points of consensus deserve mention before points of controversy. First, it is generally agreed that a harmonious two-parent home is better for children than a one-parent home — and better for parents, too, in this society. It is agreed also that fatherless homes are far more frequent among Negroes than among whites and that in both groups their frequency rises as income falls.

Another point of firm consensus is that strong action is needed to remedy adverse conditions that have existed far too long, especially for low-income Negroes; and that these conditions bear especially on the low-income Negro man, whose disadvantaged situation takes heavy toll of himself, his children, their mother, and the family unit as a whole. All these statements have long been accepted by serious students of Negro family life.[1]

The controversy centers mainly on the following points: (1) whether "the" Negro family is "crumbling" at a disastrous rate, (2) whether the amount of breakdown that exists is primarily due to poverty, or to cultural inheritance, or to a cycle of self-perpetuating pathology, (3) whether the remedy is to be sought primarily through improving the economic, social, and legal status of

---

* Reprinted with permission of the author and *Social Work*.
[1] St. Clair Drake and Horace R. Cayton, *Black Metropolis* (New York: Harcourt, Brace, and Co., 1945); E. Franklin Frazier, *The Negro Family in the United States* (Chicago: University of Chicago Press, 1939); Hylan Lewis, "The Changing Negro Family," in Eli Ginzberg, ed., *The Nation's Children, Vol. 1: The Family and Social Change* (New York: Columbia University Press, 1960); Thomas F. Pettigrew, *A Profile of the Negro American* (Princeton, N.J.: D. Van Nostrand Co., 1964).

Negroes or primarily through conducting a remedial campaign aimed directly at the Negro family.

The Moynihan Report

Impetus has been given to these and related questions by the much-discussed "Moynihan report." [2] Released to the general public in the late fall of 1965, this publication presents census figures and findings from some special studies to document the grim effects of poverty and discrimination and their impact on Negro families. It brings together all-too-familiar evidence that the frequency of broken marriage, female-headed families, births out of wedlock, and dependence on public assistance are much higher among Negroes than among whites. In doing so, it recognizes that these problems are most acute among the very poor and least acute at the middle- and upper-income levels. It points out also that they are more acute in cities than in rural areas and thus are intensified by continuing urbanization.

The report further documents the higher unemployment rates and lower wage rates among Negroes than among whites. It states, as others have done, the 2 to 1 white-Negro unemployment ratio that has persisted for years, the lower wages available to Negroes, and the fact that the median nonwhite family income is little more than half the median for white families. To this discrepancy is added the fact that the families of the poor tend to be larger than middle-class families. "Families of six or or more children have median incomes 24 percent below families with three." [3] Other sources tell how heavily this fertility differential bears on Negro families: in 1963, according to the Social Security Administration Index, 60 percent of non-white children under 18 lived in poverty as compared with 16 percent of white children. [4]

The effect on marital and family stability of the man's economic instability is also discussed. The sad cycle has become familiar in the professional literature: the man who cannot command a stable job at adequate wages cannot be an adequate family provider; the man who cannot provide for his family is likely to lose status and respect in his own eyes and in the

[2] *The Negro Family: The Case for National Action* (Washington, D.C.: U.S. Department of Labor, Office of Planning and Research, 1965).
[3] *Ibid.*, p. 24.
[4] Mollie Orshansky, "Who's Who Among the Poor: A Demographic View of Poverty," *Social Security Bulletin*, Vol. 28, No. 7 (July 1965), pp. 3–32.

eyes of others — including his family. His inability to provide drains him of the will to struggle with continuing and insuperable family responsibilities. It is an incentive to desertion, especially if his family can receive public assistance only when he is gone.

A good deal of the Moynihan report is devoted to interpretation of the documented figures and, quite naturally, it is on the interpretation that opinions diverge.[5] It is not the purpose of this paper to summarize fully, to concur with, or to take issues with the report as such, but rather to consider some propositions that were in circulation before it was published and to which it has given increased currency. With regard to the report itself, its factual summary has shocked some Americans into new recognition of old and unpalatable facts about the toll exacted by poverty coupled with discrimination; and its interpretive sections have challenged us to an assessment of evidence — two substantial services. Some of the propositions attributed to it may be misinterpretations of the author's intended meaning. In any case, they have taken on a life of their own and are met frequently in other current writings. Accordingly, they will be considered here on their own merits, without reference to any particular document.

Fatherless Families

One recurrent proposition concerns the "rapid deterioration" of the Negro family, often referred to as "crumbling" and presumably near dissolution. The incidence of fatherless families is used as the primary index of family breakdown. Although questions can be — and have been — raised about this index, such questions do not dominate the mainstream of the argument and will be disregarded here. But if one accepts the proportion of fatherless homes as a primary index of family breakdown, does it then follow, on the basis of the evidence, that the Negro family is rapidly deteriorating?

It is important to differentiate between sudden acceleration of family crisis and relatively sudden perception of a long-chronic

[5] Midway between statistical report and interpretation is discussion of a "startling increase in welfare dependency," described as occurring at a time when employment was increasing. See U.S. Department of Labor, The Negro Family: The Case for National Action, op. cit., p. 12. It would require extensive and sophisticated analysis to determine the extent to which this upswing in AFDC recipients related to changes in families, or to liberalization of AFDC policies following new legislation, or to changes in population distribution. Similarly, differentials in rates of juvenile delinquency would need to be controlled for income and analyzed in light of differential rates of apprehension and treatment of presumed offenders, white or nonwhite.

situation, since the diagnosis of a social condition influences the prescription for relieving it and the context in which the prescription is filled.

Actually, census figures do not justify any such alarmist interpretation. It seems worthwhile to review these figures, not because there is no urgent need for remedial action — the need is urgent, especially in the area of jobs for low-income Negro men. Rather it is important to keep the problem in perspective and to avoid feeding prejudices that can all too readily seize upon statistical misconceptions as reason to delay rather than to speed such action.

As already noted, census figures do show much higher rates of fatherless families for Negroes than for whites. The 1964 figures show almost 9 percent of white families headed by a woman as compared with 23 percent of nonwhite families; a difference of this order has persisted for years.[6] The figures do not, however, document a rapid increase in those rates during recent years. On the contrary — and this is a point curiously slighted by commentators on both sides of the argument — they show a gradual increase from 1949 (19 percent) to 1959 (24 percent). Moreover, from 1960 to 1964 the proportion of female-headed families among Negroes showed no net rise at all, standing at 23 percent in 1964. The total rise from 1949 to 1964 was about 5 percentage points, that is, about one-third of a percentage point a year. In 1940, the proportion was 18 percent.[7] Thus, an accurate description would be that during the past twenty-five years there has been a gradual rise, preceded and followed by a plateau, but not an acute increase in the over-all proportion of broken homes among Negroes. (Table 1)

Illegitimacy

Another generalization also related to family breakdown is met so often that by now it threatens to attain the status of "fact," namely, that there has been an "alarming rise" in illegitimacy.

[6] These figures are available for white and nonwhite rather than for white and Negro families. However, most of the nonwhite (about 92 percent) are negroes.
[7] Percentages have been rounded. The exact rise was from 18.8 percent to 23.6 percent, or 4.4 percentage points. The 1940 figure was 17.8 percent, as recomputed according to the definition of "family" introduced in 1947. Bureau of the Census, *Current Population Reports*. Series P-20, Nos. 125, 116, 106, 100, 88, 83, 75, 67, 53, 44, 33, and 26 (Washington, D. C.: U.S. Department of Commerce); Bureau of Labor Statistics, *The Negroes in the United States: Their Economic and Social Situation* (Washington, D. C.: U.S. Department of Labor, 1965); Bureau of the Census, *16th Census of the U.S. 1940. Population — Families — Types of Families* (Washington, D. C.: U.S. Department of Commerce, 1940).

Table 1.   Families Headed by a Woman as Percent of All Families by Color: Selected Periods, 1949–1964

	Families Headed by a Woman As Percent of Total	
Year	White	Nonwhite
1964	8.8	23.4
1963	8.6	23.3
1962	8.6	23.2
1961	8.9	21.6
1960	8.7	22.4
1959	8.4	23.6
1958	8.6	22.4
1957	8.9	21.9
1956	8.8	20.5
1955	9.0	20.7
1954	8.3	19.2
1953	8.4	18.1
1952	9.2	17.9
1950	8.4	19.1
1949	8.8	18.8

Source: U.S. Department of Commerce, Bureau of the Census: Current Population Reports, P-20, No. 125, 116, 106, 100, 88, 83, 75, 67, 53, 44, 33, and 26. Figures for 1963 and 1964 are drawn from Bureau of Labor Statistics, *The Negroes in the United States: Their Economic and Social Situation* (Washington, D. C., U.S. Department of Labor) Table IV, a, 1.

It is true that the number of births out of wedlock has soared. In 1964 the number was 276,000 as compared with 176,000 in 1954.[8] This is a tremendous number, and the more distressing since there has been no services explosion to keep pace with the population explosion. However, in terms of people's behavior, the only relevant index of increase in illegitimacy is *rate,* that is, the number of births out of wedlock per 1,000 unmarried women of child-bearing age.

The rise in rate (as differentiated from numbers) was relatively steady over several decades. This rise represents a long-term trend and not a sudden upsurge. Moreover, in the last seven years reported (1957–1964) the rate has oscillated within about two points, at about the same level, rising or falling one point or less annually, but in effect representing a seven-year plateau.

[8] *Monthly Vital Statistics Reports, Advance Report, Final Natality Statistics, 1964* (Washington, D. C.: U.S. Department of Health, Education, and Welfare, National Center for Health Statistics, Public Health Service, October 22, 1965); *Vital Statistics of the United States, 1963. Volume 1 — Natality* (Washington, D. C.: National Center for Health Statistics, Public Health Service, Department of Health, Education, and Welfare, 1964).

Since all national illegitimacy figures are based on estimates, with a number of states not reporting, very slight changes should not be regarded as significant. Thus, the current picture is a large rise in *numbers* and a levelling off in the *rate* of nonwedlock births.[9] Rates for teen-agers have increased less than for other groups, and for those under fifteen the rate has not increased since 1947.[10] (The ratio — the proportion of live births that are out of wedlock — has risen for both whites and nonwhites. However, *ratio* is far less meaningful than *rate* as an index of change.)

The recent relative stability of rate does not diminish the problems caused by nonwedlock births but it should affect the conclusions drawn from the statistics, the measures taken to act on those conclusions, and the attitudes of those who ponder the meaning of the figures.

Over half the children born out of wedlock are nonwhite, although only 12 percent of the population are nonwhite. The reasons for this difference have been much discussed and need only be mentioned here. They include (1) less use of contraception, (2) less use of abortion, (3) differences in reporting, (4) reluctance to lose a public assistance grant by admitting to a man in the house, (5) the expense of divorce and legal separation. It seems probable that, even if discount could be made for these and other factors, a difference would remain. It would be a much smaller, difference, however, and conceivably could still relate more to income than to color.[11]

If further evidence were needed on this virtually unchallenged relation between income and illegitimacy rates, figures on rates in high- and low-income tracts should be sufficient. Pakter and associates, for example, found that the proportion of births out-of-wedlock in relation to total nonwhite births varied from a high of 38 percent in the Central Harlem district to a comparative low of 9 percent in the Pelham Bay District.[12]

Attitudes toward illegitimacy and toward marriage are clearly linked with the economic position of the Negro male. A male head

[9] Elizabeth Herzog, "The Chronic Revolution: Births Out of Wedlock." Paper presented at meeting of American Orthopsychiatric Association, March 1965. To be published in a forthcoming issue of *Journal of Clinical Pediatrics*.
[10] Rates are not available by color except for a few years.
[11] Elizabeth Herzog, "Unmarried Mothers: Some Questions To Be Answered and Some Answers To Be Questioned," *Child Welfare*, Vol. 41, No. 8 (October 1962), pp. 339–350.
[12] Jean Pakter, Henry J. Rosner, Harold Jacobziner, and Frieda Greenstein, "Out-of-Wedlock Births in New York City. I — Sociologic Aspects," *American Journal of Public Health*, Vol. 51, No. 5 (May 1961), pp. 683–696.

of house who is not a breadwinner and provider is a hazard to
the happiness of the marriage, and his loss of economic status is
so great a hazard to his intrafamily status that he may decamp,
either to protect his own ego or to make his family eligible for
support from AFDC. Recent changes in the AFDC program are
aimed against the latter reason for family desertion.

Slavery Is Not the Explanation

Among the most frequent and most challenged generalizations
relating to low-income Negro families is the assumption that
their present characteristics are influenced more by the legacy
of slavery than by postslavery discriminations and deprivations.
The challenge rests chiefly on (1) the similarity between very
poor Negro families and very poor white families, and (2) the
fact that slavery ended a hundred years ago while the postslavery
situation is contemporary and appalling. Adequately controlled
comparisons within different income levels show that the differences associated with income outweigh those associated with
color. Family structure, for example, differs more between different income levels than between Negro and white families. The
same is true of differences between Negro and white children
in educational achievement, and — when income is controlled —
the relative position of men with respect to women, economically
and educationally, is the same for whites as for nonwhites.[13]

Descriptions of white families at the very low income levels
read very much like current descriptions of poor Negro families,
with high incidence of broken homes, "mother dominance," births
out of wedlock, educational deficit, crowded living, three-genera-
tion households, and failure to observe the norms of middle-class
behavior.[14] Such families are described by Hollingshead and Redlich:

Doctors, nurses, and public officials who know these families best
estimate from one-fifth to one-fourth of all births are illegitimate.

[13] Myron J. Lefcowitz, "Poverty and Negro-White Family Structures." Unpub-
lished background paper for White House Conference on Civil Rights, Washing-
ton, D. C., November 1965.
[14] Walter B. Miller, "Implications of Urban Lower-Class Culture for Social Work,"
Social Service Review, Vol. 33, No. 3 (September 1959), pp. 219–236; W. Lloyd
Warner and Paul S. Lunt, *The Social Life of a Modern Community* (New Haven:
Yale University Press, 1941); James West, *Plainville, USA* (New York: Columbia
University Press, 1945).

Death, desertion, separation, or divorce has broken more than half the families (56%). The burden of child care, as well as support, falls on the mother more often than on the father when the family is broken. The mother-child relation is the strongest and most enduring family tie. Here we find a conglomerate of broken homes where two or three generations live together, where boarders and roomers, in-laws and common-law liaisons share living quarters. Laws may be broken and the moral standards of the higher classes flouted before the children's eyes day after day.[15]

These are descriptions of white families in the North, with no heritage of slavery to explain their way of life. It seems unlikely that the slavery-specific thesis is needed to explain the occurrence among Negroes of patterns so similar to those produced in other groups merely by poverty, and so often described in other contexts as "the culture of poverty." [16]

It is difficult to be sure how much — if any — difference would remain in proportions of female-headed families if really sensitive comparisons were made between Negroes and whites on the same income level. Available income breakdowns employ rather broad groupings, and Negroes tend to be overrepresented at the lower layers of each grouping. It seems reasonable to assume that some differences between white and nonwhite would remain even with a more sensitive income classification. Yet it does not necessarily follow that they might be ascribed primarily to the legacy of slavery rather than to the hundred years since slavery. It seems more likely that differences between low-income white and Negro families, beyond that explained by income alone, may be attributed primarily to postslavery factors of deprivation and discrimination affecting every facet of life: occupation, education, income, housing, nutrition, health and mortality, social status, self-respect — the documented list is long and the documenting references myriad.[17]

The habit of analyzing data by color rather than by income encourages the tendency to attribute to race-related factors differ-

[15] August B. Hollingshead, *Elmtown's Youth*. (New York: John Wiley & Sons, 1949), pp. 116, 117; Hollingshead and Fredrick C. Redlich, *Social Class and Mental Illness: A Community Study* (New York: John Wiley & Sons, 1958), p. 125.

[16] Oscar Lewis, *The Children of Sanchez: Autobiography of a Mexican Family*. (New York: Random House, 1961).

[17] Dorothy K. Newman, "Economic Status of the Negro." Unpublished background paper for White House Conference on Civil Rights, Washington, D. C., November 1965; Alvin L. Schorr, *Slums and Social Insecurity*, Research Report No. 1 (Washington, D. C.: U.S. Department of Health, Education, and Welfare, Social Security Administration, 1963).

ences that may in fact be due to income level. Studies of prenatal care, for example, indicate that in effect one is comparing the prosperous with the poor in all three of the following comparisons: white mothers with nonwhite mothers; married mothers with unmarried mothers; all mothers who do with all mothers who do not obtain prenatal care.[18]

All the points mentioned here and some not mentioned are important. However, the emphasis on rapid deterioration is so central to current discussion of the low-income Negro family and to means proposed for alleviating its current problems that it deserves major emphasis — along with the slavery-specific thesis to which it is so often linked.

There has been little disposition to challenge the ample evidence that family structure and functioning in our society are strongly linked with social and economic status. The questions raised, as Robert Coles put it, have to do with which is the cart and which is the horse.[19] The alleged rapid acceleration of family breakdown has been cited as evidence that among low-income Negroes the family is the horse. Therefore it is important to recognize that according to the chief index used by proponents of this view no rapid acceleration of family breakdown is evident.

If there has been no substantial change in family structure during the past two decades, then there are no grounds for claiming that a new "tangle of pathology" has set up a degenerative process from within, over and above response to the long continued impact of social and economic forces from without; and that this process is specific to a Negro "culture" inherited from days of slavery.

Two Views — and Two Remedies

Both sides of the controversy agree that there is urgent need for strong action to increase the proportion of sound, harmonious two-parent homes among low-income Negroes. They disagree on whether that action should be focused primarily on intra-family or extra-family problems. The acute-crisis view suggests that primary attention be given to the family as such. The other view suggests that the best way to strengthen low-income families as

[18] Elizabeth Herzog and Rose Bernstein, *Health Services for Unmarried Mothers,* Children's Bureau Publication No. 425 (Washington, D. C.: U.S. Department of Health, Education, and Welfare, Welfare Administration, 1964).
[19] Robert Coles, "There's Sinew in the Negro Family." Background paper for White House Conference on Civil Rights, Washington, D. C., November 1965. Reprinted from *The Washington Post,* October 10, 1965, p. E. 1.

families is to give primary attention to building up the economic and social status of Negro men.

According to this view, a number of noneconomic supports can and should be given to low-income Negro families, pending the time when fewer of them are fatherless. Such helps should include, among other things, (1) aids for the overburdened mother in her multiple role as homemaker, child-rearer, and breadwinner; and (2) effective male models introduced into the lives of children — girls as well as boys. A number of new ways for providing both kinds of support have been proposed. In the long run, however, according to this view, what these families need most is jobs for Negro men — jobs with status, with stability, with future, and with fair wages. No one claims that this can be achieved easily, quickly, or cheaply; but many believe it can and must be done.

What is new for the white majority is not that it is suddenly faced with an explosive breakdown of "the" Negro family. What is new is the recognition of a long-standing situation, plus the determination to do something about it. If we are able to achieve that recognition and determination, however belatedly, then surely we must be able to act on this basis rather than to galvanize ourselves into action by believing that suddenly the Negro family is a bomb or a mine which will explode in our faces if it is not quickly defused. Surely we are able to act, not because of panic but because action is long overdue, and inaction flies in the face of decency.

What is new for the Negro minority is not a sudden acceleration of family breakdown. What is new is an injection of hope that attacks apathy and fatalism and sparks insistence on full justice. It is not increased family breakdown that activates outbreaks such as occurred in Harlem, Watts, and elsewhere. It is the recognition that the families of the "dark ghetto" no longer need to continue to accept the ghetto and what it does to them.

It must, of course, be recognized that "the" Negro family is itself a fiction. Different family forms prevail at different class and income levels throughout our society. In addition, at any given level a wide variety of families are found, each with its individual characteristics — some of which are and some of which are not class linked. When the great diversity among low-income families is ignored, there is danger that the deplored characteristics of some will be imputed to all.[20] At the same time, most writers — including the present one — find it almost impossible to avoid falling into the oversimplified form of reference to "'the" Negro family that constantly risks oversimplified thinking.

It is necessary also to caution one's self and others that, while problems must be discussed and attacked, strengths must not be forgotten. Problem-focused discussions, however necessary and constructive, also invite distortion. Not all fathers are absent fathers among the poor — in fact, about two-thirds of them are present among low-income Negro families. And, as Erik Erikson reminds us, there are impressive strengths in many Negro mothers.[21] Robert Coles, after living among low-income Negroes for months, wrote:

I was constantly surprised at the endurance shown by children we would all call poor or, in the current fashion, "culturally disadvantaged." . . . What enabled such children from such families to survive, emotionally and educationally, ordeals I feel sure many white middle-class boys and girls would find impossible? What has been the source of strength shown by the sit-in students, many of whom do not come from comfortable homes but, quite the contrary, from rural cabins or slum tenements?[22]

One may go on to speculate: What are the sources of strength and self-discipline that make possible a Montgomery bus boycott or a March on Washington, conducted without violence? We do well to ponder such questions, for we shall have to mobilize the strengths of families in poverty as well as the wisdom of others who ponder their problems, if we are at last "to fulfill these rights."

C. FAMILY STRUCTURE AND EMPLOYMENT PROBLEMS*

Harold L. Sheppard and Herbert E. Striner

[Editors' note: This is an excerpt from the authors' Civil Rights, Employment and the Social Status of American Negroes (Kalamazoo,

---

[20] Hylan Lewis, Culture, "Class and the Behavior of Low Income Families." Unpublished background paper for White House Conference on Civil Rights, Washington, D. C., November 1965; Elizabeth Herzog, "Some Assumptions About the Poor," Social Service Review, Vol. 37, No. 4 (December 1963), pp. 389–402.
[21] Erik H. Erikson, "The Concept of Identity in Race Relations: Notes and Queries." To be published in December 1965 issue of Daedalus.
[22] Robert Coles, op. cit., p. E 1 (Washington Post).

*Michigan: The W. E. Upjohn Institute for Employment Research, 1966),
pp. 33–45. The report was prepared for the U.S. Civil Rights Commission. The section reprinted here addresses itself to some of the issues
that had been stimulated by the Moynihan Report and controversy.*

This report places strong emphasis upon the relationship of
family structure and size to the problems of employment and job
status for many Negroes. At the outset, it should be stressed that
there is no such thing as *the* Negro family and that there is nothing intrinsically pathological about different family structures or
sizes. Because of the great lack of research and data concerning
the relationship of family structure and size to employment and
economic opportunity, much of what follows is necessarily inferential. There is great need for gathering data explicitly for the
purpose of more systematic research on this subject. Recent discussions of this topic have tended to engender acrimonious debate
instead of needed research. Unless a calmer, more empirical
analysis is undertaken, a solution to the employment problems
of Negroes will not be found.

The large-scale migration of Negroes during the forties and
fifties has had a profound effect on their families. This impact
on the families is heaped upon repercussions from the plantation
and slavery system. In any evaluation of differences between
the Negro family and the white family, it is quickly apparent that
the former is much more frequently identified with the poverty
population. But an even closer look is required. Nonwhite poverty
families have, on the average, more children that white poverty
families. There is a direct relationship between a large number
of children in a family and frustrating experience; and this correlation provides a pessimism base, an unconscious or conscious
disposition to believe that "we just can't beat the game." The
problem of planning family size, unfortunately, is being faced
very late. But it is being faced at last; and the issue of employment and economic security cannot be divorced from the outcome
of present and future family planning programs.

The following table presents the comparative distribution of
large size families among whites and Negroes, and the relationship of size to poverty:

* Reprinted with permission of the authors and The W. E. Upjohn Institute for
Employment Research.

Distribution of Negro and White Families in Poverty, by Number of Children Under 18, 1963*

All families with children under 18 (percent)	Families with 1 child (percent)		Families with 6 or more children (percent)	
	Negro	White	Negro	White
22	33	10	77	35

* Based on the less rigorous "economy" level criteria established by the Social Security Administration (Mollie Orshansky, "Counting the Poor: Another Look at the Poverty Profile," *Social Security Bulletin*, January 1965).

Such comparisons show that the larger the family the greater the poverty. Furthermore, there is a greater proportion of larger families among Negroes than among whites. *Given the continuing differential in birth rates between poor whites and Negroes, it is possible for the problem to become even more acute among Negroes.* As Philip Hauser has pointed out, "The Negro, like the inhabitant of the developing regions in Asia, Latin America, and Africa, in his new exposure to amenities of twentieth-century living, is experiencing rapidly declining mortality while fertility rates either remain high or, as in urban areas, actually increase." [6]

Furthermore, for every 100 Negroes between the ages of 20 and 64 in 1960, there were 94 under 20, while the corresponding ratio for whites in the same year was only 75. In other words, Negroes of working ages carry a greater burden of dependency than whites. As of 1965, there were 103 Negroes under 20 for every 100 aged 20–64.

In 1960, one-third of all nonwhite children under the age of 14 — as contrasted to only one-twelfth of white children in the same age group — were living and being reared in the absence of one or both parents, usually the absence of the father. About 20 percent of all nonwhite children were living with mothers only, as contrasted with less than 6 percent of white children. There are no data on how many Negroes have lived in fatherless families during all of their childhood. Living in a fatherless family is especially difficult for boys in their developmental years. The emergence of this type of pattern as an urban phenomenon is suggested by the fact that, in 1965, 25.5 percent of nonfarm Negro families were headed by females, in contrast to only 15.3 percent among farm families, according to the Bureau of the Census.

[6] "Demographic Factors in the Integration of the Negro," *Daedalus*, Fall 1965, p. 864.

With one-third of Negro children under 14 being reared in families with one or both parents absent, economic equality with whites for large numbers of Negroes (perhaps growing numbers) can only be a pious wish. There is nothing intrinsically immoral about fatherless or motherless family structures — unless we view as immoral in our type of society and economy high unemployment rates, low income, and exhausting occupations. Nor is there anything intrinsically immoral about matriarchal families if there is an adequate role for the husband and son to perform in such families and in the general society.

As long as there are large families in low-income, low-skilled, poorly schooled populations — white or Negro — we must strive to design more effective means of attaining progress in income and occupational status. Low-income rural-origin families with large numbers of children have a high rate of dropouts. And dropouts have a higher unemployment rate than high school graduates. Thus, there seems to be a definite correlation between birth in a large low-income, rural-origin family and low job status and high unemployment. In other words, the nature and size of the family can become a condition for poor jobs and unemployment. Generally speaking, birth rates actually have declined in periods of unemployment in our history; that is, extended unemployment has tended to be followed by declines in birth rates. It would be interesting, incidentally, to trace historically white-Negro differences, if any, in birth rate "adjustments" to changes in nonfarm unemployment rates.

The fact that in urban centers Negroes currently have a higher proportion of low-income recent migrant persons and larger families than whites creates the impression of a "Negro problem." Many Negroes become sensitive to such a description. Many whites use the description as a defense against any action that would change such a fact, thus indulging in a self-fulfilling prophecy. It may also be possible that some Negro leaders, by refusing to cope with these facts, are also participating in self-fulfilling of the prophecy.

In years past, we witnessed the reluctance on the part of whites and Negroes alike to accept the proposition that education is a crucial variable in the life chances of Negroes. Prejudiced whites insisted that biology was the sole underlying cause of Negro inequality, while many Negroes insisted that discrimination was the sole cause. Biology certainly was not and is not the explanation, but discrimination on the basis of skin color alone is no longer as crucial as it was in the past (although it is far from being eradicated). The main point, however, is that Negroes and whites now accept the importance of educational improvements as one of the means or conditions for equality.

Since education and training are recognized today as making a difference between success and failure in the world of work, it has become almost trite and platitudinous to state that Negroes must be given better and more education and training. What has not been recognized sufficiently is that one — and *only one* — of the obstacles to rapid progress toward this goal for more Negroes is the nature of the family structure in a significant minority of the Negro population in urban areas. This minority has a greater birth rate, and it may thus be on the way to becoming a larger minority than before — *the result of which can be a perpetuation of the very crisis we are trying to prevent or mitigate.* One statistical aspect of this differential birth rate is that 64 percent of all the nonfarm, nonwhite poor population living in families are 21 years of age or younger — a proportion 21 percent higher than that among white poor persons living in nonfarm families. Among the nonwhites who were not poor, about one-half were 21 or younger.

The modern American urban world encompasses a caste system that has emerged out of the migrations of the descendants of 19th century slavery. As St. Clair Drake has pointed out:

. . . the character of the Black Ghetto is not set by the newer "gilded," not-yet run down portions of it, but by the older sections where unemployment rates are high and the masses of people work with their hands — where the median level of education is just above graduation from grade school and many of the people are likely to be recent migrants from rural areas.

The "ghettoization" of the Negro has resulted in the emergence of a ghetto subculture with a distinctive ethos, most pronounced, perhaps, in Harlem, but recognizable in all Negro neighborhoods . . . . The spontaneous vigor of the children who crowd streets and playgrounds . . . and the cheerful rushing about of adults, free from the occupational pressures of the "white world" in which they work, create an atmosphere of warmth and superficial intimacy which obscures the unpleasant facts of life in the overcrowded rooms behind the doors, the lack of adequate maintenance standards, and the too prevalent vermin and rats.[7]

[7] "The Social and Economic Status of the Negro in the United States," *Daedalus*, Fall 1965, pp. 771–772.

About 60 percent of Negro families in the United States earn less than $4,000 per year, while 60 percent of white families earn more than that amount. Within the Negro low-income segment there is naturally a heterogeneity of social strata and styles of life. Many low-income Negroes behave within a system of what has come to be called "middle-class" values, including a stress on respectability and decorum; getting an education (if not for themselves, at least for their children); family stability; and a reasonable family size. To quote Drake, "For both men and women, owning a home and going into business are highly desired goals, the former often being a realistic one, the latter a mere fantasy." [8]

But within this same income category there are other types of families and individuals. This part of the urban Negro population and its style of life provide the flesh-and-blood world from which spring the statistics of the "Moynihan" Report:

. . . an "unorganized" lower class exists whose members tend always to become disorganized — functioning in an anomic situation where gambling, excessive drinking, the use of narcotics, and sexual promiscuity are prevalent forms of behavior, and violent interpersonal relations reflect an ethos of suspicion and resentment which suffuses this deviant subculture. It is within this milieu that criminal and semi-criminal activities burgeon. [9]

The maintenance of a middle class style of life requires more than sheer perseverance and willpower. It also calls for a certain level of income (more precisely, a certain level of purchasing power) and perhaps even a certain kind of family structure. Purchasing power is not distributed and occupational and family structure are not organized among Negroes to the same degree as they are among whites. The issue is, can one be changed without changing the others?

In this respect, a vicious circle continues to pervade the social world of many Negroes in which the number of families without fathers and a lower prestige of males among their female associates and their children are dominant features. The pattern of Negro male insecurity, sustained by other current conditions, continues to be a major obstacle to effectuating a distinct break from the disadvantaged position of a large part of the Negro population today. For one thing, "An impressive body of evidence indicates

[8] *Ibid.,* p. 779.
[9] *Loc. cit.*

that rather serious personality distortions result from the female dominance so prevalent in the Negro subculture. . . ." [10] What is not sufficiently recognized is the link between the nature of the social status of many Negro males today and their problems of employment and occupational status. Indeed, this link is often vehemently denied.

The low esteem of the Negro male, especially in the lower income strata, must be given prime attention in any serious effort to change the social structure of American Negro society which is much more like a pyramid than the white social structure. Negro occupational structure, for example, consists of a miniscule capstone of upper class families, a larger stratum of middle class families under that, and the largest class at the bottom. Conversely, white social structure is shaped more like a diamond, with a large middle-class bulge.

This situation of a large number of Negro males warrants further comment. For example, Negro boys in lower income families receive less and even inferior education compared to Negro girls. Smaller proportions enroll in college-preparatory and commercial classes in the high schools. Even if the girls in such classes do not actually enter college, they at least become more qualified for white-collar jobs — the occupational sector which is expanding at a greater rate than manual jobs. As one study has pointed out:

When more white-collar occupations open up for Negroes, the girls will be better prepared and more motivated to fill them than the boys. This is true for clerical and sales positions, but also for semi-professional and professional ones. Under these conditions Negro girls, especially those of a working class background, can be expected to achieve higher occupational status than the boys from their socio-economic category. This kind of development would tend to perpetuate the high prestige position of Negro women with the Negro group. [11]

The author of that study also confirms one of the major theses of this bulletin, namely, that the disadvantaged position of Negroes can persist even when discrimination itself declines or is actually eliminated, especially in the case of Negro males. If this is so, the civil rights movement and the drive for equal job status face some severe frustrations. Unless major changes can be

[10] *Ibid.*, p. 787.
[11] Jetse Sprey, "Sex Differences in Occupational Choice Patterns among Negro Adolescents," *Social Problems,* Summer 1962, p. 22.

brought about in the demography, sociology, and psychology of lower income Negro families, and of males in particular, civil rights legislation for fair employment practices will not soon achieve its goal. At best, the only kinds of jobs available for unskilled Negro males born and reared in such family settings are actually declining, and the large numbers involved cannot possibly be absorbed.

The adverse character of families in substantial parts of the Negro population is certainly due in large part to (1) the heritage of past decades and (2) the nature of their present environmental setting. In other words, it may be looked upon as an effect, a result. But effects can assume a causative role in human affairs.[12] Illegitimacy, many children in a family, and unstable parental relations have their effects, too; they should not be looked upon merely as results of other factors if we intend to deal with the problem and not just continue to look for someone or something to blame.

A large number of children is obviously an insuperable burden for a low-income family, regardless of racial background. In this particular instance, just on the aggregate level, the average income of Negro families is about 50 percent of the average income of white families, but the average number of children in Negro families is 30 percent more than in white families. Putting it even more dramatically, while the average number of children in upper income nonwhite families has fallen below that of whites with comparable economic characteristics, the average number of children for lower income nonwhites is above that for comparable whites. According to the 1960 Census, for every 1,000 nonwhite females aged 15–19 who had ever been married, 1,247 children had been born unto them. For comparable white females, the corresponding figure was 725.

The basic point is that the growth in the Negro population is concentrated among those with low income, inadequate education, employment insecurity, and unstable family structure.

If we are sincere in our statements about the crisis nature of Negro income, employment, and occupational status, it is not enough to be comforted by long-run predictions that, like others

[12] The family problem does exist and also does affect efforts to move the Negro into the economy and the society on a comparable footing with the white. But to be really effective, one must see the family factor not as the sole or major focus of our efforts, but as one of many crucial focuses. We are faced with a social simultaneous equation where the solution can only result if all factors are dealt with in the solving process.

before them, Negroes will decrease their rural exodus to urban areas and thus eventually produce a population "increasingly similar to others in the areas to which they have come." [13] For one thing there is nothing inevitable about such a prediction. Even if it were inevitable, the current rate of change is actually so slow that it could take more than 100 years to reach "parity." Certainly, recent trends in income and occupational status do not point to any optimistic conclusion about the future.

Hauser points to the impact of the higher birth rate among Negroes on their socioeconomic status:

High fertility with its consequent large family size handicaps the Negro by limiting the investment the family can make in human resources — that is, in the education and training of the child. Under economic pressure the Negro child, on the one hand, has little incentive to remain in school and, on the other, is often forced to leave even when he desires to obtain an education. Thus, the Negro child tends to be the high school drop-out rather than the high school graduate. Even if much more is done to remove the Negro family from the bitter consequences of raw poverty, large numbers of children will tend to set limits on the education each child in the Negro community will receive. Certainly, the family with two or three children will, for some time to come, be in a better position to support its children through high school than the family with six or more children.

The poverty of the Negro family must rank as the single most important factor preventing the Negro from developing those abilities which could help him to assume both the rights and obligations of being a first-class American citizen ... the large proportion of Negro children now under eighteen cannot possibly be expected to participate fully in the mainstream of American life so long as they are steeped in the morass of poverty. [14]

Since education is becoming a much more important requirement for eliminating Negro-white economic differentials and for increasing job opportunities, and since "large numbers of children will tend to set limits on the education each child in the Negro community will receive," we must come face to face with the subject of family structure and size. This matter is more than a spurious factor in the issue of Negro progress in employment and occupational status. To put it more directly by quoting Hauser, "As a result of a high birth rate, the Negro population retains characteristics such as inferior occupations, low income, and a

[13] Hauser, *Daedalus*, Fall 1965, p. 85.
[14] *Ibid.*, pp. 865–866.

style of life precluding association and social interaction with the dominant white society — all of which retard assimilation." [15] This statement underscores the authors' view that a high birth rate among low-income families can itself serve to perpetuate inferior occupations and high unemployment rates.

The vicious circle of poverty, large family size, poor education and skills, and high unemployment rates must be broken. It *can* be broken. And a vicious circle can be entered and broken at many points of its circumference. One of these points of entry relates to family size. We need a massive effective program aimed at helping "the relatively uneducated and impoverished Negro family to restrict its size." If all Negroes were in the upper 5 percent of the income distribution, concern about family size would, of course, be irrelevant (or indicative of fears of Negro dominance). Millionaires — Negro or white — can afford to have families of six or more children. The only adverse effect would be smaller inheritances for each child. Low-income persons — Negro or white — cannot afford large families, at least in the current stage of human history.

Poverty, poor education, punitive welfare policies (such as the "man-in-the-house" rule), and even pathological discrimination, have all contributed to the economic and social-psychological frustrations of our Negro citizens. Such frustrations are a result of these and other patterns created and sustained by dominant white beliefs and practices. But again, results can, in turn, become causes. Today, the inferior role and status of low-income Negro males contribute to the perpetuation of Negro inequality in general. "There is a great need for special efforts to enhance the role of the Negro male in the family, to concentrate on providing him with the capabilities of taking on his expected functions, responsibilities, and obligations as husband, father, and provider." [16] These capabilities also depend on the less understood, but nevertheless real, psychological phenomena such as self-identity, ego strength, etc. These factors are among the causes, as well as among the effects, of the employment problem.

The psychological literature is replete with findings about the unique personality problems of Negro males from lower income families. Department of Labor and Bureau of the Census data on economic and demographic characteristics offer only partial — and hence inadequate — information and "explanations" about

[15] *Ibid.*, p. 866.
[16] *Ibid.*, p. 867.

the employment problem of Negroes. Furthermore, the data too frequently understate the problem by being reported in the category of nonwhites instead of Negroes specifically and exclusively.

The research findings on Negro males in particular, as well as on the impact of fatherless situations on basic behavior patterns and motivations, have been summarized by Thomas Pettigrew. One of his passages supports the authors' position that the employment problems of Negroes (males in particular) cannot be separated from family structure.

. . . eight-and-nine-year-old children whose fathers are absent seek immediate gratification far more than children whose fathers are present in the home. For example, when offered their choice of receiving a tiny candy bar immediately or a large bar a week later, fatherless children typically take the small bar while other children prefer to wait for the larger bar. This hunger for immediate gratification among fatherless children seems to have serious implications. Regardless of race, children manifesting this trait also tend to be less accurate in judging time, less "socially responsible," less oriented toward achievement and more prone to delinquency. Indeed, two psychologists maintain that the inability to delay gratification is a critical factor in immature, criminal, and neurotic behavior.

. . . Various studies have demonstrated the crucial importance of the father in the socialization of boys. Mothers raising their children in homes without fathers are frequently overprotective, sometimes even smothering, in their compensatory attempts to be a combined father and mother . . . boys whose fathers are not present have initially identified with their mothers and must later, in America's relatively patrifocal society, develop a conflicting, secondary identification with males . . . .

Several studies point to the applicability of this sex-identity problem to lower-class Negro males.[17]

Lower income Negroes have experienced difficulty in the learning process, as Martin Deutsch pointed out.[18] He also described how the economic and social experiences of the low-income Negro male have influenced his "concept of himself and his general motivation to succeed in competitive areas of society where the rewards are the greatest. . . . the lower-class Negro child entering school often has had no experience with a 'successful' male model or thereby with a psychological framework in which

[17] A Profile of the Negro American (Princeton: Van Nostrand, 1964), pp. 17–19.
[18] "The Disadvantaged Child and the Learning Process," in A. H. Passow, ed., Education in Depressed Areas (New York: Teachers College, Columbia University, 1963), pp. 163–179.

effort can result in at least the possibility of achievement. . . . A child from any circumstance who has been deprived of a substantial portion of the variety of stimuli which he is maturationally capable of responding to is likely to be deficient in the equipment required for learning." Deutsch and Brown have also shown that even when income is held constant, the IQ's of Negro pupils from families without a father present are lower than the IQ's of those from families with a father.[19]

The large urban areas of the United States are fostering and are subject to a set of adverse social conditions affecting young Negroes — especially the males. These boys are too frequently in fatherless and/or unemployed families; they lack adequate stimulation for achievement, adequate occupational guidance (often nonexistent) in the families and the schools and sufficient occupational training; and they obtain only blind-end jobs, if any. The "choice" of a first job is itself a vital variable; an unskilled (or nonskilled) worker typically takes the only job he knows about when entering the labor market, and this job is stigmatized by a low wage and/or frequent spells of layoffs. If young Negroes are not poorly motivated to begin with, they inevitably lower their aspirations and efforts at self-improvement as a result of the syndrome of environmental insults. Even the pernicious system of easy credit and exorbitant interest operates to discourage their active job-seeking once unemployed, since their income from jobs would only be garnished by their creditors. The unemployed have their own version of cost-benefit analysis too.

David McClelland, of Harvard University, who has studied extensively the role of motivation in economic behavior, has pointed out that the conditions of slavery influenced the nature of American Negro adjustment conducive to obedience but not to achievement and self-betterment; and that it should not be surprising to find that many of the descendants of slavery — even though "free" — still show the effects of such adjustment. It is significant that for those few Negroes who have become middle and upper class, their achievement motivation (as measured by McClelland's projective test approach) is conspicuously high — "reflecting once again the fact that individuals who have managed to move out of a low . . . achievement [motivation] group tend to have exceptionally high motivation." [20]

[19] Martin Deutsch and Bert Brown, "Social Influences in Negro-White Intelligence Differences," *Social Issues,* April 1964, p. 27.
[20] *The Achieving Society* (Princeton: Van Nostrand, 1961), p. 377.

The relevance of the family structure to the individual's motivations to succeed — to aspire to and obtain better jobs, more education, and training — should be made clear to persons concerned with the job and income status of Negroes. A number of studies have indicated that people whose fathers were absent during their childhood tend not to develop such motivations.[21] Neither Negroes nor the nation as a whole will benefit if we create the conditions for greater opportunities in employment without preparing Negroes to take actual advantage of these conditions and opportunities. Part of this preparation must include a full-scale program of restructuring the motivational conditions of Negroes, again especially Negro males. This attack must enlist the active leadership of Negroes themselves, with the financial and organizational support from public and private sources. Some Negro leaders have already taken the initiative in the formulation of part of the issue in these terms, notably Whitney Young, Jr., of the Urban League. Since he has professional background in the field of social work and community organization, this is to be expected. We must, however, persuade others that these considerations are involved in the economic problems of Negroes, not merely as effects but as causes.

In a 1963 study, in Philadelphia,[22] it was found that lower status Negro mothers had lower educational and job aspirations for their sons than did higher status Negro mothers; they were less certain about aspirations for their sons than for their daughters (which was not true of higher status mothers). Compared to higher status mothers, a much higher percentage of these mothers said that 21 years of age or under is the best age for their sons to marry and 19 years of age for their daughters. This finding is crucial because "if a mother holds high educational and occupational aspirations for her children and at the same time thinks they should marry young and have a large family, there is often, by implication, a contradiction in her aspirations." And the younger the age at marriage, the greater the chances for bearing more children. If one keeps in mind the high percentage of mother-dominated families (even in families where the father is present) in Negro urban lower income groups, these findings have a significant bear-

---

[21] For example, W. Mischel, "Father-Absence and Delay of Gratification," *Journal of Abnormal and Social Psychology*, Vol. 63 (1961), pp. 116–124; R. L. Nuttall, "Some Correlates of High Need for Achievement among Urban Northern Negroes," *Journal of Abnormal and Social Psychology*, Vol. 68 (1964), pp. 593–600.

[22] Robert R. Bell, "Lower Class Negro Mothers' Aspirations for their Children," *Social Forces*, May 1965, pp. 493–500.

ing on the occupational and employment progress of Negro males. Given the importance of the mother in Negro lower income urban families, her aspirations can adversely influence the future of her offspring — even in the face of rising job opportunities as a result of economic growth and fair employment legislation:

. . . the relative positions of Negro mothers in the lower class may be related to different aspirational values transmitted to their children, and may also contribute to a way of life which makes any alternative aspirational levels difficult for their children to internalize and possibly achieve.[23]

If such lower aspirations operate at the lower end of the lower income group's values system, the greater is the need for agencies and institutions to exercise a positive role in reshaping the goals of Negro youths who lack such motivation. The schools, training programs, the employment service, OEO, and other agencies in the community have much to do. If they fail, the less likely will it be that values conducive to occupational upgrading can be injected into the thinking and behavior of these groups of Negroes, especially the males. Negro adults must not be excluded from such attention, either.

Much of this reshaping must be carried out by the larger society, too. Once opportunities are available, the larger society and the government in general cannot simply stand aside and watch. What whites do in addition will also play a role in the motivational environment of Negroes. What motivation is there for a young Negro to graduate from high school when he sees that whites with high school diplomas earn one-third more than Negroes with similar schooling? How can a young Negro aspire to enter an apprenticeship program when he might be required to serve for four to seven years before he enjoys the fruits of such training? How can a young Negro adult with a family to support enter a training program, instead of taking a job as a laborer, for 16 to 52 weeks if the training allowance is less than the immediate income as a common laborer, and if the job for which he may be trained seems to be a dead-end one?

The responsibility for helping low-motivated Negroes to improve themselves lies partly in community institutions such as the schools. But the teachers are not yet equipped with the appropriate techniques to perform this task. Any program aimed at raising the motivations and aspirations of those Negro youths

[23] *Ibid.*, p. 500.

who are frustrated, and who often have ample reason for frustration, will in and of itself be a motivating factor in their lives. If someone pays attention to them and is sincerely concerned about their future, a large number of them will respond favorably. There is a great urgency for a vast program to train large numbers of Negro male "motivators" to serve in this role.[24]

[24] In this connection, David McClelland now believes that he and his associates at Harvard (Sterling Livingston, George Litwin, and others) have techniques for increasing the achievement motivation of individuals. His proposals deserve serious consideration by public and private agencies concerned with the issue of employment progress among Negroes. See "Achievement Motivation Can Be Developed," *Harvard Business Review,* November–December 1965.

15

The Response of the
White House Press and a Rejoinder

A. PRESIDENT TALKS FRANKLY TO NEGROES*

Mary McGrory

[Editors' note: from The Washington Star, June 6, 1965. See pages 133–135.]

President Johnson's speech to the graduating class of Howard University Friday was a dramatic departure, both in content and context.

He was the first President to speak on civil rights at a moment of calm in the racial turmoil of the past five years. He was the first President to ask the Negroes, with their legal rights all but won, to help find the remedy for their own social plight.

In the past, whites have been asked to give Negroes justice. At Howard, the President asked them to give understanding.

* Reprinted with permission of the author and *The Washington Star.*

369

Negroes generally hear exhortations for patience and understanding and promises of relief. President Johnson suggested that
the time had come for them to come to grips with their own worst
problem, "the breakdown of Negro family life."

The President initially turned down the invitation to speak at
Howard. Ten days ago, he decided it was an opportunity to strike
out in a new direction, to proclaim in Churchill's phrase, "the end
of the beginning."

The speech was cleared with Roy Wilkins, Executive Secretary
of the National Association for the Advancement of Colored
People, and with Dr. Martin Luther King, Jr., chairman of the
Southern Christian Leadership Conference. They were both in
enthusiastic accord.

Negro civil rights leaders have soft-pedaled the ills of the Negro
community — the statistics on crime and illegitimacy among nonwhites, which have given their foes the excuse to deny them their
rights. But with total legal victory at hand they have begun to
turn their attention to the core of the Johnson speech, the failure
of Negro family life.

Since last January, they have been suggesting that self-improvement may be the key to Negro self-esteem. Participants in the
civil rights demonstrations, which have produced a new breed of
Negro, were exhilarated by their achievements. But the feeling
did not trickle down to the illiterate jobless in the slums.

The NAACP began a series of "citizenship clinics," which were
aimed at pointing out the evils of anarchy in the home, and finding social uses for political agitators.

Fearful to Speak

Even James Farmer, the leader of CORE, has been brooding
about the necessity for efforts within the Negro community to
make life better. His associates say he has been prevented from
speaking out for fear that a call to improve Negro community life
might be misinterpreted as a slowdown to integration. In the past
Negroes who have advocated the "bootstrap" approach to Booker
T. Washington have run the risk of being called "Uncle Tom."

With the President's encouragement and approval, more
Negroes are expected to speak out on this hitherto most delicate
subject.

Johnson indicated that the effort will be as before, "black and
white together." He acknowledged white guilt in bringing about

the conditions which have demoralized the Negro and continued white involvement in seeking to better his lot.

But he is determined, aides say, that the unprecedented White House conference he has called for next fall will not turn into a seminar for reliving old woes and grievances or generate only new demands for help from the federal government.

Seeks Frank Discussion

In persuading the Negroes to talk frankly about their own troubles, he hopes they will find solutions of their own.

He seemed to be trying to set the tone and even provide the agenda. He said: "Less than half of all Negro children reach the age of 18 having lived all their lives with both parents . . . . Probably a majority of all Negro children receive federally-aided public assistance during their childhood."

The first southern President in a hundred years, in other words, told the Negroes that in compassion and concern he would not be outdone. Now to be constructive, he must have their help. It was an authentic new note.

B. DRIVE FOR NEGRO FAMILY STABILITY SPURRED BY WHITE HOUSE*

John D. Pomfret

[Editors' note: from The New York Times, *July 19, 1965. See pages 137–138.]*

WASHINGTON, July 18 — A White House study group is laying the groundwork for a massive attempt to revive the structure of the Negro family.

This effort, in the view of those working on the problem, is the key to the next phase in the achievement of Negro equality —a phase, they hope, that will go far beyond merely establishing the legal rights of Negroes to make them genuinely accepted and equal members of the American community.

The study group is made up of about a dozen men. Some are on the White House staff, others work for Government agencies.

Their immediate aim is to plan for a White House conference in the fall, probably November, that will bring together scholars, experts, Negro leaders and Government officials to try to define the problems confronted by Negroes and suggest the broad outlines of solutions.

The conference was announced by President Johnson in a speech June 4 at Howard University. He declared that legal freedom and equality were "not enough" to guarantee Negroes their full share of American justice and plenty. A more profound stage of the battle for Negro rights is just beginning, he said, and the goal "is to give 20 million Negroes the same chance as every other American to learn and grow, to work and share in society, to develop their abilities — physical, mental and spiritual — and to pursue their individual happiness."

Family Plight Studied

One of the principal sources of Mr. Johnson's speech was an unpublished 78-page Government study analyzing the plight of the Negro family.

The study pulls together a variety of information from many sources and concludes that the United States is approaching a new crisis in race relations.

This, it says, is because the expectation of Negroes that equality of opportunity will yield roughly equal results as compared to other groups is not going to be fulfilled — and will not be fulfilled for a long time unless new and special efforts are made.

One reason, the study says, is that Negroes will encounter serious personal prejudice for at least another generation. Secondly, it says, "three centuries of sometimes unimaginable mistreatment have taken their toll on the Negro people."

"The harsh fact is that as a group, at the present time, in terms of ability to win out in the competitions of American life, they are not equal to most of those groups with which they will be competing," the study declares. "Individually, Negro Americans reach the highest peaks of achievement. But collectively, in the spectrum of American ethnic and religious and regional groups, where some get plenty and some get none, Negroes are among the weakest."

Situation Held Worsening

Furthermore, the study continues, the circumstances of the Negro American community in recent years have probably been getting worse, not better and the gap between the Negro and most other groups in American society is widening.

The study says that "the fundamental problem" is that of family structure.

"The evidence — not final, but powerfully persuasive — is that the Negro family in the urban ghettos is crumbling," it declares. "A middle-class group has managed to save itself, but for vast numbers of the unskilled, poorly educated city working class the fabric of conventional social relationships has all but disintegrated.

"There are indications that the situation may have been arrested in the past few years, but the general postwar trend is unmistakable. So long as this situation persists, the cycle of poverty and disadvantage will continue to repeat itself."

The study says that it is doubtful whether the establishment of equal rights and the kinds of general Government programs set up so far — manpower retraining and the antipoverty program, for example — will do much more than make opportunity available.

"They cannot insure the outcome," the study states. "The principal challenge of the next phase of the Negro revolution is to make certain that equality of results will now follow. If we do not, there will be no social peace in the United States for generations."

The study declares that the fundamental source of weakness of the Negro community is the deterioration of the Negro family. It recommends that establishment of a stable Negro family structure be made a national goal.

The study notes that the role of the family in shaping character and ability is so pervasive as to be easily overlooked.

"There is considerable evidence that the Negro community is in fact dividing between a stable middle-class group that is steadily growing stronger and more successful, and an increasingly disorganized and disadvantaged lower-class group," it says.

The study cites the following statistics to support its thesis:

Nearly a quarter of the Negro women living in cities who have ever married are divorced, separated or are living apart from their husbands. The percentage among white women is 7.9.

Between 1940 and 1963, the illegitimacy rate among Negroes rose from 16.8 to 23.6 per cent; for whites, from 2 to 3.07 per cent.

In 1940, both groups had a divorce rate of 2.2 per cent. By 1964, the white rate was 3.6 per cent, the Negro rate 5.1 per cent.

In 1950, 18 per cent of all Negro families and 9 per cent of all white families were headed by a female. In 1960, the percentage for white families was still 9 per cent but for Negro families had risen to 21 per cent.

Currently, 14 per cent of all Negro children are receiving aid to dependent children, compared to 2 per cent of white children. About 56 per cent of Negro children receive such assistance at some time, compared to 8 per cent of white children.

Until 1952 [sic], fluctuations in the number of Negro children receiving aid to dependent children paralleled the rise and fall in the unemployment rate for Negro men. Since then, the number of aid cases opened has been going up despite the fact that the unemployment rate has been going down.

Negroes, who accounted for 1 in 10 in the population in 1950, will account for 1 in 8 by 1970 if present population trends continue.

Meets with Experts

The study group has been meeting with distinguished psychologists and sociologists such as Talcott Parsons, Eric Erickson and Kenneth Clark to explore the dimensions of the problem. Later, it met with a number of economists and experts in other fields.

The group has not begun to work out firm proposals for legislation. Its members, however, have been devoting a good deal of time, for example, to the psychological impact on children of the lack of a strong father figure in many Negro families.

The question has been raised whether, through legislation and other means, steps cannot be taken to remedy this. One small step, some members of the group believe, would be to end the practice in some states of denying welfare aid to families with an able-bodied man in the house. This has the effect of forcing men to desert their families so the families can get public assistance.

The group is also exploring whether the traditional tools used to attack poverty can work for many Negroes. It is asking, for example, whether more education is the answer when children go from the classroom back into the slum and the broken home.

Members of the group are convinced that a broad consensus favoring establishment of basic legal rights for Negroes exists among white middle-class Americans.

They are not as certain that a similar consensus exists that it is necessary to go beyond this, so they are looking into steps that may be taken to increase public comprehension of the problem.

The process by which the Administration's proposals to aid the Negro community are being evolved is not the usual one. Ordinarily, legislative proposals are put forward by pressure groups and the Government acts as sort of a broker working out a politically feasible compromise between these groups.

In the present situation, the initiative so far has come largely from the Administration, which is convinced that the problem and the need for fast action are so great that it must take the lead.

C. INSIDE REPORT: THE MOYNIHAN REPORT*

Rowland Evans and Robert Novak

[Editors' note: Syndicated column of August 18, 1965. See pages 141–143.]

Weeks before tthe Negro ghetto of Los Angeles erupted in violence, intense debate over how to handle such racial powder kegs was under way deep inside the Johnson administration.

The pivot of this debate: The Moynihan Report, a much-suppressed, much-leaked Labor Department document which strips away usual equivocations and exposes the ugly truth about the big-city Negro's plight.

Some Administration officials view the report as a political atom bomb certain to produce unwanted fallout — mainly by bringing up the most taboo subject in civil rights: preferential treatment for Negroes.

But others (and they include key figures in the White House) feel that the Moynihan Report might open the door to new ideas and avert continuous guerrilla warfare in Negro ghettoes.

The report stems from the big city Negro riots last summer. That violence was deeply disturbing to Daniel P. (Pat) Moynihan,

* Reprinted with permission of the authors and The Publishers Newspaper Syndicate.

a liberal intellectual and politician who then was Assistant Secretary of Labor (he resigned last month to run for president of the New York City Council). Viewing the riots as seemingly unconnected parts of a revolution by the nation's most submerged class, Moynihan began probing unanswered questions.

He wondered, for instance, why in a time of decreasing unemployment, the plight of the urban Negro was getting worse — not better. His answer: a 78-page report (based largely on unexciting Census Bureau statistics) revealing the breakdown of the Negro family. He showed that broken homes, illegitimacy, and female-oriented homes were central to big-city Negro problems.

But when Moynihan wanted to release the report, he was stopped by his boss — Secretary of Labor Willard Wirtz. In private conversation, Wirtz expressed fear that evidence of Negro illegitimacy would be grist for racist propaganda mills. Beyond this, other officials believed Moynihan's report would stir up trouble by defining insoluble problems. As a result, the Labor Department never did release the report. But in Washington, what is suppressed almost always finds its way into print.

Thus, the Moynihan Report was raw material for an eloquent discussion of the Negro problems in Theodore White's *The Making of the President 1964*. It was the basis for a three-page spread in the Aug. 9 *Newsweek*. A UPI dispatch quoted liberally from it last weekend.

The most important "leak," however, went over Wirtz' head into the White House. Presidential advisers — particularly Bill D. Moyers, the chief policy factotum — were fascinated. This produced President Johnson's moving June 4 commencement address at Howard University here. Using the Moynihan Report as a source, the President for the first time discussed the degeneration of Negro family life and called a White House conference this fall to deal with it. Since then, sociologists, psychiatrists and Negro leaders have trooped in and out of the White House to prepare the conference.

These talks have confirmed that it's easier to define problems than solve them. They acknowledge the basic need for male-directed discipline in Negro ghettoes. But how to get it? Ideas range from the minimal (using men instead of women to deliver welfare checks) to the radical (lowering military requirements to get more Negro youths out of the ghetto and into the Army).

The heart of the problem is far tougher. Moynihan believes the public erroneously compares the Negro minority to the Jewish minority. When discriminatory bars were lowered, Jews were ready to move. But the implicit message of the Moynihan Report is that ending discrimination is not nearly enough for the Negro. But what is enough?

The phrase "preferential treatment" implies a solution far afield from the American dream. The white majority would never accept it and Administration officials keep their fingers crossed that the forthcoming White House conference won't even mention it.

Yet, the Moynihan Report inevitably leads to posing the question. Accordingly, the internal debate about how to deal with the report — and the problem — is infinitely more than a mere intrabureaucratic tiff. It may determine whether this country is doomed to succeeding summers of guerrilla warfare in our cities.

D. REPORT FOCUSES ON NEGRO FAMILY*

John Herbers

[Editors' note: From The New York Times, August 27, 1965. See pages 145–146.]

Aid to Replace Matriarchy Asked by Johnson Panel

WASHINGTON, Aug. 26 — A confidential report submitted to President Johnson last spring by a committee on civil rights has become one of the most widely discussed and quoted papers in Washington.

Still unpublished in its entirety and still officially confidential, the report has come in for new attention since the Los Angeles riots, for it pinpoints the causes of discontent in the Negro ghettos and says the new crisis in race relations is much more severe than is generally believed.

Entitled "The Negro Family — the Case for National Action," the 78-page report constitutes a devasting indictment of what white Americans have done to Negro Americans in 300 years of slavery, injustice and estrangement — the result of which is a "tangle of pathology" that will require a unified national effort to correct.

A leading role in compiling and writing the report was played by Daniel P. Moynihan, then Assistant Secretary of Labor for policy planning and research. Mr. Moynihan later resigned to become candidate for President of the New York City Council on the Democratic ticket of Paul R. Screvane.

The essence of the report, as published in the New York Times on July 19, is that deterioration of the Negro family has resulted in a deterioration in the fabric of Negro society. As a result, Negroes as a group are not able to compete on even terms in the United States. As a synthesis of the published works of a number of social scientists, reinforced by government statistics, the report contains little new information. It points out, however, that "probably no single fact of Negro American life is so little understood by whites" as the breakdown of the Negro family.

President Johnson has accepted the thesis of the report and is expected to make it the basis for White House conferences on civil rights next fall. In a speech at Howard University last June, the President said white Americans must accept the responsibility for the breakdown of the Negro family structure.

"It flows from centuries of oppression and persecution of the Negro man," Mr. Johnson said. "It flows from the long years of degradation and discrimination which have attacked his dignity and assaulted his ability to provide for his family."

The report was prepared by a committee appointed by the President to help chart the Government's course in race relations. The members came from several agencies of the Government.

"A national effort towards the problems of Negro Americans must be directed towards the question of family structure," the report said. "The object would be to strengthen the Negro family so as to enable it to raise and support its members as do other families."

Essentially what has happened, the report said, is that white Americans by means of slavery, humiliation and unemployment have so degraded the Negro male that most lower-class Negro families are headed by females.

"The very essence of the male animal from the bantam rooster to the four-star general is to strut," the authors said. "But, historically, the instincts of the American Negro male have been suppressed. Indeed, in the 19th century America, a particular type of exaggerated male boastfulness became almost a national style. Not for the Negro male. The 'sassy nigger' was lynched."

"In essence," the report continued, "the Negro community has been forced into a matriarchal structure which, because it is so out of line with the rest of American society, seriously retards the progress of the group as a whole, and imposes a crushing burden on the Negro male and, in consequence, on a great many Negro women as well."

Disintegration of the family, the report said, has been speeded by poverty, isolation and displacement of Negroes from southern farms into urban ghettoes of the north. The result has been a high rate of crime, delinquency, school dropouts and escape from reality.

E. FAMILY REPORT SPARKS DEBATE*

Jean M. White

[Editors' note: From The Washington Post, *November 17, 1965. See pages 254–255.]*

The subject of Negro "family breakdown" has proved to be a prickly issue even before today's opening of the planning session for the White House Conference on Civil Rights.

Ironically, the dissension stems from the so-called "Moynihan Report," said to have inspired the central theme of President Johnson's Howard University speech and its call for a White House conference.

The Moynihan Report traces many Negro problems back to a crumbling family structure that has resulted in an "emasculated" Negro male and a matriarchial society. The family breakdown is seen largely as a heritage of slavery.

This emphasis on family deterioration and the scars of slavery has been disquieting to many Negro leaders. Other participants have shared their fears that the conference would get sidetracked from hard-core problems if it centered on family breakdown, which some dispute anyway.

The agenda for the two-day planning session, opening today, has been broadened to include jobs, housing, health and welfare, and education among the eight study topics.

The session of "The Family: Resources of Change" will take off from a paper challenging the main thrust of the Moynihan report — that a splintering family is the root of many evils for Negroes.

The paper argues that it is more important to provide jobs than to worry about the strong male image which will take care of itself once Negro men can get better education, well-paying jobs, and provide for their families.

The discussion paper was written by Hylan G. Lewis, a Howard University sociologist. He cites evidence that income rather than color accounts for much of the instability of the Negro family.

Lewis argues that factors stemming from discrimination in housing, employment, health and education are to blame for much of the difference in family stability between whites and Negroes.

The Moynihan report — a study made by a group headed by Daniel P. Moynihan, then Assistant Secretary of Labor — described the Negro family as being in the "deepest trouble." It detailed figures that one fourth of Negro births are illegitimate, almost one-fourth of Negro families are headed by females, and that more than half of Negro children receive aid-to-dependent children assistance during their lives.

In rebuttal, Lewis notes that two-thirds of Negro families still include two parents and the female-headed family is in the minority.

He argues that many experts feel that the relatively frequent breakup of marriages among low-income Negroes can be traced to the jobless male, who is downgraded in his family, loses his self-esteem, and finally gives up the struggle to meet family responsibilities.

F. INSIDE REPORT: CIVIL RIGHTS DISASTER*

Rowland Evans and Robert Novak

[Editors' note: Syndicated column of November 24, 1965. See pages 256–257.]

Nothing in the glittering two-year history of President Johnson's Great Society has failed so dismally as his White House Conference on Civil Rights last week.

Top Administration officials had forebodings of disaster for months. That's one reason the conference was quietly changed to a "planning session" to prepare for a full conference next spring. But few were prepared for what happened at the Washington Hilton Hotel.

The main results were two-fold:

The gap between the civil rights movement and the Johnson administration is wider than ever.

A carefully planned effort to inject a new realism regarding the plight of the Northern Negro was a failure.

The reason: Shrill cries of Negro militants continued to drown out cautious attempts by more thoughtful Negro leaders to make a hard-headed appraisal of America's agonizing social problem. As a result, the country is farther than ever from even defining the boundaries of the problem.

The conference evolved last spring when the White House became engrossed in a confidential report on the deterioration of the Negro family prepared by then Assistant Secretary of Labor Daniel P. Moynihan. His report was the underpinning of an eloquent commencement address at Howard University by President Johnson, summoning the White House conference.

The President's goal was a bold one: to switch the civil rights dialogue from the easily understandable problem of dismantling Jim Crow in the South to the incomparably more difficult question of the Northern Negro ghetto. Thus, months of preparation went into researching the Negro male's loss of "manhood," the dominance of the Negro female, the breakdown of family life and the acceleration of illegitimate births.

But by the time of the Los Angeles riots in August, officials suspected Negro leaders were in no mood to discuss these realities. These suspicions were more than confirmed last week.

Sweeping the problems posed by the Moynihan report under the table, Negro leaders at the conference insisted that the Federal government and the Federal government alone could relieve the torment of the urban Negro.

In this spirit, ailing, aging Negro leader A. Philip Randolph called for a $100 billion Federal "freedom budget" to aid the Negro. The source of this plan: civil rights leader Bayard Rustin, who has never disguised his doctrinaire Socialist view that the root of the Negro's misery is the American economic system.

The implication of Rustin's freedom budget was spelled out at the White House conference by outspoken Floyd McKissick, of the Congress of Racial Equality, who insisted that to alleviate the Negro's plight, "the capitalistic system" must be changed.

And only thinly disguised was an unhealthy dose of Negro racism. Lawrence Landry, a Negro radical leader from Chicago, complained publicly that the conference was dominated by "whites and Jews."

All this was on the surface. Beneath the surface was disillusion-ment by those who had worked six months to prepare for two dismal days last week. One high policy maker in the Administra-tion grumbled bitterly that the Negro leadership knows only how to put its hand out to Uncle Sam. White intellectuals who had come to Washington to discuss Negro social disorganization were stunned by the demagoguery.

The question is why? Some disillusioned liberals hint darkly that radical white elements are at work, prodding Negroes to seek the unattainable (such as the $100 billion), thereby promoting racial discord.

Beyond this, the civil rights leadership simply cannot break the mold of its own doctrine. To examine critically the generations-old habits of the Northern Negro and seek self-improvement would be for them a return to the discredited "Uncle Tom" preachments of Booker T. Washington. Nor can even highly in-telligent leaders like Bayard Rustin free themselves from a doc-trinal belief in the class struggle.

Thus, what was boldly conceived at the White House as a fresh new look became a tired rehashing of old slogans. It will happen again at the full-dress conference unless the White House comes up with a new cast of characters willing to leave their dogmas at the door.

G. A FRUSTRATION ON RIGHTS*

John Herbers

[Editors' note: From The New York Times, November 25, 1965. See page 257.]

Parley Said to Displease White House; Subject of Families Rejected or Ignored

WASHINGTON, Nov. 24 — The Johnson Administration, hav-ing joined the civil rights movement, is learning something of its complexities and ambiguities.

The White House is said to be disappointed and somewhat bewildered at the outcome of its own conference on civil rights, held here last night. There were two general causes for displeasure. First, the conference members either rejected or ignored the subject of family stability as a starting point for bringing 12 million poor and isolated Negroes into the mainstream of American society.

Second, there was no consensus on the procedure that should be followed or explored for achieving this goal, but there was a torrent of criticism that the Administration had not done all it could to enforce civil rights laws.

Diverse Delegates

There was little reason to have expected a consensus on procedure. Delegates came from the cotton furrows of Mississippi, the slums of New York and the ivory towers of Harvard and Yale. Even among less diverse leaders and thinkers there has seldom been agreement on ways of obtaining Negro rights.

Virtually every local movement has been rent with dissension on the amount of militancy to be applied and on methods of moving against what is invariably called "the power structure."

To the White House the chief disappointment of last week's conference was that the need for family stability was dismissed virtually without debate and no other central issue agreed on.

Administration sources say the family approach as proposed by Daniel P. Moynihan, former Assistant Secretary of Labor, has been widely misunderstood.

In the first place, they point out, President Johnson is firmly committed to Negro equality. Behind this commitment is not only acknowledgement of ancient and glaring social injustices but an awareness that the racial situation bears seeds of distruction.

Where the President falls out with civil rights forces is in his unwillingness to move against public opinion. For instance, a member of the Administration told delegates to the conference that much more could have been done to speed school desegregation but that there was massive opposition against full integration, in the North and the South.

The bitterly attacked Moynihan report suggests that drastic remedies may be needed to break the cycle of poverty, broken homes and despair in which many Negroes are caught. The country must do more than provide equal opportunity, he said; it must insure "equality of results."

"If we do not," the report said, "there will be no social peace in the United States for generations."

Insuring equality of results has broad implications, and Mr. Moynihan pointed out that here is where middle-class support begins to dissipate. He provided an explanation of why self-help as used successfully by other minorities may not be possible in the Negro ghetto.

His explanation was that three centuries of oppression and injustice had created an unstable, matriarchial family structure that is not equipping its males to compete in the over-all American society.

Here, it was believed, was something white Americans could understand. Once having understood it they would be more willing to accept responsibility for the Negro's plight. Here was a means of extending new forms of assistance to the Negro without going against the majority opinion.

Many civil rights leaders, however, saw it differently. Although the Moynihan report emphasized that the Negro's problems were not racially inherent, these leaders felt that the report exaggerated Negro defects and would serve only to increase white opposition to integrated schools.

"Subtle Racism"

Writing in The Nation, William Ryan, a Harvard medical school psychologist, attacked Mr. Moynihan's scholarship and said the report "encourages a new form of subtle racism." One white civil rights leader said, "we need a new handle, a new approach, for attacking this problem, but obviously this isn't it."

Drastic remedies were suggested at the conference. A. Philip Randolph, the honorary chairman, proposed a $100 billion "freedom budget" to eradicate slums, over a period of years and provide employment.

There were several proposals for replacing welfare payments and their resultant unintended encouragement of broken homes, with a guaranteed income that "would not discourage work."

But there was no new "handle," no suggestion for winning the "understanding heart" that President Johnson has said is needed for Negroes to become first-class citizens.

The conference was billed as an idea generating session for a fuller conference next spring. Some of the ideas brought out will receive consideration. But mostly it's back to the drafting board for the White House.

H. A FAMILY POLICY FOR THE NATION*

Daniel Patrick Moynihan

[Editors' note: This article appeared in America magazine, September 18, 1966.]

Formulation of a national policy concerning the quality and stability of family life could be the cornerstone for a new era of U.S. social legislation. Former Assistant Secretary of Labor Moynihan's interpretation of current statistics on American families emphasizes the need for such a policy.

The United States is very possibly on the verge of adopting a national policy directed to the quality and stability of American family life. It would mean an extraordinary break with the past. This could be the central event of our new era of social legislation.

In the course of the past several months, in a series of specific events that mark the transition with a precision almost unknown to social history, the United States concluded one era of domestic politics and embarked upon another. Nearly a quarter century after the event, the legislative agenda of the New Deal was finally completed. The reason for the delay could not have been more simple: the New Deal lost its majority in Congress in 1938 and did not really get it back until 1965. But once it was back in power, as it were, bills were passed one-two-three-four; President Johnson, of course, was there to sign them. The Education and Medicare Acts were perhaps the most significant, but a host of measures accompanied them. At long last, the social insurance and public welfare proposals of the 1930's have become law.

In about this same period, less dramatically but more significantly, the other great objective of the New Deal has also been achieved: it is now fairly clear that the United States has at last learned how to make an industrial economy operate at a high

---

* Reprinted with permission from *America*, The National Catholic Weekly Review, 106 W. 56th Street, New York, New York 10019.

level of employment and a steadily rising level of production. The goals formally set forth in the Employment Act of 1946 are closer to reality today than at any time in history.

The components of this economic revolution have been so complex, and the results so persuasive, that it is easy to overlook it. The United States is now in the 53rd month of unbroken economic expansion—the longest and strongest in peacetime history. During this brief, fleeting period — not two thousand days, not nearly that — we have raised the level of Gross National Product by some $160 billion. In 1946, the year the Employment Act was passed, our total GNP after two centuries of growth and the enormous spurt of World War II was only $211 billion. In June of the present year, the number of industrial jobs surpassed the historic peak of November, 1943, and in July the unemployment rate for white workers dropped to the interim goal of 4 per cent.

All in all, it has been a magnificent achievement. As a result, the general quality and decency of life in the United States is incomparably greater than in years past, just as it is in almost all the industrial democracies that have been going through the same process as we.

On the other hand, there are two sets of problems very much before us. The first concerns that segment of our population whose lives have somehow not been touched by the general success — except to the extent they have fallen even farther behind the rest of the nation. The second concerns those problems brought on by success itself.

It is growth, not decline, that is turning America ugly: ride into town from any airport in the nation if you have doubts about it. It is a superabundance of goods and services and gadgets, rather than lack of them, that gives us the feeling of being hemmed in. (New York City, for example, is surrounded by water and covered by air, but somehow running out of both.)

Because it is entirely possible that many of the processes that are producing prosperity are also producing much of our poverty, it may be that both sets of problems are in fact part of a single phenomenon: the pathology of post-industrial society. It is to this continuum of issues that the next period of social policy-making in the United States must address itself.

One could hardly ask a more agreeable challenge. The resources available are unprecedented — the level of GNP is expected to rise by something like $235 billion in the next five years — and the receptivity to new ideas in Washington can hardly ever have been greater. Richard N. Goodwin, of the White House staff, spoke in a recent address of the challenge of a great society that "looks beyond the prospects of abundance to the problems of abundance" and to the reality that, for all our success, "we find discontent with what we have, dissatisfaction with the life we created, unhappiness and restlessness." The President has set moving a series of task forces pursuing just such issues.

In one sense, what is involved is a search for new definitions. It is here that the possibility of a national family policy most clearly emerges.

American social policy until now has been directed toward the individual. The individual — and the various circumstances relating to him — has been our primary unit of measurement: men, women and children are all lumped together. Thus, our employment statistics count as equally unemployed a father of nine children, a housewife coming back into the labor market in her forties, and a teen-ager looking for a part-time job after school. The minimum wage required by law to be paid to any of these persons is exactly the same. If they should somehow have the same level of earnings — which would be easy enough — and were to lose their jobs, the amount of unemployment insurance paid to each would be exactly the same. The examples are numerous; the point does not change. American arrangements pertain to the individual, and only in the rarest circumstances do they define the family as the relevant unit.

This is a pattern that is almost uniquely American. Most of the industrial democracies of the world have adopted a wide range of social programs designed specifically to support the stability and viability of the family. Except in the United States, family allowances are practically a hallmark of an advanced industrial society. In France, for example, a worker with a wife and three children, earning the average factory wage, receives about as much in family allowances as in his pay packet. Typically, the money is paid to the man, not the housewife.

It would be useful to learn more about the reasons for this situation. To state that it is in the tradition of American individualism does not explain the process, but simply restates it. I would venture that it has something to do with the extraordinarily diverse pattern of family systems in the United States, which results from the no less extraordinary pattern of immigration. About one-third of our population is descended from migrants from Great Britain and Northern Ireland. The rest come from all parts of the globe. With them they brought family structures ranging from the extremes of patriarchy to the outer reaches of matriarchy — combined with every known variant of stability and instability.

With such confusion, it was impossible to prescribe family programs that would meet the needs or desires of all groups, and all the more so since the Anglo-Saxon families were heavily concentrated in rural areas, which were opposed to all such measures on general conservative principles. (The problem is perhaps still reflected in our complex adoption procedures.)

One has the impression that a Catholic problem was also involved. Catholics made much of families, were said to have enormous ones, and — in a view that was and may still be widely held — could be counted on to compound the enormity if public funds began to subsidize "indiscriminate reproduction." And European bishops talking about *patrie, famille et travail* didn't help.

It is also quite possible that events of the New Deal era, until now the most creative period of modern American social policy, were much influenced by the anthropological orientation of American sociology at that time. Family structures could be vastly different, one from the other, but who was to say which was better or worse? They were simply different.

The sociologist Nathan Glazer has pointed out that this amiable tolerance began to break down during World War II. If the family structure of the European middle class produced personalities that were peculiarly susceptible to Fascist and Nazi ideologies, was that a matter of indifference to the world? Morever, when the colonial areas of the world began to achieve independence, the new rulers were often far less satisfied with the results of the traditional ways of life than the colonial administrators, who often carefully preserved them.

More recently, however, American social scientists have been revising their views. More and more the family is seen, as Glazer puts it, "as not only the product of social causes but as itself a significant and dynamic element in the creation of culture, social character and social structure."

As society, in the form of government, more and more acknowledges its responsibilities to the poor and disadvantaged, it follows that it must be concerned with family patterns that help or hinder efforts to bring people out of poverty and into the mainstream of American life.

The different effects of different patterns are also becoming more clear. Of the many peoples who have come to the United States, some have prospered much more than the general run, others much less. Without any question, family stability and values account for much of the difference. No people came to our shores poorer than did the Chinese and Japanese. Yet in terms of census data, they are today incomparably the highest social and economic group in the nation. Thus, twice as many Japanese and Chinese go to college as do Americans as a whole. American Jews as a group are probably even better off in socio-economic terms than the Chinese and Japanese, although the census does not classify persons by religious faith. (See Chart A.) And what have all three groups in common? A singularly stable, cohesive and enlightened family life.

It would be wrong to suggest that there is a very great deal of systematic knowledge on this subject. There is not. Typically, Catholic "teaching" abounds in moralisms about family values, but Catholic sociologists seem hardly to have touched on the question. Once again we find ourselves with a surplus of opinions, but few facts, on a subject of profound moral significance about which we should be helping to shape national policy.

Even so, general impressions surely cannot be far wrong: the stability and quality of family life are a prime determinant of individual and group achievement. This is not to argue for any one pattern — any more than to declare that there can be only

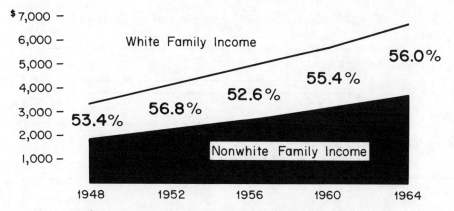

Chart A: Percent of Americans, 18 to 24, in college. According to an analysis of private surveys by Alfred Josep for B'nai B'rith, 70 to 80 per cent of college age Jews are enrolled in college.

one form of achievement. But what evidence we do have argues that social conditions ought to enable the general run of families to succeed in whatever arrangements fit their fancy. American social policy, however, ignores the question altogether: the individual rather than the family is the object of concern.

The shortcomings of this approach are beginning to be manifest. For several reasons, they have become most clear with regard to the problems of Negro Americans. This being the most pressing and grave social problem facing the American people today, it has begun — only just begun — to attract a degree of serious inquiry. Invariably, the problem of family life emerges as one of the most deep-rooted of Negro problems. Because census data distinguish between white and nonwhite families, it is possible to trace the experience of the Negro family over the past several decades and to see the effect of various economic and social developments on a group of persons of whom a high proportion live in or near to poverty. (See Chart B.) It is almost certain that many or most of the same effects would be found to occur among white families in similar circumstances, but the experience of poor whites is concealed in the affluent mass.

Our experience of unemployment in the postwar period gives perhaps the best example of how our traditional way of looking at events from the point of view of the individual has concealed many of the most important things we ought to have known. For a quarter century, the nation has been keeping ever more detailed and accurate accounts of the number of persons working and not

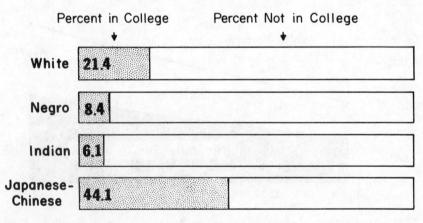

Chart B: Non-white income as percent of white income. Non-white family income fails to increase in proportion to white income.

working. For most of this period, we have had a relatively high level of unemployment. And throughout there has been a disastrous unemployment level for Negroes. It has been universally agreed that this is a bad thing. All administrations have deplored it. It has been generally depicted, however, as a bad thing for the individuals involved. Not until President Johnson rose to deliver his historic address at Howard University last June has anyone in high office in the United States even suggested that it was a catastrophe for the *families* involved.

The main outlines of the President's speech are well known to the nation. Despite spectacular progress in some areas of the Negro community, for the great majority of Negro Americans, "the poor, the unemployed, the uprooted and the dispossessed," he reminded us, ". . . the walls are rising and the gulf is widening." "Only a minority — less than half — of all Negro children," the President reported, "reach the age of 18 having lived all their lives with both of their parents." He added: "Probably a majority of all Negro children receive Federal public assistance sometime during their life."

Behind the President's speech was a body of data that reveals how the persistent, savage unemployment of the Negro male worker had contributed to this breakdown. I should not think there is another nation in the free world in which anything comparable could have occurred without the fullest national awareness and outcry. President Johnson spoke to a nation that seemed almost never to have heard of the idea — save for the leaders of the Negro community, who hailed his forthrightness and courage, and in doing so revealed not a little of their own.

The absurdities of our exclusively individual-oriented approach are also becoming clear. The most striking example is our experience with the Aid to Families of Dependent Children program. This New Deal measure, part of the Social Security Act, was primarily designed to provide income for families in which the father had died or become permanently disabled. But families in which the father was simply absent — having deserted or whatever — were also included. By 1940, there were a quarter of a million children in this latter group of families — some 30 per cent of all AFDC children. Today this figure has grown to almost 2 million children: two-thirds of the total.

In New York State, the average number of persons receiving AFDC payments rose from 177,889 in 1954 to 497,038 in 1964 — nearly three times as many. Two-thirds of the children are Negro or Puerto Rican; two-thirds of all fathers are absent from the home.

In New York City, the average number of children per AFDC case rose from 2.2 in 1950 to 3.1 in 1963.

What the AFDC program has amounted to for most of its history is a family allowance program for *broken* families. Each family is given a sum of money according to its needs, as measured by its size. But only *after* the family breaks up. (Since 1961, unemployed men can receive AFDC payments, but these are still fewer than 10 per cent of the cases.)

I venture to say that in Canada — not to mention Britain or France — such an arrangement would be viewed as a form of social insanity.

Typically, such imbalance in social values produces further contortions. Project Headstart, a program in the war on poverty, is one of the most imaginative and promising efforts to bring hope to slum children that we have seen in this generation. Even so, it must be stated that we are paying women — well-qualified, professional women to be sure — up to $9.20 an hour to look after the children of men who can't make $1.50. If the working class fathers of the city earned a steady $3.00 or $4.00 an hour, would we need a Project Headstart? Clearly we need one today, but are we going to change the system that produced the need, or merely cope with it as in the AFDC program?

The urgency of this question is compounded by a special fact of demography: as perhaps never in history, while the rich of America do whatever it is they do, the poor are begetting children. Again, the statistics about Negro Americans, because they are separated out and contain so large a proportion of poor persons, give a clue. In 1960, 1 person in 10 in the United States was nonwhite. Today it is 1 in 9. By the end of the decade, it will be 1 in 8. Of persons under fourteen today, it is 1 in 7. Of persons under the age of one, it is 1 in 6.

Given the opportunity for a stable family life, with all that this means in the way of family income, family housing and family services, there is no reason for anything but rejoicing at the prospect of an increasing number of Americans not utterly bound to middle class rigidities. But given the course of events that we have pursued until very recently — the policy of paying little or no attention to any such question — one could grow profoundly alarmed. From the wild Irish slums of the 19th-century Eastern seaboard, to the riot-torn suburbs of Los Angeles, there is one unmistakable lesson in American history: a community that allows a large number of young men to grow up in broken families, dominated by women, never acquiring any stable relationship to male authority, never acquiring any set of rational expectations about the future — that community asks for and gets chaos. Crime, violence, unrest, disorder — most particularly the furious, unrestrained lashing out at the whole social structure — that is not only to be expected; it is very near to inevitable. And it is richly deserved.

Although the Labor Department's report on August unemployment shows that the Negro jobless rate fell fairly sharply to 7.6 per cent of the Negro labor force, still the unemployment rate among adult Negro males remains deplorably high. It remains about twice that of whites. These are the very men we are expecting to rear stable, orderly, well-behaved children, and to do so in what is just about the worst urban housing in the Western world.

We are expecting the impossible, and will end up with an impossible situation unless we seriously and promptly address ourselves to the issue of what it takes for a working man to raise a family in an American city today, and then see to it that what it takes is available. What this comes to is a national family policy.

In itself, a national family policy need not be any more complex than were the provisions of the Employment Act of 1946. The point is not what answers are provided, but what questions are posed. The Employment Act said nothing about how to achieve the fullest measure of employment, but rather declared that the national government should be continually concerned with just that question, and should be constantly seeking answers.

A national family policy need only declare that it is the policy of the American government to promote the stability and well-being of the American family; that the social programs of the Federal government will be formulated and administered with this object in mind; and finally that the President, or some person designated by him, perhaps the Secretary of Health, Education and Welfare, will report to the Congress on the condition of the American family in all its many facets — not of *the* American family, for there is as yet no such thing, but rather of the great range of American families in terms of regions, national origins and economic status.

Taxation is a good example of an area of government policy in which a general pronouncement would have considerable specific relevance. General impressions to the contrary, during the postwar period indirect taxes, which bear heaviest on the families of the poor, have been *rising* as a proportion of all tax receipts. The "value" of the income tax exemption for wives and children has steadily eroded since its present level was set in 1948. Recent tax cuts certainly have not improved, and may have further worsened the relative tax burden of poor families. All these imbalances could easily be righted, however, if the tax reductions of the coming five years or so are deliberately designed to do so. The tax cuts are coming: a national family policy would help shape them in a direction they might not otherwise assume.

Whatever the specific form a national family policy might take, it is clear that President Johnson raised just such large possibilities in his Howard University speech. "The family," he said, "is the cornerstone of our society. More than any other force, it shapes the attitude, the hopes, the ambitions and the values of the child. When the family collapses, it is the children that are usually damaged. When it happens on a massive scale, the community itself is crippled."

As we enter a new era of social policy, the opportunity to overcome the one great shortcoming of the past is almost in our grasp.

16

Reaction of Civil Rights Leaders

A. NEW TRENDS IN CIVIL RIGHTS*

Benjamin F. Payton

[Editors' note: This is the second of two articles on the Moynihan Report by Dr. Payton, Director of the Office of Church and Race of the Protestant Council of the City of New York, who formerly taught at Howard University. The earlier article is unpublished, although it was distributed to the press and several hundred social scientists, civil rights and political executives in early October, 1965, and was by far the most influential of the two articles in the development of the controversy. We regret that it was not possible to obtain permission to reprint the earlier article in this volume. The two articles are discussed in detail on pages 233–244.]

An unusual kind of perplexity and frustration seems to have settled recently over segments of the civil rights movement. The phrase "an unusual kind" is used deliberately, for bewilderment

* Reprinted with permission of the author and *Christianity and Crisis*.

and even failure have never been strangers to the leaders and participants of a movement that for decades skirted along the edges of political ostracism and social obloquy.

The peculiar character of the present quandary seems to be related to the very success of the movement in dealing with past frustrations; in overcoming the reluctance of Chief Executives to act on its behalf; in persuading the Supreme Court to protect its constitutional prerogatives; in prodding a fearful Congress to institute new laws to safeguard its constituents; and finally in shaming church and synagogue into affirming the moral majesty of its cause, in deed as well as in word, with bodies as well as with testaments.

Presently there are at least two schools of thought on how this perplexity can be explained. The first assumes that in the process of undoing the above-mentioned frustrations the major obstacles to the elimination of discrimination were also eradicated. It then goes on to view the present situation as a stage "beyond discrimination." According to this view, the trouble with the civil rights movement is that it does not understand that the central issue is no longer achieving "equality of opportunity" but is instead a matter of achieving "equal results." Because the debilitating conditions of slavery and the ensuing generations of deprivation have quite effectively disorganized the institutional structure of the Negro community, the power to reach the goal of "equal results" cannot be mobilized by Negro initiative in a relationship of equality with other groups. "Cultural deprivation" within the Negro community must, therefore, be overcome in order that "the newcomers" will be adequately socialized in the proper use of power.

In this view the next steps must be taken within the context of the Negro community itself by persons more qualified than Negroes to take them. The civil rights movement can form a sometimes useful adjunct to such efforts.

The second school of thought insists that America is far from reaching a "post-discrimination" stage. It holds that much of the bewilderment in the movement is a product of the rapid entrenchment of the "how-successful-we-have-been" view, particularly as expressed in the minds of persons who claim to be friendly to the movement. Exponents of this view insist that the undoing of *past* frustrations to the achievement of racial justice merely uncovered deeper resistances that continue in complex and often devious ways from the present into the future.

This school also believes that theories of "cultural deprivation," oddly tied to a goal more impossible than "equal opportunity," are but new masks for the old face of prejudice, new rationalizations for a persistent refusal to share power and position more equally with Negroes. Just as the next stage in the struggle may not be a battle strictly for *civil* rights, so the subject of the struggle is not only the underdevelopment of the Negro community but also the immaturity of the larger society, particularly its urban areas.

We will discuss the issues here under three headings: (1) "Equality," the Problem of Definition; (2) "Negro Family Stability" and the Problem of Power; and (3) "Metropolis" and the Problem of Context. Because of its immediacy and relevance, the report prepared early this year by the U.S. Department of Labor under the title *The Negro Family: The Case for National Action* will help shape the discussion. Written by Daniel P. Moynihan and Paul Barton when the former was Assistant Secretary of Labor, the document has come to be known as the "Moynihan Report."

"Equality," the Problem of Definition

According to some observers, the civil rights movement has pushed a new definition of "equality" to the fore of American politics. While the term tends to mean "equality of opportunity" in the minds of most white people, the report says that it "now has a different meaning for Negroes. . . . It is not (or at least no longer) a demand for liberty alone, but also for equality — in terms of group results. . . . It is increasingly demanded that the distribution of success and failure within one group be roughly comparable to that within other groups. It is not enough that all individuals start out on even terms, if the members of one group almost invariably end up well to the fore, and those of another far to the rear" (p. 3).

Now "equality" is the regulative principle for the whole notion of social justice. If this transformation from equality of opportunity to equality of group results has indeed occurred, then a major change in the meaning of an important moral concept has taken place, producing as it were an ideological chasm of vast proportions between Negroes and whites. For a real conflict between the ways in which Negroes and whites understand "equality" would further exacerbate relations between the two groups and make future agreements on the nature of the moral issue all but impossible. Since the evidence brought forth to support the point is so sketchy — two quotes, one from a sociologist and another from Bayard Rustin — one may be permitted the luxury of doubting the validity of the assertion.

In the event that Mr. Moynihan is proved correct, the problem ceases to be empirical and becomes a philosophical one. Is any group, whether white or Negro, morally justified in demanding "equal rights"? Can any group or person legitimately claim more than an "equal chance" to receive life's goods and services? I think not. The problem is that the "Moynihan Report" is not thoughtful enough about the nature of and the relationship between the moral concepts it uses.

A more assiduous process of concept-clarification would show that if the meaning of "equality of opportunity" has changed, it has become not a demand for "equal results" but a claim for intergroup relationships in which *equal chances* to achieve are a social reality and not just a legal theory. As R. H. Tawney has observed, authentic equality of opportunity "obtains insofar as . . . each member of a community, whatever his birth or occupation or social position, possesses in fact, and not merely in form, equal chances of using to the full his natural endowments of physique, of character and of intelligence." By imputing to Negroes the belief that "it is not enough that all individuals start out on even terms," the "Moynihan Report" assumes that Negroes do in fact enjoy equal life chances, but that for reasons rooted in historic past discriminations, the Negro community has been so traumatized that equal life chances are not enough.

Actually, of course, this point of view unintentionally falsifies the ethical problem and renders even more impossible the critical political problem. The goal of the civil rights movement is in the succinct title of Whitney Young's book, *To Be Equal*. But, as he says therein, "our basic definition of equal opportunity must include recognition of the need for special effort to overcome serious disabilities. . . ." Nevertheless, the claim for a "special effort" in behalf of the Negro is not a demand for equal results — an awkward and impossible goal. It is, again in Mr. Young's words, a demand "to provide the Negro citizen with the leadership, education, jobs, motivation, and opportunities that will permit him to help himself. It is not a plea to exempt him from the independence and initiative demanded by our free society. Just the opposite. It is a program crafted to transform the dependent man into the independent man."

The problem, therefore, is discrimination — in the present as well as in the past — not the failure to produce equal results under the assumed conditions of real equality of opportunity. A "special effort" is required precisely in order to produce equal life chances.

The Negro Family and the Problem of Power

The most serious mistakes of the "Moynihan Report" occur in the course of its analysis of the Negro family as "the fundamental source of the weakness of the Negro community at the present time." (p. 5) While acknowledging a relationship between the rate of unemployment and family stability, the burden of the report seeks to demonstrate that in 1960 "for the first time unemployment declined but the number of new Aid to Families with Dependent Children cases rose. In 1963 this happened a second time. In 1964 a third." Therefore, he arrives at "one central conclusion," namely that "the present tangle of pathology is capable of perpetuating itself without assistance from the white world." The point being that whereas under ordinary circumstances improvement in the broader socio-economic structures would produce positive changes in family life, the "tangle of pathology" in which the Negro family is involved prevents this from happening. Therefore, the report concludes, "a national effort toward the problems of Negro Americans must be directed toward the question of family structure" (p. 47).

It should be said that the errors of the report are not rooted in any racial hostility on the part of its authors. Nevertheless, these errors have already produced quite damaging political consequences. They have led to facile "explanations" of the urban riots of 1964–65, and continue — clearly contrary to the intention of its authors — to provide ammunition to those who would deny to Negro citizens real equality of opportunity. (Southern newspapers have lifted large segments from the report and printed them.) Political consequences aside, the more important question relates to the validity of the report itself as a scientific piece of work. On this point some very glaring errors must be noted.

First, the report is much more optimistic about the employment situation among Negroes than are other observers. The crucial factor is income level, which Herman Miller, one of our most competent authorities on income statistics, believes is actually worsening rather than getting better among Negroes relative to whites.

Second, the method of analyzing family data by color instead of by income level results in an alarmist picture of differences between white and Negro family structures. Other more careful studies by Hylan Lewis at Howard University allow for income differential and reach much more sober conclusions.

Third, the analysis of illegitimacy rates among Negroes fails to analyze; it would have reached different conclusions if, rather than producing statistics without interpretation, it had taken into account these considerations: (1) the differential circumstances under which Negroes and whites report illegitimate births — the former mainly in *public* hospitals, the latter mainly in *private* hospitals where concealment is much easier; [2] the approximately 2 million abortions that are performed each year in the United States, 95–99 per cent of them on white women; [3] unequal access to contraceptive devices and information; and [4] differential rates of adoption of Negro and white illegitimate children. Analysis of data by these factors reduces considerably the difference and removes entirely the alarmist overtones of the relationship between white and Negro family structures.

More important, careful analysis would show that however pathological or disorganized the Negro community might be, the student movement, the continued power of the Negro church and the tremendous "coping skills" generated by the Negro family itself are but a few of the factors that demonstrate the community's great reserves of untapped power and health. If these were harnessed under Negro leadership but with larger and more relevant national resources and co-operation, the remaining gap between Negroes and whites — a gap caused by continuing forms of discrimination — can be rapidly closed. If the focal point of the effort to mobilize our larger resources is not the Negro family, then neither is the main context the Negro community: it is, rather, Metropolis — its incoherences, its scarcities and its continuing discriminations.

Metropolis and the Problem of Context

In a University of Michigan commencement address, President Johnson summarized the goals of his Administration in his concept of the Great Society. Whatever else the term may mean, *sociologically* it refers to those broad changes under way in modern life that — initiated by large-scale industrial and technological innovations, sustained by the migration of masses of people from different backgrounds into urban areas and, more recently, out again into the suburbs — have transformed the relationships of small community life. In the process, they have complicated interminably the problem of ordering society in terms of such concepts as "justice" and "the common good."

The root problem is not, therefore, Negro "family breakdown" rooted in past injustices but "urbanization," its conflicts, inadequate resources and injustices. Urbanization raises the problem of civil rights to a new level, for it "means the creation of multi-ethnic metropolises." [Matthew Holden, Jr., *The Journal of Politics,* Vol. 26, No. 3, Aug. 1964, p. 637.] The problem that is really basic not only to the well-being of Negro citizens but to the health and security of the body politic is that "many central cities of the great metropolitan areas of the United States are fast becoming lower-class, largely Negro slums." The civil rights movement has forced us all to confront the fact that we must view not only the rural deltas of Mississippi but "the metropolitan area as a racial problem." (Morton Grodzins in *American Race Relations Today,* Raab, Ed., Doubleday Anchor Book, p. 85.)

I have called the key problems raised acutely in this context "scarcity" and "discrimination." More accurately, they are abundant resources *scarcely used* and discrimination in Metropolis. Much of the bewilderment in the civil rights movement is rooted in the perception that even some friends find it impossible to see the issue this way.

But the facts show rather clearly that America is approaching a critical watershed in dealing with the civil rights issue. Welfare doles and social tinkering simply will not meet the crying, desperate needs heralded by the civil rights movement. A bold and imaginative statement of priorities needs to be set before the Federal Government, with a price tag attached. For municipal and state and private budgets simply do not have the resources to meet the developing crisis. The Federal Government must, therefore, make a bold entry into the whole arena of "metro-politics."

To this end, and with a view to affecting the agenda of the spring White House Conference on Civil Rights, the Office of Church and Race of the Protestant Council of the City of New York, with the cooperation of the Commission on Religion and Race of the National Council of Churches, has initiated a call for

"An Economic Development Budget for Equal Rights." With the assistance of social scientists from metropolitan New York universities, research has already been done on the basis of which an estimate of $32 billion per annum is seen as needed for housing and slum rehabilitation, education, job-training and job-creation programs, health and medical facilities. We will soon prepare a budget for the metropolitan area of New York, and we hope that social scientists and churchmen in other metropolitan areas will do the same thing.

This kind of program is designed to aid not only Negroes but all of the disinherited who have been robbed of their birthright of freedom and equal opportunity. Pushing for such a program is the next and more profound stage of the struggle for equal rights.

B. AN ADDRESS BY DR. MARTIN LUTHER KING, JR.*

[Editors' note: This address was delivered at Abbott House, Westchester County, New York on October 29, 1965. Dr. King has made essentially the same observations about the Negro family and civil rights on several subsequent occasions; for example, at the University of Chicago on January 27, 1966. See page 402.]

I have been asked to speak tonight on the subject of the dignity of family life. It is appropriate that a Negro discuss the subject because for no other group in American life is the matter of family life more important than to the Negro. Our very survival is bound up in it. It is a particular privilege to speak under the auspices of the Abbott House because they are combining the treatment of symptoms with a probing of causes. Their experimental work to discover new aspects of the dynamics of family relationships is fresh and creative.

For a number of years a good many writers have tartly denigrated the role of the family. Some have asserted the family will disappear in 50 years: others have argued its preservation is hopeless because sex is now used for recreation rather than procreation. One writer summed up the prevailing contemptuous attitude with the statement that "Family life is obviously a study in lunacy."

Some 30 years ago Malinowski refuted these pessimistic and negative appraisals with the striking statement, "The family, that is, the group consisting of mother, father and child, still remains the main educational agency of mankind. Modern psychologists agree that parenthood as the dominant influence of infancy forms the character of the individual and at the same time shapes his social attitudes and thus places its imprint upon the constitution of the whole society."

In more recent years the writings of Dr. Benjamin Spock have not only reinforced these views but extended them through popular media to hundreds of millions around the world.

I endorse these conclusions and would emphasize one in particular. Family life not only educates in general but its quality ultimately determines the individual's capacity to love. The institution of the family is decisive in determining not only if a person has the capacity to love another individual but in the larger social sense whether he is capable of loving his fellow men collectively. The whole of society rests on this foundation for stability, understanding and social peace.

At this point in history I am particularly concerned with the Negro family. In recent years the Negro as an individual and Negroes as a community have been thrust into public attention. The dignity and personality of the Negro as an individual has been dramatized by turbulent struggles for civil rights. Conditions of Negro communities have been revealed by the turmoil engulfing northern ghettos and southern segregated communities. But the Negro family as an institution has been obscured and its special problems little comprehended.

A recent study offers the alarming conclusion that the Negro family in the urban ghettos is crumbling and disintegrating. It suggests that the progress in civil rights can be negated by the dissolving of family structure and therefore social justice and tranquility can be delayed for generations. The statistics are alarming. They show that in urban cities nearly 25% of Negro women, who were married, are divorced, in constrast to a rate of 8% among whites. The rate of illegitimacy in the past twenty years rose slightly more for whites than Negroes, but the number of Negro illegitimacies in proportion to its population is substantially higher than whites. The number of Negro families headed

by woman is 2½ times that of whites and as a consequence 14%
of all Negro children receive aid to dependent children and 56%
of Negro children at some point in their lives have been recipients of public aid.

As public awareness increases there will be dangers and opportunities. The opportunity will be to deal fully rather than haphazardly with the problem as a whole — to see it as a social
catastrophe and meet it as other disasters are met with an adequacy of resources. The danger will be that the problems will
be attributed to innate Negro weaknesses and used to justify
neglect and rationalize oppression.

We must therefore, learn something about the special origins
of the Negro family. If we would understand why Negroes could
embrace non-violent protest in the South and make historic progress there while at the same time most northern ghettos seethe
with anger and barely restrained fury we will have to know
some lessons of history. The flames of Watts have illuminated
more than the western skies — they lit up the agony of the
ghetto and revealed that hopeless Negroes in the grip of rage
will hurt themselves to hurt others in a desperate quest for
justice.

The Negro family for three hundred years has been on the
tracks of the racing locomotives of American history and was
dragged along mangled and crippled. Pettigrew has pointed out
that American slavery is distinguished from all other forms because it consciously dehumanized the Negro. In other cultures
slaves preserved dignity and a measure of personality and family
life. Our institution of slavery began on the coasts of Africa
and because the middle passage was long and expensive, African
families were torn apart in the selective process as if the members
were beasts. On the voyages millions died in holds into which
blacks were packed spoon fashion to live on a journey often of
2 to 6 months with approximately the room for each equivalent
to a coffin. The sheer physical torture was sufficient to murder
millions of men, women and children. But even more incalculable
was the psychological damage. For those who survived as a
family group, once more on the auction block many families
were ripped apart.

Against this ghastly background the Negro family began the
process of organization in the United States. On the plantation
the institution of legal marriage did not exist. The masters might
direct mating or if they did not intervene marriage occured with-

out sanctions. There were polygamous relationships, fragile, monogamous relationships, illegitimacies, abandonment, and most of all, the tearing apart of families as children, husbands, or wives were sold to other plantations. But these cruel conditions were not yet the whole story. Masters and their sons used Negro women to satisfy their spontaneous lust or, when a more humane attitude prevailed, as concubines. The depth was reached in certain states, notably Virginia which we sentimentally call the state of presidents. In this state, slaves were bred for sale, not casually or incidentally, but in a vast breeding program which produced enormous wealth for slave owners. This breeding program was the economic answer to the halting of the slave traffic early in the 19th century.

Through the ante-bellum era, the Negro family struggled against these odds to survive, and miraculously many did. In all this psychological and physical horror many slaves managed to hold on to their children and developed warmth and affection and family loyalties against the smashing tides of emotional corruption and destruction.

The liberation from slavery which should have initiated a birth of stable family life meant a formal legal freedom but as Henrietta Buckmaster put it, "with Appomatox, four million black people in the South owned their skins and nothing more."

Government policy was so conflicted and disinterested that a new inferno engulfed the Negro and his family. Thrown off the plantations, penniless, homeless, still largely in the territory of their enemies and in the grip of fear, bewilderment and aimlessness, hundreds of thousands became wanderers. For security they fled to Union army camps, themselves unprepared to help. One writer describes a mother carrying a child in one arm, a father holding another child and eight other children with their hands tied to one rope held by the mother, who struggled after Sherman's army and brought them hundreds of miles to safety. All were not so fortunate. In the starvation-induced madness some Negroes killed their children to free them of their misery.

These are historical facts. If they cause the mind to reel with horror it is still necessary to realize this recital is a tiny glimpse of the reality of the era. And it does justice neither to the enormous extent of the tragedy nor can it adequately describe the degree of human suffering and sorrow. The enormity of the tragedy utterly defies any attempt to portray it in terms the human mind can comprehend.

Following this period millions were returned to a legal form of slavery, once again imprisoned on plantations devoid of human rights and plunged into searing poverty generation after generation.

Some families found their way to the North in a movement Frazier aptly describes as "into the city of destruction."

Illiterate, undisciplined, afraid, and crushed by want, they were herded into slums. City life then, as now for migrant groups, has been ruinous for peasant people. The bewilderment of the complex city undermined the confidence of fathers and mothers, causing them to lose control of their children whose bewilderment was even more acute. Once more the Negro's problem had two, rather than one cutting edge. Because the institution of marriage was not legal under slavery, and with indiscriminate sex relations often with masters, mothers could identify their children but frequently not their fathers; hence a matriarchy developed. After slavery it did not die out because in the cities there was more employment for women than for men. Though both were unskilled, the women could be used in domestic service at low wages. The woman became the support of the household, and the matriarchy was reinforced.

The Negro male existed in a larger society which was patriarchal while he was the subordinate in a matriarchy.

The quest of males for employment was always frustrating. If he lacked skill he was only occasionally wanted because such employment had little regularity and even less remuneration. If he had a skill, he also had his black skin, and discrimination locked doors against him. In the competition for scarce jobs, he was a loser because he was born that way.

The rage and torment of the Negro male was frequently turned inward because if it gained outward expression its consequences would have been fatal. He became resigned to hopelessness, and he communicated this to his children. Some, unable to contain the emotional storms, struck out at those who would be less likely to destroy them. He beat his wife and his children in order to protest a social injustice, and the tragedy was that none of them understood why the violence exploded.

Even had the Negro family been assured of adequate food on the table, it would still be insufficient to secure a constructive life for the children. In all cities they are herded through grades of schooling without learning. Their after-school life is spent in neglected filthy streets which abound in open crime. Most white people are ignorant of the extent to which crime surrounds the Negro in the ghettos, or the degree to which it is organized and cultivated there by crime syndicates. Numbers, prostitution and narcotics rackets pervade the ghettos and because they are white-owned enterprises they drain staggering economic wealth out of the community, leaving a wealth of misery and corruption behind. Even when he and his family resist its corruption, its presence is a source of fear and of moral debilitation. For many Negro children, the care and protection of a mother is unknown because she is busy caring for a white child in order to earn the money to keep her disintegrating family together. Dick Gregory, telling of his youth, describes how his mother stole food from her employer to keep the family adequately fed. When she called her children to the table to bless the food, he responded with the sardonic, poignant humor for which he is now so well-known by saying, "You come down to the basement and bless what I stole and I'll bless what you stole."

The shattering blows on the Negro family have made it fragile, deprived and often psychopathic. This is tragic because nothing is so much needed as a secure family life for a people seeking to pull themselves out of poverty and backwardness. History continues to mock the Negro because even as he needs greater family integrity because he had so little in his heritage, in the larger American society today severe strains are assailing white family life. Delinquency is not confined to the underprivileged — it is rampant among middle and upper social strata, and more than one observer argues that juvenile delinquency is a product of widespread adult delinquency. In short, the larger society is not at this time a constructive educational force for the Negro.

The dark side of the picture appears almost to make the future bleak, if not hopeless. Yet something says this is not true. Back two hundred years on the coasts of Africa mothers fought fiendish slave traders to save their children. They offered their bodies to slavers if they would leave the children behind. On some slave ships that are known, and many that will never be known, manacled Negroes crawled from the holds and fought unarmed against guns and knives. On slave plantations parents fought, stole, sacrificed and died for their families. After liberation countless mothers wandered over roadless states looking for the children who had been taken from them and sold. And finally in the modern era mothers, fathers and their children have marched together against clubs, guns, cattle prods and mobs, not for conquest but only to be allowed to live as humans. The Negro was crushed, battered and brutalized, but he never gave up. He proves again life is stronger than death. The Negro family is scarred, it is submerged, but it struggles to survive. It is working against greater odds than perhaps any other family experienced in all civilized history. But it is winning. Step by step in agony it moves forward. Superficial people may superciliously expect it to function with all the graces and facility of more advantaged families. Their unfeeling criticism may hurt, but it will not halt progress. If the Negro is called upon to do the impossible, he may fail in the eyes of those ignorant of his tortured history, but in his own eyes the Negro knows he is imperceptibly accumulating the resources to emerge fully as a total human being. In the past ten years, he has learned how to win battles against vicious adversaries. In the process he has learned also how to win battles with himself. No one in all history had to fight against so many physical and psychological horrors to have a family life. The fight was never lost; victory was always delayed; but the spirit persisted, and the final triumph is as sure as the rising sun. A hundred times I have been asked why we allowed little children to march in demonstrations, to freeze and suffer in jails, to be exposed to bullets and dynamite. The questions implied that we have a want of family feeling or recklessness towards family security. The answer is simple. Our children and our families are maimed a little every day of our lives. If we can end an incessant torture by a single climactic confrontation, the risks are acceptable. Beyond that our family life will be born anew if we fight together. Other families may be fortunate to be able to protect their young from danger. Our families, as we have seen, are different. Oppression again and again divided and splintered our families. We are a people torn apart from era to era. It is logical, moral and psychologically constructive for us to resist oppression united as families. Out of this unity, out of the bond of fighting together, forges will come. The inner strength and integrity will make us whole again.

The most optimistic element revealed in this review of the Negro family's experience is that the causes for its present crisis are culturally and socially induced. What man has torn down, he can rebuild. At the root of the difficulty in Negro life is pervasive and persistent economic want. To grow from within the Negro needs only fair opportunity for jobs, education, housing and access to culture. To be strengthened from the outside requires protection from the grim exploitation that has haunted it for 300 years.

The Negro family lived in Africa in nature's jungle and subdued the hostile environment. In the United States, it has lived in a man-made social and psychological jungle which it could not subdue. Many have been destroyed by it. Yet, others have survived and developed an appalling capacity for hardships. It is on this strength that society can build. What is required is a recognition by a society that it has been guilty of the crimes and that it is prepared to atone. With that beginning there need be no doubt about the end.

Much of the ugly experiences of Negro history have been obscured and forgotten. A society is always eager to cover great misdeeds with a cloak of forgetfulness, but no society can repress an ugly past when the ravages persist into the present. America owes a debt to justice which it has only begun to pay. If it loses the will to finish or slackens in its determination, history will recall its crimes and the country that would be great will lack the most indispensable element of greatness — justice.

I do not think that the tiny nation that stood in majesty at Concord and Lexington, that electrified a world with the words of the Declaration of Independence, will defame its heritage to avoid a responsibility. That is why I believe not only in the future of the Negro family but in the future of the family of man.

C. NEWSPAPER COLUMNS BY JAMES FARMER*

[Editors' note: These two discussions of The Moynihan Report appeared in Mr. Farmer's column, "The Core of It," on December 18 and 25, 1965. See pages 258–259.]

The Controversial Moynihan Report [December 18, 1965]

As if living in the sewer, learning in the streets and working in the pantry weren't enough of a burden for millions of American Negroes, I now learn that we've caught "matriarchy," and "the tangle of Negro pathology" . . . a social plague recently diagnosed by Daniel Moynihan in his celebrated report on "The Negro Family."

* Reprinted with permission of the author.

After tracing the long history of Negro oppression in this country, Moynihan concludes that our current difficulties are rooted in the effects of that oppression dramatized in the shattered Negro family, stripped of its male and going to Hell in a basket.

On the surface, this would seem to be a fairminded exercise in the Life Sciences but in fact the Moynihan Report, which seems to have been given a good deal of currency by the present administration, is another one of those academic efforts to get our eyes off the prize.

By laying the primary blame for present-day inequalities on the pathological condition of the Negro family and community, Moynihan has provided a massive academic cop-out for the white conscience and clearly implied that Negroes in this nation will never secure a substantial measure of freedom until we learn to behave ourselves and stop buying Cadillacs instead of bread.

This well-enough intentioned analysis provides the fuel for a new racism . . . it succeeds in taking the real tragedy of black poverty and serving it up as an essentially salacious "discovery" suggesting that Negro mental health should be the first order of business in a civil rights revolution.

Nowhere does Moynihan suggest that there may be something wrong in an "orderly and normal" white family structure that is weaned on race hatred and passes the word "nigger" from generation to generation.

Nowhere does Moynihan suggest that the proper answer to a shattered family is an open job market where this "frustrated" male Negro can get an honest day's work.

And nowhere does Moynihan suggest that high illegitimacy rates in the black community may be partly explained by the fact that birth control information and covert abortions are by and large the exclusive property of the white man.

I say all this because I'm angry . . . really angry and I intend to spell out this anger in just one more effort to convince somebody, anybody, down in the places of power that the cocktail hour on the "Negro Question" is over and that we are sick unto death of being analyzed, mesmerized, bought, sold and slobbered over while the same evils that are the ingredients of our oppression go unattended.

It has been the fatal error of American society for 300 years to ultimately blame the roots of poverty and violence in the Negro community upon Negroes themselves. I honestly felt that the Civil Rights and Voting laws indicated that we were rid of this kind of straw-man logic, but here it is again, in its most vicious form, handing the racists a respectable new weapon and insulting the intelligence of black men and women everywhere.

I intend to devote a good deal of space to this Moynihan Report for a number of reasons. First and most important, it is fast becoming the scriptural basis for several new brands of bigotry, even without the consent of its authors.

Secondly, it has been specifically hailed by the American right wing and is currently being used to "explain away" the Negro Revolution as the hysterical outburst of a mentally unbalanced sub-culture.

Third, it provides a documented basis for men in elected authority to divert practical anti-discrimination programs into an open season on "pathological" Negroes.

And fourth, the report is especially bad in that it contains a great number of statistical facts, misread, misinterpreted and warped into a series of conclusions that could make Robert Shelton into a holy prophet. In many ways, this report, when studied carefully, emerges in my mind as the most serious threat to the ultimate freedom of American Negroes to appear in print in recent memory.

I cannot possibly in the course of this article cover even a small part of the report's analyses and conclusions. I will deal with those in subsequent columns. I must say, however, that I am convinced that the author or authors of this document did not consciously intend to write a racist tract . . . but the fact that it may be used as such makes their innocence inexcusable.

They have forgotten that we are bottled into our ghetto and held down not simply by the restraints of our past, but by the clear and present acts of subtle and unsubtle discrimination that continue to destroy our option for self change and make our life a living Hell. And to forget that while focusing on "the tangle of Negro pathology" is very much like curing Yellow Fever by painting the patient white and ignoring the mosquitoes.

More on The Moynihan Report [December 25, 1965]

Contrary to most folks, I relish a good fight . . . particularly when the stakes are high enough materially to affect my life. And that's exactly what's involved in the current scramble around Daniel Moynihan's report on the Negro family. Last week, I took considerable time to classify the report as a tactical blunder, a post-facto "discovery" of Negro pathology that could easily be fashioned into a weapon of the racists. This week, I intend to challenge its accuracy and raise questions, serious questions as to the responsibility of its "proofs" and the wisdom of its authors.

Before doing that, however, I would like to discuss two points that have surfaced in the past few days of debate. First off, Daniel Moynihan did not invent candor and most certainly did not courageously "talk truth" for the first time about the American Negro family. Even beyond E. Franklin Frazier's first-rate studies of the Negro community written in 1937 and 1948, the Civil Rights movement has for nearly a decade been *demanding* that the plight of American Negroes be viewed as a hard fact of life rather than a political push-up for American reformers. The concept of preferential hiring, for example, came directly from the movement's candid assessment of a depressed Negro community, despite Mr. Moynihan's implication that we have been burying our heads in the sands of romantic protest. We know how tough it is to be black, but more important we know what continues to fence us into a circle of emotional and economic depression. In a word, we don't suffer and die by choice, we suffer and die from lack of choice. Secondly, I am pleased to report that Mr. Moynihan has broadened the conclusions of his report. In his recent public statements he has agreed with our contention that improved jobs, housing and educational options are essential in the fight to stop community erosion. These late refinements, however welcome, serve to confirm the haphazard judgement at work when the unqualified report was originally issued.

Now as to matters of "proof." In dramatizing the "tangle of Negro pathology" Moynihan relies heavily upon illegitimacy statistics from the U.S. Census, which indicates a rate of 3% illegitimacy in the white community and 22% in the black. On the face of it, this would be a sobering revelation, indicating that black folks are, among other things, a pretty promiscuous lot. But it just isn't true. And, as usual the numbers are misleading. When you begin to compute the hidden factors: the availability of contraception, divorce, abortion, and adoption advice, you suddenly discover that illegitimacy in the Negro community is not eight times as much as among whites, it simply is recorded eight times more often. White folks have access to a whole fabric of social machinery to prevent or hide the illegitimate child that is simply not widely available in the Negro community. In fact, a more complete reading would show that whites have closer to *half* as many illegitimate children as Negroes rather than an eighth. And that's about what any sociologist would expect in a 300-year-old pocket of American poverty.

The same sloppy research applies to Moynihan's statistics on criminal behavior and welfare dependency. There is no question that disproportionate illegitimacy, felony and poverty exist in America's Negro community, but it exists because of systematic and continued discrimination, and any analysis that doesn't compute the effects of discrimination in reporting Negro social statistics is irresponsible, dangerous and just plain wrong.

D. TWO NEWSPAPER COLUMNS*

Whitney Young, Jr.

[Editors' note: These two discussions of the Moynihan Report appeared in Mr. Young's column, "To Be Equal," in October, 1965 and January, 1966. See pages 265–266.]

White House Confab [October 1965]

The White House has indicated that its forthcoming conference on race relations will emphasize the tragic plight of the Negro male.

Stirred by the recent U.S. Labor Department study of widespread disorganization among the Negro poor, President Johnson has asked his braintrust to plumb beneath the surface and to produce some far-reaching solutions.

"There will be no social peace in the United States for generations" (unless the Negro male has the same opportunities as his white counterparts) the report warns. His lot is regarded as the

* Reprinted with permission of the author.

key to the future of the Negro poor — and that's every second family of color in this country.

The Urban League movement, of course, has long been trying to focus public opinion on this question. In fact, the Federal report cites these paragraphs from my "To Be Equal" book (McGraw-Hill):

"Both as husband and as a father the Negro male is made to feel inadequate, not because he is unlovable or unaffectionate, lacks intelligence or even a gray flannel suit. But in a society that measures a man by the size of his paycheck, he doesn't stand very tall in comparison with his white counterpart.

"To this situation he may react with withdrawal, bitterness toward society, aggression both within the family and racial group, self-hatred, or crime. Or he may escape through a number of avenues that help him to lose himself in fantasy or to compensate for his low status through a variety of exploits."

As I read these words again I can imagine the fresh batch of letters I will receive accusing me of "making excuses for Negro criminals" and the like.

But just as I tell Negro citizens that "We must do more than deplore injustice by whites" I say it is not enough for white citizens to "deplore" crime among Negroes.

This is a time for understanding — and for action.

African Males

Regarding the former, I found my recent trip to Africa of immense usefulness. On that continent I was deeply impressed by the heads-high attitude of ordinary Africans. The colonialism which they endured for centuries has not marked them as deeply as slavery did their American brothers.

In African society, the African male — whether he is a pilot or ditch-digger — feels his worth as an individual. His job is as steady as the next man's, and his family unit is as stable. (This is true for middle-class American Negroes, by the way.) He possesses a spirit of confidence in himself, his daily role, and his future.

The difference lies in the fact that European colonialism thirsted to exploit the land and its resources — whereas slavery sought to exploit the human person. Moreover, because of our Judeo-Christian heritage, the slaveowners had to convince the Negro that slavery was Holy Writ, and moral, in keeping with the servant mentality they forced the slave to assume.

At the same time, they fed the vanity of unthinking white people with the pipe-dream of a superior race — to justify slaveholding. Only in America has the Negro male been so deeply injured.

My understanding is that President Johnson intends to hit hard the issue of the Negro male. Hopefully, his solutions will include far-reaching meat-and-potato programs to encourage Negro youth, to rehabilitate their poverty-struck fathers, and to improve their housing and economic prospects.

Most of the signs of overt discrimination ["white" and "colored"] have been taken down. Now the unwritten sign over our ghettos must be removed. For too long it has read: "Abandon hope all ye who enter here."

The 'Real' Moynihan Report [January 1966]

Last Spring, a report published by the U.S. Department of Labor and popularly known as the Moynihan Report, after its author, received a good deal of publicity in the press. Since then it has become difficult to read about or discuss the Negro's drive for full equality without encountering references to this report or without dealing with the questions it raises.

Briefly, the point of the report, which is entitled "The Negro Family," is that as a consequence of slavery and oppression, the Negro family as an institution has deteriorated to the point where its pathological state threatens to engulf the gains Negroes may make in the future. Impressive-looking charts and graphs are presented to show that Negroes commit more crimes, have more illegitimate births, and more often unemployed, and are more often members of broken families.

Unfortunately, the report has been pressed into uses which its author, Daniel P. Moynihan, an eloquent advocate of civil rights, could not have foreseen. Both the popular press and other quarters have seized upon parts of its findings and have distorted them to the point where the record must be set right.

First of all, the report isn't about the Negro family at all, it is about some Negro families. The picture of prevalent pathology it presents just does not fit reality and is a gross injustice to the overwhelming majority of Negro families, which are as stable as any in the nation.

Further, the statistics it quotes leave out factors which put its findings in doubt. Nowhere among the many charts in the report is there a breakdown of comparative statistics which contrast figures for Negro families with those for white families of comparable income. What appear to be racial differences in regard to family stability are more probably class differences, which Negro lower-class families share with whites.

Again, figures which purport to show Negro crime and illegitimacy rates as higher than those of whites do not take into account such hidden factors as the police propensity for arresting Negroes more readily, and the ease with which better-off white families can conceal illegitimacy and abortions. Too often the figures which show such shocking disparity in family stability are the result of these "hidden" factors. The pejorative implications of the report's figures just do not stand up to examination of the causes behind them.

The findings of the report, whatever the failing of its statistics, do give a picture of some of the social ills which affect many Negroes. However, family instability has been presented in the press and elsewhere as being the cause of Negro failure to achieve equality. This is a gross distortion. It is instead the result of patterns of discrimination which deny to Negro citizens the same chance to hold a job and earn a decent living that the white American has.

The real message of the report, obscured by the unfortunate emphasis on the distorted figures, is that unemployment among Negroes, twice the white rate and affecting perhaps 25 percent of Negro men, has effects which go beyond the economic, harming the social fabric of family life. The poverty and unemployment which afflict disproportionate numbers of Negroes in the United States take a tremendous toll from the man who is jobless, the housewife who is forced into the labor market to make ends meet, and the child denied the atmosphere he needs to grow up properly motivated.

The problems the Negro family faces today are caused by its economic disadvantages, which are in turn mainly the result of the discrimination and unequal treatment of today — not chiefly the result of slavery, as the report argues. The sooner we get off the side track of peripheral issues and back on the main road of current basic causes, the sooner the Negro will attain the equality to which he is entitled.

E. WHY DON'T NEGROES . . .*

Bayard Rustin

[Editors' note: from America, June 4, 1966. Mr. Rustin has discussed the Moynihan Report and the Negro family in a similar vein in public addresses during 1966 and in an article on the McCone Report in Commentary, March, 1966. See pages 269–270.]

Why don't Negroes . . .

have more respect for law and order? . . . straighten up their family life and stop asking for handouts? . . . do something to help themselves, the way other minorities have? These questions, lurking in the minds of many white men, are answered honestly and frankly by one of the most prominent leaders of the civil rights movement

Television viewers were shocked some weeks ago to see Negroes attending a conference of the Citizens Crusade Against Poverty demonstrate against Sargent Shriver. To most Americans, I'm sure, this was another demonstration of Negro irrationality, ingratitude and lack of self-discipline.

I opposed and tried to curb that demonstration because it allowed a handful of people to obscure the fundamental criticisms most conference participants had of the antipoverty program. In Indianola, Miss., for example, the chief of police is head of the antipoverty board; in Selma, Ala., Jim Clark controls much of the funds, and for the most part the concept of maximum feasible participation has not been implemented.

I recall the incident because it brought to the fore once again the questions white people often raise about Negroes. For instance: "Why don't Negroes respect law and order?" "Why don't they straighten up their families and stop asking for handouts?" "Why don't they pull themselves up by their bootstraps as we did?"

I don't want to belittle these questions, for even religious people are deeply confused about some of them. Men of good will cannot

---

* Reprinted with permission of the author and *America*, The National Catholic Weekly Review, 106 W. 56th Street, New York, N.Y.

sit by, however, and allow programs that were well-intentioned to flounder, nor should they accept unsubstantiated or unthought-out statements about law and order, the breakdown of the Negro family and self-help.

I am going to address myself to those questions in the following pages, but before I do so, I want to say that there are two theses I believe we can all accept. The first is that the Negro family can be reconstructed only when the Negro male is permitted to be the economic and psychological head of the family. The second, that racism is a blasphemy against the fundamental oneness and unity that the world and all its people derive from their Creator; that racists are, in a very precise sense of the term, blasphemers who set themselves up as gods over their fellow men and worship not a human nature created in the divine image, but the accidents of skin color, of nation, of ethnic background. These people would annul that great and enormous truth which is so central to the Judeo-Christian tradition: that God is not the talisman of a tribe, a sort of good-luck charm for one's warriors as against the warriors of some other god, but that God is indeed one.

The racists, for all their Scriptural quoting, would belittle God, for they turn human beings into non-souls and thus seek to diminish the divine work.

Who is to Blame for Ghetto Violence?

Anatole France once wrote that it is illegal for rich men and poor men alike to sleep under bridges or to steal a piece of bread. At the heart of this wise witticism, there is an understanding of the way in which all the noble words — equality, justice, freedom — have definitions that vary according to one's misery or prosperity. And this sad truth holds most profoundly in the racial ghettos of America, where millions of black citizens live out poverty-stricken lives. In these man-made jungles, there are many who cannot comprehend the very meaning of a phrase like "law and order," for it does not correspond to anything that has ever happened in their lives. Such people are not stupid; far from it. They are being ruthlessly logical in generalizing from their own experiences, for they have seldom seen the least shred of empirical evidence that there is such a thing as "law and order."

But then, there are those who say that when I talk in this way I somehow "excuse" the violence and nihilism that sometimes erupt in the Negro slum. And that, of course, is not the case at all.

It would take a fool or a sadist to celebrate the involuntary, spastic violence of the ghetto or to say that it was a means toward any good. The real issue is: Who is to blame? Is it the Negro man or woman who was born into a miserable, vermin-infested apartment, sent to an overcrowded, inadequate school, not really taught to read, write or count, and actually educated, for all practical purposes, in the street? Is this the autonomous, morally choosing individual whom we shall not excuse for his free choice of violence?

My question should answer itself. But more than that, this line of inquiry should indicate the profound limits on the moralistic advocacy of respect for law and order. The disorder, the alienation, the violence of the ghetto are, to a considerable degree, social consequences that are imposed upon people. It is thus a waste of time to give beautiful sermons filled with words that may make some sense in suburbia, but that the daily reality of slum life has rendered meaningless. Moreover, the root of the violence is in the economic order of the ghetto. The policeman who arrests a young man for selling marijuana, numbers or women is not only preventing crime; he is in fact stopping that young man from earning a living.

The greatest lesson one could teach would be to create a decent, integrated environment in which man's potential for brotherhood, reason and co-operation was a deduction from firsthand experience, rather than an incomprehensible pronouncement broadcast into chaos by philosophers who live in ordered comfort. For, as Western philosophy has understood as far back as Aristotle, the hungry man, the freezing man, the sick man, does not have time or inclination to speculate upon the higher things. He is consumed by his immediate misery, which is the only reality he knows. And so for millions of people living in ghettos, a discussion of law and order is misleading. For where there is justice and just law, order can exist; where there is injustice and an unjust administration of law, disorder is inevitable.

What Are a Negro's Job Prospects?

Two decades ago, in the Irene Morgan case, Jim Crow was illegalized in interstate transportation. The Supreme Court decision outlawing segregation was handed down almost twelve years ago. The Montgomery bus protest was won eleven years ago. The sit-in movement swept through the lunchrooms and bus stations

of the South five years ago. The dogs were unleashed in Birmingham three years ago. It is a year since Selma. And during all this
time, while thousands and tens of thousands suffered and faced
death — and while some died — the economic and social position
of the Negro relative to that of the white has declined. When
general unemployment was high, the Negro rate was double the
white; when progress in reducing joblessness was made, as in the
last two years, the Negro gains were half those of the white. At
the same time, New York (where liberal pieties on the race issue
are required of all serious candidates for office) maintains ghetto
schools that actually work a deterioration on the intellectual
ability of a growing number of black students each year.

This situation becomes all the more pathological when one
looks at the job prospects of the young, systematically un-edu-
cated Negro from the black ghetto. In the next five years, according to the President's Manpower Report of last year, Negroes,
who are approximately 10 per cent of the population, will be almost 20 per cent of the new entrants to the labor force. In part, of
course, this figure simply reflects the ability of the whites to
prolong education (and in their case, more effective education:
Scarsdale spends twice as much per capita on education for its
children as Harlem). But beyond that, what is going to happen to
these hundreds of thousands of young Negroes?

One grim possibility is discernible in the recent government
reports of progress in reducing unemployment. The over-all jobless level has fallen to around 4.2 per cent; the Negro rate, at
well over 8 per cent, is as usual double. But — and this is an
explosive fact — the Negro teen-age percentages have hardly
declined at all, and remain in the neighborhood of 25 per cent.
In other words, at the very moment when the New Economics
was successfully rescuing whites and some Negroes from unemployment (the Negroes returning to work were laid-off workers,
usually with skills), Negro youth was continuing to inhabit a
world where work was as hard to find as in the Depression of the
1930's.

It should be emphasized, however, that even the positive figures
are overly optimistic. A number of economists have convincingly
argued that Washington's unemployment statistics do not take
into account those driven out of the labor market (there have been
estimates as high as a million and a half) and do not compute the
cumulative effect of part-time unemployment and various other
forms of under-employment. As a result, Leon Keyserling has con-

cluded that the "true" unemployment rate, even with the much vaunted progress we have recently made, is around 8 per cent and all the numbers for Negroes would show a substantial increase. Beyond this, as the testimony that Clarence Mitchell of the NAACP presented on behalf of the civil rights leadership last year shows, working Negroes are, to an unusually high degree, concentrated in "poverty jobs:" domestic work, the janitorial occupations in the service trades, laundry work, etc. These are people who often labor a full two thousands hours a year and who are, nevertheless, bitterly poor. They are in jobs not covered by Federal legislation at all, or in those that pay the official, legal and impoverishing minimum of $2,600 a year, or $500 under the poverty line for a man with a wife and two children.

But, then, perhaps Watts can be taken as a summary — and utterly persuasive statement — of my themes. The Los Angeles ghetto was, and is, a way station on the terrible above-ground railway that this economy runs for Negroes. Literally tens of thousands of black men are forced to migrate from the South. They come North to "freedom," where they are packed together in slums and sent out to compete on the labor market with the black generation that arrived a decade or two ago (Jeremy Larner has estimated that over half the adult population of Harlem is made up of migrants who were not born there). And they also must contend, of course, with white competition. In Watts, then, one found jobless rates — according to the official figures — of nearly 40 per cent. And since the flaming outburst of last summer, many agencies, public and private, have gone into Watts to talk to Negroes there about work. The one thing they have not provided is jobs.

In one form or another, the reality I have described is now common knowledge in the civil rights movement and in the Federal government. What, then, are we going to do about it — besides writing sociological descriptions of it?

The debate over the "Moynihan Report" focuses on one approach. As is generally known by now, one of the principal authors of the report was Daniel Patrick Moynihan, then Assistant Secretary of Labor.

Let me make it clear at the outset that I feel it is unfair to charge Moynihan with being a racist, open or covert, and that, as a matter of fact, he was trying in his report to insist on the social and economic dimension of the race issue — for example, in his showing that prolonged unemployment tended to disintegrate the white family structure and to place particularly difficult psychological burdens on the male. The Negro family, Moynihan shows, has lived in a depression-like atmosphere ever since the 1930's, and the result has been a predictable breakdown. Now, this point has been made previously by Negro scholars — the late Franklin Frazier comes to mind in particular — and it has also emerged from studies of the heritage of American slavery.

But the Moynihan data were presented in a form guaranteed to promote confusion. An intra-office memo on one aspect of a problem, it was taken by many, both friends and foes, as a comprehensive statement. Thus, even though the report made it clear that Negro family stability had always increased when Negro economic opportunity was on the rise, there were those who claimed that Moynihan had demonstrated that the real problem was a Negro deficiency in facing reality. Don't talk about "handouts," these sermonizers and moralists said whenever anyone spoke of the job of generating programs that could provide a basis for Negro family stability. And they concluded: just have Negroes put their own house in order! Thus chaotic aspects of Negro life that are the direct consequence of the economic and social discrimination practiced by white America were turned into bogus evidence of some kind of Negro inferiority.

And the truncated form of the Moynihan Report also meant that it concentrated almost solely upon what is negative in Negro life. There was no examination of the degree to which the "abnormality" of some of the ghetto mores, when seen from the point of view of a secure white middle class, represents a desperate, but intelligent attempt on the part of a jobless Negro to adapt to a social pathology. There was no assessment of the extraordinary accomplishment of the civil rights movement in summoning so many to sacrifice and to idealism despite these indignities.

Breakdown of the Negro Family

In 1962 [sic], Abram Kardiner, M.D., and Lionel Ovesey published their study of the personality of the American Negro, *The Mark of Oppression*. The section in their book that deals with the breakdown of the Negro family is a scientific and compassionate description; it explains a great deal about the interrelationship between personality and economics.

When a Negro male abandons his wife and children, the authors point out, he is blamed for having no sense of responsibility — something generally considered a character trait of Negroes. Research has shown, however, that such a man himself is more often than not the product of a broken home. He had no father to set him a pattern of stability and protection, and his overburdened mother was irritable and demanded strict obedience. He was thrown into competition with his mother's other children. Hearing men disparaged by his female relatives, and without affectionate attention from anyone, his self-esteem was lowered. The submissive attitude he thus developed toward women limited his ability to enter into a satisfactory marital relationship. When he married, he knew that his wife had much better chances economically than he did. Moreover, neither he nor his wife had much tolerance for each other's faults. Even if he found work, it was hardly ever permanent. Often he tried hard to fulfill his obligations, but he failed continuously. Therefore his wife began berating and browbeating him. Finally, either she invited him to leave, or he himself abandoned his family.

When a husband moves out, the authors continue, he is generally a defeated man. He drifts from job to job. Often he seeks escape in drink, or satisfaction through expensive clothes or through pleasure with women. Even if he stays married, the husband remains subordinate to his wife. Though he is submissive toward her, he may become domineering over the children. An abandoned wife, on the other hand, usually marries — and often successfully — a second time. If that marriage fails, her lot from then on is one of ceaseless toil. Usually she cannot give her child either attention or love. Ofter a sister or brother has to take care of the child, who is thus exposed to bitter rivalries with other children. The male child of a broken marriage takes to the streets. Here he elevates his self-esteem through exploits with other boys, obtaining rewards he cannot get at home. Without his knowing it, many of his satisfactions are bought through anti-social acts.

If we study this description of the breakdown of the American Negro family, we find that there is a common reality-factor in that cycle: the economic position of the Negro male. We could attempt to psychoanalyze poor Negroes, to improve their self-image and self-esteem, but in the face of the economic realities, all our effort would be futile.

That is why A. Philip Randolph has proposed a "Freedom Budget," a multi-billion-dollar social investment to destroy the racial ghettos of America, house the black and white poor decently and create full and fair employment in the process. His approach is fundamental if we are serious about reconstructing the Negro family and allowing the Negro male to be the head of the household.

"Help Yourself, Like We Did"

Misconceptions about Negro family life are often compounded by admonitions to Negroes to help themselves "like we did" (the "we" are the Poles, Jews, Irish, Italians, etc.).

Michael Harrington pointed out, in a recent issue of *Dissent*, that the old immigrant groups came to America when an expanding blue-collar economy had work for grade school dropouts and men who could not even speak English, while the Negro has come to the city as an internal alien in a time of automation, a time when the number of available jobs is decreasing. (Oscar Handlin points out in his book *Race, Nationality and American Life* that without the immigrant labor supply, the development of the cotton goods industry to its present status in New York and other North Atlantic States could not have taken place.)

Saying this does not mean that Negro self-organization is irrelevant. Far from it. It is only when the black ghetto of the North, which has yet to be organized massively by *any* civil rights group, comes to conscious political life that the full impact of the Negro revolution will be felt. But first of all, the economic and social setting in which such organization becomes possible and even probable has to be created. Just as the semi-skilled factory workers did not create the CIO at the bottom of the Depression in 1932, but only when times were getting better a few years later, so the black masses require some tangible signs of hope and success before they are going to move.

For that matter, the white immigrant groups from Europe, which are so often held up as images of the "self-help" process, benefited from massive government intervention. The great advance made by the first and second generation workers took place, of course, in the 1930's, and the most important new institutions they created were precisely the industrial unions. But this did not happen in a vacuum. There was the Wagner Act, which, if it did not immediately guarantee collective bargaining rights, put the moral and psychological authority of the government on the side of the labor movement ("Mr. Roosevelt wants you to join," John L. Lewis said in those days). And there were the various programs — the climate of economic hope. Some Negroes participated in this progress; most were excluded because racism had kept them out of the factories, where the decisive events occurred.

In short, the CIO had to organize itself, but it did so under circumstances of Federal intervention that made the momentous task easier to perform. Negroes have to organize themselves. And the Freedom Budget, which is their New Deal 30 years late, will not simply provide full and fair employment and lay the basis for the destruction of the physical environment of poverty. Like the Wagner Act and the social investments of the New Deal, it should also evoke a new psychology, a new militancy and sense of dignity, among millions of Negroes, who will see something more concrete and specific than a promise of eventual freedom.

But secondly, when I talk of the self-organization that the Freedom Budget should make possible, I am not talking about "self-help" in the neighborhood improvement sense. In *Dark Ghetto*, Kenneth Clark tells of how one New York block got together to clean up the street. In the doing, Clark rightly remarks, these Negroes gave tacit assent to the charge that it was their *fault* that the street was dirty, thus accepting one more of the white man's stereotypes about the Negro (i.e., he is guilty of non-cleanliness). What is more, the energy was misdirected. It should have been directed to City Hall as a demand that the city clean up the streets of Harlem the same way it cleans up the streets of the white middle class.

From the time of the American Revolution until the rise of the NAACP in the first decade of this century, Negroes have followed the advice of the self-helpers. When Negroes were thrown out of the Methodist Church in the 18th century, they established the African Methodist Episcopal Church. When they were not allowed to attend white universities, they set up Wilberforce University in Ohio. When insurance companies would not insure Negroes, fraternal organizations and social clubs took on the task. The history of the Negro people in the United States is a history of attempting to build separate self-help organizations. At the end of World War II, the Urban League and the National Council of Negro Women formed "Hold Your Job Committees." The committees conducted educational campaigns in the factories and the Negro community to urge Negroes not to give employers any excuse for discharging them after the war.

More recently, Black Nationalists and Muslims have believed that if Negroes would only follow the Protestant ethic and "Buy Black" (while a number of confused whites have said: "Be frugal"), they could end their economic dependence. But the fact is that if millions of Negroes are to change the conditions of their life, it will be not by becoming shopkeepers or by cleaning up their block, but by winning full and fair employment for black men as well as white.

Negroes, I am saying, should be individually virtuous — and so should whites. But the Negro movement's future does not lie along the line of making over millions of black personalities, one by one. The European immigrants and their children ceased being rude peasants not because they got religion or psychology, but because they got economic opportunity and hope. The Negro movement must now struggle against economic injustices that are more deeply rooted in the management and structure of our technology than anything the immigrants ever faced. And it can win this perilous fight only by way of militant political organization and through national programs.

[*Bayard Rustin* is the executive director of the A. Philip Randolph Institute. His article is based on a study paper that he prepared for a recent conference of the John LaFarge Institute.]

17

Intellectual Response to the Report

A. BEWARE THE DAY THEY CHANGE THEIR MINDS*

Charles E. Silberman

[Editors' note: This article, from the November, 1965, issue of Fortune is included for its excellent presentation of the state of the civil rights movement in the summer of 1965; it also contains a brief discussion of the Moynihan Report. See pages 9–16.]

The cause of civil rights, fresh from its greatest victories, is facing its greatest threat — a bitter new mood, with elements of nihilism and hopelessness, that is suddenly making headway in the Negro community.

"There is no more civil-rights movement," the Reverend James Bevel, one of Martin Luther King's principal aides, told the

---

* Reprinted from the November 1965 issue of *Fortune* Magazine by special permission; coypright 1965 Time Inc.

August convention of Dr. King's Southern Christian Leadership
Conference. "President Johnson signed it out of existence when
he signed the voting-rights bill." The Reverend Mr. Bevel's speech
was widely interpreted as reflecting an understandable, if excessive, euphoria; with the signing of the voting-rights bill just a
year after the civil-rights law of 1964, civil-rights groups certainly
had gained a considerable part of what they had been fighting
for in recent years.

In fact, Bevel's speech reflected not euphoria but a spreading
frustration and gloom. The civil-rights movement is not dead,
of course, and no one, Bevel included, really thinks it is. The
movement *is* at a dreadful impasse; its leaders, as the painting
above suggests, are estranged from their rank and file and divided and uncertain where to turn. Their frustration and confusion are widely shared, particularly in Washington. Within the
past year, as historian C. Vann Woodward writes, Congress "has
put more teeth in the law and more law on the books" regarding
civil rights than it has in the ninety years since the end of Reconstruction; insofar as federal legislation can cope with the knotty
problems of race, Congress has now done just about all that can
be done. And yet we seem to be as far as ever from having solved
the problem of race.

The reality, however, is not that the legislative victories of the
past year were meaningless but that they served to move the so-
called "Negro problem" to a new and unfamiliar plane, one in
which the problem, perhaps for the first time, is visible in all its
fullness and all its many dimensions. And so the long and tortuous
history of Negro-white relations has entered a new and radically
different stage — a stage so different from the recent or distant
past as to make the familiar approaches and solutions obsolete,
irrelevant, and sometimes even harmful. This new stage offers an
opportunity, as President Johnson has put it, "to make good the
promise of America"— an opportunity the U.S. may never have
again.

By the same token, the U.S. now faces a racial crisis every bit
as serious as, and in some ways more urgent than, the one that
tore the nation asunder a century ago. Indeed, it is no exaggera-
tion to say that unless we make the plight of the Negro American
the central concern of all Americans, there will be no social peace
in this country for generations to come.

If any evidence were needed, last summer's week-long riot in
the Watts section of Los Angeles provided it. For the riot drama-

tized a fundamental change in Negro-white relations — a change that was inevitable, and that had been clearly visible, though widely ignored, for some time. What is new is that Negroes have begun to reveal and to express — indeed, to act out — the anger and hatred they have always felt, but had always been obliged to hide and suppress behind a mask of sweet docility. (*"Got one mind for white folks to see, Another for what I know is me,"* an old Negro work song goes.) The anger was there, but it was turned inward, in the form of self-hatred, or violence against other Negroes. Now, at long last, the anger is exploding outward, against what has always been its true object: "the man," "Mr. Charlie," "Whitey," which is to say white men — *all* white men.

The change has come about in spite of, but also in a sense because of, the enormous strides Negroes have taken in recent years toward full equality. The push toward equality of opportunity has been based on the implicit assumption that something approximating equality of results would follow. It hasn't, nor is it likely to. Equality of results is impossible in a competitive society unless people enter the competition on roughly equal terms. And the harsh but inescapable fact is that all too many Negroes are unable — or unwilling — to compete. To say this is not, in any way, to suggest that Negroes are inherently inferior; it is simply to recognize that three hundred and fifty years of brutalization, humiliation, and exclusion have taken, and continue to take, a heavy toll. "The Negro, if he fails to recognize his deprivation or acts as though it doesn't exist," Whitney M. Young, Jr., executive director of the National Urban League, has written, "is guilty of stupid chauvinism. And the white person who ignores this reality or acts as though it doesn't exist is guilty of dishonesty."

Where Some Get None

Worse yet, for a great many Negroes the disparities have been widening rather than narrowing. As the U.S. Department of Labor put it in the widely publicized "Moynihan Report" (so-called because its principal author was former Assistant Secretary of Labor Daniel P. Moynihan), "Individually, Negro Americans reach the highest peaks of achievement. But collectively, in the spectrum of American ethnic and religious and regional groups, where some get plenty and some get none, where some send 80 percent of their children to college and others pull them out of school at the eighth grade, Negroes are among the weakest. The most difficult fact for white Americans to understand is that in these terms the circumstances of the Negro American community in recent years has probably been getting *worse, not better.*"

This deterioration is not only exacerbating the enormous store of anger and hatred that Negroes were already beginning to express, but is also giving it a destructive, nihilistic, sometimes even suicidal turn. There has always been a certain dualism in Negro thought; Negroes have always wondered whether they should, after all, keep banging on the doors of a society that seemed determined to keep them out, and at moments they have wanted, Samson-like, to bring the whole house crashing down. (*"If I had-a my way,"* an old spiritual begins, *"I'd tear this building down."*) Alienation and nihilistic hatred have always existed in exquisite tension with Negroes' burning desire to enter the larger society. Now the balance is shifting somewhat, as the opportunities to enter white society increase faster than a great many Negroes' ability to enter.

There is, in short, a Negro's Negro problem every bit as severe as the one with which the white man wrestles. But the grim irony of history is that whites, having created the Negro's Negro problem, are no longer in a position to solve it through their actions alone. This in no way reduces the burden or responsibility that white men have. But because Negro Americans, as novelist Ralph Ellison has put it, "are in desperate search for an identity," there is ultimately a point at which only Negroes can solve the Negro problem, by creating a sense of community that will provide the identity for which they are searching.

The irony is compounded. Since the collapse of Booker T. Washington's strategy of "self-improvement" around the turn of the century, any such ideas have been indissolubly linked with a posture of accommodation and submission. Understandably, the emphasis of the civil-rights movement has been on ending the legal system of segregation, which is to say on ending the public humiliation of Negro Americans. But one result of this emphasis has been to blur the distinction between a compulsory ghetto and a voluntary community. Because Negroes had no choice but to live in all-Negro neighborhoods, attend all-Negro schools, etc., Negro leaders were trapped in a rhetoric and a logic whose premise was that any all-Negro institution is per se degrading. They found themselves, therefore, unable to argue simultaneously *against* Jim Crow and *for* the improvement of the Negro community. And the great mass of big-city Negroes, trapped in the ghetto, became convinced that their "leaders," far from trying to help them, were merely trying to escape from being black.

The explosive increase of Negro anger is compounding both these problems. On one hand, the new mood of militancy makes it virtually impossible for any Negro leader — indeed, any Negro intellectual — to acknowledge publicly the need for change within the Negro community. And this, in turn, prevents the leaders from doing anything that might produce a change. This same mood of anger, with its black-nationalist overtones, also serves to widen the already enormous breach between civil-rights leaders and a large mass of urban Negroes who are far less concerned with where they can eat or vote than with where —or whether — they can find a decently paid job.

Decline of a Taboo

The real question, let it be acknowledged from the start, is not why Negroes are expressing their anger, but why the explosion did not occur until now — and why white men did not see the anger until it erupted, as in Watts. Its explosive nature has been a central theme of the poetry of Langston Hughes, who summed up the situation twenty-three years ago, in five spare lines:

> Negroes,
> Sweet and docile,
> Meek, humble, and kind:
> Beware the day
> They change their minds!

But why now? The change has occurred, in part, because after three hundred and fifty years of fearing whites, Negroes have discovered that it is also the other way around — that the whites are afraid of Negroes. It is hard for whites to appreciate what a tremendous liberating force this discovery of white fear is, for fear of "the man" has dominated Negro life and thought. In large areas of the South it still does, although the fear is receding. In Mississippi, Alabama, rural Georgia, and elsewhere, this fear is soundly based; whites have always kept Negroes "in their place" through sheer terror and brutality. But the southern Negro's fear of the white man went beyond the rational; it had — and still has — elements of an almost mystical or magical taboo. Even in the North the taboo has not been completely broken — witness the fact that the Watt rioters did not shoot to kill,* and that they did not venture outside the Negro district.

But the taboo is breaking down very rapidly. The hatred of everything white was much more overt and explicit in Watts this year than in Harlem last year. It was also much more carefully controlled and focused; in Watts the burning and looting for the most part were limited to white-owned businesses, frequently in a systematic way. Watts aside, Negroes generally feel much freer about admitting their anger than they did a year ago.

In large measure, however, this new feeling stems less from any change in Negro psychology than from demographic changes. These changes have been largely overlooked in discussions of the Negroes' new situation, but they are crucial. As recently as 1940, more than two-thirds of all Negro Americans lived in the eleven states of the Old Confederacy, most of them in rural areas. As a result of the tremendous migration of Negroes that occurred during the 1940's and 1950's, about half of all Negroes now live in cities outside the Deep South. This double shift — from south to north and from country to city — ranks as one of the great population changes in history. (See "The City and the Negro," *Fortune,* March, 1962.)

But even more than that is involved. Because the migrants were predominantly young people with a high birth rate, the number of Negroes who had been born outside the South increased more than 150 percent in twenty years; by 1960, in fact, according to calculations by Professor C. Horace Hamilton of the University of North Carolina, nearly three-fifths of the Negro population living in the North had been born there — hence those Negroes were relatively free of the taboo that prevents southern Negroes from expressing their anger.

The Exaggerated Americans

Then there is the teenage dimension. The combination of great social mobility, rapidly changing standards of morality and authority, and an explosive birth rate has elevated teenagers' tra-

---

* *Despite reports of "marauding mobs" that "pillaged, burned, and killed," the fact is that the rioters killed only one person, a deputy sheriff (and that killing was accidental); the police and National Guardsmen killed twenty-six rioters and bystanders, and an individual store owner shot and killed someone looting his store. (In addition, one policeman was killed when another accidentally discharged his gun; a fireman was killed when a wall collapsed; and four deaths remain unexplained.)*

ditional rebellion against their elders into something of a national problem. In this sense, Negroes have become what Gunnar Myrdal called "exaggerated Americans." Even more than their white peers, Negro teenagers and young adults feel the need to rebel against their parents — to destroy any remnants in themselves of the "Sambo image," or the meek, docile, submissive Negro. And the number of Negro teenagers in the North is increasing far more rapidly than the number of white teenagers.

What is happening, moreover, is that the expression of anger is turning out to be a cumulative rather than a cathartic process. Instead of expending itself, the anger is feeding upon itself; the more it is expressed, the more there is to express — the more reasons for anger these young Negroes begin to discover. For "with rebellion, awareness is born," as Albert Camus has put it. Before the act of rebellion, the individual had accepted all the demands made upon him — had accepted indignities, without reacting against them, that were far more terrible than the one at which he balks. "He accepted them patiently, though he may have protested inwardly . . . But with the loss of patience," Camus argues, "— with impatience — a reaction begins which can extend to everything that he previously accepted, and which is almost always retroactive."

The new anger also reflects the fact that full equality still eludes most Negroes. For all the changes that have taken place in recent years, Negroes are still excluded from many areas of American life. Housing segregation remains rigid, notwithstanding President Kennedy's "stroke of the pen" decree. The quality of education offered Negro children is still grossly inferior to that given whites. "Children who are treated as if they are uneducable," as Professor Kenneth B. Clark of New York's City College puts it, "almost invariably become uneducable." And consciously or unconsciously, a staggeringly large proportion of the teachers with whom Negro children come into contact — in the North at least as much as in the South — do treat them as if they are uneducable. Job discrimination, moreover, still bars Negroes from many occupations and industries, though the discrimination tends to be more polite. To the Negro, however, the effect is the same whether the personnel officer says, "Sorry, we have no vacancies" or simply, "We don't hire niggers." In a sense, the latter is easier to take; Negroes' uncertainty over how they will be received or treated — over where they will meet discrimination and where not — is one of the most frustrating aspects of the changes now going on.

"Blessed is he who expects nothing, for he shall not be disappointed."

Growth of an Ethic

But Negroes do expect a great deal, and their expectations are being disappointed. There is hardly a Negro who does not still meet humiliation and insult — or, what is worse, unconscious condescension — with maddening regularity. ("They"ll have to get somebody else to practice on," Sammy Davis Jr. remarked, after attending a party at which one guest assured him that he was a credit to his race, and another proudly announced, "My son goes to school with Ralph Bunche's son.") And Negroes continually come up against maddening inconsistencies in white behavior, inconsistencies that add up to a kind of double standard: for example, the government's massive failure to give southern Negroes the protection of the law, or the fact that the murder of civil-rights workers who are Negro goes virtually unnoticed, as in Selma, Alabama, whereas the slaying of a white civil-rights worker arouses the national conscience.

The result is a sense of betrayal that leads to even greater rage (it's not surprising that Negroes' bitterest anger has been directed at "the white liberal") and confirms Negroes in their conviction of the basic hypocrisy of white protestations of justice. Hence the growth of what some Negro intellectuals are calling "the new ethic," which amounts to a kind of opting out of American society and an explicit rejection of "white" (i.e., Judaeo-Christian) morality as simply hypocritical.

But Negroes' advocacy of "the new ethic" also represents — consciously or not — a cover for withdrawal from competition, the educated Negro's heroin, so to speak. If, in the past, Negroes directed the hatred they felt for whites against themselves, it is almost certainly the case that some Negroes are now directing some of the hatred they feel for themselves (for their fear of competing in a white world) against that world itself. "There comes times," James Weldon Johnson wrote in 1934, "when the most persistent integrationist becomes an isolationist, when he curses the White world and consigns it to hell."

The turn toward nihilism and despair often has a belligerent ring to it. "If we can't sit at the table, let's knock the f-----g legs off!" James Forman, executive secretary of S.N.C.C. (Student Nonviolent Coordinating Committee), shouted last March at a mass meeting in Montgomery, Alabama. Within S.N.C.C. itself, and a host of smaller groups clustered around it, there is a growing insistence — fed by such things as President Johnson's appointment of Mississippi ex-Governor Coleman to the federal judiciary and the Justice Department's failure to make real use of the voting-examiner provision of the 1965 voting-rights law — that Negro aspirations cannot be met within the existing structure of American politics and government.

S.N.C.C. members and sympathizers have been moving toward a rhetorical stance in which any cooperation with the established organs of government or the existing political parties is decried as selling out to the Establishment, though they are not above accepting governmental help when it suits their purpose. The young Negro radicals are also moving toward black nationalism. "At the mass meetings, the effort is still made to say 'white segregationist,' not just 'the whites,' " Pat Watters of the Southern Regional Council writes in *Encounter With the Future,* a perceptive (and largely sympathetic) study of S.N.C.C. published recently. "But in private conversations, it is the man, the white man, Mister Charlie, all inclusive." And they are moving away from any devotion to nonviolence; as Watters puts it, "the possibilities for success of terrorism against whites" is becoming "a topic for informal discussion."

The revulsion against nonviolence was also evident in Watts — both in the rioting itself and in the heckling Martin Luther King received when he visited the area. "We don't believe in turning the other cheek down here," one heckler told a *Fortune* reporter. "We believe in hit back when you get hit. Why should King turn the other cheek when the white man hasn't turned one? All he does is turn his head and ignore you." The temptation to violence was evident, too, in the expressions of sympathy and support for the rioters that came from Negroes of all classes and in all parts of the country. "I hate this, I deplore it," one eminently respectable Negro remarked, "but I must smile a little at getting back. I was kind of glad at first to see them beat up the police a little."

James Baldwin warned two years ago, in *The Fire Next Time:* "The Negroes of this country may never be able to rise to power, but they are very well placed indeed to precipitate chaos and ring down the curtain on the American dream." The rioting in Watts suggests that the desire to ring down the curtain is more widespread than most whites — or most Negro leaders — had been willing to admit.

Those Who "Want In"

But this destructive impulse, we have observed, exists side by side with a burning desire to enter the larger society. Indeed, some of the angriest Negroes display the most wistful yearning for the values and accouterments of the society they profess to hate; a certain ambivalence has always been part of the price of being Negro in the U.S. The rioting in Watts also reflected this ambivalence. It was simultaneously an expression of hatred for white society and an attempt at forced entry into that society; the same people who expressed their bitterness in burning and looting were almost pathetically eager to explain their point of view to any white willing to listen. Both during the riots and afterward, a reporter had only to stand on a corner and take out a pencil and notebook to be surrounded by men and women clamoring to talk. "What this is all about," one participant explained, "is the gravy from this great society. We want some of it, brother — yeah, and a piece of the steak. We want *in.*"

By some measures, a fair number of Negroes actually are getting in. Thus the number of Negro families earning $7,000 a year or more, in dollars of 1964 purchasing power, has more than tripled in the past decade to nearly one million — 20.4 percent of all Negro families. The number earning $10,000 or above has more than quintupled — from 71,500 families in 1954 to almost 400,000 (8.3 percent) last year.

The Missing Men

But most Negroes still have good reason to feel left out of the affluent society; the Negro community is sharply divided between a growing but still small middle-class group and a large and in many ways increasingly disorganized and disadvantaged lower-class group. The median income of Negro families last year ($3,893) was only 56 percent that of white families — the same ratio as ten years ago. No fewer than 45.8 percent of all Negro families earned less than $3,500 — i.e., less than a "poverty income." Unemployment among Negroes averaged 9.8 percent in 1964, versus 4.6 percent for whites. And more than one-quarter of all Negroes in the labor force were out of work at some time or other during the course of the year.

Furthermore, the measured employment rate grossly understates the number of Negro men who are idle; the government counts as unemployed only those who are both out of work and looking for work, and a substantial number of Negro men are not looking for work. They have sunk so deeply into apathy and idleness that they are not counted as part of the labor force; some are so far out that they are not even counted as part of the *population*. According to the Census of Population, there were, in urban areas, only eight-six Negro men for every 100 Negro women in the fifteen to forty-four age group. But this is impossible: there can't be significantly fewer Negro men than women, since in the age brackets below fifteen the number of males is roughly the same as the number of females. What is involved, quite clearly, is a massive error in reporting; a substantial number of Negro men simply aren't around when the census enumerator — or anyone else presumed to represent authority — comes to call.

The problem of Negro "outness' goes far beyond the income and employment data. The heart of the matter, indeed, is the deterioration of Negro family life at the lower end of the economic scale. The deterioration is rooted in slavery, which made stable family relationships impossible, and in segregation, which continued to crush Negro men's sense of manhood and to thwart their inclinations to be family providers. Today nearly 25 percent of urban Negro women who have been married are divorced, separated, or living apart from their husbands. Fewer than half of all Negro children reaching eighteen have lived all their lives with both parents; more than half (56 percent) receive public assistance at some time during their childhood — the rate is seven times that for white children. Nearly one-fourth of all Negro births are illegitimate, versus 3 percent of white births. In some cities the rates are startlingly higher. In central Harlem, for example, over 43 percent of the births that occurred in 1963 were illegitimate.

Against this background of poverty and broken homes, it is scarcely surprising that young Negroes do not compete very effectively in the white world. More than 50 percent of Negro youngsters (versus 15 percent of white) fail the Armed Forces Qualification Test, which measures ability to perform a job at an acceptable level of competence — the level that ought to be found in someone with a seventh- or eighth-grade education. This inability to compete is the heart of the Negro's Negro problem. "They *are* inferior, and they know it," a Negro reporter says of the youngsters who rioted in Watts. "It's the knowing it that makes them dangerous."

No Roots in the Ghetto

The tragedy of the civil-rights movement is that it failed to
address itself to this Negro's Negro problem, and in its failure
it has lost touch with its own constituency. "Civil-rights organizations have failed," James Farmer, national director of CORE, said
just after the Watts riot. "No one had any roots in the ghetto."
Bayard Rustin, a strategist and theoretician for the civil-rights
movement, commented about the young people of Watts: "We
must hold ourselves responsible for not reaching out to them . . .
Roy [Wilkins], Martin [Luther King], and I haven't done a damn
thing about it. We've done plenty to get votes in the South and
seats in the lunchrooms, but we've had no program for these
youngsters."

These leaders still don't; the confessions of failure are not
being followed up by any appropriate action — certainly not by
any action that gives promise of success. Items:

The N.A.A.C.P. continues to be primarily concerned with the
white man's Negro problem — i.e., with eliminating white prejudice and discrimination. The greatest present need, as Executive Director Roy Wilkins sees it, is "a teaching and educating
job on the use of the new legislation," which is to say, an
emphasis on making sure that the new laws are actually en-
forced. As to the Negro's Negro problem: "You can't persuade
the Negro that he ought to be concerned with larger issues of
the community when he still feels the billy club on his neck —
or when the banker won't give him a mortgage."

James Farmer talks of building a mass base, as he has for
some time. CORE has changed character in the past several
years, from a middle-class organization with a predominantly
white membership to an organization more and more dominated
by militant young Negroes of predominantly lower-class background. But Farmer shows no signs of being able to pull these
elements together or to develop a coherent program; CORE
remains essentially a loose collection of small and largely autonomous groups.

The radical student groups like S.N.C.C., Northern Student
Movement, and Students for a Democratic Society are trying
to build a mass base for "the movement." These tough-minded
young people have the courage and commitment to put their
lives on the line; unlike their better-known elders, they live in
the rural and urban slums they are trying to organize. And as

Robert Penn Warren writes, they are "good enough psychologists to understand that a mass base is not created by preaching abstractions; it is created by involvement, by acting out." But their rejection of "the corruption" of white society is too rigid and uncompromising to enable them to succeed. S.N.C.C.'s principal strategy of building "parallel institutions" — e.g., the Mississippi Freedom Democratic Party — may be useful as a means of exerting pressure for change, but it also dooms Negroes to the role of perennial outsiders. The militants can't have it both ways; they can't acquire the political power they consider essential unless they are willing to bring Negroes into the existing political system.

"Too much integrity," as Pat Watters writes, "can be a neurotic paralysis. You can become so right, so uncompromising that you no longer are able to function in this wicked world."

As a result of Watts and the frustrations it revealed, Martin Luther King is now turning his energies to the problem of the northern city; he expects to make Chicago something of a test of his ability to create a mass movement in the North. How much success he will have remains to be seen. Dr. King's appeal has always been much greater among southern than among northern Negroes — and greater among northern whites than among northern Negroes. His philosophy of non-violence has reassured whites; it has tended to anger lower-class Negroes, who see it as coming too close to the image of the docile Negro they have rejected. And the Negroes of the North — particularly the men — have moved pretty far away from the Negro churches, which provide Dr. King's base in the South. Dr. King, too, has had trouble developing a coherent program responsive to the new Negro mood. "Periodic mass euphoria around a charismatic leader should not be confused with building an organization," says Saul D. Alinsky of the Industrial Areas Foundation, who has built working-class organizations in various parts of the country. Dr. King says that he is "less concerned with building an organization than with building a movement," i.e., building "a national consensus that will arouse the conscience of Americans and cause them to respond creatively to Negro demands." But in the last analysis, and despite all the accompanying references to Gandhi's "constructive program" of self-improvement, this leaves the emphasis *not* on change within the *Negro* community, but on action to change the *white* community. "The power structure must help the nonviolent leaders," he says. "We need victories; until we get them, the people won't trust us." Victory, in short, is still defined as something whites give Negroes.

"A Real Ball"

How might the Negro's Negro problem be solved — or at least diminished? It is at least clear that there can be no hope of halting or reversing the breakdown of the Negro family unless Negro men can find jobs that afford them some measure of dignity and enable them to support their families. It may well be that Negro unemployment can't be solved in the short run without some expanded program of public works and training, and King and Rustin seem increasingly interested in some such program. However, they grossly exaggerate the impact of automation and grossly underestimate the private economy's ability to generate jobs — for Negroes as well as whites. As a result of the vigorous rate of growth of the past four years, the unemployment rate among Negro men aged twenty and over has dropped in half — from 12 percent in the second quarter of 1961 to 6 percent in the third quarter of this year.

But it is also clear that the problem is not just an insufficient number of jobs for Negroes. "The roots of the multiple pathology in the dark ghetto," Kenneth Clark writes, "do not lie primarily in unemployment. In fact, if all of its residents were employed it would not materially alter the pathology of the community." More important, in many ways, are the *kinds* of jobs that are made available to Negroes — and Negroes' willingness to take the jobs and their ability to hold them. After the 1964 riots in Harlem, for example, Rustin got jobs for 120 youngsters; a few weeks later, only twelve of them were still working. One boy told Rustin he could make more money playing pool than the $50 a week he had been earning; another could make more than his $60 salary selling "pot" (marijuana); another turned down a four-year basketball scholarship to a major university because he preferred to be a pimp.

The explanation of this behavior, in part, is that the life of the street appears much more glamorous and exciting than the life of work. "My childhood delinquent career was a real ball," Claude Brown, author of the searing autobiography, *Manchild in the Promised Land,* says. "It was an exciting adventure to me. I was a delinquent not because I was forced to, you know what I mean,

I was a delinquent because I wanted to be one."

In part, too, the problem is bound up with the "desperate search for identity" of which Ralph Ellison spoke — in particular, with the younger generation's attempt to escape completely from the "Sambo image" that previous generations were forced to act out. Hence, many of the jobs that are available to people with little or no skill, training, or education — e.g., hospital attendant, waiter, busboy, etc. — are spurned as "slaving," particularly if they are to be performed for whites; the jobs are just too close to the image of servility that Negro teenagers and young adults are trying desperately to escape. The problem has been compounded by the rhetoric of the Negro revolt. "To want a Cadillac is not un-American," Rustin wrote last February; "to push a cart in the garment center is."

What Negro teenagers and adults lack most, however, is not motivation but that minimum sense of competence that is pre-requisite to performing any job. By the time a good many Negro slum youngsters reach sixteen, they have been so completely beaten, so totally convinced of their own worthlessness, of their inability to succeed at anything that they are — or appear to be — unemployable and untrainable. "We are plagued, in work with these youth, by what appears to be a low tolerance for frustra-tion," Professors Richard A. Cloward and Robert Ontell have written, in commenting on the work-training experiences of Mobilization for Youth. "They are not able to absorb setbacks. Minor irritants and rebuffs are magnified out of all proportion to reality. Perhaps they react as they do because they are not equal to the world that confronts them, and they know it. And it is the knowing that is devastating."

"The Time for Failure is Gone"

And yet the situation is not entirely hopeless. As the Moynihan Report observed, "That the Negro American has survived at all is extraordinary — a lesser people might simply have died out, as indeed others have. That the Negro community has not only sur-vived, but in this political generation has entered national affairs as a moderate, humane and constructive national force is the highest testament to the healing powers of the democratic ideal and the creative vitality of the Negro people."

The manner in which the Negroes will continue to impinge on U.S. political life is still being decided. It is not likely that, in the end, many Negroes will nihilistically "opt out" of American society; but it is still unclear how — and by whose efforts — they are going to get in. Somehow, and soon, they must get in, and perhaps the real ground for optimism these days is the fact that this proposition is now accepted as obvious. "It is not enough just to open the gates of opportunity," President Johnson declared last June, in his commencement address at Howard University. "All our citizens must have the ability to walk through those gates." And so we have entered "the next and more profound stage of the battle for civil rights," in which "we seek not just legal equity but human ability — not just equality as a right and a theory, but equality as a fact and as a result." Johnson added, "The time for failure is gone."   end

B. THE MOYNIHAN REPORT*

Christopher Jencks

[Editors' note: From The New York Review of Books, October, 1965. See pages 216–218.]

After six months of private circulation among government officials and a steadily widening circle of increasingly loose-mouthed journalists, the controversial "Moynihan Report" on the Negro family has been released to the public. Actually, the name of Daniel Patrick Moynihan appears nowhere on the 78-page pamphlet. But the authorship of the former Assistant Secretary of Labor for Policy Planning (who recently ran unsuccessfully for the Democratic nomination as President of the New York City Council and is now rumor's favorite candidate for almost every important unfilled job in Washington) is no secret. Nor is it any secret that this document, while not an official statement of federal policy, has influenced recent thinking at every level of government. It lay behind the President's call for a White House

* Reprinted from The New York Review of Books. Copyright 1965 The New York Review.

Conference in November on the problems of Negroes in general and Negro families in particular.

Moynihan's thesis can be summarized as follows: 1. American slavery was the worst version of slavery in human history. 2. The legacy of Negro slavery in America was twofold: segregation and discrimination against Negroes by whites, and establishment of an American Negro culture which disqualifies many of its participants for life in modern America even when the terms of competition are fair and opportunities open. 3. The central defect of American Negro life is the "matrifocal" family, in which the male is a transient who provides neither a regular income, consistent discipline and direction, nor an example to his sons of what they might hope to become as adults. 4. The psychological, social, and economic problems generated by matriarchy are getting worse, not better. Despite all the recent civil rights and poverty legislation, the chasm separating lower-class Negroes from the mainstream of American life is growing wider and deeper. Only a minority is acquiring the more patriarchal, middle-class family style, and only a minority shows signs of participating in the middle class's increasing affluence. 5. The establishment of a "stable" (i.e., more or less "patrifocal") Negro family structure should therefore be made a national goal, and national policy in many different fields should be adjusted to promote this goal.

Moynihan's analysis is in the conservative tradition that guided the drafting of the poverty program (in whose formulation he participated during the winter of 1963–4). The guiding assumption is that social pathology is caused less by basic defects in the social system than by defects in particular individuals and groups which prevent their adjusting to the system. The prescription is therefore to change the deviants, not the system.

Two years ago the children of the poor were to be helped to escape from the "culture of poverty" by more intensive schooling, induction into the Job Corps, provision of more guidance and counselling, and so forth. Now the lower-class Negro family is to be made more like the middle-class white family — though by means which Moynihan does not specify.

Needless to say, this approach has met with enthusiastic support from those middle-class Americans who feel that if "they" were just more like "us," everything would be all right. (Many successful Negroes hold this view, and some of them are active in the civil rights movement.)

Those activists and intellectuals who instinctively defend the interests of the Negro lower classes have been irate, and to my mind somewhat paranoid, about the Report. They argue that there is nothing inherently wrong with matriarchal families, that lower-class Negro family life is in many respects similar to family life in other groups (the more divorce-ridden segments of the white upper class are often cited), and that picking out the Negro family for improvement is a subtle form of racism. They also suspect that by focusing attention on the Negro family the Johnson Administration is really trying to escape from responsibility for other Negro problems, such as unemployment, political exclusion, police brutality, poor housing, and so on. Finally, the radicals have maintained that even if the Negro family is in trouble, it is not a proper target of governmental action, and that involvement in such issues is a first step toward 1984. (This hostility to expanding the role of the federal government seems to derive largely from a fear that the government will try to impose sexual continence and fidelity — virtues which almost all critics think greatly overrated.)

Whether lower-class Negroes would be as offended by the Report as their middle-class critics is hard to tell, since they are obviously in no position to make their views known. Nevertheless, it is difficult to discuss the subject intelligently (or morally) without knowing whether the families in question are matriarchal by necessity or by choice. If they are matriarchal by choice (i.e., if lower-class men, women, and children truly prefer a family consisting of a mother, children, and a series of transient males) then it is hardly the federal government's proper business to try to alter this choice. Instead, the government ought to invent ways of providing such families with the same physical and psychic necessities of life available to other kinds of families. But there is little evidence to suggest that lower-class Negroes really prefer matriarchal families. On the contrary, there is considerable reason to suppose that they eagerly adopt the more patriarchal middle-class norm whenever they can. In that case, the government surely ought to help them do so, by attacking wholesale unemployment among Negro unskilled men, by altering welfare laws which encourage desertion, and even (as Moynihan implies) by making it easier for Negroes to get into the Armed Forces if they want to. Indeed, if the new emphasis on "stabilizing" the Negro family means giving Negroes a free choice between living as they now do or as the white middle classes do, it is hard to think that even the radicals will oppose it.

C. THE NEGRO FAMILY: REFLECTIONS ON THE MOYNIHAN REPORT*

Herbert J. Gans

[*Editors' note: This is a slightly longer version of an article published in* Commonweal, *October 15, 1965. See pages 218–220.*]

The Breakdown of the Negro Family: The "Moynihan Report" and Its Implications for Federal Civil Rights Policy

Last March, the U.S. Department of Labor published "for official use only" a report entitled *The Negro Family: The Case for National Action.* Written by Daniel Patrick Moynihan and Paul Barton just before the former resigned as Assistant Secretary of Labor to run unsuccessfully for President of New York's City Council, it was soon labeled the "Moynihan Report" by the Washington officials who were able to obtain copies.

Although not apparent from its title, the report called for a bold and important change in federal civil rights policy, asking the federal government to identify itself with the Negro Revolution, and to shift its programs from an emphasis on liberty to one on equality. "The Negro Revolution," says Moynihan, "like the industrial upheaval of the 1930's, is a movement for equality as well as liberty," but the Supreme Court decision for school desegregation, the Civil Rights Act of 1964 and 1965 and other legislation have only provided political liberty. The War on Poverty, which Moynihan describes as the first phase of the Negro revolution, makes opportunities available, but job training programs which promise no jobs at their conclusion cannot produce equality. Held back by poverty, discrimination and inadequate schooling, Negroes cannot compete with whites, so that "equality of opportunity almost insures inequality of results."

Federal policies must therefore be devised to provide equality, "distribution of achievements among Negroes roughly comparable to that of whites," for otherwise, "there will be no social peace in the United States for generations."

But according to Moynihan, a serious obstacle stands in the way of achieving equality, the inability of Negroes "to move from

* Reprinted with permission of the author and *Commonweal.*

where they are now to where they want and ought to be." This inability he ascribes to the breakdown of Negro social structure, and more particularly, to the deterioration of the Negro family. The remainder of the report is devoted to an analysis of that deterioration.

Soon after the report was published, President Johnson drew extensively on it for a commencement address at Howard University. He placed himself firmly behind Moynihan's proposal for a policy of equality of results, describing it as "the next and more profound stage of the battle for civil rights," and pointed to the breakdown of the Negro family as a limiting factor. He called for programs to strengthen the family, and announced that a White House conference would be assembled in the fall for this purpose.

During the summer, public interest in both the report and the speech declined as new speeches and reports made the headlines, but after the Los Angeles riots, the Moynihan report suddenly achieved new notoriety, for its analysis of Negro society seemed to provide the best and the most easily available explanation of what had happened in Watts. Demand for copies increased, and now the government has released it to the press. Consequently, it is worth looking more closely at its findings and their implications.

II

From a variety of government and social science studies, Moynihan concludes that the principal weaknesses of the Negro family are its instability, its proclivity for producing illegitimate children, and its matriarchal structure. Nearly a quarter of married Negro women are divorced or separated, and 35 percent of all Negro children live in broken homes. Almost a quarter of Negro births are illegitimate, and nearly one-fourth of all Negro families are headed by a woman. As a result, 14 percent of all Negro children are being supported by the Aid for Families of Dependent Children (A.F.D.C.) program.

Although these figures would suggest that a smaller proportion of the Negro community is in trouble than is often claimed, they also underestimate the extent of the breakdown, for more families are touched by it at one time in their lives than at the given moment caught by the statistics. Thus, Moynihan estimates that less than half of all Negro children have lived with both their parents by the time they reach the age of 18, and many legitimate children grow up without their real fathers. As Lee Rainwater points out in a forthcoming issue of *Daedalus,* lower class Negro women often marry the man who fathers their first or second child in order to obtain the valued status of being married, but thereafter they live in unmarried unions with other men. Also, many households in which a man is present are nevertheless headed by women, for Moynihan indicates that in a fourth of Negro families in which a husband is present, he is not the principal earner. Perhaps the best illustration of the way in which available figures understate the problem comes from unemployment statistics which show that while the average monthly unemployment rate for Negro males in 1964 was 9 percent, fully 29 percent were unemployed at one time or another during that year. Moreover, the rates of family instability among whites are considerably lower and still decreasing, while they are on the rise among the Negro population.

The population which bears the brunt of these instabilities is of course the low-income one. Although the proportion of stable two-parent Negro families is probably increasing, "the Negro community is . . . dividing between a stable middle class group that is steadily growing stronger . . . and an increasingly disorganized and disadvantaged lower class group."

In that group, a significant minority of the families are broken, headed by women, and composed of illegitimate children. The Negro woman can either obtain employment or welfare payments to support her children, while the Negro man, saddled with unstable jobs, frequent unemployment and short-term unemployment insurance, cannot provide the economic support that is a principal male function in American society. As a result, the woman becomes the head of the family, and the man a marginal appendage, who deserts or is rejected by his wife when he can no longer contribute to the family upkeep. With divorce made impossible by economic or legal barriers, the woman may then live with a number of men in what Walter Miller calls "serial monogamy," finding a new mate when the inevitable quarrels start over who should support and head the family. And because the women value children, they continue to have them, illegitimately or not.

This family structure seems to have detrimental effects on the children, and especially on the boys, for they grow up in an environment which constantly demonstrates to them that men are troublesome good-for-nothings. Moynihan's data show that Negro girls do better in school and on the labor market than the boys, and that the latter more often turn to delinquency, crime, alcohol, drugs, and mental illness in order to escape the bitter reality of a hopeless future. The girls are not entirely immune from ill-effects, however, for many become pregnant in their teens, but since the girls' mothers are quite willing to raise their grandchildren, the girls do not become a public and visible social problem.

The fundamental causes of family instability Moynihan properly traces to slavery and unemployment. Drawing on the researches of Frank Tannenbaum and Stanley Elkins, he points out that American slave-owners treated their slaves as mere commodities and, unlike their Latin American counterparts, often denied them all basic human rights, including that of marriage. More important, the structure of Southern slave economy also placed the Negro man in an inferior position. He was needed only when the plantation economy was booming, and his price on the slave market was generally lower than that of the woman. Her services were always in demand around the household—or in the master's bed—and until her children were sold away from her, she was allowed to raise them. This established her in a position of economic and familial dominance which she has maintained, willingly or not, until the present day. All the available evidence indicates that since the Civil War, Negro male unemployment has almost always been higher than female. The gap has been widened further in recent years, especially in the cities, as job opportunities increased for women, while decreasing for men due to the ever shrinking supply of unskilled and semiskilled work and the continuing racial discrimination in many trades. Since Negroes are still moving to the cities in large numbers, the trends which Moynihan reports are likely to continue in the years to come.

Slavery made it impossible for Negroes to establish a two-parent family, and its heritage has undoubtedly left its mark on their descendants. Even so, slavery is only a necessary but not a sufficient cause of the problem. Histories of the 19th century European immigration, anthropological studies of the Caribbean matriarchal family, and observations among Puerto Ricans in American cities indicate that whenever there is work for women and serious unemployment among men, families break up as the latter desert or are expelled. The most impressive illustration of this pattern is a chart in the Moynihan Report which shows that between 1951 and 1963, increases in the Negro male unemployment rate were followed, a year later, by a rise in the proportion of separated women.

Underemployment, being stuck in a dead-end job, and low wages may have similar consequences. The H.A.R.Y.O.U. report on Harlem, *Youth in the Ghetto,* reported that social pathology is as high among those holding inadequate jobs as among the unemployed, and Moynihan points out that the minimum wage of $1.25 an hour, which is all that too many Negroes earn, can support an individual but not a family.

In short, Moynihan's findings suggest that the problems of the Negro family which he sees as holding back the achievement of equality are themselves the results of previous inequalities, particularly economic ones that began with slavery and have been maintained by racial discrimination ever since. The report's concluding proposal, that "the policy of the United States is to bring the Negro American to full and equal sharing in the responsibilities and rewards of citizenship" and that "to this end, the programs of the federal government . . . shall be designed to have the effect, directly or indirectly, of enhancing the stability and resources of the Negro American family," therefore requires a drastic change of direction in federal civil rights activities.

III

The Moynihan Report does not offer any recommendations to implement its policy proposal, arguing that the problem must be defined properly first in order to prevent the hasty development of programs that do not address themselves to the basic problem. While this argument was perhaps justified as long as the report remained confidential, it may have some negative consequences now that the contents have been released to the press. The vacuum that is created when no recommendations are attached to a policy proposal can easily be filled by undesirable solutions, and the report's conclusions can be conveniently misinterpreted.

This possibility is enhanced by the potential conflict between the two major themes of the report, that Negroes must be given real equality, and that because of the deterioration of the family, they are presently incapable of achieving it. The amount of space devoted to the latter theme, and the inherent sensationality of the data make it possible that the handicaps of the Negro population will receive more attention than Moynihan's forthright appeal for an equality of outcomes.

Thus, the findings on family instability and illegitimacy can be used by right-wing and racist groups to support their claim that Negroes are inherently immoral and therefore unworthy of equality. Politicians responding to more respectable white backlash can argue that Negroes must improve themselves before they are entitled to further government aid, and so can educators, psychologists, social workers, and other professionals who believe that the Negro's basic problem is "cultural deprivation" or "ego inadequacy" rather than lack of opportunities for equality. This in turn could lead to a clamor for pseudo-psychiatric programs that attempt to change the Negro family through counseling and other therapeutic methods. Worse still, the report could be used to justify a reduction of efforts in the elimination of racial discrimination and the War on Poverty, watering down programs which have only recently been instituted and have not yet had a chance to improve the condition of the Negro population, but are already under concerted attack from conservative white groups and local politicians.

Of course, the deterioration of Negro society is due both to lack of opportunity and to cultural deprivation, but the latter is clearly an effect of the former, and is much more difficult to change through government policies. For example, poor Negro school performance results both from inadequate, segregated schools and from the failure of the Negro home to prepare children for school, as well as from low motivation on the part of Negro children who see no reason to learn if they cannot find jobs after graduation. Even so, however difficult it may be to improve and desegregate the schools and to provide jobs, it is easier, more desirable and more likely to help Negro family life than attempts to alter the structure of the family or the personality of its members through programs of "cultural enrichment" or therapy, not to mention irresponsible demands for Negro self-improvement.

In addition, it must be stressed that at present, we do not even know whether the lower-class Negro family structure is actually as pathological as the Moynihan Report suggests. However much the picture of family life painted in that report may grate on middle-class moral sensibilities, it may well be that instability, illegitimacy, and matriarchy are the most positive adaptations possible to the conditions which Negroes must endure.

Moynihan presents some data which show that children from

broken homes do more poorly in school and are more likely to turn to delinquency and drugs. Preliminary findings of a study by Bernard Mackler of the Center for Urban Education show no relationship between school performance and broken families, and a massive study of mental health in Manhattan, reported by Thomas Langner and Stanley Michaels in *Life Stress and Mental Health,* demonstrated that among whites at least, growing up in a broken family did not increase the likelihood of mental illness as much as did poverty and being of low status.

Families can break up for many reasons, among them cultural and personality differences among the parents, economic difficulties, or mental illness on the part of one or both spouses. Each of these reasons produces different effects on the children, and not all are likely to be pathological. Indeed, if one family member is mentally ill, removing him from the family and thus breaking it up may be the healthiest solution, at least for the family.

Likewise, the matriarchal family structure and the absence of a father has not yet been proven pathological, even for the boys who grow up in it. Sociological studies of the Negro family have demonstrated the existence of an extended kinship system of mothers, grandmothers, aunts, and other female relatives that is surprisingly stable, at least on the female side. Moreover, many matriarchal families raise boys who do adapt successfully and themselves make stable marriages. The immediate cause of pathology may be the absence of a set of emotional strengths and cultural skills in the mothers, rather than the instability or departure of the fathers. A family headed by a capable if unmarried mother may thus be healthier than a two-parent family in which the father is a marginal appendage. If this is true, one could argue that at present, the broken and matriarchal family is a viable solution for the Negro lower-class population, for given the economic and other handicaps of the men, the family can best survive by rejecting its men, albeit at great emotional cost to them.

Similar skepticism can be applied to premature judgments of Negro illegitimacy. Since illegitimacy is not punished in the lower class as it is in the middle class, and illegitimate children and grandchildren are as welcome as legitimate ones, they may not suffer the pathological consequences that accompany illegitimacy in the middle class. Moreover, even the moral evaluation of illegitimacy in the middle class has less relevance in the Negro lower class, particularly when men cannot be counted on as stable family members.

Finally, illegitimacy and the bearing of children generally has a different meaning in this population than in the middle-class one. Rainwater's previously cited paper suggests that adolescent Negro girls often invite pregnancy because having children is their way of becoming adults and of making sure that they will have a family in which they can play the dominant role for which they have been trained by their culture. Although many older Negro women have children because they lack access to birth control methods they can use or trust, I suspect that others continue to have them because in a society in which older children are inevitably a disappointment, babies provide a source of pleasure and of feeling useful to their mothers. If having children offers them a reason for living in the same way that sexual prowess does for Negro men, then alternate rewards and sources of hope must be available before illegitimacy can either be judged by middle-class standards, or programs developed to do away with it. Until more is known about the functioning and effects of lower-class Negro family structure, the assumption that it is entirely or predominantly pathological is premature.

It would thus be tragic if the findings of the Moynihan Report were used to justify demands for Negro self-improvement or the development of a middle-class family structure before further programs to bring about real equality are set up. Consequently, it is important to see what conclusions and recommendations emerge from the forthcoming White House conference and how the assembled experts deal with the two themes of Moynihan's Report. It is also relevant to describe some recommendations which seem to me to be called for by the findings of that report.

IV

The fundamentally economic causes of the present structure of the Negro family indicate that programs to change it must deal with these causes, principally in the areas of employment, income, and the provision of housing and other basic services. The history of the Negro family since the time of slavery indicates that the most important single program is the elimination of unemployment. If Negro men can obtain decent and stable jobs, then many — and far more than we think — can at once assume a viable role in the family and can raise children who will put an end to the long tradition of male marginality and inferiority.

Neither the current economic boom nor the present programs of the War on Poverty have yet had a significant impact on Negro employment, largely because neither have created decent jobs in sufficient numbers to help the unemployed or underemployed, and those untold many who are not counted in unemployment statistics because they have given up looking for a job. Moreover, because private industry is no longer able to create jobs in the massive numbers it once did, and because technological innovations now make it possible to increase productivity without increasing employment significantly, the federal government must deliberately create new jobs through its activities. A policy that was used initially in the Great Depression and revived this summer in finding work for unemployed adolescents should now be extended to put all able-bodied unemployed men to work.

The fastest way of doing so is a public works program designed to generate a maximum number of decent jobs and to bring about needed improvements in American society. Such a program should build the schools, hospitals, clinics, libraries, recreation facilities, mass transit systems, and the air and water purification machinery sorely needed by most American cities, but its first task should be a giant rehousing program, to provide new housing for low- and middle-income people in the cities and the suburbs, and to clear or rehabilitate the slums. As I indicated in describing such a program in the April 1965 issue of Commentary, construction is one of our most labor-intensive industries, and would create millions of new jobs.

Additional millions of jobs can be provided by raising performance standards in municipal facilities and services, in medicine, social work, the other helping professions and in the War on Poverty, by hiring and training people to function as "subprofessionals" in them. A growing body of evidence, reported in Arthur Pearl and Frank Riessman, New Careers for the Poor, indicates that poor and even previously unemployed people can serve as subprofessionals, especially in low-income neighborhoods, for they are often more able to communicate with and thus help low-income clients than middle-class professionals.

A second set of needed programs must provide equality of incomes for people who cannot work or cannot earn a living wage. Since the minimum wage will not support a family, it must either be raised, or it must be subsidized by governmental wage supplements, which would function like the recently instituted rent supplements to enable people to participate equally in the private consumer goods market.

Increases and changes ought also to be made in welfare and unemployment programs. Since the age of private charity, welfare payments have been minimal, in order to motivate the recipients to find employment instead. In an era when jobs for unskilled workers are scarce, this policy becomes ever more unreasonable and unjust. Moreover, low welfare payments are punitive, depriving people of the minimal decencies that the mass media proclaim to be necessary for everyone, and the more so when their disbursal is supervised by "investigators" who make sure that poor families do not try to earn extra income on the side or spend more than is budgeted for recreation.

The immediate need is for a welfare program based on the premise that people are poor because American society is not distributing resources properly, which would raise payments, do away with budget-setting and call off the investigators. Equally necessary is the provision of unemployment compensation for a much longer period, with payments related to the family size of the unemployed individual. This is especially important for the Negro family, for in many cases it would re-establish the man as the source of his family's income.

Similarly urgent is a change in the program for Aid to Families of Dependent Children, for at present it fosters the instability of the Negro family. By making payments dependent on the absence of the man, it forces him out of the house, and many Negro families are nominally or actually separated so that the mother will be eligible for AFDC payments. Even when this does not happen, the program supports family instability by maintaining the economic independence and thus the economic superiority of the woman. Although families with unemployed men have been eligible for AFDC payments since 1961, less than 10 percent of all AFDC cases are currently in the new program. The immediate solution is to provide payments to all families in which the men cannot provide support. By giving larger payments to households in which husbands are present, family stability and the two-parent family could be encouraged.

Welfare, unemployment and dependency payments, however

high they may be, are by their very nature degrading, thus contributing to the inferiority with which the low-income population is saddled. All of these forms of income subsidy ought
therefore to be replaced by a single system of income grants,
based on the concept of the negative income tax, to be paid to
all households below a minimum income, whatever the reason
for their poverty.

A third set of programs should aim at equality of results in
housing and other basic services. The enforcement of effective
desegregation laws would at once enable many Negro parents
who can afford to live outside the ghetto to raise their children
amidst other stable families. The previously suggested federal
rehousing program combined with an expansion of the rent
supplement scheme would make this opportunity available to
yet others, including many female-headed households who are
struggling desperately to keep their children "off the streets,"
in order to isolate them from early pregnancy, delinquency, and
despair.

The construction of new housing outside the ghetto and the
desegregation of existing housing will automatically provide
Negro children and adults with more equal access to good
schools, hospitals, and other facilities. Until this happens, however, independent steps must be taken to desegregate the schools,
so that Negro youngsters can escape the culture of inferiority
which is endemic to segregated schools, to improve school plants,
teaching methods, and teacher recruitment practices so that
children from lower-class homes are encouraged to learn, and to
so alter the school social climate that lower-class children do
not need to resort to the defensive hostility that now frustrates
attempts to teach them.

Some steps can also be taken to change the female-dominated
environment in which Negro boys grow up. While little can be
done in the home, it is possible to increase the number of men
in schools, recreation centers, settlement houses, and social work
agencies, to give the boys contact with men who have a viable
function, and to reduce the impression — and the fact — that
women are the source of all instruction, authority, and reward
in their lives. Adolescent boys and adult men can be hired as
subprofessionals for this purpose. Similarly, voter registration
and political organization programs ought to be supported, for
politics is, even in the Negro community, a male activity, and

the extension of real democracy to the ghetto would do much to make its residents feel that they have some power to change their lives and their living conditions.

Finally, a massive research program on the structure of the Negro family ought to be undertaken, to determine how and where it breeds pathology, and to permit the development of therapeutic methods to aid those who cannot adapt to programs for equality of results. There will be men who are so ravaged by deprivation and despair that they cannot hold a job even when jobs are plentiful, but I am confident that if men can be given a viable occupational role, if family income is sufficient to guarantee a decent living, if Negroes are freed from the material and emotional punishment of racial discrimination, and are allowed to participate as first-class citizens in the political community, a healthy Negro family structure — which may or may not coincide with the middle-class ideal — will develop as a result.

V

The insistence on equality of results in the Moynihan Report is therefore the most effective approach to removing the instabilities of the Negro family. Whether or not Moynihan's plea — and that made by President Johnson at Howard University — will be heeded remains to be seen. The economic, social, and political changes required to provide equality are drastic, and both the white and the Negro middle class — not to mention the white lower class — have a considerable investment in the status quo which condemns the poor Negro to membership in a powerless, dependent and deprived underclass. President Johnson's success in achieving his legislative program in Congress suggests that some change can be initiated through federal action, but the implementation of civil rights legislation and antipoverty programs also indicates that much of the federal innovation is subverted at the local level and that a significant portion of the new funds are drained off to support the very political and economic forces that help to keep the lower-class Negro in his present position.

Federal and local officials must do all they can to prevent this from happening in the future, but they must be supported — and pressured — by professional, religious, and civic groups dedicated to racial equality. Also, the civil rights movement must begin to represent and speak for the low-income Negro population more than it has done in the past, for if the Negro revolution and the social peace of which Moynihan speaks are to be won, they must be won by and for that population.

Yet inescapably, the Negro problem is primarily a white problem, for the ultimate source of change must be the white population. Of the twin ideals of American democracy which Moynihan describes, it has traditionally opted for Liberty rather than Equality, including the liberty to keep the less equal in their place. It would be hard to imagine a sudden ground swell for equality from the white population, but if it really wants to prevent the spreading of violent protest through race riots, and the proliferation of the less visible but equally destructive protest expressed through delinquency and drug addiction, it must allow its political leaders to make the changes in the American social, economic, and political structure that are needed to move toward equality. Unfortunately, so far most whites are less touched than titillated by riots and family breakdown, and more driven to revenge than to reform when Negro deprivation does reach into their lives. In this desert of compassion, the Moynihan Report is a tiny oasis of hope, and if properly interpreted and implemented, a first guide to the achievement of equality in the years to come.

D. SAVAGE DISCOVERY: THE MOYNIHAN REPORT*

William Ryan†

[Editors' note: From The Nation, *November 22, 1965. This article was widely distributed in slightly longer form in early October, 1965, and was also published in* The Crisis, *publication of the NAACP. See pages 220–232.]*

The Labor Department publication, *The Negro Family* (usually called "The Moynihan Report" in reference to its presumed chief author), had had an enormous impact on public discussion about

---

* Reprinted with permission of the author and *The Nation.*

† William Ryan, Ph.D., a psychologist, teaches in the Harvard Medical School Laboratory of Community Psychiatry, and is a mental health consultant for the Massachusetts Committee on Children and Youth.

the Negro in America. It contains frightening statistics about broken Negro families, illegitimate Negro children and Negro welfare recipients, and these have been seized on by journalists who proclaim in loud voices what the Moynihan Report states very quietly: Negro family instability is a basic cause of the Negro inequality and "pathology" that are reflected in unemployment statistics, census data and the results of sociological research.

In view of this influence, it is important to make public the serious shortcomings of the report that a careful analysis uncovers. Briefly, it draws dangerously inexact conclusions from weak and insufficient data; encourages (no doubt unintentionally) a new form of subtle racism that might be termed "Savage Discovery," and seduces the reader into believing that it is not racism and discrimination but the weaknesses and defects of the Negro himself that account for the present status of inequality between Negro and white. The document can be criticized on three levels: first, the methodological weaknesses; second, the manifest misstatements; and, finally, the naive error of interpreting statistical relationships in cause-and-effect terms; that is, of stating that, since A is associated with B, it follows that A causes B.

Among the methodological weaknesses is the use of such material as census data without apparent awareness either of its deficiencies or, more important, of the existence of other well-known or well-estimated data within whose context this material must be considered. The outstanding example of this failure is a highly sophomoric treatment of illegitimacy.

Illegitimacy looms large in the Moynihan Report, in the text and in the illustrations. Only 4 per cent of the relatively dull tables but fully 22 per cent of the large and dramatic charts and graphs concern illegitimacy, which shines through the report as the prime index of "family breakdown." This is one of the main beams in the hypothetical structure being put together. In an oversimplified way, the implicit hypothesis goes like this: the values of Negro culture (produced by centuries of slavery and mistreatment, to be sure) are such that there is little commitment to the main components of family organization — legitimacy, material stability, etc. The implicit point is that Negroes tolerate promiscuity, illegitimacy, one-parent families, welfare dependency, and everything else that is supposed to follow.

The authors of The Negro Family take at face value Census Bureau statistics that record illegitimacy rates for whites at about

3 per cent, for Negroes at about 22 per cent. More careful consideration, *in the context of other well-known facts,* would reveal not so much a careless acceptance by Negroes of promiscuity and illegitimacy, as a systematic inequality of access to a variety of services and information.

If we do not attribute the 7-to-1 difference in illegitimacy rates to Negro family instability as a subcultural trait, what does account for these differences? Here, very briefly, are a few pieces of additional data:

Reporting. Illegitimate births are significantly underreported, and are more underreported for whites than for nonwhites. This is true, first, because reporting is dependent upon discriminatory white sources. Second, white illegitimate births occur more often in private hospitals, are attended by sympathetic — and white — doctors, and involve the cooperation of social agencies, all of which work consciously to help the white unmarried mother conceal the fact of illegitimacy.

Shotgun marriages. A large portion of first-born children are conceived "illegitimately," with the parents marrying before the child's birth. Such marriages are less frequent among Negroes because of the man's financial insecurity.

Abortion. It is estimated that more than 1 million illegal and unreported induced abortions are performed each year. Authorities agree that one-fourth to one-half of these are performed for unmarried women, and that the overwhelming majority of abortion patients are white. Abortions also account for most of the differences in the census illegitimacy figures.

An attempt to calculate the "illegitimate conception" rates — an awkward but interesting term — would probably show that for whites it would be 12–15 per cent, for Negroes 25–30 per cent. The differences are clearly not so striking: the ratio drops from 7 to 1 to 2 to 1.

Contraception. Access to contraceptive information and services is also unequally distributed in favor of whites. The extent of inequality is not known, but if the differential were as low as 2 to 1 in favor of whites, we would be able to conclude that "illegitimate intercourse" — if we may push the terminology this far — is about the same among Negroes and whites.

In any case, it is not necessary to introduce a complex and highly speculative hypothesis about the malformation of the Negro family by slavery and post-Reconstruction semi-slavery — that is, the sins of our grandfathers. The facts are more easily explained as the results of straightforward discrimination — that is, the sins of ourselves and our contemporaries.

Aid for Dependent Children and Adoption. When they wring their hands about Negro family life, the journalists who have seized on the Moynihan Report are most fascinated with illegitimacy, but their next favorite is its presumed consequence: the number of Negro mothers receiving AFDC support. How, we may ask, does a Negro mother with an illegitimate child "get on" AFDC? First, of course, she must decide to keep the child; how does she make this decision? The answer is remarkably simple: she is rarely called on to make the choice. The services of adoption agencies and maternity homes are mostly for white mothers, who account for about 90 per cent of agency adoptions of illegitimate children, and probably an even higher proportion of independent adoptions. Again to oversimplify: white illegitimate babies get adopted, their Negro counterparts "go on" AFDC. And again we are faced with *contemporary* discrimination — our sins, not the sins of our grandparents.

To summarize, the reported rates of illegitimacy among Negroes and whites tell us nothing at all about differences in family structure, historical forces, instability, or anything else about which the authors speculate. From the known data, we can conclude only that Negro and white girls probably engage in premarital intercourse in about the same proportions, but that the white girl more often takes Enovid or uses a diaphragm; if she gets pregnant, she more often obtains an abortion; if she has the baby, first she is more often able to conceal it and, second, she has an infinitely greater opportunity to give it up for adoption.

The treatment of illegitimacy data in the Moynihan Report is one example of inexpert methodology. A more general defect is the subtly irrational presentation of correlational data to imply a cause-and-effect relationship. The method of argument is, first, to present data about "family breakdown" among Negroes — separation, illegitimacy, broken homes, female household heads, etc. — and then to juxtapose statistics about the "tangle of pathology" among Negroes. In the manner of a propaganda document, the report allows the reader to make the cause-and-effect connection on the basis of his own prejudice. Little or no actual cause-and-effect data is presented.

Of the total of 125 different blocks of information presented — forty-seven tables, eighteen charts and sixty pieces of data in the text — *more than 80 per cent* is purely descriptive, retailing stale and well-known sociological facts. Only nine pieces of information (a scant 7 per cent of the total) relate to the conclusions drawn by the authors. Of these nine, six are reports of studies showing a relationship between broken homes and delinquency, and one is drawn from the 1960 census to show that children with both parents present in the home are — not unsurprisingly — less likely to drop out of school. The final two pieces of evidence show that the tested IQs of children with fathers in the home are higher than those without fathers in the home.

This is the sum total of evidence from which the authors draw such sweeping conclusion as:

At the heart of the deterioration of the fabric of Negro society is the deterioration of the Negro family. It is the fundamental source of weakness of the Negro community at the present time.

Unless this damage [the deterioration of the Negro family] *is repaired, all the effort to end discrimination and poverty and injustice will come to little.*

Three centuries of injustice have brought about deep-seated structural distortions in the life of the Negro American. . . . The cycle can be broken only if these distortions are set right. In a word, a national effort toward the problems of Negro Americans must be directed toward the question of family structure.

Confronted with such enormous conclusions based on such tiny scraps of evidence, an uncharitable response would be "irresponsible nonsense!"; the most charitable possible verdict would be "not proved."

Of the other thirteen pieces of data in which evidence of relationships is presented, two are somewhat tangential, showing that poor people have larger families than rich people, a fact that has not heretofore been very well concealed. The other eleven show relationships between unemployment and broken families, unemployment and illegitimacy, income level and illegitimacy, and unemployment and public assistance under the AFDC program. These, too, are well-known relationships, and anyone with a tolerable command of social statistics could add a whole set of additional correlations: unemployment and infant mortality, income level and dilapidated housing, broken families and number of tuberculosis cases, etc., etc. What these cool correlations mean, when translated from census data to the lives of human beings, is that poor people tend to live in slums, to be oppressed and exploited and mistreated, and to experience enormous amounts of social, economic, mental and physical suffering as a result. A disproportionate share of the poor are Negro and they experience a vastly disproportionate share of this suffering. It would be far more reasonable to conclude not that "family instability" leads to a "tangle of pathology" but that poor Negro families — that is, half of all Negro families — are bitterly discriminated against and exploited, with the result that the individual, the family and the community are all deeply injured.

It is not possible to comment on this smug document without pointing out a few errors of fact. The first — "conditions in Harlem are not worse, they are probably better than in most Negro ghettos" — is followed, predictably, by data about high illegitimacy rates in Harlem to suggest apparently that even in Harlem, the very paradise of ghettos, the Negro family is falling apart.

Another stupefying statement in the report is: "It is probable that, at present, a majority of the crimes against the person, such as rape, murder, and aggravated assault, are committed by Negroes." To support this statement the authors quote *arrest* and *conviction* rates, which are notoriously different from rates of crimes committed. It is well known that Negroes — guilty and innocent alike — are more readily arrested, and convicted, than whites. To conclude from the data offered that Negroes commit the majority of significant crimes is an inept piece of interpretation.

Another fantastic error deserves to be quoted: "The white family has achieved a high degree of stability and is maintaining that stability. By contrast, the family structure of lower class Negroes . . . is approaching complete breakdown." Such a statement reflects a double standard: if we were to use the authors' indices of family stability, principally divorce and illegitimacy, we should have to say that both white and Negro families — American families in general — are "crumbling." White divorce rates have zoomed almost 800 per cent in less than 100 years, and white illegitimacy has increased more than 50 per cent in the last twenty-five years — a rate of increase greater than that of Negroes.

What we are confronted with, in fact, is another example of the authors' ineptness — the careless tying together of such vague concepts as "family stability" with a few specific measures of family composition. No sophisticated social scientist would rest a broad concept on such crude and simplistic measures. That the family is an extremely complex institution is almost too well known to require restatement. Its structure and function vary in subtle ways, over time, and from one culture to another. If we were to adopt *The Negro Family*'s narrow and wholly inadequate framework for evaluating family stability, we could raise an equally sensational storm about the urban family falling apart when compared with the farm family; or the modern family when compared with the family of our grandfathers' day. Which may suggest why it is unwise to take a few pieces of census data and draw forth portentous conclusions about "the fabric of society" and "family structure" and "structural distortions in the life of the Negro American." It takes more than a desk calculator to make such judgments.

Evidence of improvements in American race relations is to be found all the way from Birmingham lunch counters to national television commercials. As yet, however, the change has had little impact on the life of the average American Negro. He remains badly housed, badly educated, underemployed and underpaid. The terms of the discourse change, but the inequality persists; and we spend more time in explaining this inequality than in doing something about it.

The explanations almost always focus on supposed defects of the Negro victim as if those — and not the racist structure of American society — were the cause of all woes that Negroes suffer. The Moynihan Report, following this line of thinking, singles out the "unstable Negro family" as the cause of Negro inequality. But the statistics, as has been suggested, reflect current effects of contemporaneous discrimination. They are results, not causes.

The new ideology, accepted now even by some liberals, would make it seem that unemployment, poor education and slum conditions result from family breakdown, "cultural deprivation," and lack of "acculturation" of Southern rural migrants.

To sustain this ideology, it is necessary to engage in the popular new sport of Savage Discovery, and to fit the theory, savages are being discovered in great profusion in the Northern ghetto. The all-time favorite "savage" is the promiscuous mother who produces a litter of illegitimate brats in order to profit from AFDC. Other triumphs of savage discovery are the child who cannot read because, it is said, his parents never talk to him, and the "untenantable" Negro family (apparently a neologism for "unbearable") that is reputed to throw garbage out the window.

If we are to believe the new ideologues, we must conclude that segregation and discrimination are not the terrible villains we thought they were. Rather, we are told the Negro's condition is due to his "pathology," his values, the way he lives, the kind of family life he leads. The major qualification — the bow to egalitarianism — is that these conditions are said to grow out of the Negro's history of being enslaved and oppressed — *generations ago.*

It is all an ingenious way of "copping a plea." As the murderer pleads guilty to manslaughter to avoid a conviction that might lead to his being electrocuted, liberal America today is pleading guilty to the savagery and oppression against the Negro that happened 100 years ago, in order to escape trial for the crimes of today.

The theme is: "The Negro was not initially born inferior, he has been made inferior by generations of harsh treatment." Thus we continue to assert that the Negro is inferior, while chastely maintaining that all men are equal. It is all rather painful, as well as fallacious. For the fact is that the Negro child learns less not because his mother doesn't subscribe to *The Reader's Digest* and doesn't give him colored crayons for his third birthday, but because he is miseducated in segregated slum schools.

The Negro is more often unemployed because he is last hired and first fired — not because his mother preferred a succession of temporary lovers to a permanent husband. Whenever we move toward full employment, the Negro is employed, usually, of course, at the bottom of the status ladder. When workers are needed badly enough, the supposed lack of skills of the Negro suddenly becomes less inhibiting. This was shown during the war, when it was more important to have someone operating the lathe, even if Negro, than it was to preserve the myth of Negro inability.

And the squalor of the Negro family's home in the Northern slum requires no farfetched explanations about Southern rural background. In the first place, most of these families are not recently from the South and few are rural. In the second place, the condition of the housing is more easily explained by the neglect of slum landlords, and the crowding caused by the criminal shortage of decent low-income housing.

It is tempting, when faced with a complex problem, to wallow in the very chaos of complexity rather than to begin the task of unraveling and analyzing and, ultimately, of acting. It is obviously true that the Negro suffers from a never-ending cycle of oppression not only from generation to generation but, in the case of many individuals, from medically uncared-for birth to premature death. Each condition has its labyrinth of causation, and we soon discover that the Negro family of six in the three-room apartment has been placed there not only by the greedy slumlord and the barbarous realtor but also and equally by the venal housing inspector, and even by the noble women leagued with her sisters in voting for a "progressive" zoning ordinance in her trim suburban town.

But to move from the recognition of infernal complexity to the refuge of damnably inaccurate simplicity is surely heresy. Much has to be done. All of it is difficult, tangled and anxious-making. Still it must be done; there's no escape in the world of sociological fakery.

Time after time, the Negro has had to deny in action the myths and lies that have been constructed to soothe the conscience of his oppressor. He had to deny his supposed docility, first by hopeless revolts against his slave-master, and then by fighting in blue uniforms by the hundreds of thousands; his lack of interest in education by almost magically expanding the few dollars he could lay hands on to send his sons through high school and his granddaughters to graduate school. He had to deny the myth of apathy both by the organized brilliance of a Woodlawn organization in Chicago and the Mississippi Freedom Democratic Party in Mississippi, and by the unorganized bursts of blind energy that we called riots in Los Angeles, Philadelphia, Harlem and Rochester.

If we persist in creating a new set of myths to justify the *status quo*; calling on the sociologists and their friends to give us the ammunition of "family disorganization" and "cultural deprivation," the Negro will doubtless destroy these too. But when we've started to move toward ending the myths that have bound us so long, to end the racism that has truly caused a "breakdown" in our community and our nation, why turn back?

Obviously, if we stop discriminating tomorrow, great damage will remain — damage ranging from miseducation that is at best partly reversible, to hatred and bitterness that may be unalterable. This damage calls for correction and compensation. But we must be clear what we mean by "compensatory programs" and we must face directly what we are compensating for. Compensation *should* mean that we give back what we took away. For the millions of grown and half-grown Negro Americans who have already been damaged, we must make up for the injury that we did to them. This is what we must compensate for; not for some supposed inherent or acquired inferiority or weakness or instability of the victim whom we injured.

What, then, is to be done? The young Negro man who dropped out of school or, worse, graduated from high school with a seventh-grade education, represents a specific example of damage done — in *his* lifetime, in *our* lifetime. The damage must be corrected to the greatest extent possible, by re-education, by training, by any means that become necessary. If a result of the demoralizing experience of growing up Negro is that a man does not in fact have the skills to obtain available work, he cannot be written off and relegated to a life of welfare subsistence. And it is almost as cruel to go through the motions of furnishing him irrelevant skills for imaginary jobs.

But the first order of business remains, now and in the near future, to bring a real end to real discrimination and segregation. These are the major causes of the conditions which the Moynihan Report so easily labels "family instability" and the "tangle of pathology." We must not forget to end discrimination or all our good works will amount to very little.

E. THE NEGRO FAMILY AND THE MOYNIHAN REPORT*

Laura Carper

[Editors' note: From Dissent, March–April, 1966. See pages 266–267.]

When discussed among the editors of Dissent, the following article aroused unusually strong reactions, pro and con. We print it because it focuses

* Reprinted with permission of the author and Dissent.

sharply on controversial matters. Several editors have declared their inten-
tion to dispute Mrs. Carper in a subsequent issue; and a copy of the article
has been sent to Mr. Moynihan with an invitation to reply. — Ed.

      MRS. BOYLE: We'll go. Come, Mary, an' we'll never come back here
agen. Let your father furrage for himself now; I've done all I could
an' it was all no use — he'll be hopeless till the end of his days. I've
got a little room in me sisther's where we'll stop till your throuble is
over, an' then we'll work together for the sake of the baby.
      MARY: My poor little child that'll have no father!
      MRS. BOYLE: It'll have what's far better — it'll have two mothers.
                          (*Juno and the Paycock*, Act III, Sean O'Casey)

The culmination of intensive efforts to codify the life of the
hapless is a document published by the Department of Labor
entitled *The Negro Family: The Case for National Action* and
commonly referred to as "The Moynihan Report," after the
reputed head of the investigation — the sociologist Daniel Moynihan. With the publication of this document a sociological theory
which borders on an ideology has become a political weapon
which we are all obliged to examine. In order to understand the
theoretical framework within which this document was written,
we must take a cursory look at sociological thought in the recent
period.

In 1960, Dreger and Miller published in the *Psychological Bulletin* a critical evaluation of the "Comparative Psychological
Studies of Negroes and Whites in the United States," which was
an examination of the relevant contributions in the field between
1943 and 1958. They concluded that "in the areas of psychological
functioning most closely related to the sociological, social class
differences show up more clearly as a basis for differentiation
between the two groups. Leadership, family life, child rearing
practices, fertility and mate selection all seem to conform to social
structure rather than to racial lines per se."

Dreger and Miller's conclusion reflected the intensive efforts
of liberal sociological and psychological thought of the period. It
was the culmination of a thoroughgoing examination of the corrosive effects of our peculiar social organization and value system
on the Negro as compared to the white. They were unable to
find a uniquely Negro personality or Negro psychology in any
class. Their conclusion became a landmark in the field with which
every investigator has been forced to contend.

In April 1964, however, *The Journal of Social Issues* published
a collection of studies with an introduction by Thomas Pettigrew
and Daniel C. Thompson and a lead article by Thomas Pettigrew

which sought to delineate what Dreger and Miller were unable
to locate — a Negro personality and a Negro psychology. Frankly
admitting that in this effort social psychology was whistling in
the dark since the Negro was notorious for his refusal to reveal
his inner self to the social investigator and since it was virtually
impossible to establish control groups of whites, Pettigrew nevertheless argued that past findings have "underestimated the corrosive effects on young children of impecunious ghetto living."
This may indeed be true, but the theoretical basis of the issue
is that due to the vicissitudes of his history and the brutality of
white society, the Negro has developed a recognizable psychology
and a recognizable personality which emerged under slavery, and
that this psychology is self-sustaining and transmitted from generation to generation. The studies, together with the introduction,
almost seem to argue for the existence of a racial unconscious.

The thinking here represents a powerful tendency in modern
sociological thought; and it is this thinking, shorn of its somewhat
hesitant and carefully hedged tone, which characterizes the ideological commitment of The Report on the Negro Family and the
direction its authors feel national action should take.

The thesis of the Report is that the Negro poor "confront the
nation with a new kind of problem. Measures that have worked
in the past, or would work for most groups in the present will not
work here. A national effort is required that will give unity and
purpose to the many activities of the Federal government in this
area, directed to a new kind of national goal: the establishment
of a stable Negro family structure." The presumption is that the
Negro poor are no longer merely the victims of white institutional
corruption but also, to an undetermined extent, of their corrosive
family life; that despite the enactment of the voting rights bill,
the creation of the "Manpower Retraining Program, The Job
Corps, and Community Action — et al," fifty per cent of the
Negro population is incapable of profiting because of a psychological distemper.

The argument is supported with an array of statistics but without any effort to come to terms with the fact that variations in
life style and social adjustment within the ghetto and between
the Northern and Southern Negro poor are far more varied than
between all of them and society at large. Fifty per cent of the
Negro population is identified as reflecting the "social pathology"
these statistics itemize, and the Negro family is recognized as its
"source."

On page thirteen of the report there is a graph charting the non-white male unemployment rate and the number of AFDC (Aid to Families with Dependent Children) cases opened each year. This graph is the strongest argument the report offers to substantiate its thesis that the Negro poor have been so crippled by their situation and history that ordinary measures — which I suppose would be full employment, a radical revision of the ghetto school system, integrated education, decent housing, and a rigorously controlled police force — will no longer suffice; that what is now needed is a national effort not to alter our white social institutions but the way the Negro poor relate to each other on the primary personal level — the family.

The graph shows a direct correlation between the non-white male unemployment rate and AFDC cases opened each year between 1948 and 1961. As the unemployment rate drops, AFDC cases drop; as the unemployment rate rises, AFDC cases rise. But in 1962 a negative correlation begins to emerge; in 1963 the lines for each cross; in 1964 AFDC cases continue to rise as the unemployment rate continues to drop. Presumably, the negative correlation after 1962 shows or suggests that giving the Negro male a job will no longer insure or help insure family stability. The conclusion is that something more is needed.

I am not prepared to argue an economic determinist thesis. It is not my contention that the area of full employment is the only front on which we should fight. But I would like to attempt to explain the graph, particularly since the authors of the report direct the readers attention to the negative correlation and argue that no government program should be instituted which aims at relieving the plight of the Negro poor until the reasons for the reversal are understood.

The first consideration in evaluating statistics is to understand their relevance. *New* AFDC cases must therefore be compared with the unemployment rate of young Negroes. A little investigation shows that the unemployment rate for non-white males as a whole is not reflected in the unemployment rate of non-white youth. Non-white youth, male and female, show a radically different set of statistics; and it is of course the young and not the mature Negro woman who would be a new AFDC case. The unemployment rate for eighteen and nineteen year old non-white men rose from 23.9% in 1961 to 27.4% in 1963, and for eighteen and nineteen year old women who would be obliged to assist in the support of their families from 28.2% to 31.9%. Taken as a whole, the unemployment rate of non-white men between the ages of sixteen and twenty-four during the years in question fluctuates but shows little over-all change. In 1963, the year the lines for AFDC cases and the unemployment rate converge, the rates were especially high. Where the over-all non-white male unemployment rate went down in 1963, the unemployment rate for youth went up and then went down a little in 1964. The picture for young non-white women is comparable. Their rate showed a general tendency to increase.

These figures, although they radically temper the implications of the graph, do not account for the extent of the reversal. A complete explanation must include the famous 1962 change in the social security law. There is a remarkable correlation between AFDC figures and the date of the new law, which authorized greater social and case work service to the poor. In the state of Michigan at least (I choose Michigan arbitrarily, only because I live there and was in a position to discuss the graph with the welfare department), the department has interpreted this law as a directive to alter its standards. Prior to 1962, if an applicant was a poor housekeeper, mentally disturbed, or evidence of a male friend could be found, her application for AFDC was denied; after 1962 she was accepted if she showed need, regardless of her housekeeping practices, her mental health or her social life. Whereas between July 1960 and June 1961 33.4% of the applications were denied, only 28% were denied between July 1963 and June 1964. The strange graph in the Moynihan Report is the result of graphing the wrong things. The negative correlation is due to an inconsistency between youth unemployment rate and the unemployment rate of the non-white male population as a whole and to an important change in policy on the part of the welfare authorities. As a staff member of the department informed me, "it is our policy to give everyone a chance now." The thinking behind the new policy is that by accepting the "undeserving" poor as well as the "deserving" poor, case-work service is made available to those who need it most. It is inevitable that as news of this policy change spreads among the Negro poor and as each of the states slowly alters its policy to conform to this new view, AFDC cases will continue to rise.

The Negro family is not the source of the "tangle of pathology" which the report attributes to the Negro community. It is the pathological relationship between white social institutions and the Negro community which has bred the statistics the report cites — from low scholastic averages to drug addiction to arrest records to illegitimacy to unemployment rates. This is the reason the Black Muslims have chosen to withdraw, and this is the reason the civil rights movement has chosen to confront us.

The statistics I have tried to examine are the supportive evidence the report offers in defense of a social psychological theory. In brief the argument is that American slavery stripped the Negro of his culture and his most minimal human rights; and that the Negro, under continued oppression, developed a matriarchal family organization within which the male played an inadequate role, if any. The argument continues that since American family life is patriarchal, the matriarchal family formulation is pathological and is perpetuating a pathological Negro culture — as the statistics show. But I cannot help wonder with James Tobin, who published an interesting economic study in the Fall 1965 issue of *Daedalus,* why "personal attributes which doom(ed) a man to unemployment in 1932 or even 1954 or 1961 did not handicap him in 1944 or 1951 or 1956." Peter Townsend has pointed out that in 1930 many Englishmen estimated that as many as a million of their fellow-countrymen were unemployable because of their personal problems and only a decade later found that only 100,000 could be characterized in this way. There was a manpower shortage in 1940. What appears to be a social malformation in one period becomes the problem of isolated individuals in another.

The Negro poor are distinguished from the middle class primarily by the fact that they are poor. The father is haphazardly employed and at a very low wage. He is frequently absent from the family scene. He has either deserted or been thrown out by the mother. If he is present and works, he may squander his income. The children are raised by an extended family of adult women. This picture does not focus on fifty per cent of the Negro families. But it does include a significant section of the Negro poor. Is it peculiar to them?

"Matriarchy" is a cultural formation common to many oppressed people throughout the history of western civilization — regardless of their own past history and regardless of the values they themselves held. A brilliant and moving characterization of how and why such a family constellation developed among the Irish poor can be found in Sean O'Casey's play *Juno and the Paycock,* from which I took the quotation which precedes this piece. The Irish matriarchal family formation is noteworthy because it existed in conflict with an Irish patriarchal ideal.

Both Patricia Sexton and Oscar Lewis have shown that the poor Puerto Rican family is beginning to move toward the same "pathology" as the Negro: illegitimacy and families with a woman at the helm.

The same can be said of Jewish family life in the shtetl. Although illegitimacy was not a problem (partly because divorce merely involved a witnessed statement placed in the hand of the wife; the father was frequently absent, either as a peddler on the road, as an immigrant in America, or as a permanent resident of the house of study who came home only to eat). Newly married couples usually moved into the home of the bride's parents. Among the Hassidic Jews (Hassidism was a movement initiated by the poor), it was common for the father to leave his wife and children without a kopek or a groshen in the house and depart for the Rebbe's court where he would dance and drink and spend all his money. As among the American poor, relations between husband and wife were cold and the roles of each clearly defined. The wife worked and assumed the main burden of supporting the family, and children became adults before they had ever had an opportunity to be children. The man either struggled desperately to make a living with little success or withdrew entirely into a private male society based on discourse or ecstacy and left the family to shift for itself. What the Jewish man succeeded in doing that the Negro man has failed to do is place a positive value on family desertion and personal withdrawal.

Since the Negro man does not rationalize his role as being a desirable religious achievement, it seems to me he would be easier to integrate into the surrounding culture than the Jew. After all, once integration became a viable possibility, even the shtetl Jew cast off what no longer served him. And the depth and extent to which oppression and poverty reduced the Jew can be measured by the disintegrative effects of the widespread Messianic movements, two of which emphasized orgiastic sexual practices as a means of insuring the coming of the Messiah.

I have chosen to detail the matriarchal organization of the Jewish family life not because it corresponds to the Negro family but because sociologists look upon Jewish family life as remarkably cohesive. Is the caricature I have drawn of the shtetl family accurate? Of course not. I have applied Mr. Moynihan's method of describing the Negro to a description of the Jew. I lumped a few hundred years of history together and failed to distinguish between people. Pathology is in the eye of the beholder. If one eliminates the positive social function of a cultural constellation, if one ignores the meaning personal relations have to the people involved, if one, in short, uses science to depersonalize, what emerges is always pathology. For health involves spontaneous human feelings of affection and tenderness which the Moynihan Report, like my deliberate caricature of Jewish family life, cannot encompass.

Let me also add that I am not trying to draw any direct analogies between the Irish poor, the Jewish poor, or even the Puerto Rican poor, and the Negro poor. I am seeking to show the "matriarchy" within the larger social context of what the report calls "patriarchy" is common to the way of life of poor people. And further, that people living under oppression always develop social formations which appear to the surrounding oppressive culture to be excessive or pathological. The form these so-called excesses take varies from culture to culture and person to person within the culture — but no matter how extreme the nature of the adjustment, once the social pressure which created it is removed, a new adjustment develops. A people is not destroyed by its history. What destroys a people is physical annihilation or assimilation, not its family life.

The question the report raises is the direction a government program would take to insure family stability. What is the quality of the solutions Mr. Moynihan has in mind? The report includes a detailed description of the therapeutic effects of military service. Mr. Moynihan argues that the armed forces are educational and that they "provide the largest single source of employment in the nation." He admits that "for those comparatively few who are killed or wounded in combat, or otherwise, the personal sacrifice is inestimable. But on balance, service in the Armed Forces over the past quarter-century has worked greatly to the advantage of those involved. . . . Service in the United States Armed Forces is the *only* [author's italics] experience open to the Negro-American in which he is truly treated as an equal: not as a Negro equal to any white, but as one man equal to any man in a world where the category 'Negro' and 'white' do not exist." Mr. Moynihan further states that for the Negro "the armed forces are a dramatic and desperately needed change: a world away from women, a world run by strong men of unquestioned authority, where discipline, if harsh, is nonetheless orderly and predictable and where rewards, if limited, are granted on the basis of performance." This view of the desirability of army life is patently absurd. Underlying the Report's understanding of the problems of the Negro family is its author's concept of masculinity. According to the Report "the essence of the male animal, from the bantam rooster to the four-star general, is to strut."

I cannot here counterpose my taste in men or my concept of the good life against Mr. Moynihan's — but it seems clear to me that it is for the Negro male himself to determine his sexual and social style — whether strutting or not.

The challenge to the Negro community is political. It remains to be seen whether we can make room for the poor to acquire social and economic power. This is our social problem — and not the existence of a matriarchal family organization. What is more, Frank Riessman has found that involving emotionally disturbed people among the Negro poor in the civil rights movement can resolve their personal problems. What is destructive to the Negro man and woman is social impotence here and now, and what rehabilitates them is social power and the struggle for it. It is not new for a ruling elite to characterize its poor as incontinent and shiftless. It is the characteristic way in which those on top describe those on the bottom, even when sincerely trying to uplift them. My Negro landlady encountered a helpful woman who tried to tell her that Negro culture was rooted in the life style of slavery and fixed by history. In telling me about the conversation my landlady said, "That woman thinks that if she handed me a bail of cotton, I'd know how to make a dress out of it!" The Negro is not grappling with the social system under which he lived over a hundred years ago, or even with the social system under which he lived ten years ago. He is grappling with the social system under which he lives today.

F. IN DEFENSE OF THE NEGRO FAMILY*

Frank Riessman

[Editors' note: From Dissent, March–April, 1966. See pages 266–267.]

> I am convinced that Daniel Moynihan is sincerely opposed to discrimination and his report is intended to document its negative consequences

* Reprinted with permission of the author and Dissent.

for the Negro. From my point of view, however, the report represents a highly inappropriate approach to the development of programs and policy to fulfill the rights of the Negro. — F.R.

The Moynihan Report employs supposed inadequacies of the Negro family as an explanatory tool for understanding why the Negro has not taken his place fully in the economic structure of our society. Presumed family pathology, particularly illegitimacy, is said to be an important cause for the under-employment and inadequate education of the Negro.

The questions raised by Moynihan and many others at the White House Conference on Civil Rights are crucial ones: Would the removal of all forms of discrimination enable the Negro to take his place economically in American society? Has the Negro been so damaged by discrimination that even if these barriers were removed, he could not be adequately employed and educated? Perhaps full employment and the removal of discrimination would bring the Negro into the mainstream far more rapidly than is assumed. But one thing seems clear: if Negroes are offered more of the same in the way of education, training and employment, they will be less than responsive. They are not terribly interested in training which does not lead to jobs or which leads at best to dead-end menial jobs. They are not attracted to the summer programs of the busy-work, anti-riot type. And they have not been receptive to "compensatory education" which constantly stresses their deficits.

The basic defect in the Moynihan thesis is a *one-sided presentation of the consequences of segregation and discrimination.* That damage has been done to the Negro as a result of discrimination cannot and should not be denied. But the Negro has responded to his oppressive conditions by many powerful coping endeavors. He has developed many ways of fighting the system, protecting himself, providing self-help and even joy. One of the most significant forms of his adaptation has been the extended, female-based family.

To overlook this adaptation and instead to emphasize one-sidedly the limiting aspects and presumed pathology of this family is to do the Negro a deep injustice. And it is most inappropriate to attempt to involve people in change by emphasizing some alleged weakness in their make-up. People are much more readily moved through an emphasis on their strengths, their positives, their coping abilities. Thus Dr. John Spiegel, in providing psychotherapy for low-income populations, is most concerned to work with the extended family rather than ignore it or stress its difficulties.

Conceptualizations developed in psychiatry have important bearing on this issue of strength and weakness. For example, it has come to be recognized that *mental health and mental illness can co-exist in the same individual — that a person may have considerable pathology and at the same time have considerable strength;* one is not the inverse of the other. In other words, it is not accurate to assume that because an individual has more pathology, he has less strength or health. Health and pathology are two continuums, albeit overlapping ones. This concept has enormous implications for social action because it draws attention to the need for concentrating on the health-producing aspects of an organism or group.

Moynihan's stress on pathology and deficit is not unique. The HARYOU Report similarly stresses various indices of pathology in Harlem and fails to accent the strengths, the cohesion, etc. It is thus no accident that the Haryou Report misinterprets the low rate of suicide among the Negro population. If it followed the classic Durkheim theory, it would note that a low rate of suicide is generally an index of the *cohesion* of a group.

The Limitations of "Compensatory Education"

In the field of education there is a widely heralded, although essentially unsuccessful approach, which, like Moynihan's one-sidedly attempts to develop a theory of action based on deficits. This is the "compensatory education" thesis. It does not build on the action style, the cooperative (team) learning potential, or the hip language of the poor. Instead, "compensatory education" stresses deficits and attempts to build an entire program on overcoming these deficits.* Like the Moynihan family approach, it is one-sided in principle and doomed to failure in practice.

---

* One should be very careful to specify what the presumed deficits are. It is not correct to talk about language deficiency as a general defect among low-income populations. It is more accurate to speak about deficiency in syntax and formal language. But in other aspects of language, such as the use of metaphor, rich adjectives, hip language, the connection between verbal and non-verbal communication, there is positive strength. A much more significant deficit of low-income populations is lack of school know-how and lack of system know-how. Similarly, in relation to the family, it is very important to specify what the supposed weaknesses are, and how these supposed weaknesses are translated into preventing the individual from functioning in the employment and education structures. The mechanism of this connection is often vague.

As long ago as 1955 I reported that Negro families in large numbers stated that education was what *they had missed most in life and what they would like their children to have.* These matriarchal Negro families are very pro-education, although they have long criticized I.Q. tests, all-white readers, condescending PTA's, and together with their children have indicated a strong desire for a livelier, more vital school. Their surprisingly tough, masculine youngsters would like a more male-oriented school. This can be achieved by hiring large numbers of males as non-professional teacher aides, recreation aides, parent education coordinators. Since much of the learning in the family comes less from the parents and more from the brothers and sisters and friends on the street, this method of peer learning might be well adapted in the school itself. (Lippitt has demonstrated how disadvantaged 6th grade youngsters helped 4th grade youngsters for a short time during the week and both groups dramatically improved in their performance!)

If one wants to improve the educability of the Negro, it would seem much more relevant to stress changes in school practice and to develop this practice so that it is more attuned to the style and strengths of the population in question rather than to emphasize the reorganization of the family. The latter emphasis seems much more indirect and less likely to produce the desired result. Similarly in the employment area, it would appear more appropriate to develop meaningful jobs for large numbers of low-income Negroes — e.g., non-professional jobs, where the job is provided first and the training built-in, rather than being concerned about the family. In the Howard University Community Apprentice Experiment, it was demonstrated that highly delinquent functionally illiterate Negro youngsters were able to function in non-professional jobs when the training was built into the job. Their life patterns and work patterns were markedly changed as a result of this new non-professional job experience even though there were no changes in their family pattern.

The emphasis on the deficits and damages of the Negro people kept sociologists from predicting the powerful Negro upheaval that developed into the Civil Rights Movement. This behavior could not be accounted for by an emphasis on the weaknesses, deficiencies and supposed lack of bootstraps. The uprising evolved from the Negro's *strength,* his protest, his anger, and when the conditions were ripe, these traits produced a powerful movement.

In response to the deficiencies of the system the Negro has

developed his own informal system and traditions in order to cope and survive. Storefront churches, the extended family, the use of the street as a playground, the block party, the mutual help of siblings, the informal know-how and self-help of the neighborhood, the use of peer learning, hip language, the rent strike and other forms of direct social action are just a few illustrations.

The community action phase of the anti-poverty program is attempting to build on these positive traditions; thus the use of neighborhood service-center storefronts and non-professional neighborhood helpers are strategic features of the new community action program.

Only by calling upon these traditions can the Negro move into the mainstream of our society and, not incidentally, can our society benefit enormously from incorporation of some of these traditions. It is the Negro who is basically challenging our educational system and producing the demand for changes in educational technology and organization that will be of benefit to everyone.

There is increasing evidence that the integrated education drive is actually powering educational benefits for *all* children, not only Negro children. For example, the great hue and cry that arose regarding the "segregated," white face, white theme "Dick and Jane" readers, has led to the development of a variety of new "urban" readers that appear not only to improve the reading ability of the Negro children but also the white children's reading. Even more dramatic, the *Wall Street Journal* (Jan. 20, 1965) reports that in approximately 10% of *Southern* schools where some desegregation has taken place, not only do the Negro pupils improve rapidly but the white youngsters appear to advance also.

It is only through full recognition of strengths that the condescension of welfarism can be avoided. Because if the have-nots have nothing — no culture, no strength, no anger, no organization, no cooperativeness, no inventiveness, no vitality — if they are only depressed, apathetic, fatalistic and pathological, then where is the force for their liberation to come from?

Epilogue
November 1966

The development that began in the fall of 1965 toward governmental withdrawal from the prospect of aggressive policy making in the area of Negro rights and poverty now seems complete.

Three days following the closing of the White House Conference, James Meredith began his "March Against Fear." Not until he was shot on the second day of his march did the Meredith March receive public attention. Suddenly, with the overt manifestation of racism and violence, the Meredith March grew from less than half-a-dozen marchers to several thousands who gathered in Jackson, Mississippi, under the banner of "black power."

The Meredith March and the subsequent rise of black power as a nationwide public issue and civil rights slogan completely preempted whatever developments might have followed the White House Conference and the issue of change in the Northern ghettos.

The pendulum of primary definition of the Negro problem as a problem of northern ghettos or southern Jim Crow had swung back south again, as it had at the time of Selma. Southern-style caste terrorism was not to be bypassed by the issues of northern-style ghetto victimization, and issues of liberty again seemed more immediately salient than those of equality.

The black power and black nationalist thinking that had been slowly growing among Negro civil rights activists, and which had played a subdued and by and large unnoticed role in the Moynihan controversy* now catapulted into the spotlight of the national media, much to the consternation of more conservative civil rights leaders, and to the mixed gratification and amusement of the younger, more radical activists. As a national issue, the problem of Negro rights was now defined by concerns with black power, with black autonomy, with black secession from white-dominated structures — and issues of resource allocation for individual Negro families had perforce to take a back seat.

Then, in response to Martin Luther King's first excursion into the northern ghettos, Chicago and Cicero whites showed their "southern" face by responding violently to Negroes' assertion of their rights to the resource of decent housing. For anyone who had forgotten it, the television screen brought home the fact that the deepest of prejudices sustained patterns of housing discrimination and segregation. These whites would "put their bodies on the line" to deny equal (housing) opportunity to Negroes; they certainly would not support programs for equal results.

As the summer wore on, the frustration and rage engendered by ghetto living spawned a series of little Watts across the country, and fear and the desire to contain came to dominate the thinking of those in government and in the white community.

By the early fall of 1966, governmental attention in the area of civil rights was turned to the effects of black power, the riots, and the white "backlash" on the November elections. The "watered-down" open housing legislation that was before Congress during the summer of 1966 was never truly pushed by the White House, as had been predicted by some of our informants at the beginning of the year. Even though the delegates to the White House Conference had insisted that this bill be both strengthened and passed, the President made little more than public gestures in support of it. As Everett Dirkson indicated to a reporter after a visit with Johnson: "The President said he wanted the bill passed, but he didn't say it very strongly."

After the White House Conference, the central civil rights problem in the White House was "how to stop the riots, without doing too much." To allow the riots to continue would mean "white

* See pages 295–296.

backlash" and increased Republican support in the November
election. Implementing social and economic change in northern
ghettos, which was required in order to prevent riots, would
also result in additional Republican support.

The shooting of Meredith, the subsequent rise of black power,
the white racism that was made explicit in the Chicago and
Cicero marches, the increased fear of additional backlash in the
November elections, and the increasing escalation of Vietnam
resulted in the Johnson Administration moving still further away
from the policy-action lines indicated in the Howard speech.

One additional casuality of the turn to the right presaged by
these events seemed likely to be the war on poverty and its
bureaucratic embodiment, the Office of Economic Opportunity.
From the spring of 1966 on, more and more authoritative sources
were predicting the demise of OEO as its programs were absorbed
into other agencies or allowed to die on the vine. Efforts like
Moynihan's to shift the direction of the war on poverty were
becoming increasingly overshadowed by the question of whether
or not there were to be any meaningful financed antipoverty
programs.

The Republican victories in 1966 are a further stimulus for
increased stagnation of governmental action in the areas of
poverty and civil rights. Whether these victories can be attributed
to white backlash, the rising cost of living, or increased concern
over the Viet Nam War, it is unquestionably true that the watered-
down Housing bill that failed to get through the 89th Congress
will have an even more difficult time in the 90th Congress. The
chances of implementation of present programs, much less the
establishment of new ones, grow slimmer.

The Moynihan Report and the government's use of it were a
response to a situation in which the government sought to be
venturesome, instead of simply reacting to the civil rights movement. The administration felt it was prepared politically to implement new policies. Now, from the point of view of independent
governmental action, one might say that the issues raised by the
Moynihan Report are dead. The Randolph Freedom Budget, an
effort to describe in some detail the kind of program that Moynihan's efforts pointed toward, made its public appearance in the
same week that the Republican-southern conservative coalition
regained its congressional hegemony. But, it is probably more
accurate to say that these issues have merely been suppressed
for the moment. The conditions of life in the northern ghettos

remain, and the need for broad social and economic changes remain. It is not likely that the civil rights movement or the increasing aspirations and demands of the Negro American will decline. While the issues raised by the Moynihan Report are overshadowed for the moment, at some future time they will be raised again, debated and fought over, and, hopefully, bear fruit in meaningful programs to provide the kind of social and economic resources that must exist if Negroes are to have the chance to climb out of the degradation into which white society has forced them.

Index